HOW DOES LAW MATTER?

FUNDAMENTAL ISSUES IN LAW AND SOCIETY RESEARCH

Bryant G. Garth and Austin Sarat, Editors

HOW DOES
LAW MATTER?

Edited by
BRYANT G. GARTH
AUSTIN SARAT

NORTHWESTERN UNIVERSITY PRESS
THE AMERICAN BAR FOUNDATION

Northwestern University Press
Evanston, Illinois 60208–4210

Printed in the United States of America

ISBN 0-8101-1434-8 (cloth)
ISBN 0-8101-1435-6 (paper)

Library of Congress Cataloging-in-Publication Data

How does law matter? / edited by Bryant G. Garth, Austin
    Sarat.
        p. cm. — (Fundamental issues in law and society
    research ; v. 3)
        Includes bibliographical references and index.
        ISBN 0–8101-1434-8 (cloth : acid-free paper). — ISBN 0–8101-1435-6 (paper :
    acid-free paper)
        1. Sociological jurisprudence.   2. Culture and law.   3. Law—Philosophy.   4. Law—
    United States.   I. Garth, Bryant G.   II. Sarat, Austin.   III. Series.
    K370.H69 1998
    340'.115—dc21   98–23815
                                                                                          CIP

This material is based on work supported by the National Science Foundation under
Grant Nos. SBR-9410902 and SBR-9422669. Any opinions, findings, conclusions, or
recommendations expressed in this material are those of the authors and do not necessarily
reflect those of the National Science Foundation.

CONTENTS

STUDYING HOW LAW MATTERS:
AN INTRODUCTION

❖

BRYANT G. GARTH

AUSTIN SARAT

T he question of how law matters has long been fundamental to the field of law and society. Going back to Pound's (1917) famous identification of the gap between law on the books and law in action, social science scholarship has repeatedly demonstrated that law matters less, or differently, than those who study only legal doctrine would have us believe (see Abel 1973; Sarat 1985). That scholarship has shown how people order their affairs without law (Macaulay 1963; Ellickson 1991), or in the "shadow" of law (Mnookin and Kornhauser 1979), how when law seems to fail as an instrument of social change, it may nonetheless succeed in constituting social consciousness (Gordon 1984). The claims that law matters less or in different ways are so common that it can fairly be said that they help to define the academic authority of social scientists who study law.

At a relatively abstract theoretical level, research in this field depends on a belief in the relevance of law to major economic, political, and social issues, regardless of how often gaps are identified. If law, whether law on the books or law in action, were thought to be irrelevant, or merely the reflection of other causal factors, law would not only be uninteresting as a matter of social scientific concern, but it also would be a bad investment for ambitious scholars. This is the case because the careers of those who do law and society

I

research depend, to some extent, on their research being taken seriously by the broader scholarly community. In an increasingly competitive academic market, decisions to take the time to develop expertise in any field may depend to a significant degree on how that expertise appears likely to be valued. This relationship between the perceived value of research domains and the value of researchers is not of course unique to the field of law and society (Bourdieu and Wacquant 1992). And it does not mean that individual scholars in any sense skew their results to exaggerate or distort the impact of law. What matters for scholarly careers is that the issue of how law matters must matter, and that what law and society scholars can contribute to our understanding of that issue, in general, must be distinctive. Debates about the question of how law matters are therefore not only characteristic of the field (see Tyler 1990; Sarat 1993) but also necessary to its continuing development. This volume focuses on those debates and the means by which scholars seek to resolve them.

We will refer later in this introduction to the position of the field of law and society, but we wish to begin by examining the basic debates within law and society about how law matters. The vitality of law and society, as we have already suggested, is found in these debates, and we can organize major scholarly positions into two basic approaches. The two approaches, usually termed the instrumental and the constitutive (Sarat and Kearns 1993), have some very different characteristics, described below; and they can roughly be linked to separate generations of law and society research. Instrumentalist research characterized the early period of law and society, in particular the 1960s, while the constitutive approach has developed more recently (Munger 1997). As we will see, however, neither position is static. Today both are evolving rapidly and aggressively importing new disciplinary tools. This volume thus provides a slice of life into the history of an academic field and, in so doing, illustrates the methods and approaches used by law and society scholars to identify how law matters.

The basic question guiding the instrumental approach is what social results can be attributed to law or legal reforms. We might ask, for example, whether the Clean Air Act made the air cleaner or if any improvement in air quality outweighed the costs of making the improvements through law. Or we might ask how *Miranda* influenced the behavior of the police or their understanding of the nature of their role and responsibility. In the framing of these questions, law can be seen as the independent variable. Law is viewed as something that is brought to an already constituted social situation and either does or does not make a difference.

The constitutive approach sees law more as a pervasive influence in structuring society than as a variable whose occasional impact can be measured. Law is seen as a way of organizing the world into categories and concepts which, while providing spaces and opportunities, also constrains behavior and serves to legitimate authority. Rather than asking what the Clean Air Act accomplished, this approach focuses more on what it means to frame the problem of air quality in legal terms, and how that framing structures both thought and action with respect to the quality of air that we breathe. It asks how *Miranda* organizes the way all of us think about law enforcement.

In general, our own research is probably closer to the constitutive than to the instrumental approach, but we do not think the question of one versus the other can be debated usefully in the abstract. Neither approach, as noted above, stands still. Scholars who neglect developments that seem conveniently to be assigned to one or another camp are depriving themselves of potentially valuable theoretical and analytical tools—and missing the creative tension that the juxtaposition of instrumental and constitutive approaches plays in developing the field.

This creative tension can be seen in part by providing some information on the intellectual context in which each approach developed. In the 1960s, at the time of the creation of the Law and Society Association, the challenge for many of the early organizers was to get the legal profession and the legal academy to take social science seriously. The dominance of legal realism in the 1930s and into the 1940s in a few elite law schools had ended, and with it went the realists' brief forays into social science (Kalman 1986; Schlegel 1995). The law schools were once again dominated by lawyers who, in one way or another, could be described as legal formalists (Shamir 1995). While many aspects of legal realism had been reincorporated into the world of legal formalism, social science had been pushed to the margins both of the legal academy and the courts. The challenge of a new generation sympathetic to social science in law—with some law school allies preserving the link to legal realism—was therefore to show that social science mattered in the study of law.

One way the new generation made its place was to argue on the basis of historical and social scientific techniques that law was in a sense the dependent variable, explained relatively easily through the analysis of the other factors that produce it. A key contribution of such scholars as Willard Hurst (1982), Lawrence Friedman (1973), and Stewart Macaulay (1963), in particular, was to show that *doctrine*—once again the dominant subject in law schools—did not really matter very much as a factor producing social or economic change. Legal changes merely reflected changes that took place essentially in other spheres. Other scholars coming to this area of research made a similar argument but framed it more as a challenge to those engaged in setting policy (Sarat and Silbey 1988). From a perspective closer to advocacy than that of the scholars just mentioned, they argued that the measured gap between the law on the books and the law in action, as revealed by social science, gave rise to "legal needs" that the state—acting through law—must find a way to meet. If law was not succeeding in effecting social change, in other words, new efforts should be put into place.

The emphasis on gaps between law and social life, coupled with the powerful work proclaiming the formal law's relatively marginal position, helped to build and solidify the status of a generation of law and society scholars in and out of the law schools. Outside of this community clustered around law, other social scientists used these findings to help build an identity distinct from that of traditional legal academics. In studies precisely parallel to those in law and society, for example, "law and economics" scholars could argue that the common law was best explained by economic theory, or that economic theory showed its own "gap"—that is, economic growth and efficiency demanded that the role of the state and state law be reduced in economic matters. It is fair to say, in fact, that arguments coming from relatively conservative economists provided the academic support for the many efforts to deregulate the economy during the 1980s. A notable recent example is Richard Epstein's (1991) attack on legal regulation as a way to eliminate racial and gender discrimination in employment. According to Epstein, such regulation is, at best, unnecessary, given that the efficiency of the market would eliminate any "irrational" discrimination, and, at worse, a way to stifle productive economic decision making. Economic theory is thus used to argue that law is irrelevant or destructive.

Political scientists and anthropologists—coming from two disciplines that until the 1950s and 1960s placed law at the center of their fields—made similar moves, concentrating their attention increasingly on factors other than law. Anthropologists shifted their focus from "disputes" to studies that broadened the focus to take account of phenomena like colonialism itself (Comaroff and Comaroff 1991). Influential scholars in political science, most notably Gerald Rosenberg (1991), pushed law away more directly. Rosenberg carefully argued for the nonimportance of law compared to political and cultural factors in social change. According to *The Hollow Hope*, *Brown v. Board of Education* and its progeny made no positive contribution to African American educational improvement.

These positions suggesting that law matters less or differently than many thought, while adopted in the name of other disciplines, have had a strong impact in the legal academy, showing that the debates about how law matters continue to matter. Just as lawyers representing clients can prosper using arguments that there is too much legal regulation, professors can gain prominence in law by helping to frame similar arguments against law. However, it may also be—to move ahead somewhat in the story—that, reminiscent of the reassertion of formalism after the period of active engagement with social science in the 1930s (Shamir 1995), there is a reassertion today of more traditional legal approaches (Kronman 1993; Edwards 1992) and new resistance to the way social scientists have understood the impact and influence of law on society.

The focus on "law as constitutive," in a very different way, also returns law to the center of attention. A new generation in social science is reacting to the movement away from law reflected in the examples from anthropology, economics, and political science noted above, and is now calling for recognition of the importance of law for the social science disciplines themselves. If law is itself constitutive of economics, politics, and society, then social scientists cannot fully understand these domains without taking the active role of law—if not causal, at least constitutive—into account. This generation's work, therefore, can be seen as both against and in support of the earlier generation of law and society research. While against instrumentalism, it reaffirms both the importance of social science to law and the importance of law to social science. These new developments also redirect our attention to the social scientific disciplines that are located around law and to the role of legal discourses and institutions in the core of those disciplines.

As the previous paragraphs suggest, developments in the social science disciplines and in the legal academy are closely related to the development of "law and society"—both as a general field of study and as represented by institutions like the Law and Society Association. It is not simply a matter of instrumental versus constitutive approaches, but rather of complex developments within the core of the disciplines that make up law and society. Before we turn to a brief discussion of the way that the essays in this volume exemplify our general themes, we should note that throughout this volume we have tried to maintain the tension between the defined academic disciplines and the issues that are more closely linked to the interdisciplinary field of law and society. The authors for this volume were chosen not only because their research sheds particular light on how law matters but also because of their disciplinary ties. They represent law, political science, economics, sociology, anthropology, and psychology. We can thus approach them from the perspective of particular disciplines, from the perspective of the debates within law and society revolving around instrumental and constitutive approaches, and for what they show substantively about the role of law in society.

We begin with three essays that address in different ways the question of how law matters in one area, namely in attacking discrimination. We chose this area because it has been a traditional concern for law and society scholars and a domain where legal intervention and regulation has been particularly controversial. Lauren Edelman and Mia Cahill, each trained in both sociology and law, combine a neoinstitutional approach grounded in sociology with a more instrumental focus. They examine a contest within business enterprises over the orientation of the professionals charged with enforcing laws against discrimination in employment and find structural reasons why a therapeutic approach has gained precedence over a more legalistic one. From this perspective, they make a very strong case that the antidiscrimination values of the law are not as fully vindicated as they would be if the institutional structures in which those values are embedded presented different sets of incentives. The tilt of business interests, they argue, favors the therapeutic, integrative approach in discrimination matters because it is less disturbing to organizational hierarchies and priorities. The market orientation and the therapeutic orientation work together to limit legal effectiveness. Nevertheless, Edelman and Cahill also suggest, the institutional impact of the law cannot be neglected. Institutional studies, they might say, are important tools for understanding the role of law, and, furthermore, sociologists of institutions who neglect the role of law will not be able to understand fully the dynamics of institutional change and stability (see Suchman and Edelman 1996).

The second essay focuses less on the gap between the laws' promise and institutional structures and more on the problem of measuring the impact of civil rights laws and Supreme Court decisions on the lives of the intended beneficiaries. John Donohue, an economist and lawyer, illustrates a relatively complicated empirical approach that marks a significant advance for the instrumental side of law and society research. This approach combines microstudies with analyses based on national census and other large data sets. The impact of any law, including civil rights laws like Title VII of the Civil Rights Act of 1964, can never be isolated completely. It is extremely difficult to rule out competing explanations, for example, to account for actual changes that took place after the implementation of the law. One reason for institutional studies, in fact, is to try to develop other tools.

Donohue and his collaborators, including especially James Heckman (e.g., Heckman and Payner 1989), concentrate their focus on trying to find the most precise measures for all the potential causes of the phenomena captured in the census data—in particular, the undeniable increase in the wages of African American males in the South immediately after the passage of the Civil Rights Act of 1964. Their high-tech positivism examines each potential cause—educational improvement, migration, urbanization—in order to ascertain as precisely as possible how it affected wages in that period and at other times. Working as "positivist detectives," they assess the potential causal impact of every plausible "suspect" on the way to a powerful conclusion, namely that the law—at least to an important extent—"did it." Law remains as the unexplained variance, but the argument for its positive impact is extremely difficult to refute. Law clearly mattered in producing wage increases. More generally, this research suggests that economists who, on the basis of economic theory, dismiss the role of law, can be refuted through sophisticated empirical research (see Donohue 1992; Siegelman 1995).

Another study of how law matters in antidiscrimination efforts comes from political science. Michael McCann, the author of the third essay, has studied how social movements use law in pursuit of political goals. Using detailed case studies, his work also helps to bridge two generations of political science work on law and social change. An earlier generation, best exemplified by Stuart Scheingold (1974), argued that "the myth of rights" led social movements to adopt strategies based on law rather than to adopt potentially more effective political strategies. This work, in fact, became one of the foundations of the "critique of rights" associated with one dimension of the critical legal studies movement in the law schools. The point was that politics mattered more than law in movements for social change or, relatedly, that law constrained social change by constituting boundaries that circumscribe social action. From the side of political science, as noted before, Rosenberg recently made a significant entry into the "how law matters" debate.

6

McCann's work (also 1994) is addressed more to the Scheingold analysis than to Rosenberg's kind of political science that minimizes the importance of law, yet clearly he speaks to both literatures. On the basis of a relatively diverse set of case studies, McCann found that the social movements he studied used law strategically to build their political power, that they were successful in many respects, and that they did not make bad strategic choices in combating discrimination through a misguided belief in the myth of rights. McCann thus concluded that law could matter positively in social movements. Not surprisingly, McCann's scholarship has also led him to defend, against the position of Rosenberg, the importance of law (McCann 1996; Rosenberg 1996). Again, we can see two voices in McCann's work, one grounded in a law and society tradition which explores how law matters, and the other speaking to a political science discipline that has pushed law further and further to the margin.

Both McCann and Edelman and Cahill draw on the idea that law can be constitutive of certain social relations, but, like Donohue, they use their disciplinary tools to try also to see whether it matters instrumentally in effecting social change on behalf of disadvantaged groups who may use the law's potential antidiscrimination machinery. The effects, to repeat, are seen through a new generation of studies of institutions, of economic analysis of all hypothesized causes, and of detailed, politically oriented case studies of social movements and the law in action. Not only do these scholars develop new tools for seeing empirically what the impact of law might be, but they also argue powerfully for the relevance of law to the disciplines from which they came.

The next three chapters—by David Engel, Jane Collier, and Kristin Bumiller—move beyond the issue of how law matters in the arena of discrimination and also provide an opportunity to focus more specifically on the constitutive perspective. Engel takes up the topic of "legal consciousness," drawing on legal history, anthropology, and more generally what has been called the Amherst Seminar in his assessment of a number of key works in developing the constitutive approach. Legal consciousness could refer to a variety of possible attitudes and practices. As Engel suggests, legal consciousness, if defined as people's ideas, understandings, and opinions in relation to the law, may suggest a naive belief in the rule of law—akin to Scheingold's "myth of rights." More expansively, he suggests, legal consciousness may simply be another way to express the constitutive role of law in the realm of ideas and practices. Paraphrasing Jean Comaroff and John Comaroff, we might say that "law colonizes consciousness" (1991), embedding thought and action within the categories and assumptions of law. Most of the writers that Engel discusses recognize that those who use the law successfully often do not actually believe in the myth of rights. They use law strategically, as McCann also suggests. It makes sense therefore to use legal consciousness in the more general and inclusive sense to coincide with the way that law constitutes the categories of thought and analysis of social issues and possibilities.

7 ↳ same old ambiguity

Framed this way, the constitutive perspective opens up new ways of considering the relationship between law and social change. Part of the politics of law, for example, involves who controls definitions and categories. The constitutive perspective, however, points also to new kinds of empirical research. In particular, it opens up the possibility of revealing through empirical study how particular categories and assumptions, generally taken for granted in the law, may limit the possibilities of those whose lives are shaped by the law. Progressive struggle for social change, from this perspective, comes in part through resistance and transformation of seemingly taken-for-granted categories and terms.

A well-known article by Lucie White (1991) makes precisely this argument. Written in part in the form of a self-criticism, White tells the story of a client who refused to follow the script that she, the legal services lawyer, had written to make an argument for certain basic necessities. The client insisted on making her own argument based on the necessity of proper shoes for church on Sunday, even though this was not recognized by prevailing legal doctrine. As it turned out, however, the resistance of the client to the law, in this account, became a way to resist a conservative view of the law—making it more receptive to an argument that recognized the world as the client saw it. Law matters very much in this example and in general. It matters both because law limits possibilities for social change and because sophisticated challenges—based, for example, on a close empirical or empathetic study of what clients might really want or expect—can open up new possibilities for social change through law.

Kristin Bumiller's essay is, like White's work, very much within the constitutive approach, yet is also far from the advocacy tradition with which White is associated. Taking a view based especially on Foucault, whose work has influenced a number of scholarly disciplines and the constitutive approach more generally, Bumiller examines how very different approaches to social issues involved with the "regulation"—in the very broad sense—of the body share certain assumptions inherent in law. She thus introduces the question of law itself as a "discipline." In other words, the discourse of law, she argues, imposes certain requirements on those who seek to craft legal approaches to social problems; and the social implications of this discourse are quite profound. Colonizing the body with legal regulation brings the body into the market as a commodity or form of property.

Bumiller's careful analysis of seemingly diverse approaches to the question of how law matters in the constitution of the body raises the question of whether it is in fact "progressive" to bring an area of social life under a regime based on law. Regardless of whether we accept the pessimistic implications of Bumiller's approach, it does put law into a different analytical framework. We can see that "legal consciousness" or the "constitutive role of law" is not simply a matter of uncontested fact. In order for law to "colonize consciousness" or, to put it another way, to become constitutive of social relations, there must be some human agency at work. For law to be central to social control and perhaps also social change, in other words, someone, or some groups, need to spread "the word" of law. Whether the language that comes with those words is helpful or harmful in a particular context, however, is not easy to say.

A new generation of anthropological studies, exemplified here in Jane Collier's chapter, examines these issues both historically and comparatively. The question of how law matters can be treated by recognizing that "law" is only one form of social regulation. In addition, we can see law's invasion into new geographies as analogous to Bumiller's study of the "colonization" of the body. Thus Collier notes that law was brought to the English colonies, and it competed in those colonial outposts with other forms of regulation—tribal, familial, religious, bureaucratic—that already existed or were also imported. One way to treat law would be to condemn it for its genealogy, since it was part and parcel of colonialism, whether imposed directly or by mimicry, but Collier suggests a more subtle approach. With the new awareness of the importance of human rights (even given the dangers of claiming universal validity) in the struggles of many indigenous groups to resist new colonial activities (Sierra 1995), anthropologists are now more receptive to the notion that law must become an important focus of disciplinary attention.

The general question that Collier's essay highlights is whether the development of a legal order, or the legalization of a particular issue, can lead to social progress by some relevant criterion. To answer this question Collier suggests that analysis must go beyond romanticizing a nonlaw or prelaw existence and also beyond taking for granted the idea of progress through law's universals. There are winners and losers under the regime that exists prior to the imposition and legitimation of the colonial order based on law, and there are winners and losers through the new colonial order. Those who "play the law" and in the process import legal institutions have always been an ambiguous group of double agents. They legitimate foreign domination by adopting the foreign terms of legitimacy, but they also may succeed in disrupting established hierarchies—for example, some of the domination inherent in traditional paternalism.

Collier's approach, therefore, suggests another way to examine how law matters, this time drawing on a historical and anthropological approach. Using this approach we can see legal regulation as one possible form of authority—and a form that, while certainly not "neutral," has impacts that depend very much on the specific social context in which it may be imported or sustained. These contexts include the domain outside of the Western centers of power, but also newly recognized territories of regulated social life—such as the body. We should not assume, however, that law inevitably "constitutes" reality in all forms of social life. Instead, we should see law as supplementing and sometimes competing to constitute reality with other forms of authority and legitimacy—for example, economic growth, personal relations, family, religion, science, marketing. We cannot take for granted that one form will triumph out of a competition that affects and transforms all of them. But we can examine the competition and the impact that it has on how social relations are constituted and governed.

This approach is complementary to those that we have already seen in our discussion of the chapters in this book. Edelman and Cahill, for example, show the competition between a therapeutic and legal approach in the regulation of the workforce; although their questions are somewhat different, their work is not inconsistent with that of Donohue or McCann in trying to understand how issues in employment came to be contested on the terms of the law. The same is true of Bumiller and Engel in their discussions focusing on the constitutive approach. Struggles about the role of law in shaping social practice fit well with questions about the implications of legal consciousness or legal discourse.

What is somewhat different, however, is the place of the research itself in this analysis. We have been talking of social change and change in the role and substance of the law. Seeing law as one form of authority suggests that the question of how law matters is not only a question of instrumental versus constitutive views of the law. Given the competition we can observe in how and whether law matters, it is appropriate to ask whether the law and society community has a stake in the competition. We believe that it can advance research to admit to such a stake. Professional expertise and status, as noted before, both depend on how expertise is valued—on whether it is perceived to matter. Again, that does not mean that the field of law and society intentionally or unintentionally skews the results of research to favor a finding that law matters. If there is a tilt to law and society perspectives, it is somewhat different. We may as a field overinvest in finding ways and places to debate how law matters, and we may underinvest in expertise about other places and forms of authority that matter in both the instrumental and constitutive senses. If this is true, it is not surprising. For purposes of research, however, it may be useful to explore how our field is embedded in a larger professional competition for status and academic authority.

It is important, in other words, not only to see the powerful arsenal of tools that we have developed to show when law matters, and how. We should also see how the fate of law in its competition with other forms of authority is tied up with our own careers and the field of law and society. Law and social science—and social science about law—are quite closely intertwined, and it is essential to try to develop a social science that takes that complex relationship into account. Social science analysis of law should try also to explain how social science is used by law (Sarat and Silbey 1988).

The close relationship between law and social science is quite evident in Shari Diamond and Jason Schklar's essay on how law matters in the structure and function of the jury. In one sense, of course, it is obvious that the law constitutes the jury and also that law matters in the ways that juries deliberate. However, very sophisticated methodological tools, especially experimental studies, make it possible to give more precision to such statements. Diamond, trained as a psychologist and lawyer, and Schklar, a psychologist, thus explore the way in which jury instructions (the representation of "the law") are perceived and used by juries. There is a considerable amount of remediable confusion in how that law is understood and used, but the appellate courts have so far been reluctant to address it. The related issue, which they also consider, is how evolving legal principles affect the selection of juries and how those juries represent the communities from which they were selected. Jury scholars from a variety of disciplines, including psychology, have pioneered in demonstrating the adverse impact of nonrepresentative juries, especially in death penalty cases.

Without repeating the points made earlier, it is obvious that the legal principles and the institution of the jury itself have evolved partly through a dialogue with social science researchers (Constable 1994). While the efforts of social science researchers have not always been successful when research has moved to legal advocacy, social scientists have succeeded in making their research matter. The relevance of the research is clear in the long effort to subject the administration of the death penalty to constitutional scrutiny on equal protection grounds (cf. Acker 1993). And social science is also quite relevant to the questions of how law matters in jury deliberations. Jury research, beginning with Hans Zeisel, has made the issue of "juries and the law" an issue that can be studied systematically using social science methodologies. Indeed, not only is social science relevant to debates about jury reform, but it is also part of a burgeoning business of jury consultants.

Richard Lempert's essay on criminal justice concludes this volume by reminding us that law matters especially in legitimating the authority that is used by the state for social control. Drawing on criminology and a variety of studies of criminal justice and police behavior, he states that law matters "of course," because it provides a framework and discourse that is oriented toward restraining power. Lempert's training is both as a lawyer and a sociologist, but we might characterize his essay as a new legal-realist account of criminal justice. Law can be constitutive of the categories, institutions, and processes used by the state for social control, but that does not mean that "the law" dictates the outcome of particular activities subject to regulation.

We have already suggested that different means of legitimating authority compete for ascendency in regulating and justifying power. Lempert's major point is consistent with the fact that law may matter less in some circumstances because of the importance of competing sources of legitimacy. It could be that the authority of the law is rejected at times because of other authorities— religious, familial, patrimonial, political. Lempert's point, however, is more to contrast pure law with power. No matter what hierarchy of legitimation is in place at a particular time and place, he suggests, there will be times when those in power choose not to comply. In terms of legal authority, they simply use their power to go outside or beyond the law. How they act may be shaped by the law, since they may circumvent the law or try to avoid detection. The point, however, is that they use their power to get their way despite what the law might have provided.

To the extent that they act in regard to law, even if hypocritically, they may help to build the legitimacy of law (Hay 1975; Ewick 1998). But they also may resist in the manner described earlier for the client represented in a welfare hearing. When the powerful use or even challenge the prevailing legal discourse, they may succeed in changing the meaning of the legal terms in their favor (Galanter 1974). They can invest in the rules or take advantage of the investments of others who compete for the social and economic rewards of representing the powerful. That is to say, they can help to reshape the categories of law in their favor. The relative autonomy of law from power, however, must be understood realistically. The powerful have a much better chance of having their resistance and challenge to legal hegemony reframed into new and more favorable (to them) legal rules. The favorable rule change seen in Lucie White's study, for example, may illustrate an exceptional occurrence in the welfare context, but similar phenomena may be relatively commonplace in matters involving powerful businesses and the state.

One other way to study how law matters, therefore, is to focus on law's relationship to power. The law, of course, is constantly changing, even if certain aspects of law as a discourse remain constant. But it is relatively easy to see that the change from the 1960s to the 1990s in the law in the United States and elsewhere was not merely a product of a change within the legal system. Changes in the world economy—stagflation, the oil crisis—were translated into a restructuring designed to restore business profits and economic growth. In the process, those who had been given more state attention in the 1960s— the poor, the employed, the unemployed, immigrants—were redefined to fall further outside of the protective umbrella of the state. Law changed to accommodate the new economic understanding of those in power, and social science—especially economics—participated actively in keeping law in tune with the changing times. Lempert's focus is on the criminal justice system, but his realist observations can be used more generally to focus on the role of law in relation to power. Law is not so much a fixed set of rules as a space that can be found between economic (and political) power and the state. Law's relative autonomy can be positioned very close to business interests, or it can reinforce a more independent state.

The essays in this volume illustrate and take part in recent debates about whether it is better to study law from an instrumental or constitutive approach. But they also highlight complex and changing relationships involving the legal academy, the law and society community, social science disciplines around law, and other forms of authority that in some sense compete with law. Our purpose here is in part to illuminate some of those relationships. However, these essays, drawing on a wide variety of new approaches and disciplinary tools, provide one means to gain access to the methods, debates, and issues involved in studying a fundamental question: How does law matter? That question, we believe, is fundamental to the position of law and society but also, more importantly, to the position of law in society.

BIBLIOGRAPHY

Abel, Richard. 1973. Law Books and Books about Law. 26 *Stanford Law Rev.*, 175.

Acker, James. 1993. A Different Agenda: The Supreme Court, Empirical Research Evidence, and Capital Punishment Reform. 27 *Law and Society Rev.*, 65.

Bourdieu, Pierre, and Loic Wacquant. 1992. *An Introduction to Reflexive Sociology.* Chicago: Univ. of Chicago Press.

Comaroff, Jean, and John Comaroff. 1991. *Of Revelation and Revolution.* Chicago: Univ. of Chicago Press.

Constable, Marianne. 1994. *The Law of the Other: The Mixed Jury and Changing Conceptions of Citizenship, Law, and Knowledge.* Chicago: Univ. of Chicago Press.

Donohue, John. 1992. Advocacy versus Analysis in Assessing Employment Discrimination Law. 44 *Stanford Law Rev.*, 1592.

Edwards, Harry. 1992. The Growing Disjuncture between Legal Education and the Legal Profession. 91 *Michigan Law Rev.*, 34.

Ellickson, Robert. 1991. *Order without Law.* Cambridge, MA: Harvard Univ. Press.

Epstein, Richard. 1991. *Forbidden Grounds: The Case against Employment Discrimination Grounds.* Cambridge, MA: Harvard Univ. Press.

Ewick, Patricia. 1998. Punishment, Power, and Justice. In *Justice and Power in Sociolegal Studies,* ed. B. Garth and A. Sarat. Evanston, IL: Northwestern Univ. Press.

Friedman, Lawrence. 1973. *A History of American Law.* New York: Simon and Schuster.

Galanter, Marc. 1974. Why the "Haves" Come Out Ahead: Speculations on the Limits of Legal Change. 9 *Law and Society Rev.*, 95.

Gordon, Robert. 1984. Critical Legal Histories. 36 *Stanford Law Rev.*, 57.

Hay, Douglas, et al., eds. 1975. *Albion's Fatal Tree: Crime and Society in Eighteenth-Century England.* New York: Pantheon.

Heckman, James, and Brook Payner. 1989. Determining the Impact of Antidiscrimination Policy on the Economic Status of Blacks: A Study of South Carolina. 79 *American Economic Rev.*, 138.

Hurst, James Willard. 1982. *Law and Markets in United States History: Different Modes of Bargaining among Interests.* Madison: Univ. of Wisconsin Press.

Kalman, Laura. 1986. *Legal Realism at Yale, 1927–1960.* Chapel Hill: Univ. of North Carolina Press.

Kronman, Anthony. 1993. *The Lost Lawyer.* Cambridge, MA: Harvard Univ. Press.

Macaulay, Stewart. 1963. Non-Contractual Relations in Business Disputes: A Preliminary Study. 28 *American Sociological Rev.*, 59.

McCann, Michael. 1994. *Rights at Work: Pay Equity Reform and the Politics of Legal Mobilization.* Chicago: Univ. of Chicago Press.

———. 1996. Causal versus Constitutive Explanations (or, On the Difficulty of Being So Positive). 21 *Law and Social Inquiry,* 457.

Mnookin, Robert, and Lewis Kornhauser. 1979. Bargaining in the Shadow: The Case of Divorce. 88 *Yale Law Journal,* 950.

Munger, Frank. 1998. Mapping Law and Society. In *Crossing Boundaries: Traditions and Transformations in Law and Society Research,* ed. A. Sarat et al. Evanston, IL: Northwestern Univ. Press.

Pound, Roscoe. 1917. The Limits of Effective Legal Action. 27 *International Journal of Ethics,* 150.

Rosenberg, Gerald. 1991. *The Hollow Hope: Can Courts Bring about Social Change?* Chicago: Univ. of Chicago Press.

———. 1996. Positivism, Interpretism, and the Study of Law. 21 *Law and Social Inquiry,* 435.

Sarat, Austin. 1985. Legal Effectiveness and Social Studies of Law: On the Unfortunate Persistance of a Research Tradition. 9 *Legal Studies Forum,* 23.

———. 1993. Authority, Anxiety, and Procedural Justice: Moving from Scientific Detachment to Critical Engagement. 27 *Law and Society Rev.,* 647.

Sarat, Austin, and Thomas Kearns. 1993. Beyond the Great Divide: Forms of Legal Scholarship and Everyday Life. In *Law in Everyday Life,* ed. A. Sarat and T. Kearns. Ann Arbor: Univ. of Michigan Press.

Sarat, Austin, and Susan Silbey. 1988. The Pull of the Policy Audience. 10 *Law and Policy,* 97.

Scheingold, Stuart. 1974. *The Politics of Rights: Lawyers, Public Policy, and Political Change.* New Haven, CT: Yale Univ. Press.

Schlegel, John Henry. 1995. *American Legal Realism and Empirical Social Science.* Chapel Hill: Univ. of North Carolina Press.

Shamir, Ronen. 1995. *Managing Legal Uncertainty: Elite Lawyers in the New Deal.* Durham, NC: Duke Univ. Press.

Siegelman, Peter. 1995. Shaky Grounds: The Case against Antidiscrimination Laws. 19 *Law and Social Inquiry,* 725.

Sierra, Maria Teresa. 1995. Indian Rights and Customary Law in Mexico: A Study of the Nahuas in the Sierra del Puebla. 29 *Law and Society Rev.,* 227.

Suchman, Mark, and Lauren Edelman. 1996. Legal Rational Myths: The New Institutionalism and the Law and Society Tradition. 21 *Law and Social Inquiry,* 903.

Tyler, Tom. 1990. *Why People Obey the Law.* New Haven, CT: Yale Univ. Press.

White, Lucie. 1991. Subordination, Rhetorical Survival Skills and Sunday Shoes: Notes on the Hearing of Mrs. G. In *At the Boundaries of Law: Feminism and Legal Theory,* ed. M. A. Fineman and N. S. Thomadsen. New York: Routledge.

HOW LAW MATTERS IN DISPUTING AND DISPUTE PROCESSING (OR, THE CONTINGENCY OF LEGAL MATTER IN INFORMAL DISPUTE PROCESSES)

❖

LAUREN B. EDELMAN

MIA CAHILL

1. INTRODUCTION

Formal legal rules create rights that are in theory designed to realize socio-cultural notions of morality and justice. Liberal legal theory holds that these rights apply generally and universally; they need not be renegotiated by each set of disputing parties. A quarter century of law and society scholarship has tempered our faith in the liberal legal model, in particular with respect to dispute resolution. Research shows that most disputes are handled in the shadow of the courts, where formal rules operate only at the margins (Macaulay 1963, 1966; Mnookin and Kornhauser 1979; Erlanger, Chambliss, and Melli 1987; Miller and Sarat 1981). There are substantial structural and social-psychological barriers to the mobilization of law in response to grievances, and those barriers cause disproportionate attrition among the most socially burdened (Felstiner, Abel, and Sarat 1981; Bumiller 1987, 1988). A stratified legal profession exacerbates social advantage and disadvantage (Carlin 1966; Heinz and Laumann 1982) and legal services for the poor are limited in their capacity to overcome the disadvantages associated with poverty (Handler, Hollingsworth, and Erlanger 1978; Wexler 1973). Parties with greater legal experience and resources enjoy great advantage both in the courts and in out-of-court settlements arranged in the shadow of law. The legal system favors those who use the courts on a repeated basis—offering economies of scale, the ability to maximize long-term gain, and the ability to structure both transactions and rules (Galanter 1974). Legal ambiguity provides opportunities for powerful parties to influence judicial constructions of law (Edelman 1992) and for judicial politics to reinforce social biases (Schultz 1990). Critical legal theorists further challenge the liberal legal model, arguing that rights are ambiguous, unstable, indeterminate, contingent, and often politically ineffectual (Scheingold 1974; Kennedy 1979; Gabel 1980; Tushnet 1984). In short, law and society scholarship shows that the liberal legal model is deeply flawed and that dispute resolution through the formal legal system systematically favors parties with greater social, political, and economic clout.

Given these problems, informal dispute resolution seems quite seductive at first blush. Informal dispute resolution is a broad term referring to alternative dispute resolution forums that assist parties in negotiation, generally do not require lawyers, and do away with the procedural rules of courts and adherence to precedent. In place of the adjudicators in formal litigation, informal dispute resolution involves third party facilitators; their roles and authority vary across settings, but in general they have less decision-making authority than do legal adjudicators. Mediation, the most popular form of informal dispute resolution, is characterized by a third party who has no authority to render binding judgments but rather seeks to help the parties reach an agreement. In other forms of informal dispute resolution, such as internal dispute resolution in the workplace, the third party often investigates complaints and may have authority to make decisions or to recommend outcomes to a higher administrator.

A growing literature supporting informal dispute resolution, written largely by practitioners but also by some academics, suggests that by moving away from formal procedural rules and the constraints of precedent, informal forums provide greater access and a process that is faster, cheaper, less adversarial, more empowering, and capable of producing flexible, creative solutions (e.g. Fisher and Ury 1981; Menkel-Meadow 1984; Westin and Feliu 1988; Bush and Folger 1994; Bush 1989; Rosenberg 1991). But there is also a large literature critical of informal dispute resolution, written primarily by academics but including a few critical mediators. This literature suggests that informal dispute resolution exacerbates the inequities of the formal system by seriously undermining legal rights, discounting the force of precedent, privatizing and depoliticizing disputes that address important public values, and allowing social biases and power differences to influence outcomes to an even greater extent than in formal dispute resolution (e.g., Abel 1982; Fiss 1984; Delgado, et al. 1985; Silbey and Sarat 1989; Hofrichter 1987; Amy 1987b; Fineman 1988; Nader 1993a, 1993b; Edelman, Erlanger, and Lande 1993).

This essay elaborates the critique of informal dispute resolution by analyzing the impact of the legitimating ideology that supports it. We contend that informal dispute resolution draws on an ideology of community rather than liberal legal ideology. As we show below, the ideology of community rests on different underlying values, modes of discourse, and logics of action than does liberal legal ideology. Rights and legal principles matter less and matter differently in informal dispute resolution because the ideology of community draws on a different set of symbolic resources or constructs that provide legitimacy. Because the formal legal system is grounded in liberal legal ideology, "rights" are its principal symbolic resource. But the ideology of community, and therefore informal dispute resolution, draws on the notion of "community" as its symbolic resource. We argue below that adherence to rights is unnecessary to the ideology of community, and in fact thwarts its goals; therefore, informal dispute resolution can move quite far from a semblance of attention to rights without losing legitimacy.

However indeterminate and politically manipulable rights may be, their status as a symbolic resource matters. The formal universality of rights in liberal legal ideology allows parties to ground their claims in those rights and in the principles of social justice that underlie them. The language of rights makes political arguments more potent, partly because even skeptics have some ambivalent faith in rights, and even more because the language of rights has a deep appeal for most of the public to which judges, juries, and attorneys have to be responsive to some degree. Thus, even where the political contingency of rights is widely understood and the realization of rights rare, rights can be empowering to disputants who lack the political clout to be heard in the absence of those rights (Minow 1987; Williams 1987). Even where rights have not been legally recognized, disputing parties may articulate their claims in terms of recognized rights, arguing for expanded interpretations and new understandings, and legitimating new claims by reference to legally recognized ones (Minow 1987). Even though courts are political institutions and have a strong capacity to undo the rights created by progressive legislatures (Klare 1982; Freeman 1990; Schultz 1990), courts must be formally attentive to rights because their legitimacy depends on it. Because formal legal processes draw legitimacy from liberal legal ideology, they are somewhat constrained by notions of law and rights even where elite classes retain a large measure of control over legal institutions (Thompson 1975; Genovese 1976). Liberal legal ideology may be myth, but that myth matters because, in return for legitimacy, it provides a mild constraint on power and a tool for social change.

Informal dispute resolution is not, of course, an entirely separate legal order; rather, it is an enclave within a broader culture in which liberal legal ideology is well institutionalized. Law matters as culture even where rights do not carry strong ideological force. Culturally, law matters constitutively and normatively. Constitutively, law helps to define and legitimate the social wrongs that give rise to disputes in the first place. Law structures what is and is not in fact grievable by legitimating certain claims and certain parties. Because law provides the language and psychological tools that empower people to frame their problems as rights violations (Williams 1987; Minow 1987), the sociolegal processes that determine whether problems evolve into disputes also tend to construct disputes in the dominant legal form of rights violations. Because informal dispute resolution is an enclave within a culture where liberal legal ideology is dominant, the disputes that enter that forum are likely initially to be framed in terms of rights.

Normatively, law and legal institutions cast a shadow on informal dispute resolution because disputants and dispute handlers tend to consider legal positions when they are bargaining (Mnookin and Kornhauser 1979). Since parties usually retain the formal option to litigate, and in some cases have already filed lawsuits, estimates of the outcome in litigation may influence both the parties and the dispute handler in the informal setting. Further, informal dispute handling professionals work closely with court and public officials, they seek and receive referrals from public legal forums, and they seek to institutionalize their role in the "market" of legal disputes. As informal alternatives to litigation draw growing support from the American Bar Association, the institutional ties between formal and informal dispute resolution blur the distinction between their logics.

We contend that although law matters culturally through its constitutive and normative roles in informal dispute resolution, a key component of law—rights—becomes highly contingent on compatibility with the ideology of community. Where rights can be framed in ways that build on and support community, they may be important considerations in informal dispute resolution processes. But where rights come into conflict with norms of community, they are relegated to a subordinate status.

In the sections below, we first elaborate the ideology of community and then examine the various effects of the ideology of community on how law matters within informal dispute resolution. We use the academic literature on dispute resolution to elaborate the ideology of community that underlies informal dispute resolution and to explain its implications for how law matters in informal forums. We elaborate that literature with an analysis of, and examples from, the dispute resolution practitioner literature. We treat the practitioner literature as data on the professional orientations and ideologies of dispute handlers.[1] Our analysis of the practitioner literature focused on three areas of informal dispute resolution: family mediation, internal workplace dispute resolution, and environmental mediation. All are informal in that they are explicit alternatives to the formal legal system and do not require attention to the Rules of Civil Procedure, to constitutional principles of due process, or to legal precedent.

Divorce custody mediation is becoming increasingly popular as an alternative to litigation and to bilateral negotiation by lawyers. A growing number of states have court-annexed divorce mediation, which in some cases is mandatory (Grillo 1991). Custody agreements reached through mediation must be approved by the courts, but judges seldom alter or even seriously review those agreements (Bryan 1994).

Internal workplace dispute resolution is also becoming increasingly common for handling a wide variety of workplace issues involving conditions, wages, promotions, discipline, and dismissal (Westin and Feliu 1988; Edelman 1990). Employers are especially interested in using internal dispute resolution for handling discrimination-related complaints that could produce administrative complaints or lawsuits under the 1964 Civil Rights Act, the Age Discrimination in Employment Act, and other civil rights mandates (Edelman, Erlanger, and Lande 1993). Employers generally believe that internal dispute resolution procedures are rational means of avoiding litigation and improving employment relations (Edelman, Erlanger, and Lande 1993; Edelman, Uggen, and Erlanger 1995). Organizations use a variety of dispute resolution techniques to resolve employee complaints against their superiors and against other employees, including open-door policies in which a high-level manager is available to look into and handle complaints, multistep appeals procedures, and mediation or similar forms of nonbinding facilitation. Internal workplace dispute resolution occasionally involves management and employee representatives and/or facilitation or decision making by a third party, but more often the decision maker or facilitator is structurally part of management.

Environmental mediation is increasingly being used on a case-by-case basis to resolve questions involving land use, including neighborhood and housing issues, urban and commercial development, parks, regional planning, natural resource management (including issues regarding fishing, mining, timber, and wilderness areas), energy, air quality, and hazardous waste (Bingham and Haygood 1986). Many environmental disputes arise due to the complexity and ambiguity of Environmental Protection Agency (EPA) regulations, federal laws such as the Resource Conservation and Recovery Act of 1976 (RCRA), and the Comprehensive Response, Compensation, and Liability Act of 1980 (CERCLA), as well as a plethora of state and local laws. Further, a number of federal administrative agencies, including the EPA, use mediation in the formulation of administrative regulations (or "reg-neg") (Amy 1987b; Holznagel 1986). We do not address reg-neg mediation in this essay. Environmental mediation is often very complex, involving multiple parties and technical issues with which at least some of the parties are unfamiliar. Indeed, one of the primary issues in environmental mediation is who ought to be at the bargaining table.

2. THE IDEOLOGY OF COMMUNITY IN INFORMAL DISPUTE RESOLUTION

The ideology of community celebrates a Durkheimian notion of social solidarity that treats harmony, cooperation, and compromise as morally superior to any substantive claims derived from rights. Informal dispute resolution seeks to promote inclusiveness, involvement, and empowerment of participants because those attributes are held to create consensus, harmony, and, ultimately, community (Abel 1981; Harrington and Merry 1988; Hofrichter 1987; Nader 1993a; Yngvesson 1993; Bush 1989). For example, Lederach and Kraybill (1993: 359), two mediation practitioners, define community as "people bonded by a common core of values." They portray conflict not as dissensus over values but rather as exclusion from community, arguing that conflict exists when people are excluded from the decision-making process, leading them to "react in ways that appear childish, irresponsible, or terroristic."

The ideology of community envisions a processual form of justice that depends on community participation: if through participation and communication consensus is achieved, then the substance of the agreement is assumed to be good for the community. Cooks and Hale (1994: 56–57), for example, argue that the goal of mediation is "in most instances, preservation of the disputants' relationship, rather than the 'defeat' of an 'opponent'" and that, in achieving this goal, communication is not only a tool but rather is "both the means and the ends of social interaction." The import placed on participation, moreover, envisions a local form of justice: the ideology of community is explicitly critical of formal law and the state because the formal legal system involves an imposition of state power on local citizens and relies on trained professionals rather than disputant participation (Abel 1982; Yngvesson 1993). Harrington and Merry (1988), for example, argue that an important motivation for early forms of alternative dispute resolution was the ideal of social transformation, a goal involving community participation, developing social networks and empowering them to handle local conflicts, and more generally moving away from the idea of justice imposed by the state on the citizenry. Thus, just as "rights" are a symbolic resource in the formal legal system, "community" is a symbolic resource in informal dispute resolution.

The ideology of community has six interrelated implications for how law matters in dispute resolution: (1) the construction and reification of relationships; (2) the institutionalization of a therapeutic paradigm of disputes and dispute resolution; (3) an ethic of reasonableness, which results in the systematic exclusion of extreme positions and undermining of legal rights; (4) a de-emphasis of the public values underlying legal rights and a concomitant emphasis on the private interests of the parties; (5) a myth of empowerment, as mediators structure the discourse of mediation in an effort to achieve agreement; and (6) remedies that emphasize relationships, compromise, individualization, and privacy. As we discuss in the next section, attention to legal issues in informal dispute resolution becomes highly contingent on its congruence with the ideology of community.

3. THE MATTER OF LAW IN INFORMAL DISPUTE RESOLUTION

A. THE CONSTRUCTION AND REIFICATION OF RELATIONSHIPS

The ideology of community assumes that community will emerge from harmonious relationships, and that conflict resolution should repair relationships.

But informal dispute resolution must often construct, transform, or reify the relationships in order to preserve them (Lederach and Kraybill 1993; Yngvesson 1993). In family mediation, the disputants seek to end their relationship, but mediators seek to transform the marital relationship into a "post-dissolution divorce relationship" (Fineman 1988). In employment, a relationship between employer and employee (or supervisor and subordinate) does exist prior to the dispute, but it is primarily a contractual relationship; social relationships, if they exist at all, are conditioned by the hierarchical and legal nature of the employment contract. Workplace dispute handlers, however, superimpose a social relationship in order to manufacture a workplace community. And in environmental mediation, the dispute itself often creates the relationship among the parties: developers and environmental groups are brought together only because they disagree about the use of environmental resources. Mediators, however, seek to sustain and improve the relationship between disputants in an effort to foster cooperation in the future. Regardless of whether the parties have or desire a relationship, mediation celebrates social relations. Where they do not exist, mediators construct them; where they do exist, they become central.

Articles on family mediation frequently emphasize the changing nature of the divorce relationship. Milne (1983: 22), for example, points out that family mediation works toward "an exploration of the potential for reconciliation, and a focus on the future relationship between the couple." And Harrell (1995: 374) argues:

> [F]amily law mediation does not involve opponents; it involves parties to a relationship that is going through a major change. When these clients are faced with post divorce events such as the birth of their first grandchild, their child's wedding, or their child's college graduation, their advocates will not be there to speak for them or control the situation on their behalfs. . . . If handled by a qualified mediator, the family mediation process can help parties achieve the confidence that they are able to work toward compromise and reach agreements even after their marital relationship has ended.

Similarly, an article in *Social Work* refers to the "co-parental divorce" and discusses the "changing relationships of each parent to his or her children" (Weingarten 1986). Another article also exemplifies mediation's effort to construct a future relationship.

> In contrast to the tension and trauma created by the adversarial approach, mediation, through its capacity to reorient the parties towards each other, creates an atmosphere in which the parties may solve their immediate disputes and at the same time lay a solid foundation for their future relationship. . . . But in cases where issues are hotly contested or, perhaps more importantly, where children are involved, providing for future communication is of critical importance. (Egle 1983: 697).

In environmental disputes, where the parties have often never interacted socially, Amy (1987b) discusses the tendency of environmental mediators to emphasize the import of the future relationship.

> Mediation does not lead to a resolution of the basic differences that separate the parties in conflict. Rather, in situations where none of the parties perceives that it is able to gain its goals unilaterally, mediation can help the parties agree on how to make the accommodations that will enable them to co-exist despite their continued differences. (Cormick 1982: 307)

Employment mediation seeks to create or preserve relationships in order to protect their investment in human capital. A dispute handler in a bank, for example, explains: "[Dispute resolution] is like recycling. You'd rather try to recycle, to save that relationship because we've invested time and money rather than just crumple it up and throw it away" (Edelman, Erlanger, and Lande 1990, bank interview, p. 32). And a dispute handler in a health care organization describes the relation between people in the workplace as marriage-like: "There's usually often a continuing issue between people. It's a marriage that has problems. You could fix a few of them but there's still going to be some other things that are going to be out there" (Edelman, Erlanger, and Lande 1990, health care interview, p. 43).

These examples suggest that the symbolic resource underlying an ideology tends to be reified. Critical legal scholars point out that liberal legal ideology reifies rights (Tushnet 1984; Gabel 1980). Similarly, the ideology of community reifies relationships. As a consequence, relationship issues tend to trump legal issues in informal dispute resolution.

B. THE THERAPEUTIC PARADIGM: PSYCHOSOCIAL VISIONS OF RELATIONSHIP PROBLEMS

The focus on relationships moves informal dispute resolution toward a therapeutic paradigm, which sees psychosocial problems as underlying most conflicts, and conflict resolution as a form of therapy for those problems. The therapeutic ideal is perhaps best characterized by former Chief Justice Warren Burger's plea that instead of participating in adversarial modes of dispute resolution, lawyers should serve as "healers of human conflicts" (quoted in Nader 1993b: 442). Whereas the liberal legal paradigm envisions plaintiff and defendant as having different visions of social or legal codes, and the third party as the adjudicator of those codes, the therapeutic paradigm envisions the participants as unhealthy and in need of therapy and the third party as healer. By healing interpersonal relationships, informal dispute resolution seeks to improve the overall health of the community. Mediators believe, moreover, that personal empowerment, improved communication, and dispute resolution techniques form the basis of a healthy community.[2]

The shift to a therapeutic model appears to have been greatly influenced by the helping professions. Professions gain status and jurisdiction by asserting expertise over a new area or reconstructing social understandings of extant problems (Larson 1977; Abbott 1988). The helping professions legitimate their role in dispute resolution by constructing disputes as more psychological than legal in nature (Fineman 1988; Edelman, Erlanger, and Lande 1993; Nader 1993a). Further, the helping professions criticize lawyers for failing to understand the psychological basis of disputes and the emotional needs of their clients, and they charge that the focus on rights and adversary techniques defeat the therapeutic ideal (Fineman 1988; Nader 1993a). For example, in an article titled "That Highly Emotional Client: All Hell Breaks Loose When Lawyers Resolve Legal Problems, But Fail To Deal With Emotional Needs," Feiger (1987) argues that lawyers must learn to deal with clients' emotional and legal problems as interrelated. As evidenced by Warren Burger's remark, many lawyers are disillusioned with adversarial techniques and appear to welcome the alliance with the helping professions and their therapeutic paradigm. Thus, the therapeutic logic of the helping professions is increasingly displacing traditional legal logic and legal rights as the dominant paradigm in informal dispute resolution.

The therapeutic view of mediation is characterized in a book titled *The Promise of Mediation* by Bush and Folger, both of whom are academics with involvements in clinical mediation programs.

[T]he mediation process contains within it a unique potential for transforming people—engendering moral growth—by helping them wrestle with difficult circumstances and bridge human differences, in the very midst of conflict. This transformative potential stems from mediation's capacity to generate two important effects, empowerment and recognition. In simplest terms, empowerment means the restoration to individuals of a sense of their own value and strength and their own capacity to handle life's problems. (Bush and Folger 1994: 2)

Illustrating the tendency of the therapeutic paradigm to consider notions of personal and relational fulfillment more important than social justice, Bush and Folger argue later in the book (p. 29) that engendering moral growth should take precedence over other goals of mediation, including fairness. They contend that although fair solutions may render people better off temporarily by changing situations, transformation achieves the more important goal of creating a better society.

Therapeutic thinking is perhaps most institutionalized in divorce mediation, where divorce tends to be characterized as an emotional crisis (Fineman 1988). Divorce mediation seeks to create communication between the parties, which is seen as a basis for a healthy postdissolution relationship. In this view, mediation is not only a therapeutic intervention for that emotional crisis, but can potentially turn divorce into a positive, growth-promoting experience. The following examples illustrate the therapeutic basis of divorce mediation.

1. The role of the mediator, like that of a therapist, is to understand the root cause of the parties' anger, for example, and its expression. Invariably, there

are triggers for anger from other emotions such as fear, anxiety, and a sense of betrayal. Anger is often the mask. (Zlatchin 1986: 41)

2. Mediators can aid spouses going through the emotional process of divorce by such therapeutic techniques as reflecting back to the client the current situation as it is described by the parties and providing an accepting atmosphere that allows the spouses to reveal their awful self and worst fears as well as their hopes for the future. (Lemmon 1983: 49)

3. [W]hile trauma and distress are recognized as modal components of divorce for both adults and children, it is also being realized that long-term debilitating consequences need not be inevitable. Indeed, it is the increasingly substantiated hope that innovative services, such as child custody mediation, which reflect in a clinical setting the insights gained from research and contemporary reconceptualizations of law and conflict resolution, can contribute much. (Koopman and Hunt 1988: 380)

Hofrichter (1987) notes similar trends in the interpersonal orientation in neighborhood dispute resolution (NDR). He argues that state-sponsored neighborhood mediation programs ignore the social bases of conflict and assume instead that the individual disputants are the problem: they, not the social problems that gave rise to their claims, require professional intervention. As in divorce mediation, NDR promotes communication as a means for achieving a more amiable relationship.

The focus on relationships also pervades internal workplace dispute resolution procedures in private work organizations (Edelman, Erlanger, and Lande 1993). Here internal dispute resolution recasts legal claims of discrimination as the types of interpersonal and psychological problems that managers routinely handle. Complaint handlers in organizations seek primarily to heal relationships and restore good employee relations rather than to end discrimination. Grounded in the therapeutic paradigm, internal dispute resolution focuses on feelings and emphasizes communication as a means of resolving problems. Therapeutic language and approaches are common (Edelman, Erlanger, and Lande 1993). Edelman, Erlanger, and Lande report the following statement by a complaint handler in a clinic (1993: 526–27):

Typically the first session is what I call "get it all out." . . . You let them dump the load and you know that's a very tense, difficult, session. . . . It's part of what in this grieving process you call stages and these types of things you have to kind of follow stages. . . . Part of it is just a lay it out on the line and . . . then break it into pieces, you know, look at the different parts of what the cause of some of these things are. . . . And then, there's usually follow up meetings. If it's that involved and that deep of a problem, I would try and have one of the professional staff here handle it because . . . I don't have the time to deal with that kind of ongoing therapy.

In environmental mediation, there is somewhat less of a tendency to see the parties as having underlying psychological problems, perhaps because the parties are usually organized political or corporate interest groups as opposed to individuals. But the therapeutic paradigm materializes as mediators claim that the process of conflict resolution contributes to health of the community. For example, Scott Mernitz (1980: 62–63) in *Mediation of Environmental Disputes: A Sourcebook* says: "[C]onflict has some positive attributes, but continued conflict produces an imbalance and irregularity which society cannot tolerate. The presence of conflict is healthy; eventual settlement is prerequisite to maintenance of health. . . . Mediation is a useful procedure for fulfilling this need with respect to environmental conflicts."

The ideology of community, then, gives rise to a therapeutic paradigm by recasting social problems as psychologically based problems; by curing those psychological pathologies, mediation can return relationships—and ultimately communities—to a healthy state. Whereas social problems require legal solutions such as the assignment of rights and formulation of policies, relationship problems invite therapeutic solutions and efforts to establish communication and consensus. Once legal relationships have been transformed into communication problems and social problems—that is, stripped of legitimacy as a basis for individual claims—legal principles and rights have far less place in the dispute resolution process. The therapeutic focus strips disputants of their status as rights-bearing subjects who may be involved in a legal relationship (e.g., as landlord and tenant) and reconstitutes them as individuals who need help getting along with one another (Hofrichter 1987; Silbey and Sarat 1989). In so doing, it places the focus on relationships rather than root causes of problems and on interpersonal conflict-resolution skills rather than power inequities or injustice (Nader 1993a).

C. The Ethic of Reasonableness

The logic of community promotes an ethic of reasonableness in informal dispute resolution which systematically suppresses extreme positions, even when those positions are supported by legal rights. Through their constructions of "rational behavior," mediators exert various forms of control over the issues and options that may be discussed, and they apply considerable pressure on parties to accept particular settlements (Silbey and Merry 1986; Fineman 1988; Bryan 1994; Grillo 1991). Because mediation depends on consensus, mediators tend to construe nonnegotiable positions as unreasonable and positions conducive to compromise as reasonable, largely without regard to the legal or ethical validity of the position. As a result, positions that deviate from the status quo tend to be constructed as unreasonable simply because they make negotiation and compromise more difficult (Silbey and Merry 1986; Hofrichter 1987). Where legal rights challenge the status quo, the ethic of reasonableness tends to pressure parties to forgo their rights. Reasonableness is, after all, a social construct: "extreme positions" or "unreasonable positions" are defined by their deviation from the status quo.

In child custody cases, for example, divorce mediators construe claims for sole custody as unreasonable, regardless of the conditions that may support such a claim. In fact, mediators often construe even the discussion of factors that might support sole custody as unreasonable, and thus discourage parties from raising past offenses (Grillo 1991; Greatbatch and Dingwall 1989), suggesting that the woman has been the primary caretaker (Fineman 1988) or suggesting moral blame on the part of the other party (Grillo 1991; Silbey and Merry 1986). Bryan (1994) reports that divorce mediators sometimes even construe hesitancy to agree to settlements or the desire to resort to more adversarial methods of dispute resolution as unreasonable, thus applying considerable pressure on disputants to accept settlements that courts would be unlikely to order.

Similar coercive patterns emerge in environmental and employment dispute resolution. Amy (1987b) reports that mediators consider demands by environmental groups for no development or no pollution as unreasonable, regardless of the environmental damage that may occur. And in employment, reasonableness may mean accepting employers' efforts to reduce discrimination rather than demanding an immediate cessation of all discrimination (Edelman, Erlanger, and Lande 1993).[3]

In addition to discouraging extreme political stances or nonnegotiable positions, the reasonableness ethic construes certain behavior patterns as unreasonable. Both emotional outbreaks or severely detached behavior can hinder settlement; thus, informal complaint handlers tend to sanction such behavior as unreasonable (Grillo 1991; Silbey and Merry 1986; Amy 1987b). Yet, especially in divorce, past events and conditions (such as abuse or patterns of control) may lead one party (often the woman) to behave more emotionally or to become numb. Employment discrimination claims may also involve explosive emotions (Bumiller 1987). And Amy (1987b) points out that members of environmental groups are often angry and emotional over developers' or polluters' actions, which violate their deeply held beliefs about the importance of environmental preservation. He contends that pressure toward reasonableness therefore tends to constrain environmentalists more than it constrains their opponents.

To the extent that mediators interpret extremes in emotion as evidence of unreasonableness rather than a result of social conditions, they systematically disadvantage disputants with less social status or weaker bargaining positions, as well as disputants who are suffering rights violations, all of whom are more inclined to become emotional or numb during negotiations (Bryan 1994; Bumiller 1987; Chambliss 1989). By labeling and sanctioning such behavior as unreasonable, the ethic of reasonableness is likely further to discourage the expression of claims by those parties.[4]

Mediators seek to create reasonableness primarily through the technique of "redirection." Through redirection, mediators direct disputants away from extreme positions, irrespective of the legal or ethical validity of those positions. As the following excerpt from *Earth Law Journal* illustrates, adherence to particular positions thwarts consensus and, thus, the success of informal dispute resolution. "As groups and individuals become characterized as 'good' and 'bad' and issues as 'right' and 'wrong,' positions become 'non-negotiable.' Unless the dynamics of such a situation can be redirected, there is little or no scope for mediation" (Cormick 1976: 217). The practitioner literature reflects three techniques of redirection: reframing disputants' statements to promote consensus, threatening dire results should the parties maintain extreme positions, and sanctioning behavior that is not conducive to compromise (Silbey and Merry 1986; Bryan 1992).

Reframing techniques, in which mediators construct disputants' positions in ways that encourage agreement, shared values, and shared experiences, may subtly discourage attention to legal rights by shifting disputants' attention to those elements of their disputes that are most conducive to compromise. Robert D. Benjamin, a mediator who analogizes the role of the mediator to that of a trickster, observes the following in an article titled "The Constructive Uses of Deception: Skills, Strategies, and Techniques of the Folkloric Trickster Figure and Their Application by Mediators."

> The mediator, like the trickster, takes the communication of a party and, without abrogating his or her meaning entirely, alters and redirects that meaning to allow for its more constructive use in the settlement process. Thus, when parties are actively fighting, the mediator might compliment the parties on how well they fight and then go on to reframe their negative statements into positive meanings by noting that "people who fight well can negotiate well." The mediator . . . twists their words and shifts the context of the discussion. . . . In reframing, the mediator operates to reposition each of the antagonists so that the dispute is amenable to a resolution. (Benjamin 1995: 9)

Another redirection technique consists of threats, such as those exemplified by Judge Welch and Hugh McIsaac, director of family services for a state court in Oregon, which seek to create fear in parties who might maintain "irrational" positions. The following examples are from mediation orientations for parties. The first threatens psychological damage.

> The one thing that I know for sure from my experience in this field is that if you have a battle over your children, your children are going to be damaged. It's only a question of how severe and how long lasting the damage is going to be. . . . When [parents] behave like immature, out-of-control adolescents, then the message to your child is that the world is a very unsafe place. . . . So, we are saying to you, take the responsibility and resolve these issues for their sake because the alternative is very damaging to your children. (Welch, Herrell, and Koch 1994: 300)

The second threat relates more to the pocketbook: "If you go to court, it can be very expensive. Some kids will be going to college, but it's not going to be your kids. You can spend a lot of money in this courthouse fighting over custody. It's expensive, it's costly, and it can be very damaging" (McIsaac 1994: 59).

Sanctioning techniques, in which mediators label certain substantive positions as irrational or unreasonable, can be subtly or overtly coercive. Mediators may threaten a party who is acting "unreasonably" with negative recommendations to a judge or recommendations favoring the other party. Fineman (1988) reports that mediators sometimes treat one parent's request for sole custody as a sign of unwillingness to cooperate and sanction such requests by threatening to recommend sole custody for the other parent.

By discouraging the expression of extreme positions, then, the ethic of reasonableness—enforced through redirection—may systematically undermine legal rights. Claims based on legal rights may be extreme (as in the claim to a harassment-*free* workplace or to development policies that *do not threaten* endangered species), and where they protect weaker parties, they are likely to threaten the status quo and to entail emotional appeal. Legal rights tend to place one party in the right and the other in the wrong, a result that would harm rather than promote harmonious relationships and would interfere with mutual assent in the immediate case. For example, Stier and Hamilton (1984: 699) argue: "The mediation process is designed to help parties move away from taking antagonistic positions and arguing in terms of rights. This shift in perspective is accomplished by assisting the parties to identify their interests and to find ways to mutually accommodate them. The agreement, therefore, should represent a win-win outcome." The claims of groups without clout, moreover, whether or not they are supported by legal rights, are likely to be construed as extreme—and will be disfavored in informal dispute resolution—simply because they challenge the extant power structure.

In cases where legal rights support extreme positions, the normative effect of law provides a force counter to the reasonableness ethic: because they usually retain the right to resort to the formal system, parties may bolster their extreme claims by references to law or threats of litigation. However, since both structural and psychological barriers to the mobilization of legal rights tend to preclude socially disenfranchised groups from asserting their legal rights (Bumiller 1987, 1988; Felstiner, Abel, and Sarat 1981), these threats may often be, or appear to be, idle. Further, the reasonableness ethic's construction of inflexible demands for legal rights as illegitimate, inappropriate, and selfish seriously compromises the normative impact of law in informal settings. The normative effect of legal rights is contingent on those rights not bumping up against the ideology of community.

D. INATTENTION TO PUBLIC VALUES

Most disputes involve, and can be framed in terms of, both private interests and public values. A dispute over the building of a convention center on a lakefront park, for example, involves private issues affecting the developers who stand to gain money, the local politicians who stand to gain prominence, and the local residents who stand to lose access to and views of the lakefront and who would endure noise and congestion. But there are also public values at stake—the normative beliefs or claims regarding the interests of society or principles of social justice; in this case, urban and economic development, on the one hand, and environmental concerns such as the preservation of land, water, and wildlife and the avoidance of pollution, on the other.

Whether disputes are framed in terms of private interests or public values is a function in part of prevailing notions of social justice and strategic political rhetoric; framing the convention center dispute as a matter of economic prosperity or environmental preservation is likely to carry significantly greater legitimacy in the public eye than framing it as a matter of developers' wealth or residents' loss of view. But prevailing notions of social justice and strategic political rhetoric are themselves dynamically intertwined with legal culture; law provides a powerful language in which to articulate public values and, at any particular time, supports certain public values over others. When lawyers, politicians, and political interest groups frame disputes in terms of public values, they are both constructing and responding to legal notions of rights.[5]

Informal dispute resolution does not ignore public values altogether, but it favors those public values such as harmony and cooperation which are consistent with the ideology of community (Bush 1989). Public values such as civil rights, environmental preservation, and gender equality, however, tend to involve nonnegotiable positions that thwart harmony. Informal dispute handlers are likely, therefore, to construe these positions as extreme or unreasonable, and appeals to those public values carry little weight. Using redirection techniques, informal dispute handlers tend to shift the focus from such "unreasonable" public values toward values that are consistent with the ideology of community; thus, mediators focus on relationships and (what they see as) the parties' underlying private interests and needs, which may be more susceptible to settlement (Aubert 1963; Menkel-Meadow 1984; Ury, Brett, and Goldberg 1988; Silbey and Sarat 1989; Hofrichter 1987; Amy 1987b; Fineman 1988; Edelman, Erlanger, and Lande 1993).

In the three types of disputes we consider, the nature and extent of the shift away from public values differs, in part due to differences in the public conceptions of these types of disputes and in part due to characteristics of the parties typically involved. In family mediation, the shift from public values to private interests may be the least noticeable since the realm of family tends to be socially constructed as a private matter, a phenomenon that some feminists believe contributes to the repression of women in society (see, e.g., MacKinnon 1984). Because of this social construction, courts as well as family mediators tend to focus on the needs and preferences of the individuals involved. The primary public value that pervades the divorce custody arena, for example, is reflected in the "best interest of the child" standard. References to this standard are common in both courts and family mediation, which is likely due to the significant and growing normative overlap in the family arena.[6] In family mediation, however, even this standard may be abandoned in favor of the parents' negotiation based on private interests. One article advocating custody mediation, for example, suggests that mediation avoids "the imposition of the judge's values upon a family system" (Pruhs, Paulsen, and Tysseling 1984: 533). It further argues: "A sophisticated blend of values governs the operation of each family. . . . An imposed decision based upon values of an evaluator or judge, values which may be fundamentally in opposition to those of the family, is more likely to upset these balances than a settlement reached by the parents utilizing the family's own values" (Pruhs, Paulsen, and Tysseling 1984: 533–34).

Within family mediation, the transformation from public to private is especially evident in the arena of property distribution, where state laws increasingly prescribe equal distribution of property between husband and wife. The public value here is economic equality for women. But in family mediation, the public value of women's economic status is ignored as individuals mediate based on their own private interests and needs (Bryan 1994). The mediation literature generally sees negotiations based on private interests as advantageous for both parties. Dworkin and London (1989: 8), for example, point out that although California marital property law requires a fifty-fifty property division, "in mediation the couple has an opportunity to develop their own standards of equity, which may not be the same."

In the employment context, informal dispute resolution involves a shift from issues of workplace fairness and discrimination to managerial issues. Discrimination complaints tend to be recast as problems typical of the managerial realm: poor management, interpersonal difficulties, or social-psychological problems (Edelman, Erlanger, and Lande 1993). For example, a complaint handler in a medical clinic reported: "[Sexual harassment] had nothing to do with it—it was a larger work group issue in terms of how these people work together so I brought in a psychologist who worked with the group on how to . . . work together as a team" (Edelman, Erlanger, and Lande 1990, clinic interview, p. 22). Similarly, an article by a mediator suggests that for mediators in sexual harassment cases, "[I]t is important to examine the parties' underlying interests, especially intangible concerns such as privacy, publicity, and reputation" (Winograd 1995: 42).

The shift from public to private is also quite noticeable in the realm of environmental disputes, where mediation tends to recast issues of pollution, development, and preservation into the private needs of the parties involved (Amy 1987b). In an article on environmental mediation in the *Journal of Applied Behavioral Science*, Lentz (1986: 132) suggests that, because public values tend to involve nebulous goals that defeat settlement, "[m]ediators must begin the process by helping the parties define their bargaining positions out of hard-to-quantify values. To do this, mediators may encourage the parties to separate their bargaining position from their values." Similarly, Bingham (1986: 109), in an article on environmental mediation, argues that: "Mediators commonly stress the importance of using 'interest-based negotiation' instead of 'positional bargaining,' believing that various parties' ability and willingness to identify the interests that underlie each other's positions and to invent new alternatives that satisfy those interests helps enormously in resolving disputes."

The ramifications of the shift from public to private values go beyond the immediate case; claims based on rights are more often generalizable (Minow 1987; Hofrichter 1987; Silbey and Sarat 1989). By framing issues as private rather than public, informal dispute resolution tends to separate each instance of conflict from other similar cases and from the structural setting in which it occurs. This privatization of conflict inhibits social reform by making similar experiences by other members of a social group irrelevant.

To be sure, appeals to public values will have some effect in informal dispute resolution because of the constitutive and normative effects of law. But within the context of informal dispute resolution, pressures to leave certain public values behind are strong. Public values have legal, social, and intellectual appeal in legal forums because they are grounded in liberal legal logic. In a forum that celebrates the ideology of community, public values carry little legitimacy unless they can be linked to the values of harmony and future relationships.

E. THE MYTH OF EMPOWERMENT

The ideology of community seeks to build community by empowering individuals to handle conflict and thus to achieve harmony. Whereas liberal legal ideology locates fairness in formal procedure, the ideology of community seeks to place the responsibility for fairness squarely in the hands of the disputants and dispute handler. In an article in *Mediation Quarterly*, Folberg (1983: 9) makes this point:

> Mediation offers these advantages because mediation is less bound by the rules of procedure and substantive law and by the assumptions or norms that dominate the adversary process. The ultimate authority in mediation belongs to the parties themselves, and they can fashion a unique solution that will work for them without a concern for existing precedent or for the precedent that they may set for others. With the help of the mediator, the parties can consider their needs, their interest, and whatever else they deem to be relevant regardless of rules of evidence or substantive law.

In mediation, then, the parties—rather than the law—determine the scope of negotiations and the outcome.

But parties are often unequal in power. Two family lawyers highlight the problem of party inequality in family mediation. "In many marriages the partners are not equal: One makes the decisions, the other complies. Generally the decision-maker also has greater negotiating skill and more information about the couple's finances. With an impartial mediator who withholds personal judgements, resolution of the issues is likely to favor the dominant partner" (Diamond and Simborg 1983: 37). Along these lines, critics of informal dispute resolution argue that, even though formal due process protections fail to place unequal parties on equal footing, the absence of those protections perpetuates and exacerbates the advantages of parties who enjoy greater social, political, and economic clout (Silbey and Sarat 1989; Fiss 1984; Delgado et al. 1985; Grillo 1991; Bryan 1992, 1994; Edelman, Erlanger, and Lande 1993).

Delgado et al. (1985) argue that informal dispute resolution may foster racial and ethnic prejudice because there are few rules to constrain conduct and no explicit policies condemning racial discrimination. Grillo (1991) and Bryan (1992, 1994) discuss the emotional and societal disadvantages of women in the context of family mediation. They argue that women generally are disadvantaged in mediation for several reasons: men tend to possess greater tangible resources such as income and education, which give men greater social power, and therefore negotiating power[7]; women are more likely to consider the situation of the other and therefore to give in to others' desires; women often are more reluctant to be assertive or aggressive because their past experience suggests that such behavior produces negative consequences; and women often are conditioned to defer to their husbands in the marital relationship.[8] Bryan (1992) also argues that sex role ideologies that support male dominance, women's lower reward expectations, women's greater likelihood of depression, and women's greater fear of achievement all tend to place women at a disadvantage in mediation. Thus, social stratification and status differences, while problematic in formal adjudication, tend to be exacerbated in informal dispute resolution because of the lack of due process protections and the greater responsibilities placed on the parties.[9]

Disparities are especially problematic where the more powerful party is also a repeat player and the less powerful party a one-shotter (Galanter 1974), as is often the case in employment and environmental disputes.[10] The advantages Galanter points to in formal litigation seem even more compelling with respect to informal dispute resolution where repeat players still have greater expertise and resources but are less constrained by rights and precedent. Although some repeat player advantages, such as playing for the rules, may have less effect in informal dispute resolution, repeat players may attempt to use the formal system where rules favor them or they can influence rules but use the informal system to avoid rules or setting of unfavorable legal precedent. Employees and environmental groups may choose informal dispute resolution because they fear or cannot afford litigation. But this gives greater bargaining power to employers, developers, and polluters, because they can withhold concessions that a court might order, knowing that their opponents cannot afford to fight them in court. Where one party enjoys power over the other, it is better able to circumvent legal requirements and to exclude legal issues from the bargaining table. In environmental mediation, moreover, an important issue is who is at the bargaining table. Many environmental disputes involve multiple parties, including public interest groups, business organizations, and local, state, and federal government agencies (Cormick 1976; Lentz 1986; Leipmann 1986).

One party may gain substantial advantages simply by managing to exclude or include another interested party from the process.

Given that the parties in informal dispute resolution have responsibility for the agenda and results, dispute handler neutrality rises in importance because it is central to fairness of both process and outcome. There are two problematic issues here: (1) neutrality is difficult to define, especially where parties are unequal; and (2) mediators' interest in settlement often motivates them subtly to structure the discourse of mediation.

First, with respect to the meaning of neutrality, Cobb and Rifkin (1991) point out that mediators are asked simultaneously to be formally neutral and to balance the power between the parties. The practitioner literature frequently addresses the problematic nature of neutrality but generally suggests that mediators, if sensitive, can both maintain impartiality and help weaker parties overcome deficiencies. Bryan (1992) argues that such sensitivity is unlikely due to insufficient attention to power issues and insufficient training.[11]

Even with substantial training, compensating for power differences would be extremely difficult in a society where power operates in subtle ways. Mediators may not always be able to take all interests into account. Parties may behave opportunistically, hiding their true interests. Further, mediators are not immune from social cues and the effects of social status; just as people of lower status defer to those of higher status, mediators are likely to defer to persons of higher status (Bryan 1992, 1994). To the extent that mediators reinforce or fail to compensate for women's disadvantages in negotiating, mediation outcomes are likely to replicate gendered power relations of wider society. Although social power relations also affect outcomes in courts, lawyers may rely on legal entitlements created over the past two decades that offer greater protections to the financial position of women (see Bryan 1992 for a discussion of these changes). To some extent, these entitlements may also enter into negotiations in divorce mediation through the normative and institutional effects of law. However, the "empowerment" of parties means that the more powerful party may be able to narrow the scope of negotiations in a way that minimizes the value of appealing to those legal rights. The ethic of reasonableness and delegitimation of public values make this easier.

Second, mediators' professional interest in producing a settlement often leads them to exert considerable force in trying to shape both the discourse of mediation and the parties' views of what constitutes a fair settlement. Cobb and Rifkin (1991: 60) argue that "narrative processes, mediator participation, mediators' psychologized vocabulary, and the structure of the mediation process itself all contribute to the production of consensus (the dominant story) in ways that are not available for discussion by the mediators or the disputants." Greatbatch and Dingwall (1989) also challenge the notion of client control in informal dispute resolution; in their study of family mediation, they argue that mediators use selective participation to encourage some options and discourage others, often exerting a great deal of pressure on the parties. Fineman (1988) argues that members of the helping professions who serve as informal dispute handlers often have institutional and professional biases toward certain outcomes; for example, one reason why the helping professions favor joint custody is because it ensures their continued role in custody decision making. And Edelman, Erlanger, and Lande (1993) point out that in the workplace, internal dispute handlers are prone to divert attention from law-based claims because they are structurally part of management and depend for pay and career advancement on the approval of management.

One strategy mediators use to shape the discourse of mediation and the nature of claims that parties make is to invoke the ethic of reasonableness, treating extreme positions and behaviors that are not conducive to settlement as "unreasonable" or "irrational." In the example below, a mediator explains her strategy for "handling" an "unreasonable" client in a family mediation case. "A client who was a college professor regularly launched into a diatribe of 'I can't believe you are doing this to me' whenever his wife brought an issue to the bargaining table. When I asked if, as a favor, his higher intelligence could address the issue on the table, he understood immediately and offered a reasonable proposal" (Gold 1993: 63). The same mediator suggests strategic use of information in explaining the mediation process:

> During times of emotional crisis or life transition, the unconscious mind is looking for information to help resolve developmental demands and ease psychological pain. People are more suggestible and are likely to be deeply receptive to suggestions. The introductory informational "monologue" can be strategically used to convey information conducive to negotiating success, cooperation, and healing, because the unconscious is paying close attention. You can embed suggestions about healing and higher purpose . . . [and] preempt potential roadblocks by describing a set of behavioral norms associated with successful outcomes. (Gold 1993: 64)

In one employment example, the complaint handler discusses using mediation as a means of convincing the employee that no discrimination occurred.

> One example . . . was age discrimination . . . when an individual claimed he or she did not get a particular promotion. We investigated that . . . in seeking the support material to convince . . . the complainant that was not the case. [The complainant] didn't accept it totally and we therefore had to, in essence, mediate the conclusion by drawing the supervisor in. (Edelman, Erlanger, and Lande 1990, utility interview, pp. 26–27)

The empowerment of disputants in informal dispute resolution is largely a fiction, then, because "neutrals" cannot in reality be neutral. Informal dispute handlers necessarily assert control and necessarily impose their unarticulated biases in the process of conciliation. Disputants compete to assert their versions of the story and informal dispute handlers either subtly or not so subtly choose and build on some stories over others. Participants are legally disempowered because they lack lawyers to assert their legal arguments and because the ethic of reasonableness delegitimates many law-based arguments. Empowerment means that participants can talk more, but their words mean less. Substantive and procedural biases are of course inherent in any legal process; judges are no more neutral than mediators and lawyers. But the "empowerment" of participants in informal dispute resolution may exacerbate the power of the "haves" by locating fairness in the hands of the participants; thus social power differences are held in check only by the (problematic) neutrality of the dispute handler.

F. Resolutions That Build Community

Under the ideology of community, the moral import of cooperation and harmony are compelling. Remedies are designed to further the values we have discussed in previous sections: preserving relationships, healing psychological pathologies, ensuring reasonableness, emphasizing private needs and interests, and above all reaching a compromise settlement. Resolutions attentive to legal theories are disfavored because they are detrimental to relationships, neglect underlying pathologies, are viewed as extreme, emphasize values unrelated to individual needs, and assign right and wrong.

In family mediation, there is a strong preference for joint custody because mediators claim that it preserves relationships and simply assume that joint custody is in the best interest of the child, irrespective of past actions of the parents (Fineman 1988; Bryan 1992; Grillo 1991; Vanderkooi and Pearson 1983). This bias is reflected in the tendency for divorce mediators to refer to custody as "co-parenting." In an article in *Trial*, for example, Ruman and Lamm (1983: 84–85) provide the following advice for mediators: "The mediators hope to help the couple work out co-parenting agreements that truly make 'best interest' a viable concept. . . . The mediator tries to help the couple brainstorm possible alternatives and encourages the couple to continue to work out a draft of the 'co-parenting agreement.' " Similarly, an article in *Mediation Quarterly* equates joint custody with successful mediation: "Arrangements concerning child custody and visitation can be an accurate barometer of successful mediation. . . . Joint legal custody, joint physical custody, or both can be considered a positive outcome of mediation" (Lemmon 1983: 49).

In informal employment dispute resolution, Edelman, Erlanger, and Lande (1993) report that remedies tend to be designed to preserve smooth employment relations rather than to end discrimination. Whereas remedies in court are framed in terms of rights violations and are therefore designed to declare acts as discriminatory and preclude their recurrence, informal remedies are primarily educational, pragmatic, and therapeutic, designed to improve relationships. Punitive remedies are common in some organizations, but they are generally mild and often consist of required apologies; even here, the purpose is primarily to preserve or improve relationships. For example, a complaint handler in a public utility describes common types of resolutions as follows: "We try to resolve it within the company and resolve it based on working conditions, not as a situation whereby the company or the defendant owes them money for ill feeling or whatever. . . . They just want to get the issue resolved and resume . . . normal working conditions. That's their main objective" (Edelman, Erlanger, and Lande 1990, utility interview, pp. 40–41).

In employment, the ideology of community dictates discretion as well as privatization: communities must be concerned about the privacy and reputation of their members, and public declarations of wrongdoing would compromise these concerns. Thus, remedies in employment dispute resolution tend to be quiet and discreet. Edelman, Erlanger, and Lande (1993) report that in one of the rare cases in which a manager was fired for sexual harassment, the employer was careful not to use the punishment as an example to others, and in fact refrained from informing other employees as to why the manager was fired out of concern for his privacy. The concern for privacy and discretion led eight of the ten companies in this study to have explicit policies about keeping complaints and their resolutions confidential. This concern fosters community but diminishes the definition and elaboration of rules.

Environmental mediation also seeks to produce working relations between the parties, to diffuse adversarial feelings, and to emphasize common interests (Amy 1987a). Environmental mediators often emphasize the value of working relationships in avoiding future conflicts.

> [I]f potential conflicts are identified before major investments have been made . . . and opposing views have hardened, the various interests can often be organized to work together with the assistance of a third party. Potential areas of dispute can be identified, information and viewpoints can be shared, and questions can be answered early enough in the project planning process that the proposed design itself can reflect mutually acceptable solutions. (Bellman et al. 1981: 4)

Amy points out that environmental mediations are likely to produce compromise agreements that result in less pollution, less development, or compensation for loss but are unlikely to result in projects being stopped entirely. He also suggests that by emphasizing harmony, environmental mediation all but eliminates the possibility that environmentalists will continue to demand that development projects be stopped because it effectively diffuses their antagonism, which is often the basis for their stamina; environmental activists therefore more easily give up their goals. This, of course, is the goal of mediation: relationships triumph over political goals.

4. CONCLUSION

In sum, we argue that the ideology of community operates at loggerheads with liberal legal logic. Informal dispute resolution treats community as a symbolic resource and therefore lessens the import of rights and legal principles without suffering significant loss of legitimacy. Because it is grounded in the ideology of community, informal dispute resolution tends to construct and reify relationships even where they do not exist or are over, to recast legal problems as psychosocial problems in need of therapeutic solutions, to impose an ethic of reasonableness that systematically discourages extreme positions, to emphasize private interests and principles over public values (except where those public values incorporate notions of community), to replace legal principles with the preferences and social biases of the disputants and the dispute handlers, and to produce resolutions that promote compromise, harmony, and future relationships. Thus, informal dispute resolution tends systematically to render legal rights and legal principles contingent on their congruity with the ideology of community.

At the same time, informal dispute resolution exists within a larger culture in which liberal legal ideology is highly institutionalized: thus, law does matter. Formal law matters most in its constitutive role; by reifying social ideas of wrongs and rights, law suggests what experiences ought to generate disputes and influences the issues that are brought to informal dispute resolution. Although informal dispute handlers tend to minimize the relevance of legal principles and rights, the culture of liberal legalism influences the language and logic of disputants and dispute handlers.

Nonetheless, because the ideology of community is the prevailing logic within the enclave of informal dispute resolution, legal claims can easily be rendered illegitimate and forceless. As we stated early in the essay, many legal rights are also extremely difficult to assert and realize through formal legal forums. The same social biases, inequities between the parties, and characteristics of decision making and conciliation exist as in informal dispute resolution, causing the "haves" almost always to come out ahead. Our claim is that law matters less, and matters differently, in informal dispute resolution because the ideology of community gains legitimacy from a different set of symbolic resources. Whereas liberal legal ideology derives legitimacy from its attention to rights, the ideology of community derives legitimacy from the ideal of harmonious communities.

The contingency of legal matter that pervades informal dispute resolution, however, seems to be making its way into the formal legal realm. As the growing popularity of informal dispute resolution engenders increasing institutional alliances between the informal and formal systems, constitutive and normative forces in both directions operate to blur the distinctions between the liberal legal logics and the logics of community in all dispute resolution arenas.

NOTES

We wish to thank Penelope Bryan, William C. Burns, Murray J. Edelman, Howard S. Erlanger, Marc Galanter, Neil Gross, Harvey Jacobs, Joyce Sterling, Jessica Trubek, Christopher

Uggen, and participants in the 1993 Law and Society Institute for Sociolegal Studies for helpful comments on earlier versions of this essay.

1. To collect the practitioner articles, we used computer searches on Legaltrack and the Index of Legal Periodicals as well as follow-up citations we found in the original articles. We chose articles based on their apparent relevance to our research question. We make no claims about the representativeness of these articles but see no reason why our search strategy should have produced a biased sample of articles.

2. Of course, not all mediators are equally prone to embrace the therapeutic model (Silbey and Merry 1986). It is also important to note that the therapeutic paradigm is not unique to informal dispute resolution; it is also found in formal legal institutions, especially the lower courts (Merry 1990).

3. The ideal of compromise is so institutionalized that it is often hard to see how an ethic of reasonableness could be problematic. But our ideas of reason are conditioned by the social context. Today a prohibition against slavery seems reasonable, but 150 years ago, a demand for the total abolition of slavery would have seemed extreme, as too much of an economic burden on the plantation system. The question for a mediator at that time would have been: How much slavery is reasonable and under what conditions is it reasonable?

4. Research on the traditional lawyer-client relationship suggests that lawyers also discourage emotional behavior and attention to emotions (Sarat and Felstiner 1989). But in traditional litigation, the client's emotional behavior is less likely to affect her ability to achieve her goals since her attorney handles the litigation and any settlement negotiations.

5. Public values, and therefore rights, matter because of the legitimacy of liberal legal ideology, which gives import to rules that apply generally to all classes of cases and universally to all classes of litigants. Thus, in a court, it would be more effective to frame the convention center dispute in terms of public values than in terms of private interests. Private interests are generally relevant in formal law only where they derive from public values such as liberty and freedom. To be sure, as critical legal theorists point out, liberal legal ideology focuses on individual rights grounded in public values, not on class rights, and therefore tends to inhibit class-based social reform (Freeman 1990). But the appeal to public values inherent in individual rights nonetheless provides more potential for social reform than is the case in informal dispute resolution where most public values do not matter.

6. Many states are now mandating mediation as part of formal divorce and custody proceedings.

7. Bryan (1992) points out that the wage gap between husbands and wives is even greater than that between men and women generally. She reports that approximately 50 percent of married women earn no income. When wives do work, their incomes average less than half that of married men. Greater income allows parties to purchase expert advice and to threaten termination of negotiations, since a lawsuit would be less burdensome. Bryan also reports that although men and women tend to marry those of similar education levels, where a difference exists, women tend to have lower educational attainment than their husbands. Education may create direct negotiation advantages such as better knowledge of the tax consequences of property division and may indirectly create confidence that increases bargaining power.

8. McCarrick et al. (1991) report that in troubled marriages, wives have more difficulty expressing and asserting themselves in discussions with their husbands than they do in conversations with other men. Further, social psychological research on expectation states shows that social status greatly affects social interactions and that both race (white)

and sex (male) operate as status cues independently of other characteristics, enabling higher-status individuals to direct and dominate interaction (Ridgeway and Berger 1986). See Bryan (1992) for a detailed discussion of research showing that social status affects negotiation success.

9. Some readers will no doubt be uncomfortable with the argument that women or minorities are likely to do less for themselves in mediation than are men or whites. But to be uncomfortable with the result does not justify ignoring social patterns of gender and race dominance. Our argument is not that there are any innate differences between these social groups, but rather that historical patterns of repression and discrimination have created a social hierarchy that replicates itself in any dispute resolution forum. Lawyers can rely on formal entitlements and professional training to mitigate these patterns; lay people are less likely to be able to do so.

10. Galanter (1974) argues that repeat players (those who anticipate repeated litigation) enjoy a number of advantages over one-shotters in formal litigation, including lower start-up costs, greater expertise, a greater ability to withstand delay, the ability to use a long-term strategy by focusing on more important cases, the ability to lobby for rule change, and the ability to structure future transactions to gain legal advantages.

11. Bryan (1992: 499) reports that the better divorce mediation programs require trainees to devote a maximum of forty hours, usually over a five-day period, to becoming a mediator. She also argues that there is a lack of standards for divorce mediation.

BIBLIOGRAPHY

Abbott, Andrew. 1988. *The System of Professions.* Chicago: Univ. of Chicago Press.

Abel, Richard. 1981. Conservative Conflict and the Reproduction of Capitalism: The Role of Informal Justice. 9 *International Journal of the Sociology of Law*, 245.

Abel, Richard L., ed. 1982. *The Politics of Informal Justice.* Vols. 1 and 2. New York: Academic Press.

Amy, Douglas. 1987a. The Politics of Environmental Mediation. 14 *Ecology Law Quarterly*, 751.

——. 1987b. *The Politics of Environmental Mediation.* New York: Columbia Univ. Press.

Aubert, Vilhelm. 1963. Competition and Dissensus: Two Types of Conflict and of Conflict Resolution. *Journal of Conflict Resolution*, 26.

Bellman, Howard, Gail Bingham, Ronnie Brooks, Susan Carpenter, Peter Clark, and Robert Craig. 1981. Environmental Conflict Resolution: Practitioners' Perspective of an Emerging Field. *Resolve* (Winter) 1, 3–7.

Benjamin, Robert. 1995. The Constructive Uses of Deception: Skills, Strategies, and Techniques of the Folkloric Trickster Figure and Their Application by Mediators. 13(1) *Mediation Quarterly*, 3.

Bingham, Gail. 1986. *Resolving Environmental Disputes: A Decade of Experience.* Washington, DC: Conservation Foundation.

Bingham, Gail, and Leah V. Haygood. 1986. Environmental Dispute Resolution: The First Ten Years. 41(4) *Arbitration Journal*, 3.

Bryan, Penelope. 1992. Killing Us Softly: Divorce Mediation and the Politics of Power. 40 *Buffalo Law Rev.*, 441.

————. 1994. Reclaiming Professionalism: The Lawyer's Role in Divorce Mediation. 28(2) *Family Law Quarterly*, 177.

Bumiller, Kristin. 1987. Victims in the Shadow of the Law: A Critique of the Model of Legal Protection. 12 *Signs*, 421.

————. 1988. *The Civil Rights Society*. Baltimore: Johns Hopkins Univ. Press.

Bush, Robert Baruch. 1989. Defining Quality in Dispute Resolution: Taxonomies and Anti-Taxonomies of Quality Arguments. 66 *Denver Univ. Law Rev.*, 335.

Bush, Robert Baruch, and Joseph P. Folger. 1994. *The Promise of Mediation: Responding to Conflict through Empowerment and Recognition*. San Francisco: Jossey-Bass.

Carlin, Jerome E. 1966. *Lawyers' Ethics: A Survey of the New York City Bar*. New York: Russell Sage Foundation.

Chambliss, Elizabeth. 1989. The Role of Confrontation in Equal Employment Advocacy. *Institute for Legal Studies*, Working Paper 4–6.

Cloke, Kenneth. 1993. Revenge, Forgiveness, and the Magic of Mediation. 11 *Mediation Quarterly*, 67.

Cobb, Sara, and Janet Rifkin. 1991. Practice and Paradox: Deconstructing Neutrality in Mediation. 16 *Law and Social Inquiry*, 35.

Cooks, Leda M., and Claudia L. Hale. 1994. The Construction of Ethics in Mediation. 12 *Mediation Quarterly*, 55.

Cormick, Gerald W. 1976. Mediating Environmental Controversies: Perspectives and First Experience. 2 *Earth Law Journal*, 215.

————. 1982. The Myth, the Reality and the Future of Environmental Mediation. 24 *Environment*, 14.

Delgado, Richard, C. Dunn, P. Brown, H. Lee, and D. Hubbert. 1985. Fairness and Formality: Minimizing the Risk of Prejudice in Alternative Dispute Resolution. 1985 *Wisconsin Law Rev.*, 1359.

Diamond, Ann Lugas, and Madeleine Simborg. 1983. Divorce Mediation's Strengths . . . and Weaknesses. 3 *California Lawyer*, 37.

Dworkin, Joan, and William London. 1989. What Is a Fair Agreement? 7(1) *Mediation Quarterly*, 3.

Edelman, Lauren B. 1990. Legal Environments and Organizational Governance: The Expansion of Due Process in the Workplace. 95 *American Journal of Sociology*, 1401.

————. 1992. Legal Ambiguity and Symbolic Structures: Organizational Mediation of Civil Rights Law. 97 *American Journal of Sociology*, 1531.

Edelman, Lauren, Steven Abraham, and Howard Erlanger. 1992. Professional Construction of Law: The Inflated Threat of Wrongful Discharge. 26 *Law and Society Rev.*, 47.

Edelman, Lauren, Howard Erlanger, and John Lande. 1990. Transcripts of Interviews with Complaint Handlers. Unpublished.

————. 1993. Internal Dispute Resolution: The Transformation of Civil Rights in the Workplace. 27 *Law and Society Rev.*, 497.

Edelman, Lauren, Christopher Uggen, and Howard S. Erlanger. 1998. The Endogeneity of Legal Regulation: Grievance Procedures as Rational Myth. Manuscript in progress.

Egle, Gilbert. 1983. Divorce Mediation: An Innovative Approach to Family Dispute Resolution. 28 *Land and Water Law Rev.*, 693.

Erlanger, Howard S., Elizabeth Chambliss, and Margo S. Melli. 1987. Participation and Flexibility in Informal Processes: Cautions from the Divorce Context. 21 *Law and Society Rev.*, 585.

Feiger, Lynn. 1987. That Highly Emotional Client: All Hell Breaks Loose When Lawyers Resolve Legal Problems, But Fail to Deal with Emotional Needs. 9(3) *Family Advocate*, 28.

Felstiner, William L. F., Richard L. Abel, and Austin Sarat. 1981. The Emergence and Transformation of Disputes: Naming, Blaming and Claiming. 15 *Law and Society Rev.*, 631.

Fineman, Martha. 1988. Dominant Discourse, Professional Language and Legal Change in Child Custody Decisionmaking. 101 *Harvard Law Rev.*, 727.

Fisher, Roger, and William Ury. 1981. *Getting to Yes: Negotiating Agreement without Giving In.* Boston: Houghton Mifflin.

Fiss, Owen. 1984. Against Settlement. 93 *Yale Law Journal*, 1073.

Folberg, Jay. 1983. A Mediation Overview: History and Dimensions of Practice. 1 *Mediation Quarterly*, 3.

Freeman, Alan. 1990. Antidiscrimination Law: The View from 1989. In *The Politics of Law: A Progressive Critique*, ed. David Kairys. New York: Pantheon.

Gabel, Peter. 1980. Reification in Legal Reasoning. 3 *Research in Law and Sociology*, 25.

Galanter, Marc. 1974. Why the "Haves" Come Out Ahead: Speculations on the Limits of Legal Change. 95 *Law and Society Rev.*, 95.

Genovese, Eugene. 1976. *Roll, Jordon, Roll.* New York: Pantheon.

Gold, Lois. 1993. Influencing Unconscious Influences: The Healing Dimension of Mediation. 11 *Mediation Quarterly*, 55.

Greatbatch, David, and Robert Dingwall. 1989. Selective Facilitation: Some Preliminary Observations on a Strategy Used by Divorce Mediators. 23 *Law and Society Rev.*, 613.

Grillo, Trina. 1991. The Mediation Alternative: Process Dangers for Women. 100 *Yale Law Journal*, 1545.

Handler, Joel F., Ellen Jane Hollingsworth, and Howard S. Erlanger. 1978. *Lawyers and the Pursuit of Legal Rights.* New York: Academic Press.

Harrell, Susan. 1995. Why Attorneys Attend Mediation Sessions. 12 *Mediation Quarterly*, 369.

Harrington, Christine B., and Sally Engle Merry. 1988. Ideological Production: The Making of Community Mediation. 22 *Law and Society Rev.*, 709.

Heinz, John P., and Edward O. Laumann. 1982. *Chicago Lawyers: The Social Structure of the Bar.* New York: Russell Sage Foundation.

Hofrichter, Richard. 1987. *Neighborhood Justice in Capitalist Society: The Expansion of the Informal State.* New York: Greenwood.

Holznagel, Bernd. 1986. Negotiation and Mediation: The Newest Approach to Hazardous Waste Facility Siting. 13 *Environmental Affairs*, 329.

Kennedy, Duncan. 1979. The Structure of Blackstone's Commentaries. 28 *Buffalo Law Rev.*, 209.

Klare, Karl E. 1982. Critical Theory and Labor Relations Law. In *The Politics of Law: A Progressive Critique*, ed. David Kairys. New York: Pantheon.

Koopman, Elizabeth J., and E. Joan Hunt. 1988. Child Custody Mediation: An Interdisciplinary Synthesis. 58 *American Journal of Orthopsychiatry*, 379.

Larson, Magali Sarfatti. 1977. *The Rise of Professionalism*. Berkeley: Univ. of California Press.

Lederach, John Paul, and Ron Kraybill. 1993. The Paradox of Popular Justice: A Practitioner's View. In *The Possibility of Popular Justice: A Case Study of Community Mediation in the United States*, ed. Sally Engle Merry and Neal Milner. Ann Arbor: Univ. of Michigan Press.

Leipmann, Karen. 1986. Confidentiality in Environmental Mediation: Should Third Parties Have Access to the Process? 14 *Boston College of Environmental Affairs Law Rev.*, 92.

Lemmon, John Allen. 1983. Dimensions and Practice of Divorce Mediation. 1 *Mediation Quarterly*, 45.

Lentz, Sydney Solberg. 1986. The Labor Model for Mediation and Its Application to the Resolution of Environmental Disputes. 22 *Journal of Applied Behavioral Science*, 127.

Luban, David. 1989. The Quality of Justice. 66 *Denver Univ. Law Rev.*, 381.

Macaulay, Stewart. 1963. Non-Contractual Relations in Business: A Preliminary Study. 28 *American Sociological Rev.*, 812.

————. 1966. Law and the Balance of Power: The Automobile Manufacturers and the Dealers. In *Law and the Behavioral Sciences* (1977), ed. Lawrence Friedman and Stewart Macaulay. Indianapolis: Bobbs-Merrill.

MacKinnon, Catharine. 1984. Difference and Dominance: On Sex Discrimination. In *Feminist Legal Theory: Readings in Law and Gender* (1991), ed. Katherine T. Bartlett and Roseanne Kennedy. Boulder, CO: Westview.

McCann, Michael. 1992. Reform Litigation on Trial. 17 *Law and Social Inquiry*, 715.

McCarrick, Anne K., et al. 1991. Gender Differences in Competition and Dominance during Married-Couples Group Therapy. 44 *Social Psychology Quarterly*, 164.

McIsaac, Hugh. 1994. Orientation to Mediation in Portland, Oregon. 32 *Family and Conciliation Courts Rev.*, 55.

Menkel-Meadow, Carrie. 1984. Toward Another View of Legal Negotiation: The Structure of Problem Solving. 31 *UCLA Law Rev.*, 754.

Mernitz, Scott. 1980. *Mediation of Environmental Disputes: A Sourcebook*. New York: Praeger.

Merry, Sally Engle. 1990. *Getting Justice and Getting Even: Legal Consciousness among Working Class Americans*. Chicago: Univ. of Chicago Press.

Miller, Richard E., and Austin Sarat. 1981. Grievances, Claims, and Disputes: Assessing the Adversary Culture. 15 *Law and Society Rev.*, 525.

Milne, Ann. 1983. Divorce Mediation: The State of the Art. 1 *Mediation Quarterly*, 15.

Minow, Martha. 1987. Interpreting Rights: An Essay for Robert Cover. 96 *Yale Law Journal*, 1860.

Mnookin, Robert, and Lewis Kornhauser. 1979. Bargaining in the Shadow of the Law: The Case of Divorce. 88 *Yale Law Journal*, 950.

Nader, Laura. 1993a. Controlling Processes in the Practice of Law: Hierarchy and Pacification in the Movement to Re-Form Dispute Ideology. 9 *Ohio State Journal on Dispute Resolution*, 1.

———. 1993b. Why Is Popular Justice Popular? In *The Possibility of Popular Justice: A Case Study of Community Mediation in the United States*, ed. Sally Engle Merry and Neal Milner. Ann Arbor: Univ. of Michigan Press.

Pruhs, Ane, Mary Lou Paulsen, and William R. Tysseling. 1984. Divorce Mediation: The Politics of Integrating Clinicians. 1984. *Social Casework: The Journal of Contemporary Social Work* (Nov.), 532.

Ridgeway, Cecilia J., and Joseph Berger. 1986. Expectation, Legitimation, and Dominance Behavior in Task Groups. 51 *American Sociological Review*, 603.

Rosenberg, Joshua D. 1991. In Defense of Mediation. 33 *Arizona Law Rev.*, 467.

Ruman, Marilyn, and Marcia Lamm. 1983. Divorce Mediation: A Team Approach to Marital Dissolution. 1983 *Trial* (March), 80.

Sarat, Austin, and William L. F. Felstiner. 1989. Enactments of Power: Negotiating Reality and Responsibility in Lawyer-Client Interactions. 77 *Cornell Law Rev.*, 1447.

Scheingold, Stuart A. 1974. *The Politics of Rights: Lawyers, Public Policy, and Political Change*. New Haven, CT: Yale Univ. Press.

Schultz, Vikki. 1990. Telling Stories about Women and Work: Judicial Interpretations of Sex Segregation in the Workplace in Title VII Cases Raising the "Lack of Interest" Argument. 103 *Harvard Law Rev.*, 1749.

Silbey, Susan S., and Sally Merry. 1986. Mediator Settlement Strategies. 8 *Law and Policy*, 7.

Silbey, Susan, and Austin Sarat. 1989. Dispute Processing in Law and Legal Scholarship: From Institutional Critique to the Reconstruction of the Juridical Subject. 66 *Denver Univ. Law Rev.*, 437.

Stier, Serena, and Nina Hamilton. 1984. Teaching Divorce Mediation: Creating a Better Fit between Family Systems and the Legal System. 48 *Albany Law Rev.*, 693.

Thompson, E. P. 1975. *Whigs and Hunters: The Origin of the Black Act*. New York: Pantheon.

Tidwell, Alan. 1994. Not Effective Communication but Effective Persuasion. 12 *Mediation Quarterly*, 3.

Tushnet, Mark. 1984. An Essay on Rights. 62 *Texas Law Rev.*, 1363.

Ury, William L., Jeanne M. Brett, and Stephen B. Goldberg. 1988. *Getting Disputes Resolved: Designing Systems to Cut the Costs of Conflict*. San Francisco: Jossey-Bass.

Vanderkooi, Lois, and Jessica Pearson. 1983. Mediating Divorce Disputes: Mediator Behaviors, Styles and Roles. 32 *Family Relations*, 557.

Weingarten, Helen. 1986. Strategic Planning for Divorce Mediation. *Social Work* (May–June), 194.

Welch, Elizabeth, Stephen Herrell, and Dale Koch. 1994. Judicial Orientation. 32 *Family and Conciliation Courts Rev.*, 299.

Westin, Alan F., and Alfred G. Feliu. 1988. *Resolving Employment Disputes without Litigation*. Washington, DC: Bureau of National Affairs.

Wexler, Robert. 1973. Practicing Law for Poor People. 79 *Yale Law Journal*, 1049.

Williams, Patricia J. 1987. *The Alchemy of Race and Rights.* Cambridge, MA: Harvard Univ. Press.

Winograd, Barry. 1995. Men as Mediators in Cases of Sexual Harrassment. 50 *Dispute Resolution Journal,* 40.

Yngvesson, Barbara. 1993. Local People, Local Problems, and Neighborhood Justice: The Discourse of "Community" in San Francisco Community Boards. In *The Possibility of Popular Justice: A Case Study of Community Mediation in the United States,* ed. Sally Engle Merry and Neal Milner. Ann Arbor: Univ. of Michigan Press.

Zlatchin, Carl. 1986. Divorce Mediation: A Psychologist's View. 9 *Family Advocate,* 38.

THE LEGAL RESPONSE
TO DISCRIMINATION:
DOES LAW MATTER?

❖

JOHN J. DONOHUE

Т he topic of the legal response to discrimination is broad and growing. It includes everything from hate crime legislation and governmental prohibition of discrimination in the purchase of housing, cars, and loans, to restrictions on discrimination in the provision of government services and benefits as well as in employment.[1] In the latter category alone, the body of law banning discrimination in the workplace has both deepened as the original prohibitions against discrimination on the basis of "race, color, religion, sex, or national origin" (Section 703(a)(1) of Title VII of the Civil Rights Act of 1964) have been interpreted to prohibit a greater array of employer actions and widened as protections have been extended to new classes of workers. Thus, the passage of the Age Discrimination in Employment Act, the Americans with Disabilities Act, and a large array of state and local employment discrimination laws that are more expansive than Title VII have greatly broadened the number of workers falling into some protected category. As a result of the enormous expansion, it is no longer possible to speak about "discrimination" in the abstract: discrimination against older or disabled workers is obviously very different from, say, discrimination against cigarette smokers—who are now protected by numerous state laws—which, in turn, is different from discrimination on the basis of race, sex, or religion (Donohue 1992:1614 n. 147).

But while the very concepts of discrimination against the elderly or the disabled, let alone against cigarette smokers, have only recently entered the legal consciousness,[2] the issue of race discrimination has been a central focus of U.S. law for over two centuries. In fact, the history of this country could be written by focusing on how race discrimination has shaped law and how those opposed to such discrimination have tried to fight it through resort to law. From such a historical perspective, the question of whether law matters in the area of discrimination would reveal many negative contributions of the law, for there is little debate that the existence of slavery and the creation of Jim Crow legislation were profoundly legal developments that mattered greatly and whose pernicious effects will not soon disappear. From the contemporary perspective, though, the question has largely focused on whether the entire civil rights apparatus, or specific parts of it, has generated any positive benefits.

One of the enormous advantages of this particular topic is that virtually any conceivable statement can be backed up with appropriate supporting citations. For example, all of the following propositions have recently been advanced by prominent academics:

1. The Civil Rights Act of 1964 and the decision in *Brown v. Board of Education* (1954) were the crowning achievements of the law in this century.

2. The Civil Rights Act of 1964 and the decision in *Brown v. Board of Education* were utterly tragic events for the entire country.

3. *Brown v. Board of Education* was wholly ineffective, and it is only the Civil Rights Act of 1964 that generated any noticeable changes in the treatment of blacks.

4. The Civil Rights Act of 1964 has had virtually no impact on the economic welfare of blacks.

5. The entire federal civil rights edifice has been a sham designed to provide legitimacy to an essentially racist system by both concealing discriminatory behavior and justifying discriminatory outcomes.

6. The law is helping blacks at the expense of everyone else.

7. The law is hurting blacks more than anyone else.

This paper attempts to sort through some of these highly contentious positions. Section 1 will explore whether law has had any impact on black education in the South. The section critiques the conflicting positions of Michael McConnell (1995), who finds tragedy in the failure of the Supreme Court in *Brown* to offer an originalist justification for its holding that racial segregation of schools violated the Equal Protection Clause of the Fourteenth Amendment, and of Gerald Rosenberg (1991), who finds that *Brown* had no impact on black schooling. Interestingly, while the current debate has been framed to ask whether the decision in *Brown* enhanced the welfare of blacks, the evidence is probably stronger in support of the proposition that pre-*Brown* litigation had a more immediate impact in improving the schooling of

Southern black children. The reason for this potentially anomalous finding is that Southern whites considered improved schooling for blacks as the price they had to pay to maintain the segregationist way of life; *Brown* sought to improve black schooling further by eliminating segregation, but this was a penalty Southern whites were not willing to bear. The focus on the law and Southern black school quality reveals that law can matter in different ways: during a period when the constitutional doctrine of *Plessy v. Ferguson* (1896) was buttressing the racist social structure of the South, it was simultaneously used to elevate the welfare of blacks within that system; when that constitutional doctrine was ultimately rejected, however, further Southern black educational gains were halted until the segregationist regime itself was toppled.

Section 2 begins with a discussion of the conflicting assessments of federal employment discrimination law offered by the libertarian Richard Epstein (1992) and the critical race theorist Richard Delgado (1993). In Epstein's opinion, the law matters because it imposes large burdens on employers that undermine productivity, thereby impairing the economic well-being of the society at large, and because the intrusion of government into workplace decision making creates inevitable tensions between different groups and lamentably transfers wealth from blacks who are already most disadvantaged to those who are already most privileged. Conversely, Delgado believes that current employment discrimination law matters in much the way that the doctrine of separate-but-equal mattered: it enables the dominant class to legitimize inequality while ostensibly prohibiting it. Interestingly, their profoundly different worldviews lead Epstein and Delgado to contradictory predictions about the degree of affirmative action on behalf of—or racism against –black candidates for teaching positions in law schools. The section ends with an examination of the empirical evidence on this question, which underscores that ideology is often a poor substitute for knowledge.

Section 3 widens the focus beyond possible discrimination in the hiring of law professors to explore whether the racial discrimination that plagued the American South prior to the passage of the 1964 Civil Rights Act was the product of racist law or racist custom. The question is central to the libertarian claim that, without the pernicious influence of government in the first place, there would have been no need for federal intervention in 1964. Somewhat surprisingly, while many aspects of the Southern segregationist regime were maintained through legal restrictions, there were relatively few such restrictions in the area of employment. In all likelihood, the continuing nature of employment relationships made it virtually certain that the hiring of blacks in "inappropriate" positions would become known, thereby enabling the community to enforce its norms without resort to more formal legal regimes. Of course, this fact takes us beyond the question of whether law matters to the question, "What is law?"

Section 4 ends with an overall assessment of whether federal law has improved the economic position of black Americans. Certainly, a very sharp increase in the relative earnings of blacks occurred in the decade after the effective date of Title VII of the 1964 Civil Rights Act and the promulgation of the federal government contract compliance program. But it is no simple matter to link this gain with these legal interventions. Were the forces that led to the passage of the Civil Rights Act the primary contributors to the gain, or was it other factors such as the unusually tight labor markets of the late 1960s, black migration out of agricultural labor, or improving black schooling? The fact that almost all of the jump in black earnings came in the South—where the law was resisted and had to be imposed—coupled with evidence that migration and schooling improvements are unlikely candidates for the discontinuous jump in the earnings of Southern blacks, provides persuasive, albeit indirect, evidence that federal civil rights policy mattered in a very important and tangible way. Whether the law is capable of providing additional benefits to blacks at acceptable costs is a question that has yet to be determined.

1. BLACK EDUCATION IN THE SOUTH: DID LAW MATTER?

The contemporary perspective on the effect of law in the area of discrimination is primarily focused on the major legal events following World War II. The simplified story might be that in the late 1940s New York and New Jersey began a fifteen-year trend that led to the enactment of employment discrimination laws in most non-Southern states. Meanwhile, the avenue of petition to state legislatures being closed in the South, the civil rights movement focused on the federal government, winning major Supreme Court victories against the system of segregation before achieving the significant legislative triumphs of the passage of the 1964 Civil Rights Act and the 1965 Voting Rights Act.

But this simplified overview obscures the fact that law and legal doctrine mattered in important positive ways to victims of racial discrimination even during times when the overall thrust of the law was hostile to these victims. An interesting illustration of this phenomenon arises from the litigation pursued by the National Association for the Advancement of Colored People (NAACP) on behalf of black victims of discrimination in the South. Launched in 1922 with a gift of $800,000 from a Harvard undergrad who had just inherited a fortune (Sunstein 1992), the NAACP's struggle to achieve racial equality through law is probably the most famous sustained litigative effort in our nation's history. The NAACP consciously adopted a two-step strategy in an effort to achieve the equal protection of law for black Americans.

First, the NAACP relied on the equality component of the separate-but-equal doctrine of *Plessy v. Ferguson* (1896) to seek improvements in the treatment of blacks. Given the egregious character of the racial injustice in America over the period from the early 1920s through the early 1950s, this protracted phase of the legal attack might seem to have been completely ineffective. In fact, this period was one of substantial black progress in Southern education if measured by the convergence toward equality in schooling inputs, such as the wages paid to black teachers, the length of the school year for black pupils, and the pupil-teacher ratios for black students. Despite the fact that Southern blacks were without significant electoral power during this period, the NAACP's efforts to achieve "equal," albeit separate, schooling for blacks did generate considerable improvements in virtually all educational inputs. By the early 1950s, when this first phase of the litigation strategy was ending, most Southern states had nearly equalized these measured inputs for black and white students (Card and Krueger 1992; Donohue and Heckman 1991). These gains were remarkable in that only twenty years earlier, Southern black teachers had only earned half the salary of Southern white teachers, and the pupil-teacher ratio for Southern black school children had been 33 percent higher than that for Southern white school children. Thus, working within the confines of a racist legal doctrine, during a time when blacks had virtually no political or economic power, NAACP lawyers did achieve significant gains for black school children in the segregated South.

Having achieved this degree of racial equality, the NAACP then switched to its second phase of the legal strategy by attacking the constitutionality of the doctrine of separate-but-equal itself. Interestingly, the NAACP sought to achieve equality first by using the existing legal framework to push for what the law had grudgingly allowed at the level of constitutional doctrine but not in practice, and then by forcing the law to grant much more. Certainly, the relative gains in black education in the segregated South prior to the decision in *Brown* were dramatic, and they represented movements in the direction of equality. Yet only by thinking of equality as something more than the formalistic achievement of equal measured educational inputs was the Supreme Court able to advance racial equality in a much more profound way than would have been possible under the doctrine of legal segregation.

Forty years after the Supreme Court handed down its monumental decision in *Brown v. Board of Education* (1954), a curious combination of conflicting criticisms has emerged from the law school and the political science department of the University of Chicago. As I will discuss below, law professor Michael McConnell (1995) is decidedly of the opinion that law matters. In fact, the law articulated by the Supreme Court is so important that good or ill will flow from major decisions, such as *Brown*, based not only on what the court holds, but also on the persuasiveness of the judicial rationale in support thereof. Unfortunately, McConnell laments, the rationale of *Brown* was so inadequate that its consequences were tragic.

On the other hand, political scientist Gerald Rosenberg (1991) has a quite different view of the *Brown* decision. Not only does he fail to share McConnell's interest in the articulated rationale for the holding of *Brown*, but he also finds the holding itself to be without significance. *Brown* was tragic only because it accomplished nothing. Subsections A and B will discuss the competing positions of McConnell and Rosenberg, and will argue that, while McConnell has an excessively grandiose vision of the power of judicial pronouncements, Rosenberg has a peculiarly stunted conception of that power.

A. A LAW PROFESSOR'S NIGHTMARE

Michael McConnell (1995) has written an interesting and illuminating article analyzing whether there is an originalist argument in support of the Supreme Court's decision in *Brown v. Board of Education* (1954). McConnell believes that constitutional provisions should be intepreted in accordance with the original intent of the authors of the provisions, and he explores whether an argument based on original intent can be constructed in support of the holding in *Brown*. This important topic has particular significance to those on the Right because the traditional view has been that *Brown* cannot be justified on originalist grounds. This has led some—such as Robert Bork (1990) and William Rehnquist—to flirt with the idea that *Brown* was wrongly decided (Posner 1990). Conversely, numerous scholars have used this same premise to mount a powerful syllogistic argument against originalism: we know that *Brown v. Board of Education* was correctly decided, and that the case would have been decided the other way using an originalist interpretation. Therefore, originalism must be a flawed theory of constitutional interpretation because, in the most important case of the last half century, its application would have led to an erroneous decision.

The evidence against the originalist position is compelling: the same Congress that voted for the passage of the Fourteenth Amendment in 1868 also voted for segregated schools for the District of Columbia. As McConnell (1995) notes, scholars as diverse as Alexander Bickel, Robert Bork (1990), and Michael Klarman (1991) have found the originalist argument in support of the decision in *Brown* to be utterly unpersuasive. As Klarman writes, "Virtually nothing in the congressional debates suggests that the Fourteenth Amendment was intended to prohibit school segregation, while contemporaneous state practices render such an argument fanciful; twenty-four of the thirty-seven states then in the union either required or permitted racially segregated schools" (1991: 252). Similarly, Bork states that "[t]he inescapable fact is that those who ratified the amendment did not think it outlawed segregated education" (1990: 75–76).

McConnell disputes this consensus. Based on an impressive and comprehensive historical assessment, he concludes that a substantial majority of the political leaders who supported the Fourteenth Amendment also believed that school segregation violated the amendment. This assessment leads him to believe that a proper originalist interpretation of the amendment would have provided the appropriate doctrinal basis for the decision in *Brown*.

Despite the impressive thoroughness of his research, there are some heroic leaps in McConnell's analysis. For example, the proponents of desegregation never secured a two-thirds vote in either house of Congress, as required to obtain a constitutional amendment, and therefore it is difficult to argue that the two-thirds majority of the Congress that supported the passage of the Fourteenth Amendment also intended to ban school segregation. Nonetheless, McConnell's article does provide a fascinating depiction of the horrible discriminatory attitudes that were once prevalent and openly articulated in this country. For example, during the school desegregation debates of 1871–75, Congressman William Robbins of North Carolina declared that it was "time to recur to the doctrine in which is bound up the salvation of this country—the doctrine that this is the white man's land and ought to be a white man's government." Senator Francis Blair criticized the Fifteenth Amendment for conferring the vote "upon a mass of ignorant, uneducated, semi-barbarous people." Eli Saulsbury of Delaware questioned whether the Fourteenth Amendment had any "legal or binding force in law" and announced: "I am placed under the most binding obligation to maintain for my race that superiority to which it is entitled by the decrees of God Himself, and here in the council of my country I proclaim that no act of mine shall assist to drag it down and place it on an equality with an inferior race."

At one point in the Congressional debate, John Harris of Virginia stated that "there is not one gentleman upon this floor who can honestly say he really believes that the colored man is created his equal." When Alonzo Ransier, a black congressman from South Carolina, responded by shouting "I can," Harris sneered: "Of course you can; but I am speaking to the white men of the House; and Mr. Speaker, I do not wish to be interrupted again by him." Harris then went on to offer this response to the argument that opposition to the desegregation bill was a product of prejudice:

> MR. HARRIS. Admit that it is prejudice, yet the fact exists, and you, as members of Congress and legislators, are bound to respect that prejudice. It was born in the children of the South; born in our ancestors, and born in your ancestors in Massachusetts—that the colored man was inferior to the white.
>
> MR. RANSIER. I deny that.
>
> MR. HARRIS. I do not allow you to interrupt me. Sit down; I am talking to white men; I am talking to gentlemen. (McConnell 1995:1067)

This outrageous conduct, perpetrated by members of Congress speaking openly during public debate, powerfully testifies to the virulence and widespread acceptance of racial prejudice that existed during the decade following the end of the Civil War. But while McConnell obviously finds these racist statements to be lamentable, he reserves his most intense antagonism for the Supreme Court of the 1950s and its "shocking" and "irresponsible" opinion writing. McConnell criticizes the Supreme Court's decision in *Brown* for relying on psychological evidence that segregated schools adversely affected black children.

This purchased trouble for future cases. Education may well be "the most important function of state and local governments," but in the years immediately after *Brown*, plaintiffs brought cases involving segregation of some distinctly less important functions of government, from airport coffee shops to municipal auditoriums. What would be the Court's answer to those cases? It decided these cases—among the most controversial in its history—by per curiam orders and summary dispositions, without any serious discussion of the merits. Never did the Court get around to informing the nation of the legal basis for desegregating the South, outside of the context of education. In Johnson v. Virginia, a case involving a segregated courtroom decided eight years after *Brown*, the Court finally announced that "a State may not constitutionally require segregation of public facilities." The only reason the Court gave, however, was that this issue "was no longer open to question." (McConnell 1995: 1136–37; emphasis in original)

It is interesting that McConnell deems these cases to have been correctly decided, yet he believes that the failure to base these opinions on what he deems to be the appropriate originalist footing has had serious consequences. In McConnell's view, law—and by this he means not just the rule of law that racial segregation of public facilities violates the Equal Protection Clause of the United States, but in addition the articulated rationale for this rule of law—really matters. Even when the court is right, it can be wrong—with tragic consequences.

But what are the consequences? My guess is that McConnell's implicit view is that *Brown*, tragically, has come to stand for the proposition that originalism is not invariably the appropriate basis for constitutional decision making. He argues that the unpersuasive rationale for the equal protection cases "contributed to the feeling in the South that the desegregation decisions were illegitimate." Perhaps true—for a very select minority. How many Southerners were sufficiently interested in the legal niceties to even contemplate the constitutional rationale for the holding that segregation violates the Equal Protection Clause? I would imagine that, of those who fell into this category of concern for the legal rationale as opposed to the final outcome of the decision, many would have found the interpretation that the Equal Protection Clause prohibits segregation to be a self-evidently correct interpretation requiring little further elaboration.

Somehow I find it unlikely that a more persuasive opinion based on the original intent of the architects of the Fourteenth Amendment would have softened Southern opposition to the holding of *Brown*. Could the court, through tighter legal reasoning, have prevented the formation of the White Citizen's Councils that emerged to offer massive resistance to the Brown decision? Would such improved reasoning have prevented counties in Virginia from abolishing their public schools and converting them into white private academies, leaving thousands of poor black school children with no schools for a number of years? Would James Meredith have been welcomed into the

University of Mississippi in 1962 had the court only offered an originalist rationale for its decision?

I am dubious. To believe that the law would have had this degree of power would be to ignore the implication of the language quoted above from various Congressional debates: segregation was about white supremacy and intentional racial subjugation. Such ingrained racist sentiments could not have been quickly shed, even with the aid of what to McConnell would have been a more persuasive constitutional rationale.

As Oliver Wendell Holmes wrote one hundred years ago in trying to offer a rationale for statutes of limitations, "A thing which you have enjoyed and used as your own for a long time, whether property or an opinion, takes root in your being and cannot be torn away without your resenting the act and trying to defend yourself, however you came by it" (Holmes 1897: 477). Holmes called this feeling to be among "the deepest instincts of man," and his viewpoint suggests that, even though Southern whites had come upon their position of racial superiority unjustly, this deep-seated belief could not be taken away from them without prompting resentment and counter-attack. McConnell's position could only have merit if both Holmes's assessment of human nature were groundless and if the Southern resisters to the *Brown* decision were principled originalists who would have fallen into line had the Supreme Court only articulated a more compelling judicial rationale.

Lawrence Friedman makes the point colorfully:

> In my view, arguments based on text wildly exaggerate the impact of text. They assume that the language and the reasoning made a critical difference, as opposed to what the decision *did*, that is, its result, outcome, or decree, as the lay public understands and understood it. But anybody who feels that a more tightly crafted and better reasoned opinion in *Brown* would have had a bigger (or even different) impact on life in rural Mississippi (or Washington, D.C., for that matter) than what Warren actually wrote, can't be living on this planet. (Friedman 1997: 51; emphasis in original)

B. A POLITICAL SCIENTIST'S DREAM

While McConnell has written a lament over the unintended harmful consequences of the *Brown* decision, he does not mention that his University of Chicago colleague Gerald Rosenberg has argued that *Brown* accomplished nothing (1991). That McConnell could write his article without addressing Rosenberg's work illustrates the factual void that characterizes most purely legal assessments of the importance of law, litigation, and judicial interpretation in promoting black economic and social progress. Rosenberg directly challenges the notion of the efficacy of court-initiated civil rights activity, claiming the *Brown* decision had no important impact on the civil rights movement or on the evolution of black economic and social progress. Unlike some of the admirers of his work, however, Rosenberg does not deny that civil rights legislation contributed to black social and economic progress.

In Rosenberg's view, nothing of importance would have changed had the court ruled differently in *Brown*. The following two quotes capture his broad thesis. Rosenberg writes:

> I have found little evidence that the judicial system, from the Supreme Court down, produced much of the massive change in civil rights that swept the United States in the 1960s. . . . The combination of all these factors—growing civil rights pressure from the 1930s, economic changes, the Cold War, population shifts, electoral concerns, the increase in mass communication—created the pressure that led to civil rights. The Court reflected that pressure; it did not create it. (1991: 157–69)

The political scientist Robert Dahl is quoted on the cover of Rosenberg's work as saying:

> Rosenberg not only demonstrates convincingly that the Supreme Court has not brought about the broad social reforms often attributed to it, but also shows why it cannot do so, except under highly unusual conditions. Hereafter, anyone who defends the view of the Court as a force for basic reforms will have to confront and rebut the evidence and argument of this book. This is not going to be an easy task.

There is a great deal of truth to Rosenberg's hypothesis if it is modified to state that the Supreme Court cannot spontaneously generate broad social change simply by rendering a single legal decision. In fact, a decade after the decision in *Brown*, virtually no school desegregation had yet occurred in the Deep South (Donohue and Heckman 1991: 1627). The contrast with McConnell's view that tragedy would have been avoided had the court only adopted a more jurisprudentially sound justification for its decision could not be more striking. Perhaps McConnell might seek to reconcile the two works by contending that the *Brown* decision was as ineffective as Rosenberg argues *because* the opinion was not better reasoned. Yet, that position would be counter to Rosenberg's broader thesis that the Supreme Court is unable to bring about social change on its own initiative.

Rosenberg deserves considerable credit for going beyond mere doctrinal analysis to examine the empirical evidence concerning the impact of judicial decisions. But his tools are not always well suited to ascertain whether those decisions generated any significant consequences. One illustration of the type of causal empirical argumentation to which Rosenberg succumbs is his citation analysis of *Brown*. Rosenberg finds that *Brown* was rarely cited in newspapers, political rhetoric, or public opinion polls during the turbulent civil rights era of the late 1950s and early 1960s. This methodology of assessing the frequency of citations leads him to conclude that more "immediate"—that is, more recent—causes were of greater significance than *Brown*. By this standard, a decision that spawned a whole host of subsidiary decisions and legislation, as *Brown* did, would be unimportant because the subsidiary decisions and legislation would appear more important in any particular instance. The "causal analysis" employed by Rosenberg is methodologically flawed because it confuses immediate causes and ultimate causes. His approach cannot capture the slow-moving forces set in motion by *Brown* that took more than a decade to unfold in the manifestations of the Civil Rights Act and the Voting Rights Act. An application of his method of dismissing the significance of *Brown* might well lead to dismissal of the fundamental legal importance of the Magna Carta or the United States Constitution and the Bill of Rights.

In what at times appears to be a somewhat procrustean attempt to fit the evidence to his overarching hypothesis, Rosenberg selectively reports the evidence against the importance of *Brown*. For example, he ignores the well-documented rapid compliance with *Brown* that occurred in the border states. Moreover, he ignores the role played by the judiciary in the late 1960s and early 1970s initiating court-ordered busing plans (Wasby, D'Amato, and Metrailer 1977). These court-ordered desegregation plans resulted in the relocation of hundreds of thousands of school children in the middle of an ongoing school year. Yet, Rosenberg dismisses these judicially decreed plans as merely the product of attempts by school systems to avoid losing federal funds for failure to desegregate. It is quite likely, though, that, had the Supreme Court in *Brown* endorsed the racially segregated school systems of the South as constitutionally permissible, Congress in the mid-1960s would have felt far less pressure to provide financial incentives to desegregate.

Even accepting Rosenberg's proximate cause approach, he can at times apply it inconsistently. He claims that there was no immediate response to *Brown*—yet his own table 4.4 depicts an obvious jump in NAACP contributions in 1954 and afterwards. The role of subsequent court cases in interpreting and extending *Brown* produced an understandable delay as both sides waited for the Supreme Court and the Executive Branch to determine exactly what "with all deliberate speed" actually meant.

His analysis of the rise of the racist white Citizens' Council movement—within two months of the *Brown* decision—is equally unconvincing (Martin 1970). He accepts the fact that *Brown* played an important role in stimulating the movement but says only that, as a consequence, *Brown* slowed the progress of blacks. He does not address the key question raised by this analysis: Why were the white citizens so concerned if *Brown* was such a minor decision?

Rosenberg also argues that desegregation and the breakup of the American version of apartheid were inevitable, and of course with a long enough time horizon this is almost certainly true. Nonetheless, this claim of inevitable change enables Rosenberg to ignore the long-term stability of segregation and discrimination in employment and social practices despite the massive economic and social change accompanying the Southern transformation from agriculture to industry (Heckman and Payner 1989).

A more systematic assessment of the impact of *Brown* would trace its immediate litigative impact by examining fully the array of NAACP and other state and federal litigation concerning school desegregation. Moreover, it would reveal the unfolding effort to apply the core tenet of *Brown*—

that official racial discrimination violated the Equal Protection Clause—to a wide variety of contexts outside the area of public education.[3] Furthermore, in determining the effect of *Brown* one must also consider the growth of white resistance—including the growth of a new round of segregation laws in schooling, accommodation, services, and employment—as the South responded to the challenge of desegregation. This response implies either that white Southerners were moved by irrational paranoia or else that *Brown* posed a real threat to the segregated Southern way of life.

2. EMPLOYMENT DISCRIMINATION LAW FROM THE RIGHT AND LEFT

The preceding section focused on how the Fourteenth Amendment guarantee of equal protection of the law affected the behavior of the officials charged with running public schools in the South. Prior to the decision in *Brown*, NAACP litigation led to improvements in the separate schools that blacks attended, even though blacks had no political power to back up their appeals to the judiciary. Following *Brown*, the prior improving trends were halted, but the longer-run process of dismantling the entire segregationist regime was launched. In the short run, the negative consequences of *Brown* probably outweighed the positive consequences for black school children, although in the long run, this accounting was reversed.

Just as the Supreme Court's decision in *Brown* has recently been assailed from different perspectives, the law of employment discrimination has come under attack from scholars on both the far Right and far Left. Much of this literature has proceeded without reference to the available empirical evidence, which accordingly explains why such contradictory claims can be offered with such bold confidence. Subsection A discusses Richard Epstein's libertarian attack on all employment discrimination laws, and subsection B offers a contrary critical race theory perspective from Richard Delgado. Subsection C offers empirical evidence on one of the precise disagreements between Epstein and Delgado—the degree of discrimination, either for or against, that a minority candidate for a law school teaching position would experience.

A. THE TRAGEDY OF EMPLOYMENT DISCRIMINATION LAW

Disapproval concerning the legal interventions designed to address the problem of discrimination seems to be a recurring theme among conservative scholars at the University of Chicago. Professor Richard Epstein has recently documented his complete opposition "to the entire complex of modern civil rights laws and their administration." In his view, "the only hard questions about the employment discrimination laws concern the types and magnitudes of the social dislocations that result from their vigorous enforcement" (1992: xii). He writes:

> The gains recorded under [Title VII] are only the gains received by blacks who are skillful enough or lucky enough to remain in the hiring market. The figures on relative wages do not reflect the increased unemployment rates for black labor, which can plainly be tied to the minimum wage law, and probably to the anti-discrimination law as well, as the data on the decreases in black labor force participation illustrate. . . . As with the minimum wage, Title VII works a redistribution from worse-off to better-off blacks, which is surely far from what its principled supporters intended.

To Epstein, the "modern civil rights laws [not only] strangle the operation of labor and employment markets, [but] are a new form of imperialism that threatens the political liberty and intellectual freedom of us all" (1992: 505). He asserts that "as a matter of first principle . . . discrimination by private parties [is not a wrong] requiring state intervention or correction" (1992: 351). Moreover, society should "exclude *all* instances of mere offense born of moral outrage or bruised sensibilities from the class of actionable harms, however deeply felt the hurt" (1992: 415). "There are many areas in which the employer has no rational reason to discriminate on the basis of race or sex; such discrimination will not be found to any systematic or large degree, even if some discrimination will (and should) survive." (1992: 447).

These conclusions stem from his belief that:

> The problem of social governance . . . requires that we make peace not with our friends but with our enemies, and that can be done only if we show some respect for their preferences even when we detest them. Using the principle of exclusion allows both groups to go their separate ways side by side. The anti-discrimination laws force them into constant undesired interaction. The totalitarian implications become clear only when one realizes the excessive steps that must be taken to enforce the anti-discrimination principle in favor of some groups while it is overtly ignored relative to other groups. It is not the least of the ironies of the study of Title VII that it has brought in its wake more discrimination (and for less good purpose) than would exist in any unregulated system. (1992: 497)

He continues:

> The great tragedy of the American experience with segregation was that our nation lost sight of [the principle that civil rights refers to the civil capacity to contract], and substituted an expansive regime of government activity . . . which injected governmental influence and governmental favoritism into every transaction. (1992: 497)

Epstein is certainly provocative. The suggestion that different racial groups should be allowed "to go their separate ways side by side" will evoke unpleasant memories of lunch counter owners in the South informing blacks that they were not welcome to dine with whites.[4] Linking federal civil rights with totalitarianism will rankle many, and the thought that the "great tragedy" of the American version of apartheid was that we lost sight of a legal definition—a sentiment evocative of McConnell's attack on *Brown*—will appear insensitive in light of the enormous human suffering that white oppression inflicted on Southern blacks.

Note that in Epstein's account, law matters strongly in the effort to dismantle racial discrimination because it follows a conceptually flawed path— and tragedy follows. But while McConnell is somewhat cryptic in defining the harm that flowed from the poor reasoning of the *Brown* decision, Epstein is much clearer about the vast array of undesirable consequences that result from the attack on employment discrimination. In particular, Epstein believes that the effort to ban discrimination has merely changed the identity of the victims:

> Anyone who works in academic circles, and I dare say elsewhere, knows full well that *all* the overt and institutional discrimination comes from those who claim to be the victims of discrimination imposed by others. It is a sad day when any effort to defend the traditional norms of a discipline, profession, trade, or craft exposes the defender to withering political attack for a covert form of discrimination under the guise of excellence and neutral standards. In all too many cases honorable people are attacked as racist or sexist when the charges often apply with far greater truth to the persons who make these charges than to the persons about whom they are made. (1992: 502)

Epstein goes on to say that he is happy to tolerate affirmative action on behalf of whatever group private employers wish to advance, but only if there is no trace of governmental pressure prompting the preferential treatment. The great problems with affirmative action in his view are that (1) it is often undertaken under the threat or fear of litigation, (2) it is often used as a principled pretext for self-interested special pleading, and (3) it is at times conducted by governmental authorities, who Epstein believes should be held to a strict color-blind standard.

B. WIDESPREAD DISCRIMINATION IN THE LEGAL ACADEMY?

Interestingly, Epstein's strong prediction that *all* the overt discrimination comes from those who claim to be the victims of discrimination directly conflicts with the predictions of one of the major critical race theorists, Richard Delgado. Consider Delgado's statements, written in dialogue form:

> "So the informal nature of equality of opportunity allows members of an em-powered group to call upon and invoke the many culturally established routines, practices, and understandings that benefit them.
> "Take our earlier [example] of the law school that can only hire one professor. There are two finalists, a Black and a white. The formal job description contains

the standard criteria: potential for scholarship, teaching, and public service. The two finalists seem equally qualified in each of those respects. Equality of results would dictate that the Black applicant get the job because of the small number of African-Americans on the faculty. That is, the approach would strive for equality, for proportional representation, or some similar measure. But . . . under equality of opportunity *the white will inevitably get the position*. Equality of opportunity only guarantees that both will receive initial consideration. And when both candidates are considered, a myriad of factors, some conscious, some unconscious will come into play: inflection, small talk, background, bearing, social class, and the many imponderables that go into evaluating 'collegiality'. Critical Race Theory argues, and the battle for civil rights demonstrates, that such a regime is exactly the opposite of fair and neutral. . . .

"So, equality of opportunity really just amounts to affirmative action for whites. . . . It builds in a background of unstated assumptions that confer a consistent advantage in all the competitions that matter. If society were serious about equality, it would abolish this way of doing things and opt for equality of results. But this is something our culture will never do. . . ."

"It has defined equal opportunity, the approach which permits its members to win, as legal, principled, and just. If one were to devise a system that would, first, produce racially discrepant results, and, second, enable those who manage and benefit from the system to sleep well at night, it would look very much like the present one." (Delgado 1993: 1150–51, emphasis added)

It would seem that Delgado—like McConnell and Epstein, albeit for very different reasons—conceives of the current state of the law as tragic and hypocritical. His example of the job selection decision between identical black and white law professor candidates appears to be premised on the view that the critical choice for law is between equality of opportunity and equality of result, and the law has erred in opting for equality of opportunity. But the problem that concerns Delgado is actually broader than this somewhat limited example would suggest. Delgado predicts that, when the standard objective employment criteria are in equipoise, subjective factors will dominate and the white will always be hired. Delgado does not make clear whether he thinks that, even when the objective criteria favor the black candidate, the white will still be likely to get the job. Obviously, the most egregious form of discrimination would exist if the standard criteria frequently favored the black candidate, but the white candidate was routinely selected because of the other "imponderables." But this situation is not sanctioned by law, and indeed it would define a classic successful employment discrimination lawsuit under the equality of opportunity doctrine.

The third possibility is that the white applicant is superior on the standard criteria. In this case, the white would get the job under equality of opportunity, but under equality of result, there would be some advantage given to the black to offset the disadvantage on the standard criteria. One of the hard questions of law is how far employers should be free, or encouraged, to seek equality of result by favoring the black candidate. Since Delgado believes that the balance is invariably tipped in favor of the white candidate, he does not appear to be concerned with this case.

In any event, the issue is now joined. We have the prediction from Epstein that all the discrimination in academic circles will be in favor of the black candidate, and we have the prediction from Delgado that all the discrimination in this setting will favor the white candidate. But while McConnell, Epstein, and Delgado have articulated broad and provocative empirical claims, the empirical evidence does exist that can and should be examined to sort out which claims are deserving of support.

C. WHAT DOES THE EVIDENCE TELL US?

A recent study by Deborah Merritt and Barbara Reskin (1994), which analyzes law school hiring over the period from 1986 through 1991, has examined precisely the issue raised by the opposing statements of Delgado and Epstein. The study examined the 1,094 professors who were hired into their first tenure-track position during these years, and used a regression model to predict the institutional prestige of the first school to hire them. The explanatory variables employed in the regression were race, sex, prestige of the undergraduate institution and law school, membership on the law review, type of judicial clerkship, possession of a doctorate or master's degree in a field other than law, and whether the individual previously worked for a law firm, used the AALS recruitment process, was hired by his own law school, previously had a nontenure-track job, or imposed a major geographic limit on his or her job search. Merritt and Reskin conclude that men of color did obtain tenure-track positions at significantly more prestigious institutions than the schools that hired comparably credentialed white men. Based on their constructed law school prestige scale ranging from a low of -4.81 to a high of 4.03, the authors found that white women and men of color both obtained jobs at significantly more prestigious institutions than did white men. For white women, their sex conferred an advantage of about four-tenths of a prestige point, which was roughly comparable to the advantage gained by having a master's degree in a nonlaw field. Men of color had a somewhat greater advantage—almost seven-tenths of a point in institutional prestige, which was about the same advantage as that conferred by having a doctorate in a nonlaw field.

In other words, Merritt and Reskin found that if two candidates, a black male and a white male, had equivalent objective credentials, the black male would be hired at a law school that was .68 prestige points higher (on the roughly nine-point scale) than the white male. To put in perspective the .68 and .4 advantages enjoyed by black men and white women, consider some of the other features that generated benefits in law school hiring: the bonus conferred for membership on the law review was .45, for having a nonlaw doctorate was .67, for having a nonlaw master's degree was .40, for clerking on the Supreme Court was 1.28, and for clerking for the Court of Appeals was .65.[5] This study tends to refute Delgado's speculation that law schools confronted with black and white candidates with equal objective credentials would always hire the white candidate. In fact, there is significant evidence in law school hiring of affirmative action in support of black male applicants.[6]

On the other hand, while Delgado appears to be wrong,[7] Epstein is not exactly right. His animated contention that all of the bias is in favor of blacks and women must be put in context. In the law school hiring process, there does seem to be a considerable advantage to being a black man, but many other factors such as clerkships and more and better education can offset this advantage. Moreover, the .4 point advantage garnered by white women is substantially less than that secured by black men, and black women actually had no statistically significant advantage over white men in the law school hiring process.[8] Thus, it is inaccurate to claim that blacks and women are advantaged in law school hiring, since black women appear to get no such advantage.[9]

The finding that black men receive a substantial boost in the law school hiring market while black females receive no such advantage is surprising. This is particularly the case because other studies have suggested that firms that are interested in securing workers that can meet affirmative action guidelines will be most interested in hiring black women, since one worker can fill two quota categories (Smith and Welch 1984). The presence of this effect in the economy at large, coupled with its absence in the legal academy, may suggest that law school hiring is less influenced by the external legal pressures of Title VII and the federal government contract compliance program. It would be interesting to explore whether this phenomenon is unique to law school hiring or applies more broadly to hiring of highly educated workers.

There is an important prudential consideration that should be stressed at this juncture. Claims about bias in favor of or against certain demographic groups can be highly inflammatory. Serious scholars would be well advised to consult carefully the available empirical evidence before making hyperbolic speculations about the extent and nature of discrimination in employment.

3. LAW OR CUSTOM?

While the matter of ascertaining whether there is discrimination for or against certain groups in the law professor hiring market is by no means trivial, it is vastly easier than determining whether employment discrimination positively influences the hiring of black labor, and if so, by what mechanism. An article of faith among certain academics and policymakers has been that if productive workers are not being hired because of labor market discrimination, competitive market pressures will ensure that they will be snapped up quickly by other employers. Senator Orrin Hatch has asserted that "The EEOC has sometimes been credited with opening up new pools of labor that corporations somehow contrived to ignore, and occasionally with hastening the breakdown of traditional barriers to labor mobility. . . . But in the context of the market's endless search for efficiency, these anomalies would have been eliminated anyway, leaving only the question of whether they were worth the expenditures compelled by law" (Leonard 1984).[10]

A major empirical challenge to this view was presented by the work of Heckman and Payner analyzing the employment of blacks in the South Carolina textile industry over most of this century.[11] Heckman and Payner demonstrate that black employment levels rose dramatically at about the time that Title VII went into effect and the federal government contract compliance program was initiated in 1965. Heckman and Payner carefully document the share of black employment by sex in the textile industry of the state over the period 1910–74. Through two world wars, the Great Depression, and the Korean War, the share of blacks remained low and stable, despite the expanding employment in the industry throughout this period. Regardless of the degree of labor market tightness or slackness, one fact emerges with remarkable clarity: virtually no black women and only a small portion of black men worked in the textile industry in the fifty-five years before 1965. After that date, black male and black female wages and employment levels (relative to those of white males) suddenly accelerated in the industry. Heckman and Payner (1989) concluded that the breakthrough in black employment in South Carolina occurred shortly after the implementation of Title VII civil rights legislation. The highly synchronized breakthrough in black employment that occurred in all counties of the state irrespective of the tightness or slackness of county local labor markets and the available supply of blacks suggests a common factor was present in all counties—federal pressure.

The experience of the virtually complete exclusion of blacks from the Southern textile industry followed by a major breakthrough in black employment in 1965 challenges the view that the problem of employment discrimination is largely self-correcting. The challenge has elicited two major responses: one critique, advanced by Epstein, concedes that federal intervention was needed in 1965 and did succeed in advancing black economic welfare, but it then argues that this intervention was only necessary and successful to the extent that it eliminated the coercive power of racist Southern state and local government. In other words, according to this view, if the market had been unimpeded by the restrictions of government in the first place, there would have been no need for federal intervention in 1965, and a fortiori there is no case for federal intervention in labor markets today. Subsection A outlines this libertarian argument, and subsection B raises some doubts about its validity. The second critique does not directly address the experience of the South Carolina textile industry, but rather seeks to demonstrate that, from a statistical perspective, any black gains that occur in the post-1965 period are better explained by supply-side factors, such as more and better education for blacks, than by any federal antidiscrimination policy. I will address this argument in section 4.

A. PRIVATE DISCRIMINATION IS NOT A SERIOUS THREAT

A major theme of Richard Epstein's book is that there is little to fear from purely private discrimination. Epstein argues that blacks were excluded from the textile industry for so long only because Southern segregationist legislation and other governmental restrictions kept blacks from being hired: remove the government restrictions and blacks will do fine without any additional antidiscrimination protection. The unfettered market will protect blacks far better than federal law, according to this libertarian view.

Interestingly, while Gary Becker (1971) writing in 1957 observed that the Southern textile industry was "extremely competitive,"[12] Epstein paints a very different picture of the Southern labor market. In his view, "[f]or much of the period before 1965, segregation pursuant to statute, the very antithesis of a market system, was dominant in the South" (1992: 251). Epstein blames a 1915 South Carolina statute that mandated racially segregated facilities for textile workers for undermining competitive employment practices in the industry (1992: 246).[13] It should be noted that this Jim Crow statute did not mandate the exclusion of blacks, but simply required that black and white textile workers be kept strictly segregated. Epstein argues that the higher costs that would be imposed by having to maintain segregated facilities made the hiring of black workers financially impossible.

Of course, if the libertarian view were correct, then policymakers should try to protect competitive forces and eliminate any governmental restrictions. But if custom and private discrimination alone can maintain widespread exclusion of blacks over long periods of time, then the case for libertarianism is undermined and the argument for governmental antidiscrimination law is strongly buttressed. The question is both enormously important and largely unstudied. As Howard Rabinowitz, one of the primary Southern historians focusing on this period, has observed: "Strange as it might seem, during the entire debate over [C. Vann Woodward's thesis advanced in *The Strange Career of Jim Crow*], there has been remarkably little interest in the Jim Crow statutes themselves, and no one has satisfactorily followed the life of a statute from its origins through passage and the effects of implementation" (1988: 850). The reason for the lack of investigation into the comparative significance of custom versus legally enforced segregation is not wholly surprising. Many scholars have been interested in the question of whether federal intervention was needed and whether, once it came, it was successful. With this goal in mind, these scholars have not focused on whether the nature of the problem was Southern custom or Southern legislation. But Epstein's libertarian argument has brought this understudied issue to the fore. His argument that federal intervention was necessary and beneficial in 1965 in that it restored free labor markets to the South is central to his view that such intervention cannot be helpful today.

According to the libertarian view, the South did not have free labor markets, and therefore discrimination could thrive and harm blacks. But the evidence of explicit racial restrictions in the arena of employment is lacking, although Epstein has postulated that, through the ability to deny permits and other regulatory measures, racist governments could make life hard on firms that hired blacks. Moreover, there was an array of ostensibly neutral legal restrictions—such as the antienticement and antirecruitment laws discussed by Zeichner (1940) and Cohen (1976)—that to some degree restricted the free flow of black labor in the South throughout the twentieth century. While the libertarian position is that these restrictions prevented the market from eliminating the patterns of discriminatory exclusions of blacks from higher paying jobs and industries, there are reasons to doubt this view. Many of the legal restrictions were primarily designed to protect the interests of landowners in ensuring that their farm laborers would not accept advances from them and then fail to work on the farm through the end of the harvest (Zeichner 1940: 30). This meant that, once a labor contract was signed, black agricultural workers were restricted in their mobility, but this restriction only lasted for a year. Thus, in the late nineteenth century, large numbers of blacks seeking higher wages moved from Georgia, Alabama, and other southeastern states to Arkansas, Louisiana, and Mississippi, and, after World War I, blacks fled the South entirely. With so much black mobility across and within states, it is hard to believe that the legal restrictions tying sharecroppers to their farms for the one-year contract duration kept blacks from moving into low-skilled manufacturing employment in the South.

To date, the evidence on the enforcement of the Jim Crow statutes that were specifically directed toward the Southern textile industry provides no credible evidence that legal restrictions were responsible for the maintenance of a virtually all-white industry from 1910 to 1965. The most interesting unresolved question is why the pattern of black employment in the South was so stable despite the absence of explicit Jim Crow restrictions, while such racist legislation was common in restricting black conduct in the social sphere.

B. EVIDENCE AGAINST THE LIBERTARIAN HYPOTHESIS

Much evidence conflicts with the libertarian view that racial exclusions were purely the product of private violence and Jim Crow laws. For example, within two months after the decision in *Brown*, the Citizens' Councils of white segregationists were formed to seek legislation that would maintain the Southern segregated way of life. With this system under stress from the federal government, the Citizens' Councils sought to buttress segregation by resort to legislation. The libertarian hypothesis may have it exactly backward: rather than racist legislation being the central problem thwarting the operation of the market, it may have been the federal governmental threat to the continued operation of a custom-driven economy that generated racist legislation designed to thwart the federal civil rights initiative.

Moreover, the libertarian hypothesis does not seem to align well with a number of facts. To the extent that racial exclusions from the Southern textile industry were generated by segregationist legislation, one would imagine that (1) such exclusions would not be found prior to passage of the segregationist law or during periods when the law was not enforced, (2) the exclusion would occur only in areas subject to such legislation, and (3) when the segregationist law ultimately came to be seen as unconstitutional, the racial exclusion would quickly be undone by competitive pressures. Yet the evidence seems to contradict all three points. First, the South Carolina law requiring separate but equal facilities in textile firms was not adopted until 1915 and seems not to have been enforced after the 1920s, yet Heckman and Payner document that the exclusion of blacks in the industry was complete from 1910 to 1915 and continued until 1965.[14] Second, despite the fact that other leading textile states such as North Carolina, Georgia, and Virginia had no such Jim Crow legislation,[15] one finds the same pattern of racial exclusion in the textile industry followed by a pronounced black breakthrough beginning in 1965. Specifically, between 1964 and 1965 black employment in the textile industry increased by 59 percent in South Carolina and by 73 percent in North Carolina (Butler and Heckman 1977: 245). Third, the unconstitutionality of the segregationist legislation pertaining to the South Carolina textile industry, if not immediately apparent after the 1954 decision in *Brown v. Board of Education*, would have been uniformly recognized considerably before the passage of the 1964 Civil Rights Act, but the employment gains documented by Heckman and Payner only came in 1965. Where was the vaunted power of the market to break down discriminatory exclusions?

Moreover, if Jim Crow restrictions alone impaired the ability of the market to protect blacks, then we should not see similar systematic exclusions in the North, which with only rare exception had no such segregationist legislation governing the employment relationship. But recent work by Whatley and Wright finds significant discrimination against blacks in the Northern auto industry. In fact, one of the most discriminatory firms—General Motors—enjoyed considerable growth during its period of racial exclusion (Whatley and Wright 1991; see also Donohue 1992). Northrup documents widespread exclusions in airplane manufacturing in such states as New York, New Jersey, Connecticut, and California (1968). In both cases, these exclusions existed prior to the emergence of unions in these industries. Accordingly, evidence of wholesale racial exclusion outside the South is inconsistent with the libertarian hypothesis that such exclusions cannot exist in the absence of the constraints that characterized the Jim Crow South.

Another interesting question is, When did the significant racial exclusions outside the South begin to crumble? Jim Heckman and I have documented that a black breakthrough in relative earnings did not occur after 1965 except in the South, which might be deemed to support the libertarian hypothesis (Donohue and Heckman 1991). The argument would be that federal antidiscrimination law brought no relative gains for non-Southern blacks since the market had already protected them. On the other hand, at the time of the passage of the 1964 Civil Rights Act, virtually all Northern states had adopted state fair-employment practice laws forbidding discrimination on the basis of race, so that whatever gains that could have been achieved through antidiscrimination law might have been generated outside the South well before 1964.

Therefore the effectiveness of state antidiscrimination laws turns out to be a critical piece in the puzzle of resolving the subsequent effectiveness of federal antidiscrimination law. Yet only a single study has tried to assess the impact of these state laws on black earnings. William Landes found that the state antidiscrimination laws elevated black incomes but also increased black unemployment. But there are two dimensions of his study that are questionable.

First, Landes did not distinguish among state antidiscrimination regimes based on the degree of enforcement authority and the types of sanctions available. Specifically, states such as New York had relatively strong laws that were quite aggressively enforced, while states such as Kansas had laws that were largely hortatory. Yet in Landes's analysis, all of these states are treated monolithically as having employment discrimination laws.[16] Second, an examination of the impact of state antidiscrimination laws over the period from 1945 (when New York and New Jersey became the first states to adopt such laws) until 1965 when federal law extended the legal prohibition on discrimination to the entire country must control for black migration from the South. The reason can be illustrated with reference to Landes's study. He finds in a cross-section study that in 1959, states with antidiscrimination laws had higher unemployment rates than states without such laws. However, conducting the same regression in years prior to the passage of the laws—such as 1949 and 1939—generates similar significant coefficient estimates. That is, blacks already experienced higher wages and unemployment in states that subsequently adopted employment discrimination laws. In other words, the explanation for the higher black unemployment in various states is not that they have antidiscrimination laws, but rather they have a different labor economy that generates higher unemployment. Specifically, the South, where no such state laws were found, was a largely subsistence agricultural economy for blacks with low wages and little unemployment.

Landes recognized this problem but contended that the estimated coefficients grew in size over time. He considered this growth to be a measure of the effect of the state laws. But even if the state antidiscrimination laws had no effect, black migration from the South would tend to cause the estimated black unemployment coefficient to grow. Over the entire period covered by Landes's study, blacks continued to leave the South for the industrialized urban North (which largely had antidiscrimination laws by 1959), where wages were higher and unemployment was significant. Therefore, black migration to the higher-pay Northern states undoubtedly led to higher black unemployment rates, as it took time for the new arrivals to be absorbed into the labor market. Thus, black migration may well be the true explanation for a spurious correlation between high black unemployment rates and the presence of state antidiscrimination law.

4. HAS FEDERAL CIVIL RIGHTS POLICY AIDED BLACKS?

The tension created by the sharply conflicting academic research prompted Jim Heckman and me to critically evaluate the existing literature to ascertain the state of the evidence on the effects of the federal civil rights regime on the economic status of blacks (Donohue and Heckman 1991). This section draws on that evaluation.

A number of works, including the U.S. Civil Rights Commission report of 1986, have advanced the view that the long-term trends of migration and improving education are the primary determinants of black economic progress: "The racial wage gap narrowed as rapidly in the 20 years prior to 1960 (and before affirmative action) as during the 20 years afterward. This suggests that the slowly evolving historical forces we have emphasized in this essay—education and migration—were the primary determinants of the long-term black economic improvement. *At best, affirmative action has marginally altered black wage gains around this long-term trend*" (Smith and Welch 1989: 555; emphasis added). Smith contends that throughout this century there has been "gradual but significant improvement in the quality and quantity of the skills that blacks are able to carry with them into the labor market to compete with white workers, [a]nd as the human capital of blacks increased relative to whites, so also did their earnings" (Smith 1984: 698). This body of research has created the impression of an inexorable narrowing of the gap between black and white earnings as blacks have developed greater marketable skills. But is the impression correct?

A. BLACK PROGRESS, 1940–1960 AND 1960–1980

There is indirect evidence supporting the view that the skill advantage of whites has continuously narrowed for much of this century. As mentioned earlier, Card and Krueger (1990; 1992) document the rather dramatic if relative improvements since 1910 in the quality of black education as measured by three variables: the student-teacher ratio, the length of the school term, and teacher salaries. But the relentless narrowing in the black-white wage differential that the human capital story would lead us to expect is far more difficult to discern.

Over the seventy years from 1920 to 1990, measured black incomes rose relative to white incomes in only two periods: during the economic rebound from the Great Depression induced by World War II, and in the decade following the launching of an intensive federal effort to guarantee the civil rights of blacks.[17] Because measured black gains from 1939 to 1949 were comparable to the gains from 1965 to 1975, the simple equivalence that Smith and Welch (1977; 1978; 1984) observe between black advances over the period from 1940 to 1960 and the gains in the next twenty-year period, during which time the law went into effect, is correct but highly misleading.

Moreover, the measured relative gain for blacks for the decade beginning in 1939 may be exaggerated for two reasons. First, the higher wages earned by Southern black migrants to the North are not adjusted downward for cost-of-living increases, nor do the census income figures correct for the value of farm production consumed by Southern agricultural workers. Second, black incomes may well have been artificially depressed by the Depression and subsequently elevated by the war. Without a sizable gain during the 1940s, though, we would be left with a very different story than the one offered by the advocates of long-term continuous progress: the long period of narrowing skill differentials between blacks and whites would be linked with only one decade of relative black progress—that following the passage of the 1964 Civil Rights Act, when the aggregate black/white earnings ratio rose from .62 in 1964 to .72 by 1975, before falling to .69 in 1987.

B. THE EFFECT OF MIGRATION

The long-term historical factors that the U.S. Civil Rights Commission study and others offer as the basis for the black gains after 1960 do not appear to justify their strong conclusions about the ineffectiveness of the law. Consider first the issue of migration: enormous numbers of blacks were fleeing the South. One would expect this massive exodus of young blacks to contribute to narrowing the racial wage gap because blacks were largely leaving low-paid agricultural jobs in the South and securing higher-paid industrial jobs in the North. In the decade of the 1940s and again for the 1950s, roughly a quarter of young black men living in the South migrated North. This amazing black exodus grew at an even faster pace in the first half of the 1960s, but then suddenly the outflow slowed to a trickle. Over the decade of the 1970s the flow was reversed, as the South experienced net black in-migration. Thus, while black migration is an important explanation of black progress in the period prior to the passage of the 1964 Civil Rights Act, it cannot serve as an explanation for the substantial black gains in the aftermath of the civil rights legislation. Indeed, rather than undermining the case that federal civil rights policy aided blacks—as the above quote from Smith and Welch would suggest—the story of black migration powerfully buttresses it. Something very dramatic happened in the mid-1960s to make Southern blacks decide to remain in the South. It is quite likely that the cause of this sudden shift was the perception that the comprehensive federal effort, directed primarily at the South, to eliminate barriers to blacks in housing, voting, schooling, and employment would improve the quality of black life in the South.

C. THE EFFECT OF SCHOOLING

In addition to migration, the improvement in the relative education of blacks has been offered as an explanation of black progress in the decade following passage of the 1964 Civil Rights Act. But the continuous relative improvements in black education going back to the 1920s cannot explain fully the large black economic advances in the post-1965 decade, even though they contributed to those gains. First, the black economic gains following 1964 were across-the-board: young blacks as well as old blacks experienced substantial jumps in income relative to that earned by whites. Second, gains achieved through improved schooling tend to be gradual over time rather than discontinuous, and therefore improved schooling is unlikely to explain the sharp jump in post-1965 black income.

Both of these factors suggest that the elevation of black income at the time of the adoption of Title VII of the 1964 Civil Rights Act and the promulgation of the federal government contract compliance program calling for affirmative action in the hiring of black workers likely came from a sudden demand-side influence such as would be created by new legal requirements, rather than an evolving factor such as better education or declining discrimination. Moreover, it should also be underscored that the gains to black income that did occur via the mechanism of the evolving supply-side factor of improved black education, while not the product of employment discrimination law, were largely engineered through litigative efforts to enforce the dictates of the Fourteenth Amendment.

5. CONCLUSION

In examining a few areas in which law has affected the well-being of black Americans, I have tried to convey some sense of the many critical aspects of life—public schooling, legal education, the labor market—that have been touched by law. At times, particular legal interventions—witness the NAACP schooling litigation under the doctrine of separate-but-equal—brought benefits to blacks, even though the overall character of Southern law was racist and harmful. Richard Delgado would probably view the current law of employment discrimination as simply a continuation of a situation that is basically racist while holding out the unrealized promise of equality. On the other hand, there are signs of some genuine gains through law. As the decade of the sixties came to a close and the seventies began, the South went from being the area of the country with the most segregated schools to being the area with the least segregated schools. Moreover, there is evidence of sharp gains in the relative earnings of blacks during the decade after 1965 that is most likely caused by federal civil rights law.

Yet achieving consensus within the academic community concerning the influence of antidiscrimination law on black welfare will not be easy. The subject is so controversial, the pathways of causal influence are so manifold, the data contain so many unfillable holes, and the rewards to contrarian scholars are so great that there remains a rich ground of uncertainty from which inflated claims and extreme propositions can blossom. More disturbing than the inflated rhetoric that often accompanies these speculations, however, is the fact that the scholars who announce them often pursue a theoretically driven vision of the impact of civil rights law even when the ultimate questions on which they opine so strongly are empirical matters that are susceptible to verification—or refutation. For example, many law and economics scholars have endorsed an idealized view of the market that virtually rules out the possibility that governmental action may serve a useful social function in addressing the problem of employment discrimination. Conversely, other scholars are content to make theoretically driven claims about the pervasiveness of discrimination despite the presence of strong empirical evidence to the contrary. The appropriate strategy for research in this area is to remove the strong ideological lenses and systematically to examine the evidence in an effort to distinguish the rhetoric from the reality.

NOTES

1. Recent additions to the literature concerning discrimination in education and housing include Deborah Mayo-Jeffries (1994) and Thomas Kingsley and Margery Austin Turner (1993).

2. Broad involuntary sterilization laws that led to the sterilization of sixty thousand individuals between 1907 and 1960 would likely now be viewed as "discriminatory," although at the time their opponents attacked them as violations of personal rights (Larson and Nelson 1992). Of course, had the Supreme Court ruled differently in the 1927 case of *Buck v. Bell,* many of those sterilizations would never have occurred (Gould 1985).

3. In the years immediately following the 1954 *Brown* decision, the Supreme Court struck down a number of state-assisted segregationist practices in a series of one-sentence per curium orders issued in 1955, 1956, and 1958. *Mayor and City Council of Baltimore v. Dawson,* 350 U.S. 877 (1955) (beaches); *Holmes v. City of Atlanta,* 350 U.S. 879 (1955) (golf course); *Gayle v. Browder,* 352 U.S. 903 (1956) (buses); and *New Orleans City Park Imp. Ass'n v. Detiege,* 358 U.S. 54 (1958) (parks).

4. No law—other than the unwritten Southern code of racial segregation—prevented the private store owners from serving blacks.

5. In addition, each increase of 1 point in the prestige index of one's law school increased the prestige of the hiring law school by .48.

6. The evidence is strong and statistically significant, but the study does not address the possibility that some explanatory variables could have been influenced by prejudice or affirmative action. For example, if Supreme Court justices are biased against black men, then fewer blacks would have achieved this highly beneficial credential. This could lead to a spurious finding of an advantage in black male hiring when in fact it simply implied bias in securing Supreme Court clerkships. Conversely, if there is affirmative action operating to secure some of these credentials, such as in admission to law school, college, or graduate school, then the estimated amount of affirmative action in law school hiring could be biased downward.

7. Assuming that the attainment of some of the "objective" credentials is not itself tainted by discrimination and the results of the Merritt and Reskin study hold up, then Delgado's claim that the white male candidate for a law school teaching position would always be hired instead of the objectively equivalent black male candidate is false. On the other hand, one might well ask why law professors with certain credentials, such as a Ph.D. in a nonlaw field or a Supreme Court clerkship, should be favored in the law school hiring process. Would such reliance on credentials have a disparate impact on the hiring of black candidates? Could law firms justify such credentials as consistent with business necessity?

8. The study found that black women had a .1 advantage over white men in terms of the prestige of the institution in which they were hired, but this advantage was not statistically significant. This finding would seem to show that both Epstein and Delgado were wrong.

9. This finding vindicates the concerns expressed by Kimberle Crenshaw (1989), that there is a tendency "to treat race and gender as mutually exclusive categories of experience and analysis." One might reformulate Crenshaw's concern in econometric terms by pointing out that a regression equation of law school hiring must include not only race and gender dummies but an interaction term to identify the experience of black women as well. The interaction term that Merritt and Reskin wisely included turned out to have an exceptionally significant coefficient, and of course it revealed the important finding that black women fare worse than either black men or white women in securing law school teaching jobs.

10. For an argument that this position follows from the incorrect premise that labor markets are as effective as more perfect markets, such as capital markets, in guaranteeing the equality of price and value, see Donohue 1994.

11. Textiles has long been the major manufacturing employer in the state, accounting for 80 percent of all manufacturing employment in 1940 and more than 50 percent in 1970 (Heckman and Payner 1989).

12. Others have suggested that some textile plants in isolated areas enjoyed monopsony power over the available labor supply.

13. The law was formally repealed by the South Carolina legislature in 1972. Act No. 1049—An Act to Repeal Section 40–452, Code of Laws of South Carolina, 1962, Relating to Separation of Employees of Different Races in Cotton Textile Factories. March 8, 1972.

14. Indeed, there was a modest increase in the percentage of blacks hired in the industry following the enactment of the law. The data that Heckman and Payner used in their study only went back to 1910, five years prior to the passage of the 1915 textile segregation act.

15. North Carolina did have a law that required separate toilet facilities for blacks in manufacturing firms, but we doubt such a law was responsible for the industry's strict racial exclusion.

16. This problem would tend to bias downward the estimated coefficients in Landes's regression.

17. Absolute black progress was enormous over the entire seventy-year time period, since the real wages of all workers were climbing significantly.

BIBLIOGRAPHY

Becker, Gary. 1971. *The Economics of Discrimination*. Chicago: Univ. of Chicago Press.

Beller, Andrea. 1978. The Economics of Enforcement of an Anti-discrimination Law: Title VII of the Civil Rights Act of 1964. 21 *Journal of Law and Economics*, 359.

Bork, Robert H. 1990. *The Tempting of America: The Political Seduction of the Law*. New York: Free Press.

Bound, John, and Richard Freeman. 1989. Black Progress: Erosion of The Post-1965 Gains in the 1980s? In *The Question of Discrimination: Racial Inequality in the U.S. Labor Market*, ed. S. Shulman and W. Darity. Middletown, CT: Wesleyan Univ. Press.

Brown, Charles. 1982. The Federal Attack on Labor Market Discrimination: The Mouse That Roared? 5 *Research in Labor Economics*, 33.

Bullock, Henry. 1967. *A History of Negro Education in the South*. Cambridge, MA: Harvard Univ. Press.

Bullock, Henry, James Heckman, and Brook Payner. 1989. The Impact of the Economy and State on the Economic Status of Blacks. In *Markets in History: Economic Studies of the Past*, ed. D. Galenson. Cambridge: Cambridge Univ. Press.

Butler, Richard, and James Heckman. 1977. The Government's Impact on the Labor Market Status of Black Americans: A Critical Review. In *Equal Rights and Industrial Relations*, ed. L. Hausman. Madison, WI: Industrial Relations Research Association.

Cameron, Stephen, and James Heckman. 1991. Dynamics of School Attendance for Blacks, Whites, and Hispanics. Under review.

———. 1993. The Nonequivalence of High School Equivalents. 11 *Journal of Labor Economics*, 1.

———. 1998. Life-Cycle Models of Schooling Attainment. Forthcoming in *Journal of Political Economy*.

Card, David, and Alan Krueger. 1990. Does School Quality Matter? Returns to Education and the Characteristics of Public Schools in the United States. MBER Working Paper 3358.

———. 1992. School Quality and Black/White Relative Earnings: A Direct Assessment. 107 *Quarterly Journal of Economics*, 151.

Cohen, William. 1976. Negro Involuntary Servitude in the South, 1865–1940: A Preliminary Analysis. 42 *J. S. Historya*, 31.

Coleman, James. 1966. *Equality of Educational Opportunity*. Washington, DC: U.S. Government Printing Office.

Crenshaw, Kimberle. 1989. Demarginalizing the Intersection of Race and Sex: A Black Feminist Critique of Anti-discrimination Doctrine, Feminist Theory and Antiracist Politics. 1989 *Univ. of Chicago Legal Forum*, 139.

Delgado, Richard. 1993. Rodrigo's Fourth Chronicle: Neutrality and Stasis in Anti-discrimination Law. 45 *Stanford Law Rev.*, 1133.

Donohue, John. 1992. Advocacy versus Analysis in Assessing Employment Discrimination Law. 44 *Stanford Law Rev.*, 1583.

Donohue, John. 1994. Employment Discrimination Law in Perspective: Three Concepts of Equality. 92 *Michigan Law Rev.*, 2583.

Donohue, John, and James Heckman. 1991. Continuous versus Episodic Change: The Impact of Civil Rights Policy on the Economic Status of Blacks. 29 *Journal of Economic Literature*, 1603.

Duncan, Greg, and Saul Hoffman. 1983. A New Look at the Causes of the Improved Economic Status of Black Workers. 17 *Journal of Human Resources* (Spring), 268.

Edds, Margaret. 1987. *Free at Last*. Bethesda, MD: Adler and Adler.

Epstein, Richard. 1992. *Forbidden Grounds: The Case against Employment Discrimination Laws*. Cambridge, MA: Harvard Univ. Press.

Farley, Reynolds, and Walter Allen. 1987. *The Color Line and the Quality of Life in America*. New York: Russell Sage Foundation.

Fligstein, Neil. 1981. *Going North*. New York: Academic Press.

Freeman, Richard. 1973. Changes in the Labor Market for Black Americans, 1948–1972. 1 *Brookings Papers on Economic Activity*, 246–95.

————. 1981. Black Economic Progress after 1964: Who Has Gained and Why?" In *Studies in Labor Markets*, ed. S. Rosen. Chicago: Univ. of Chicago Press.

Friedman, Lawrence M. 1997. *Brown* in Context. In *Race, Law and Culture*, ed. Austin Sarat. New York: Oxford Univ. Press.

Garrow, David J. 1986. *Bearing the Cross*. New York: Vintage.

Gould, Stephen Jay. 1985. Carrie Buck's Daughter. 2 *Constitutional Commentary Summary*, 331.

Hamilton, C. Horace. 1959. Educational Selectivity of Migration from the South. 38 *Social Forces*, 38.

————. 1965. Educational Selectivity of Migration from Farm to Urban and to Other Nonfarm Communities. In *Mobility and Mental Health: General Conference on Community Mental Health Resources*, ed. Mildred B. Kantor. Springfield, IL: Charles Thomas.

Heckman, James. 1989. The Impact of Government on the Economic Status of Black Americans. In *The Question of Discrimination*, ed. S. Shulman and W. Darrity. Middletown, CT: Wesleyan Univ. Press.

Heckman, James, and Brook Payner. 1989. Determining the Impact of Federal Anti-discrimination Policy on the Economic Status of Blacks: A Study of South Carolina. 79 *American Economic Rev.*, 138.

Holmes, Oliver Wendell. 1897. The Path of the Law. 10 *Harvard Law Rev.*, 457.

Johnson, George, and Frank Stafford. 1973. Social Returns to Quantity and Quality of Schooling. 8 *Journal of Human Resources*, 139.

Juhn, Chinhui, Kevin Murphy, and Brooks Pierce. 1989. Accounting for the Slowdown in Black-White Wage Convergence. In *Workers and Their Wages: Changing Patterns in the U.S.*, ed. M. Kosters. Washington, DC: American Enterprise Institute Press.

Kingsley, Thomas, and Margery Austin Turner. 1994. *Housing Markets and Residential Mobility*. Washington, DC: Urban Institute Press.

Klarman, Michael. 1991. An Interpretive History of Modern Equal Protection. 90 *Michigan Law Rev.*, 213.

Landes, William. The Economics of Fair Employment Laws. 76 *Journal of Political Economy*.

Larson, Edward J., and Leonard J. Nelson III. 1992. Involuntary Sexual Sterilization of Incompetents in Alabama: Past, Present, and Future. 43 *Alabama Law Rev.*, 388.

Lawson, Steven. 1976. *Black Ballots: Voting Rights in the South, 1944–1969*. New York: Columbia Univ. Press.

Leonard, Jonathan. 1984. Antidiscrimination or Reverse Discrimination: The Impact of Changing Demographics, Title VII, and Affirmative Action on Productivity. 19 *Journal of Human Resources*, 145.

Lieberson, Stanley. 1980. *A Piece of the Pie: Blacks and White Immigrants Since 1880*. Berkeley: Univ. of California Press.

Long, Larry, and Lynne Heltmann. 1975. Migration and Income Differences between Black and White Men in the North. 80 *American Journal of Sociology*, 1391.

Mandle, Jay R. 1992. *Not Slave, Not Free: The African American Economic Experience Since the Civil War*. Durham, NC: Duke Univ. Press.

Margo, Robert. 1990. *Race and Schooling in the South, 1880–1950: An Economic History*. Chicago: Univ. of Chicago Press.

Martin, John. 1970. *The Deep South Says Never*. Westport, CT.: Negro Universities Press.

Mayo-Jeffries, Deborah. 1994. *Equal Educational Opportunity for All Children: A Research Guide to Discrimination in Education* (1950–1992). Buffalo: W. S. Hein.

McCauley, Patrick, and Edward Ball. 1959. *Southern Schools: Progress and Problems*. Nashville, TN: Southern Education Reporting Service.

McConnell, Michael. 1995. Originalism and the Desegregation Decisions. 81 *Virginia Law Rev.*, 947.

Merritt, Deborah, and Barbara Reskin. 1994. Sex, Race, and Credentials: The Truth about Affirmative Action in Law School Hiring. 97 *Columbia Law Rev.*, 199.

Myrdal, Gunnar. 1944. *An American Dilemma: The Negro Problem and Modern Democracy*. New York: Harper and Row.

Northrup, Herbert R. 1968. *The Negro in the Aerospace Industry*. Philadelphia: Univ. of Pennsylvania Press.

Orfield, Gary. 1983. *Public School Desegregation in the United States, 1968–1980*. Washington, DC: Joint Center for Political Studies.

Osofsky, Gilbert. 1971. *Harlem: The Making of a Ghetto: Negro New York, 1890–1930*. New York: Harper and Row.

Posner, Richard. 1987. The Efficacy and Efficiency of Title VII. 136 *Univ. Pennsylvania Law Rev.*, 513.

———. 1990. Bork and Beethoven. 42 *Stanford Law Rev.*, 1365.

Rabinowitz, Howard N. 1988. More Than the Woodward Thesis: Assessing *The Strange Career of Jim Crow*. 75 *Journal of American History*, 842.

Rosenberg, Gerald. 1991. *The Hollow Hope: Can the Courts Bring about Social Change?* Chicago: Univ. of Chicago Press.

Smith, James. 1984. Race and Human Capital. 74 *American Economic Rev.*, 685.

Smith, James, and Finis Welch. 1977. Black/White Male Earnings and Employment: 1960–1970. In The *Distribution of Economic Well-Being*, ed. F. T. Juster. Cambridge, MA: National Bureau of Economic Research.

———. 1978. *Race Differences in Earnings: A Survey and New Evidence.* Santa Monica, CA: Rand Corporation.

———. 1984. Affirmative Action in Labor Markets. 2 *Journal of Labor Economics*, 269.

———. 1986. *Closing the Gap.* Santa Monica, CA: Rand Corporation.

———. 1989. Black Economic Progress after Myrdal. 27 *Journal of Economic Literature*, 519.

St. John, Nancy. 1975. *School Desegregation: Outcomes for Children.* New York: Wiley-Interscience Publication.

Sunstein, Cass. 1992. How Independent Is the Court?" 39 *New York Review of Books*, 47.

U.S. Commission on Civil Rights. 1986. *The Economic Progress of Black Men in America.* Washington, DC: U.S. Government Printing Office.

Wasby, Stephen, Anthony D'Amato, and Rosemary Metrailer. 1977. *Desegregation from Brown to Alexander.* Carbondale: Southern Illinois Univ. Press.

Welch, Finis. 1967. Labor Market Discrimination: An Interpretation of Income Differences in the Rural South. 65 *Journal of Political Economy*, 3.

———. 1973. Education and Racial Discrimination. In *Discrimination in Labor Markets*, ed. Orley Ashenfelter and Albert Rees. Princeton, NJ: Princeton Univ. Press.

Whatley, Warren, and Gavin Wright. 1991. Getting Started in the Auto Industry: Black Workers at the Ford Motor Company, 1918–1947. Unpublished manuscript.

Wilson, William. 1987. *The Truly Disadvantaged: The Inner City, the Underclass and Public Policy.* Chicago: Univ. of Chicago Press.

Woodward, C. Vann. 1974. *The Strange Career of Jim Crow.* 3d rev. ed. New York: Oxford Univ. Press.

———. 1988. *Strange Career* Critics: Long May They Persevere. 75 *Journal of American History*, 857.

Zeichner, Oscar. 1939. The Transition from Slave to Free Agricultural Labor in the Southern States. 13 *Agricultural History*, 22.

———. 1940. The Legal Status of the Agricultural Laborer in the South. 55 *Political Science Quarterly*, 412.

HOW DOES LAW MATTER
FOR SOCIAL MOVEMENTS?

MICHAEL W. McCANN

1. INTRODUCTION

Much recent scholarship has contributed to our understanding of how law matters for social movements in U.S. history. Two rather different, and so far mostly independent, scholarly traditions have proved most directly relevant to the topic.

A. LEGAL SCHOLARSHIP

One salient disciplinary tradition of studying law and social change has been staked out by legal scholars. While there is much variation in the approaches directed to the subject, three general types of studies have been most common and influential among legal scholars. The first of these are judicial impact studies. The primary aim of these studies has been to examine the degree to which various target populations comply with, or otherwise respond positively to, important judicial rulings. One finding of many such studies is that a wide gap separates the promises of reform litigation initiated by social movements and the minimal effects on behavior actually generated by judicial decisions.[1]

A second category of study has focused on the ideological biases of law. Although such studies vary widely in kind, most—especially those associated with critical legal studies scholarship—have labored to demonstrate the degree to which specific doctrines of official law are ideologically biased in support of status quo hierarchies (see Kairys 1982; Kelman 1987). As such, legal norms, logics, and practices are reproached for either preempting or coopting struggles by oppressed groups (Gabel 1982, 1984; Freeman 1982; Tushnet 1984; see Bartholomew and Hunt 1990). An important ancillary argument of many such studies is that most legal reform efforts thus unwittingly tend to rationalize, legitimate, and "mystify" rather than to challenge existing injustices and hegemonic relations.

A third category involves what we might call "cause lawyer" studies. These studies focus on the contributions of progressive lawyers to reform organizations, social movements, or general political causes. Although again variable in conclusions, most such studies have emphasized the limitations, burdens, and biases inherent in most cause lawyers' propensity to litigate for change rather than to press for alternative, more "political" reform tactics.[2]

Although methodologically and analytically distinct, these various types of studies both separately and together have proved very influential among legal scholars in recent years (see Scheingold 1974; McCann 1986; Rosenberg 1991).[3] As such, it is worth noting some conceptual assumptions regarding "how law matters" for social movements that inform all three frameworks to some degree. Most important, all three approaches typically begin with clearly definable exogenous legal forces (legal norms, legal institutions, lawyers) and examine their effects on social actors and activities (e.g., state officials, social elites, public opinion, reform movement constituencies, etc.). Officially sanctioned legal norms or actions are the starting point; their unidirectional impact (or lack thereof) on various target populations is the focus of concern. Similarly, assessing the instrumental effectiveness of official legal policies rather than understanding the complexities of legally constituted action for movement politics receives the bulk of attention in most of these studies. Finally, as suggested above, the bulk of existing scholarship is highly critical about the pervasive constraints, costs, and obstacles that law imposes on reform movement efforts to transform society. Whether demonstrating that legal norms and practices are a "hollow hope" or a co-optive trap for social movements, most such studies suggest that the promise of legal justice is a nefarious myth. Some exceptions to this generalization exist (see below), but the majority of prominent studies in the last three decades fit this general mold.

B. SOCIAL MOVEMENT SCHOLARSHIP

Another relevant scholarly literature focuses social scientific analyses directly on social movements themselves. This expanding intellectual field is diverse and difficult to characterize in general terms. For example, considerable disagreement and uncertainty exists regarding just how the very concept of "social movement" itself should be defined.[4] For the purpose of this paper, I will use political scientist Sidney Tarrow's often cited definition. He characterizes social movements as "groups possessing a purposive organization, whose leaders identify their goals with the preferences of an unmobilized constituency which they attempt to mobilize in direct action in relation to a target of influence in the political system" (1983: 7).

Despite the wide range of such approaches to the study of social movements, however, one broad tradition has come to dominate work by sociologists and political scientists. This research tradition has developed around what usually is called resource mobilization (RM) theory (see Tarrow 1983). It is important to emphasize that there are many versions of this general approach which vary quite dramatically. Perhaps the most dramatic line of division is between "rational choice" and more culturally oriented and institutionally focused types of study (see Fireman and Gamson 1979; Ferree 1992; Chong 1991).[5] My own work is most influenced by McAdam's "political process" version of resource mobilization (1982; Tarrow 1983; Costain 1992; Klandermans 1992), supplemented by various analyses addressing activist consciousness, solidarity, and other aspects of the intersubjective "movement culture."[6]

Social movement studies in this broadly defined tradition have recognized the importance of legal norms (especially rights claims), tactics, institutions, and experts in many social movement struggles. Just how law matters rarely is addressed in any sustained, theoretically rigorous way by this literature, however. In fact, while case studies often attribute considerable significance to legal factors, most social movement scholars tend to highlight (often somewhat romantically) those unconventional resources and tactics that distinguish social movements from other forms of political activity (see McAdam 1982: 42; Piven and Cloward 1979). In short, even though many scholarly narratives about movements demonstrate the common connection between "law and disorder" (Lowi 1971), their formal theoretical frameworks tend to emphasize the tension between defiant movement activity and order-affirming law.

C. TOWARD A SYNTHESIS

The analysis in the following pages will attempt to synthesize these two traditions. Specifically, my aim is to specify how social movement scholarship can reorient inquiry regarding how law matters in social struggle. In other words, I attempt to develop the implications of social movement theorizing and empirical study for analyzing law in ways that scholars in this tradition themselves have not done. The resulting framework aims to provide a somewhat different, more nuanced view than that offered by much of the conventional, court-centered legal analysis briefly summarized above. At the same time, however, my argument also draws on and converges with a variety of other less traditional modes of legal analysis. These include especially recent scholarship on civil dispute processing, interpretive studies of everyday legal resistance, and maverick cultural analyses of law and political struggle.[7]

This discussion will begin by outlining a broad theoretical framework for legal analysis, and then proceed to develop secondary conceptual issues and empirical findings from social movement experience. Although both social movement theorizing and case studies will draw primarily on U.S. experience, the rapidly increasing scholarship on movements around the world will be acknowledged at various points.

2. LEARNING FROM SOCIAL MOVEMENT MODELS: TOWARD A DECENTERING OF LAW

A. Social Movement Analyses

Several basic features of prevailing theories regarding social movements are worth noting at the outset. Perhaps most important is to recognize that such analyses typically begin with the primary constituent group of victimized or oppressed citizens that forms the core of the social movement itself. In short, the starting point and focus of most studies is the discrete social actors engaged in ongoing struggle with dominant groups or institutional relations. The perspective thus is a mostly bottom-up, nonstate-centered view of power relations.

Moreover, most studies emphasize that these group struggles involve inherently dynamic and volatile life histories. As such, most analyses at least implicitly recognize various stages or phases of social movement activity (see McAdam 1982; Tarrow 1983; Chong 1991). These stages are variously defined, but usually include (1) initial group identity formation, consciousness-raising, and movement organizing; (2) early battles to win recognition by dominant groups or to get on the public agenda; (3) struggles over policy development and implementation; and (4) eventual movement decline, transformation, "hibernation," or rebirth (see Taylor 1989).

Scholars have discerned that movements generally undergo a variety of internal changes during this evolutionary process. Two types of transformations are especially important. The first involves the shifting roles and relations among different movement groups. This is important, for it underlines the often neglected point that most movements are pluralistic, volatile alliances of differently situated, often competing groups whose contributions vary at different points of struggle (Morris 1984; Tarrow 1983; Freeman 1975). Most "contemporary social movements . . . rarely, if ever, take a single organizational expression," notes Alan Hunt. "They are characterized by their multiplicity of organizational expressions" (1990: 318). The second related aspect of internal flux concerns movement tactics. Just as group roles and relations typically vary over time, so do most social movements deploy multiple types of resources and tactical maneuvers in diverse venues over the course of struggle.

Scholarly studies in this tradition likewise give considerable attention to features of the larger social context that affect movement development. While traditional structuralist concerns regarding macrolevel socioeconomic and

state factors usually receive attention (Skocpol 1979), so are more meso-
and microlevel factors considered important in understanding the multiorganizational field constituting movement activity (Klandermans 1991; Zald
1992). The political process approach categorizes such dynamics in terms of
changing (1) systemic opportunities for, and vulnerabilities to, challenge from
traditionally marginalized citizens; and (2) movement resources, including
financial resources, cultural discourses, indigenous associations, and third-
party support from government, elite patrons, allied groups, and so on (see
McAdam 1982; Tarrow 1983). In this view, such factors do not determine
the rise and fates of social movements in any mechanical fashion. Rather, the
assumption is simply that increased opportunities and resources for action
enhance the likelihood that struggles of aggrieved citizens will escalate into
movements and have an impact on the larger culture, while the opposite is
true as well.

These points suggest a final relevant issue. In short, most movement scholars recognize that human subjectivity is a crucial independent factor in social
action. This reflects, on the one hand, the tendency of most contemporary
theorists to emphasize the inherent rationality of social movement activists.
Understandings of activist rationality vary widely from the methodological
individualism of public choice theory (Taylor 1988; Chong 1991) to more
culturally embedded views of subjectivity (Ferree 1992; Fireman and Gamson
1979; McAdam 1982; Klandermans 1992; Morris 1992; Fantasia 1988).
But all of these approaches at least emphasize that movement activists are
(1) regularly engaged in self-critical dialogue about how to define their
interests in a hierarchical social environment; (2) relatively skeptical about
dominant cultural norms and discourses sustaining the hierarchies in which
they are embroiled; and (3) at least moderately sophisticated about the
limited tactical options for collective action available to them in a constrained but volatile environment. As such, most empirical studies reject
explanations of movements as either inherently irrational and dysfunctional
(McAdam 1982) or diverted by co-opted false consciousness (Scott 1985,
1990; Cocks 1989).

On the other hand, a growing literature has emphasized that activist
interests, demands, and identity are socially constructed over time. The focus
of such an understanding thus goes beyond documenting changes in the
external structure of social conditions to changes also in the perceptions,
meanings, and consciousness that develop among key actors regarding social
relations, power, and injustice. Rationality is, in short, understood as situated
and historical in character, the product of practical material experience over
time in particular institutional settings (see Ferree 1992; Fantasia 1988).
Moreover, while shaped and constrained by specific cultural conventions,
citizen consciousness is presumed to be inherently heterogeneous and oppositional in character. "New social movement" studies in particular focus
on how movement participants over time must constantly work to construct
from prevailing cultural norms a common framework of defiant demands,

alternative group identities, and "ideological packages" to sustain movement action (Scott 1990; Gamson 1988; Snow and Benford 1988; Melucci 1989).

B. A Social Movement Approach to Legal Mobilization

These tenets of social movement theorizing can be helpful for conceptualizing how law matters in social reform activity.[8] Most fundamentally, this approach emphasizes the value of beginning not with official legal texts or institutions, as does most conventional legal scholarship, but with the wide variety of legally oriented practices and understandings generated among movement participants engaged in social struggle. That is, this approach urges a decentered view of how law becomes meaningful through the practical material activity of citizens (Harrington and Yngvesson 1990; Brigham 1988; McCann 1994).

Such an approach stresses further that law is inherently multidimensional in its practical manifestations and hence becomes meaningful in varying forms and ways. It is useful to recall in this regard the distinctions urged by E. P. Thompson—a pioneering movement scholar who wrote brilliantly about legal relations—between law as (1) institutions (courts, etc.); (2) personnel (lawyers, judges, etc.); and (3) ideology (1975: 260). While the first two manifestations of law emphasize the official side of law, the ideological dimensions of legal norms, discourses, and conventions convey the relatively autonomous legal power that permeates social interaction at multiple levels and in various degrees. The relative weight of specific legal forms in society is, of course, influenced by and loosely tethered to official state practices. Yet legal practices are more indeterminate, mutable, and pluralistic than is recognized by positivist models (see Merry 1990; Ewick and Silbey 1992).

An important corollary of this point is that the indirect and radiating symbolic effects of official legal actions (e.g., by courts) often are far more important than their direct, command-oriented effects (see Handler 1978; Galanter 1983; McCann 1993a; 1994). As Galanter has argued, law should be understood capaciously "as a system of cultural and symbolic meanings (more) than as a set of operative controls. It affects us primarily through communication of symbols—by providing threats, promises, models, persuasion, legitimacy, stigma, and so on" (1983: 127). Evaluations of how reform litigation and other institutional activities matter thus require accounting for the variable ways that differently situated groups interpret and act on those signals sent by officials over time (Brigham 1987; Galanter 1983).[9]

If the political process approach emphasizes the complex multiplicity and relative autonomy of legal norms, it also emphasizes their contingency and interdependence with other social factors in shaping social struggle. In this view, legal norms and tactical manipulations typically are located in complex environments characterized by multiple hierarchical axes, plural institutional discourses, and differently situated groups (Bourdieu 1987; Merry 1988). Both the content and relative power of legal meanings always vary among citizens as they are differently and unequally located in specific institutional settings. It likewise follows that legal norms, conventions, and tactical maneuvers vary in significance over time as well. We thus might expect that particular discursive strategies or institutional ploys become more significant for some forms of struggle than for others.

This points to the further assumption that law (the aggregate of legal conventions) can at once both empower and disempower variously situated social groups in different types of relations. Legal "cultures provide symbols which can be manipulated by their members for strategic goals," notes anthropologist Sally Engle Merry, "but they also establish constraints on that manipulation" (1985: 60; Scheingold 1989). As such, legal norms in general may tend to sustain hegemonic hierarchies, as critical legal scholars contend, but they also can provide sources of opposition and change within particular institutional terrains (Hunt 1990; Scheingold 1989; McCann 1994). The key question is not whether legal conventions limit the potential for social resistance and transformation: of course they do. The more important but difficult challenge is to determine how and to what degree groups can work within and through these legal traditions to advance their causes. A social movement approach would specify two levels in which legal power can be relevant to action—first, in shaping the overall "structure of opportunities" facing movements; and, second, in the various legal resources available to different parties struggling for position.

And this, finally, underlines the fact that law should not be considered as external to, or simply imposed on, citizens (Thompson 1975). A conflict-centered, political process approach would emphasize that movements from the start are embedded within a (more or less) legally constituted environment rather than as outside of law. As such, legal norms should be viewed as an intersubjective force that mediates meaning-making activity among and within contending groups. It follows that activists themselves should be viewed as relatively (but unequally situated) legal actors rather than merely as consumers and recipients of law handed down from above (see Brigham 1988; McCann 1993a). Scholars thus must be attuned to how legal norms play a role in shaping and expressing the terms of resistance, aspiration, and tactical struggle for institutional transformation. We must, in Michel de Certeau's words, analyze law's "manipulation by users who are not its makers" (1984: xiii). As such, the dynamics of "legal consciousness" require attention in any assessment of how law matters for social movements (Ewick and Silbey 1992; Sarat 1990; McCann 1994).

All in all, the approach outlined here alerts us to the many ambiguous, shifting, complex ways in which law can become manifest in social struggles. With these general premises in mind, we now turn to a more focused theoretical and empirical inquiry regarding actual social movement experiences with law. The following sections will be organized according to the temporal scheme of stages in movement development outlined earlier, beginning with initial movement formation and proceeding through the legacy left by movement action.

3. LAW AND THE FORMATION OF MOVEMENTS

Perhaps the most significant point at which law has mattered for most social movements in the United States is during the earliest phases of organizational and agenda formation. Some legal scholars have recognized and explored this relationship in general terms. However, both social movement theory and empirical study suggest the need for a more refined analysis.

A. Legal Consciousness and Movement Building

We can begin with Stuart Scheingold's well-known argument regarding the "politics of rights." As he puts it, it is possible for marginalized groups "to capitalize on the perceptions of entitlement associated with (legal) rights to initiate and to nurture political mobilization" (1974: 131; see also Handler 1978; Olson 1984; Milner 1986). This process can be understood to involve two separate, if often intimately related, processes of cognitive transformation in movement constituents.

The first of these entails the process of agenda building by which movement actors draw on legal discourses to name and to challenge existing social wrongs or injustices. As such, legal norms can become important elements in the process of forging a sense of collective aspiration and identity among diversely situated citizens. Elizabeth Schneider's provocative argument regarding the "dialectic of rights and politics" in the evolving women's movement provides some very useful insights into the logic of this process. Schneider's primary argument is that the practice of rights advocacy by feminist activists has been a self-generating process that has "energized the women's movement" over time (1986: 550; see also McGlen and O'Connor 1983; Rupp and Taylor 1987). Emphasizing that rights advocacy is a dynamic, dialogic, and relatively indeterminate process, she outlines how new rights claims of women have developed from the tensions between past gains and newly perceived challenges, and between the personal empowerment experienced by a politicized few and the still disempowered many available for movement mobilization. As she describes it, "the assertion or 'experience' of rights can express political vision, affirm a group's humanity, . . . and assist in the collective political development of a social or political movement, particularly at its early stages" (Schneider 1986: 590). Such movement building around particular rights claims can emerge in a variety of ways, she suggests: by exploiting the conflict between already settled rights claims and practices violating those rights; by identifying implicit contradictions within settled discursive logics of rights; or by developing logical extensions or new practical applications of settled rights claims.

John Brigham has similarly explored how "rules made by government infuse and inform the movements themselves by becoming an essential part of their thought, their identity, and their social boundaries" (1988: 304). He identifies three different forms of legal practice around which social movements mobilize. Not surprisingly, he begins with rights claims, which entail reliance on governmentally promulgated rules backed up by threats, as one expression of movement identity. But he also adds two other forms: "rage," which involves struggles against legally sanctioned oppression and the effort to transform it, as in feminist antipornography campaigns; and "remedy," which expresses the desire for conflict resolution, as in the alternative dispute resolution movement.

Social movement scholars likewise have provided much evidence for the role of legal norms in framing movement demands, articulating a larger causal story about existing relations, developing a larger sense of purpose over time, and hence forging a common group identity (see Stone 1989; Snow and Benford 1988). Perhaps nowhere was this process more striking than in the civil rights movement. Leading sociological interpreters have explored at length how legal norms both framed movement demands and shaped movement identity over time (McAdam 1982; Morris 1984; Tushnet 1987). Legal conventions shaped evolving demands in similar ways for the early American labor movement (Forbath 1991; Tomlins 1985), the women's movement (Costain 1992; McGlen and O'Connor 1983; Freeman 1975; Evans 1980), the welfare rights movement (Piven and Cloward 1979), the animal rights movement (Silverstein 1996), and the gay and lesbian rights movements. Although always a matter of contestation, legal norms, discourses, and practices in each case were an important constitutive element of evolving movement understandings, aspirations, and strategic action.

A second related way in which legal practices can contribute to movement building is by shaping the overall "opportunity structure" within which movements develop. As noted above, most scholars agree that movement formation and action is more likely in periods when dominant groups and relationships are perceived as vulnerable to challenge (Piven and Cloward 1979; McAdam 1982). Advances through formal legal action—and especially by high-profile litigation—many times have contributed to this sense of vulnerability among both state and nonstate authorities. In particular, judicial victories can impart salience or legitimacy to general categories of claims (for example, antidiscrimination rights) as well as to specific formulations of challenges within these broad legal traditions. Indeed, many scholars have noted a sort of "contagion effect" generated by rights litigation over the last forty years in the United States (see Tarrow 1983). As Charles Epp has argued, "rights consciousness develops in conjunction with the development and clarity of legally enforceable rights" sanctioned by officials (1990: 150; Burstein and Monaghan 1986).

The movement-centered approach tends to interpret this latter aspect of legal consciousness-raising somewhat differently than many characterizations by legal scholars. For one thing, the cognitive transformation at stake typically involves less enlightenment about new values, understandings, or wants among oppressed groups than an increasing recognition that long-evolving grievances are more realistically actionable at particular points in time. In short, judicial victories (or other legal actions) do not reveal injustice so much as improve the chances that such injustices might be effectively challenged by movement action in and out of the courts (McCann 1994). Moreover, formal legal action alone rarely is likely to generate this catalytic or triggering effect on movement constituents (Rosenberg 1991). Only when concerted efforts are made by movement leaders and organizations to publicize such evolving opportunities and to use legal resources for movement building purposes is successful organizing likely (McCann 1994).

It is important to emphasize, furthermore, that these two dimensions of legal catalysis are often interrelated in social movement development. For example, formal legal actions (litigation) can work initially to expose systemic vulnerabilities and to render legal claims more salient. As long-marginalized groups act on these opportunities, they often gain sophistication and confidence in their capacity to mobilize legal conventions to name wrongs, to frame demands, and to advance their cause. Piven and Cloward recognize this in their classic discussion of consciousness-raising in protest politics. When citizens "begin to assert their 'rights' that imply demands for change," there often develops "a new sense of efficacy; people who ordinarily consider themselves helpless come to believe that they have some capacity to alter their lot" (1979: 4; see also Minow 1987; McAdam 1982).

This complex process of legal catalysis was again well evidenced by the civil rights movement. As sociologist Aldon Morris (1984) analyzes it, the legacy of cases leading up to *Brown v. Board of Education* was vital to the evolving civil rights movement in two ways. First, it sparked Southern blacks' hopes by "demonstrating that the Southern white power structure was vulnerable at some points" and providing scarce practical resources for defiant action.

> The winning of the 1954 decision was the kind of victory the organization needed to rally the black masses behind its program; by appealing to blacks' desire to enroll their children in the better equipped white schools it reached into black homes and had meaning for people's personal lives. (1984: 34)

Second, the increasing "pressure on the Southern white power structure to abolish racial domination" led to a massive, highly visible attack—including legal assaults as well as physical violence—on the National Association for the Advancement of Colored People (NAACP). These reactions in turn forced a split between local, church-affiliated NAACP leaders urging more radical forms of protest action and the more bureaucratic, legally oriented national organization. The result was a swell in both the momentum of the grassroots protest campaign among Southern blacks generally and frustration about the effectiveness of legal tactics alone. "The two approaches—legal action and mass protest—entered into a turbulent but workable marriage" (1984: 26, 39). Moreover, it was the resulting escalation of conflicts between whites and blacks on both fronts that "expanded the scope" of the dispute to include Washington officials, federal courts, the Northern media, and national public opinion (McAdam 1982). Court decisions thus did not unilaterally cause, by moral inspiration, defiant black grassroots action or, by coercion, federal support for the civil rights agenda (see Rosenberg 1991). But legal tactics pioneered by the NAACP figured prominently in elevating civil "rights" claims and intensifying the initial terms of racial struggle in the South. As Morris counsels, "It would be misleading to present the courtroom battles in narrowly legal light" (1984: 81).[10]

Similar dynamics have been evident in the movements for the rights of the disabled (Olson 1984), for animal rights (Silverstein 1996), and for gender-based wage equity (McCann 1994). These examples are especially interesting because they demonstrate that conclusive, far-reaching judicial victories are not necessary to achieve this legal catalyzing effect. The wage equity issue, for example, largely developed in response to the limitations of traditional court-approved affirmative action policies for remedying discrimination against women workers locked into segregated jobs (Blum 1991). After a string of defeats in the 1970s, the wage equity movement won a small advance in wage discrimination law at the Supreme Court level and one pathbreaking lower court ruling, which later was overturned on appeal. But in the five-year interim between the first and the last of these three rulings, movement leaders effectively used successful legal actions—despite their doctrinal limitations— to organize women workers in hundreds of workplaces around the nation. A massive publicity campaign focusing on court victories initially put the issue on the national agenda and alerted leaders that wage equity was "the working woman's issue of the 1980s." Lawsuits were then filed on behalf of working women as the centerpiece of a successful union and movement organizing strategy in scores of local venues around the nation. Again, the evidence suggests not that court decisions worked to "enlighten" working women about their subordination, as sometimes is claimed. Rather, sustained legal action over time worked to render employers vulnerable to challenge, to expand the resources available to working women, to provide them a unifying claim of egalitarian rights, and to increase both their confidence and sophistication in advancing those claims (McCann 1994).

B. RETHINKING LEGAL CO-OPTATION

The perspectives outlined above provide reason to rethink familiar arguments alleging that legal experts, tactics, and norms tend to preempt or co-opt the formation of grassroots movements. We can begin with the claim that lawyers tend to dominate movements in ways that privilege litigation-oriented strategies over other grassroots alternatives (Scheingold 1974; O'Neill 1985;

McCann 1986; Rosenberg 1991). Few social movement studies have found much evidence of this tendency. Lawyers have played prominent roles in many movements, including the early civil rights movement (Morris 1984; McAdam 1982; Chong 1991), the women's movement (Freeman 1975; Costain 1992), the environmental movement (McCann 1986), and the animal rights movement (Silverstein 1996). But in none of these did lawyers prevail over rival leaders or dominate movement strategizing to any significant degree.

In some movements—the civil rights, women's, and environmental movements, for example—it is true that lawyers have acted somewhat independently from grassroots activity and other tactical engagements. This fact may reflect their professional legalistic proclivities and a lack of overall movement coordination in some cases. But this also only underlines the point that movements are often pluralistic alliances of different actors and groups each engaged in different modes of struggle. Although lawyers may dominate some aspects of movement activity on which legal scholars focus, lawyer control over entire movements has been rare.

Moreover, there is much evidence of what Susan Olson has called a new style of cause lawyering in many movements. Attorneys who fit this mold are more inclined to coordinate legal tactics with other, political tactics, to take an active role in leading those nonlegalistic activities, and to do whatever contributes to overall movement success (1984; McCann and Silverstein 1997). In sum, few studies of social movements in the broad resource-mobilization tradition have confirmed legal scholars' fears about oligarchic lawyers and the "lure of litigation" that they pose. It is true that many movements decline after years of struggle, thus giving way to more bureaucratic interest-group organizations in which lawyers play significant roles (Goodwyn 1978; McAdam 1982). But this process has much more to do with extralegal factors of movement life history than with lawyers' imperial designs (Taylor 1989).

Arguments that legal norms, logics, and strategic practices tend to limit and co-opt movements are more difficult to assess. There are some cases where legal actions have seemed to conflict with movement building. Probably the best example is the women's movement. Jane Mansbridge (1986) argues convincingly that successful litigation before the Supreme Court took much of the steam out of the movement for an Equal Rights Amendment (ERA) in the 1970s. Her point, however, is not to assail reform litigation; but rather it is to show that the ERA movement was lacking in clear aims and obsessed with "empty" symbolic gains. Anne Costain, following Mansbridge, argues that equal rights norms moderated women's demands and constrained the larger women's movement in the 1970s and 1980s, especially by downplaying "difference" issues (1992). But the women's movement actually has relied very little on litigation overall, except for specialized goals of abortion rights, which has not been framed as an equality issue, and for enforcing civil rights legislation. Moreover, arguments that equal rights discourse inherently discounts or obscures concerns for difference tend to overdetermine legal norms and identify them too narrowly with official legal endorsement. Many other scholars have demonstrated that debates about equal rights have encompassed a wide variety of claims addressing both gender difference and economic redistribution that go well beyond "equal (same) treatment" norms (see Minow 1990; Williams 1989; Kessler-Harris 1990; McCann 1994). In fact, it often is argued that difference issues came to dominate debates over equality within as well as outside of official legal circles by the late 1980s.

Legal tactics and norms often have proved nearly irrelevant or ineffectual as movement building resources, it is true. Both "rights talk" and judicial tactics arguably provided limited support for the welfare rights movement and other antipoverty campaigns (see Piven and Cloward 1979; but see Bussière 1997). At other times, legal norms and institutions have posed formidable obstacles to various movements. In the terms outlined earlier, law can constrain opportunities when legal norms are biased against certain types of claims, and especially when courts back up this bias by explicitly denying desired judicial remedies or invalidating movement advances in other institutional sites. One of the most dramatic historical examples of this involved the Populist movement in the late nineteenth century. In a series of dramatic decisions in the 1890s invalidating state regulations as a violation of private property rights, the Supreme Court virtually took away the farmers' grassroots strategy of expanding democratic regional control and forced them into a national electoral campaign that spelled their doom (Westin 1953; Goodwyn 1978). Parallel actions by the courts had much the same influence on the radical wings of the early labor movement, whose most basic claims were invalidated and dismissed as unrealistic by moderates within the movement (Forbath 1991). In short, legal norms and institutions work to restrict as often as to open up opportunities for mounting challenges to dominant institutional relations.

Finally, even where legal norms, tactics, and rights contribute to the construction of viable movements, there often is reason to question whether constituent interests, needs, and even wants have been well served by these legal frameworks. Critical legal studies scholars have been perhaps most persistent in raising such questions. These are important reservations that are difficult to address generally in this paper. However, it is worth noting that most social movement scholars rarely pose the issue in the same way as do radical legal scholars. The former are far more likely to assume that movement actors are relatively sophisticated (rational) in their choices, and that any question about optimal strategies must be related to the often highly limited options available to them (see Thompson 1975). Moreover, it is presumed that all oppositional tactics are limited, limiting, even costly. This, after all, is the logic of systemic hegemony—not that the oppressed are routinely duped into consent, but that the options for concerted challenge are few in number, modest in promise, high in risk, and often contradictory in implications (see Scott 1985). Where radical challenges do occur, they usually begin with moderate demands concerning everyday issues framed in fairly traditional terms—such as demands for "equal rights," for fair treatment, or for safe conditions at work and in the general environment. As Alan Hunt has argued, counterhegemony "has to start from that which exists, which involves starting from 'where people are at.' . . . [A]ll struggles commence on old ground" (1990: 313; Piven and Cloward 1979).

Movement scholars frequently cite the Italian theorist Antonio Gramsci on this point. He argued that the most promising strategy for disadvantaged groups is to pursue an ongoing "war of position" that attacks the most vulnerable points within the existing ideological terrain. To take advantage of contradictions, to open up silences, to turn the rules against the rulers, to work for change within existing traditions—these generally are the most common and effective strategies available to traditionally oppressed and marginalized groups. In this view, the fact that movements frequently construct their claims from legal conventions and deploy legal tactics reflects less the mystifying tendencies of law than its modest utility for defiant groups short on alternative strategies of action (Hunt 1990; Thompson 1975; Crenshaw 1988).

C. CONTEXT AND EXTRALEGAL FACTORS

The preceding questions regarding whether law constrains or empowers movements cannot, finally, be separated from matters of broader social context. A political process model emphasizes the fact that how (how much and in what ways) law matters is always contingent on a variety of extralegal factors. As noted earlier, legal factors should be viewed as just a partial dimension of the overall opportunity structure and resource base from which movements act. For example, McAdam's analysis specifies a variety of factors that contributed to the emerging African American movement for civil rights in the mid-twentieth century (1982). These include a variety of broad socioeconomic changes (the decline of "King Cotton"), favorable political opportunities (created by wartime contributions of blacks; cold war ideology celebrating freedom and equality; Democratic Party dynamics), and developing political resources among blacks (new religious leaders; indigenous church and social associations; white allies in the North). While McAdam does not develop the point, these factors themselves not only provided an extralegal context favorable to legal rights mobilization, but they themselves were constituted in part by prevailing legal norms and practices.

This emphasis on context again places a premium on analyzing law within a densely mapped terrain of social practices and relations. It means that we cannot understand legal significance by focusing on official texts alone or abstracting legal ideology from particular social settings of practical interaction. Legal consciousness does not develop—or fail to develop, or even arrest political development, for that matter—in a vacuum. We must study law as it becomes meaningful in social practice rather than simply its mechanical behavioral effects as an alien force interjected into struggle from without (Thompson 1975; Brigham 1987).

Social movement scholarship has pointed to some important generalizations in this regard. For one thing, such studies emphasize that movement development is highly unlikely in the absence of preexisting indigenous associational bonds and relations among group members. This means that legal consciousness-raising and mobilization are likely to be least effective among diffuse groups of isolated individuals, regardless of how victimized or oppressed they may be (see Bumiller 1988). Conversely, existing forms of association and organization are likely to shape the relative significance of legal norms, tactics, and experts in specific movements. For example, we might expect certain types of middle class movements—such as national environmental, consumer, and other public interest groups—to emphasize professional staff–led actions in which lawyers and litigation play more prominent roles than do grassroots mobilization, protest, or even electoral tactics (McCann 1986). By contrast, movements that have large, well-organized constituent bases but are short on financial resources—the civil rights and early labor movements, for example—are likely to employ litigation more as a secondary tactic.

4. LEGAL MOBILIZATION AS POLITICAL PRESSURE

A. LAW AS A SYMBOLIC CLUB

Another general way in which law and legal advocacy often matter to social reform movement activity is as a source of leverage against recalcitrant opponents. This leveraging role is closely related to—indeed, it is the flip side of—law's catalytic contributions to movement building. Just as legal rights advocacy can pull in strong affirmative support for reform goals from various groups, so can it be employed as a weapon to push otherwise uncooperative foes into making concessions or compromises. As in movement-building efforts, this second dimension of legal mobilization usually entails some measure of litigation or other formal legal action. Nevertheless, triumph in the courts is not necessarily pivotal to either short- or long-term successful legal leveraging. Again, this is because judicial actions typically are less significant in their direct, command-oriented aspects than in their indirect interaction with other political tactics such as lobbying, negotiations, or mass demonstrations.

In some respects, this is hardly a pathbreaking insight. The use of legal tactics and threats to compel informal resolution of everyday private disputes regarding divorce settlement, contractual obligations, liability for property damages, and the like is familiar and well documented (see Mnookin and Kornhauser 1979). However, the dialectical relationship of formal and informal legal action in social reform politics has generally received less scholarly attention (but see Handler 1978; Olson 1984; McCann 1994; Silverstein 1996).

There are several ways in which litigation often offers formidable tactical leverage for social movements. For one thing, organizations targeted by reformers often are well aware that litigation can impose substantial transaction costs in terms of both direct expenditures and long-term financial burdens. Indeed, court costs in major public disputes—over race and gender discrimination, unsafe workplaces, or environmental damage, for example—often run in the millions of dollars, and the litigation can tie up economically vital operations for years. More important, powerful public and private interests typically fear losing control of decision-making autonomy—whether concerning capital investment, wage policy, externalized costs, or the like—to outside parties such as judges, and hence have a stake in cutting potential losses by negotiated settlements of conflicts with movements (see Handler 1978).

Finally, the symbolic normative power of rights claims themselves should not be discounted. This point links Scheingold's "myth of rights" and "politics of rights" analysis (1974). Because citizens in our society are responsive to (legally sensible) rights claims, defiant groups often can mobilize legal norms, conventions, and demands to compel concessions even in the absence of clear judicial (or other official) support. This power of legal discourse has several related and indistinguishable dimensions, including abstract appeals to the moral sensibilities of dominant groups; more concrete appeals to the interests of dominant organizations in maintaining cooperative relations with victimized groups, such as workers or consumers; and, perhaps most important, indirect appeals for moral censure from the general public regarding the actions of specific powerful groups. This latter factor of stigmatizing publicity distinguishes the potential impact of legal action in high visibility social struggles from that in everyday disputes. Formal legal actions by movements threaten to transform disputes by mobilizing not just judges as third-party intervenors, but also a variety of social advocacy groups, nonjudicial state officials, and broader public sentiment or voting power through the catalytic dynamic discussed in the last section. In other words, litigation often provides a powerful means for, in Schattschneider's terms, "expanding the scope of conflict" in ways that augment the bargaining power of disadvantaged groups and raise the perceived risks of hard-line opposition from their foes (1960).[11]

The implicit promise at stake here is that political struggles may advance more quickly, cheaply, and effectively when conducted in the shadow of favorable legal norms and threats of judicial intervention. Such legal gambits are hardly costless guarantees of success for social reformers, of course. Initiating legal action often does not generate concessions from powerful opponents, and thus may commit movement supporters to long, costly, high-risk legal proceedings that they can afford far less than can their institutional foes. Even more important, eventual defeat in court can sap movement morale, undercut movement bargaining power, and exhaust movement resources. Consequently, legal leveraging is most successful when it works as an unfulfilled threat, but activists must be willing to follow through occasionally with action or lose considerable clout. In any case, the symbolic manifestations of law, as both a source of moral right and threat of potential outside intervention, imbue rights discourse with its most fundamental social power.

One final general point is relevant here. I have chosen to emphasize in this essay how the leveraging power of law sometimes can be deployed directly in efforts to transform existing relations—that is, to augment worker power, to challenge racial and gender hierarchies, to redistribute wealth, to compel environmentally responsible action, and so on. At the same time, however, we should not forget the important secondary ways that legal leveraging tactics often are employed to defend advocates of change from overt repression by dominant groups and state officials. On this front, I refer especially to the crucial battles for protection of both radical advocacy—including protest and acts of civil disobedience—as constitutionally privileged political speech and procedural rights for those radicals whose actions have been deemed criminal or otherwise punishable by authorities. While such protections have proved highly fragile in moments of dramatic social struggle, legal claims of basic rights surely have helped to expand some space for radical challenge by workers, people of color, women, gays and lesbians, peace activists and others (see Kairys 1990). Revolution in our own streets—as well as those around the world—surely has often been aided, although hardly secured, by claims of conventional liberal legal rights by dissident citizens (see, e.g., Lefcourt 1971).

The deployment of legal resources to pressure dominant groups often takes place at several different, if often continuous, stages of movement struggles. Movement experiences with leveraging action at two of the general stages demarcated earlier will be briefly discussed.

B. COMPELLING POLICY CONCESSIONS

One general affirmative use of legal leveraging by many movements has been to "get on the public agenda" recognized by dominant groups. That is, legal tactics often have proved useful in forcing attention to movement demands and compelling at least some general policy concessions from state officials or other powerful actors.

Silverstein (1996) has demonstrated how this tactic has generated some relatively important advances by the animal rights movement in recent years. In a variety of instances, she illustrates how litigation has been used to dramatize abuses of animals, to embarrass particular institutional actors, and to win favorable media attention. When carefully coordinated with demonstrations, pranks, and other media events, high-profile litigation worked as a double-barreled threat—at once mobilizing public opinion against targeted "abusers" and threatening both costly legal proceedings and possible defeats in court. Overall, such legal tactics have proved to be one of the movement's most effective modes of forcing change by state and nonstate authorities alike. My own study of gender-based pay equity revealed a similar dynamic

(McCann 1994). Pay equity activists repeatedly used litigation not only to mobilize women workers but also to pressure employers indirectly by both branding them as "discriminators" in the public eye and posing the risk that judges might impose new wage structures on them. In dozens of cases, legal tactics worked to draw attention to the issue, to break collective bargaining or legislative deadlocks on wage policies, and to secure wage advances for workers in female-intensive occupations.

Both of these studies confirm again some often overlooked aspects of legal leveraging tactics. First, they illustrate that repeated clear victories in court are not necessary to effective legal mobilization. In neither movement did lawsuits generate appellate decisions directly authorizing many of the new rights and remedies that activists sought. However, the ability at least to win some small advances on related issues and to win standing for major claims posed enough actual costs (bad publicity, legal fees) and potential risks (of judicially imposed policies) to pressure opponents into making significant concessions. Second, legal tactics again were useful primarily only in concert with other tactics, such as demonstrations, legislative lobbying, collective bargaining, and media mobilization. The fact that legal norms and institutional maneuvers constituted only one dimension of movement strategy complicates evaluation of their independent contributions, to be sure. But, in each movement, both activists and specific case histories confirmed the importance of such contingent, ancillary legal actions.

The legacy of the civil rights movement again represents an even more complex example of such dynamics. On the one hand, Supreme Court rulings outlawing public segregation in the 1950s mostly generated hostility or apathy in the South. Compliance with the courts was very low (see Rosenberg 1991). On the other hand, much evidence suggests that *Brown* and other decisions helped to force growing federal intervention by escalating volatile confrontations, catalyzing Northern public opinion, and bolstering the resolve needed for action among key federal officials. Judicial action alone did not determine these outcomes, of course; increasing demonstrations and white violence were probably even more important. Yet most social movement scholars have not discounted the importance of legal actions for the evolving struggle (see Morris 1984; McAdam 1982). Rather, the civil rights movement represents a classic case of how "law and disorder" can be joined in social movement strategies for change (Lowi 1971).

Important examples where legal tactics either failed to generate, or even impeded, progressive change are notable as well, however. The abortion case arguably offers a revealing example. While feminists won support for women's "right to choose" in *Roe v. Wade*, the provision of both medical services and financial aid to pay for exercising those rights did not materialize to any great degree. What is more, *Roe* generated a significant conservative countermovement bent on denying, or at least substantially restricting, the capacity of women to choose the abortion option (Rosenberg 1991). Finally, the "privacy" logic adopted to secure women's rights occluded key issues of power at stake and undercut prospects for winning state financial aid to low-income women (Copelon 1989). In short, legal tactics not only failed to leverage real change; they arguably undermined the potential for change that alternative tactics (legislation, grassroots organizing) might have produced.[12]

Backlashes against both race and sex-based affirmative action policies authorized by the courts likewise have rendered mixed, at best, those efforts at leveraging social change in recent decades as well. And other cases are even more subtle. For example, litigation by Northwest Indian tribes seemingly won major policy victories over the predominantly white fishing industry in the 1970s. However, several studies demonstrate that Native Americans were forced to frame their claims in legal terms of property rights that both obscured the larger resource planning issues at the heart of the debate and ended up exacerbating inequalities of private wealth among the indigenous peoples themselves (Bruun 1982; Anderson 1987). The net result, so to speak, was hardly an improvement at all.

Finally, it is worth noting that legal leveraging tactics by opponents can significantly undermine and even destroy social movements. The successful mobilization of courts by business interests beginning in the late nineteenth century again significantly throttled both the Populist and radical labor movements. Court alliance with conservatives not only took away legal resources from "the common people," but it invited overt repression, sanctioned violence, and advantaged moderate wings of both movements who urged accepting the hierarchical terms of emerging corporate relations (Westin 1953; Forbath 1991; Goodwyn 1978). This history affirms the fact that legal leveraging tactics, like law generally, are mobilized as resources by opponents more often and more effectively than by advocates of egalitarian change (Scheingold 1989). Not the least of the factors at stake in any particular historical moment are the reigning ideological propensities and partisan allegiances of judges on the bench. While judicial support hardly assures movement advances, hostility from the courts surely can, and often does, contain reformers on many fronts.

C. POLICY DEVELOPMENT AND IMPLEMENTATION

Legal leveraging often figures prominently at the policy development and implementation stages as well. Somewhat surprisingly, however, both social movement scholars and legal scholars have provided only limited insights about these dynamics. In most scholarly portrayals, social movements—which usually are defined by disruptive tactics of mass organization, public protest, and the like—give way to more conventional hierarchical organizations and interest groups that then carry on bureaucratic battles for final policy formulation, execution, and enforcement (Piven and Cloward 1979; Goodwyn 1978; Tarrow 1983). By definition, then, implementation politics is nonradical, co-opted, "nonmovement" activity. Such a romance with mass action strikes this author as narrow and misguided, however. The reason is that it is precisely at these phases of struggle that the social ramifications of official policy changes often are most determined (Lowi 1979).

Legal scholars, by contrast, often do focus much attention on implementation politics, but only to show that legal tactics are relatively futile. The most common explanation for this tendency is that courts lack the independence and resources to enforce their decisions on recalcitrant groups in government and society alike (Rosenberg 1991; Horowitz 1977; Dolbeare and Hammond 1971; see also Handler 1978). While largely valid in itself, such a focus ignores the degree to which legal norms and tactics can matter even in the absence of judicial enforcement action and simple citizen compliance (see Brigham 1987). Focusing on courts rather than on movement politics provides a truncated understanding of how the shadow of law and legal tactics matters at implementation as well as at other phases of struggle (McCann 1993a).

Nevertheless, many studies in both traditions have provided some useful insights into how law matters for policy implementation battles. In particular, a host of empirical inquiries document how legal tactics—and especially actual or threatened litigation—can help movement activists to win voice, position, and influence in the process of reform policy implementation, whether sanctioned by state or nonstate authorities. These include policy areas regarding the environment (Sax 1971; Melnick 1983; McCann 1986), gender (Blum 1991; Gelb and Palley 1982) and race discrimination (Burstein and Monaghan 1986), and the rights of the disabled (Olson 1984), among others (Lowi 1979; Handler 1978). Indeed, the continuing salience of such public policy issues itself stems in large part from their definition as legal injuries or wrongs.

Law is especially important to one specific aim of many "outsider" groups—that of formalizing policy formulation and implementation processes. Formality, as understood here, refers to the degree to which relations are conducted according to procedures and standards that are public, general, positive, and uniform (Lowi 1979; see Scott 1985: 194). The key supposition here is that dominant groups tend to prefer relatively insular modes of highly discretionary policy implementation unhampered by standardized procedures, substantive guidelines, high visibility, and outside supervision. In such informal settings, established prerogatives of prevailing elites can more easily prevail to minimize costs, maintain control, and protect their own privileges while granting empty symbolic gestures to challengers. By contrast, marginalized groups usually benefit from more formalized processes where codified procedural rights and substantive standards can be employed to restrict the discretion of dominant interests who control the bulk of material and organizational resources (Lowi 1979; Delgado et al. 1985).

Social movement groups often use litigation specifically to create such institutional access as well as to apply pressure to make that access consequential. In this way, legal resources often provide a series of more refined tools—a template of procedures, standards, and practices—along with blunt leveraging tactics for shaping the structure of ongoing administrative relations at the remedial stage of struggles over policy (see Galanter 1983). For example, charges of unfair labor practices, reliance on arbitration and grievance mechanisms, and other related tactics have constituted a routine strategy for labor radicals in the post–New Deal era (Fantasia 1988). This tactic also comprised the primary agenda of liberal public interest (environmental, consumer, good government) groups who, in the 1970s, tried to open up the administrative state to greater democratic participation (McCann 1986; McCann and Silverstein 1997). Similar efforts likewise defined one of the primary tactics of gender-based pay equity reformers seeking to prevent employer co-optation of wage restructuring implementation (McCann 1994). One final example is noteworthy. Sociologist Lauren Edelman has demonstrated how employers routinely established in-house offices to avoid litigation and maintain an appearance of good faith compliance with race-based affirmative action principles in the 1970s. While established for largely deceptive or defensive purposes, however, such offices (in alliance with minority groups) sometimes mobilized antidiscrimination norms and the specter of litigation to force real changes from within many corporate and state institutions (1990).

Of course, as judicial impact studies suggest, legal leveraging often offers as little to reformers in policy implementation battles as at earlier stages of struggle (Handler 1978). The fact that judges shrink from cases requiring great technical knowledge and experience may make legal leveraging tactics less effective generally. Moreover, openly hostile courts again often greatly undercut opportunities and deny resources in ways that actually disempower movement actors in the policy process. And, again, even where courts weigh in favorably for disadvantaged groups, injustice in most institutional settings will go unchallenged in the absence of well-organized constituencies willing to mobilize legal resources for change. Indeed, apparent advances in official law may even add insult to injury for marginalized citizens lacking organizational resources (Bumiller 1988). In short, law often does not help reformers and may constitute a considerable constraint on action. Again, understanding these variations requires analysis of law's workings within the larger web of social relations where struggle occurs.

5. THE LEGACY OF LAW IN/FOR STRUGGLE

Perhaps the least fully explored aspect of social movement politics concerns the legacy of particular struggles. Many movement scholars and legal scholars, we have seen, work from the assumption that movements tend to follow a linear pattern of development and have finite life histories (Tarrow 1983; McAdam 1982). That is, they rise, peak, and then fade into oblivion, leaving perhaps only a highly co-opted residue of interest group representation in their place. But other scholars have challenged this scenario. Verta Taylor's (1989) provocative analysis of the women's movement, for example, suggests that indigenous associations forming the core of social movements may recede from public struggle for periods of time, but they often continue quietly to thrive over time, only to resurface as opportunities arise for defiant action at later dates. In short, movement associations do not live and die so much as alternately howl and hibernate according to changes in the larger political climate. James Scott's research linking routine patterns of everyday private resistance by marginalized or oppressed groups to occasional explosions on the public stage suggests much the same dynamic (1985; 1990).

This insight suggests the need for a complex assessment of social movement dynamics. Rather than focus merely on whether movements succeed or fail with regard to their primary short-term policy aims (which almost always fall short), we need also to assess how those struggles affect movement constituents and their relations with dominant groups over the long haul. Did a specific movement struggle pass quietly, leaving basic relations with dominant groups virtually intact? Or did struggles escalate, shift to new fronts, and fundamentally alter social relations in a variety of empowering ways for movement constituents? Or did the movement retreat, only to recharge and reemerge again in powerful form at a later date? In sum, has the movement been contained or expanded over time (McCann 1994)?

These basic questions are important for assessing the changing character of law's constitutive power in different social terrains. Social movement theory suggests three ways in which the legal dynamics of power relations can change through ongoing struggle. First, we might ask whether movement efforts altered the legal (or rights) consciousness of constituents and other publics. That is, have understandings, expectations, and ideological solidarity of disadvantaged groups and their allies been altered in ways that contribute to subsequent development of group struggle? Second, it is worth inquiring whether specific movement struggles contributed to the development of new legal resources for disadvantaged groups. This might include new statutes, specific advances in judicial constructions, and broader ideological advances in prevailing legal norms signaled by such specific advances. Third, it is relevant to query whether both types of gains might expand the opportunities for action by creating new vulnerabilities in institutional power. Such types of transformations again shape and reshape the context from which ongoing struggles—whether covert or overt—are waged by oppressed peoples. In sum, the focus on such changes underlines the complex ways in which legal conventions at once express, channel, and contain citizen efforts to achieve justice over time.

We have already noted arguments that various movements during the 1960s contributed to changes at all three levels (Epp 1990; Burstein and Monaghan 1986; see also Garth 1992). Schneider's (1986) earlier noted argument about the ongoing dialectic between rights and politics in the women's movement offers a particularly interesting angle on this issue. Crenshaw's incisive account regarding the civil rights movement and the relentless struggles of African Americans makes a similar case (1988). My own study of comparable-worth wage reform found extensive evidence that continuing change at all three levels was an important part of the legacy left by the politics of legal mobilization among women workers during the last two decades (1994). This understanding is developed most broadly in Sidney Tarrow's theory of reform/protest "cycles."

> Stretching the definition of reform to include Supreme Court decisions—which is not unfair in the American context—the 1954 decision on equal education was a reform which clearly helped to trigger the Civil Rights movement. It also is likely that, within the American cycle of protest, policy innovations directed at one group gave rise to both new channels of access and to generalized expectations about elite responsiveness among others that led to new stages of protest which in turn evoked new policy reponses. This seems to have been the relationship between the black movement and other movements for minority rights which followed similar strategies and succeeded—at a much lower cost— in achieving many of the gains that blacks fought for in the 1960s. (Tarrow 1983: 47)

Once again, it is important to emphasize that legal conventions and institutions just as often contain or deter expansion of struggles in our society. The legacies of the Populist, labor, and various poor people's movements clearly underline this fact. Indeed, virtually all movements have left a legacy to some degree constrained by our limited and limiting legal inheritance that thrives within and without the state. Sorting out this mix of potentially transformative and hegemony-affirming implications over time is one important dimension of assessing how law matters for specific movements.

6. SUMMARY AND CONCLUSIONS

This essay has attempted to accomplish two interrelated goals. My first aim has been to sketch a general framework for analyzing how law matters for social movements. Such a framework synthesizes elements of prevailing political-process models of social movements with those of interpretive legal studies. The result is a decentered, conflict-oriented approach that emphasizes how legal conventions at once construct and, in turn, are reconstructed by the political struggles of social movements. In this view, law is understood as distinctive forms of intersubjective knowledge whose relative power and meaning varies among differently situated groups in different institutional contexts.

My second aim derives from the first. In short, I have attempted to outline some of the insights generated by recent empirical research on social movements and legal mobilization activity. Overall, while informed by a similar critical spirit, my analytical review has offered a more complex, dynamic, and contingent view regarding how law matters than that provided by most top-down, court-centered studies of legal reform politics. I thus conclude here by highlighting a few salient generalizations based on the preceding discussion.

These comments will be directed to elucidating my differences with other modes of critical legal scholarship on the subject.

Most important, my review confirms that there is good reason to urge skepticism regarding the extent to which legal tactics can advance social change. Critical legal scholars surely are correct that radical court decisions are rare, while even moderately progressive judgments alone directly cause little social change (see Rosenberg 1991; Horowitz 1977). However, conventional behavioral accounts discount many of the fundamental ways in which law matters in social struggle. Above all, before we even get to the question of tactical effectiveness, we must recognize the extent to which legal norms routinely shape the very terms of citizen identity, position, and power in various institutional contexts. This point identifies the essence of the cultural view urged here—that law is manifest as a complex array of relatively independent conventions and practices that infuse material relations. Such legal power is expressed in both the palpable shadows cast by official actions on citizen calculations and the broader constitutive force of legal discourses themselves that are variously embedded within social life and citizen consciousness. That so many recent movements have defined themselves as (civil, women's, gay and lesbian, animal) "rights" movements animated by legally derived claims is one obvious manifestation of this latter point.

Once legal resources become mobilized or appropriated within specific institutional terrains, moreover, it is crucial to recognize that their significance depends on a variety of contextual factors.[13] The social meaning of law varies not only with official actions, but more broadly with the interaction of specific legal norms with other legal and extralegal factors in particular institutional settings. As such, I have argued that legal forms should be viewed as an integral part of the larger social fabric of changing (micro-, meso-, and macrolevel) opportunities and resources within which social movements develop and maneuver for position. For example, we noted earlier that the mobilizing potential of legal claims and tactics is to a large degree contingent on existing indigenous associational bonds among constituents. Moreover, the effectiveness of continued legal action depends on the capacities for coordination with other tactical maneuvers. Movement experiences suggest that the more varied the available tactics and resources, the more likely is movement vitality and success (Tarrow 1983; Hunt 1990). In short, we should expect that law generally is least instrumentally significant as a primary or solitary resource, and most likely to matter as an ancillary component of a larger multipronged political strategy (Scheingold 1974).

These understandings highlight two further generalizations often neglected by behavioral social scientists. On the one hand, as Handler (1978) long ago counseled, analysts need to focus study more on the indirect, symbolic (rather than on direct, coercive) effects and significance of legal actions—whether court decisions, institutional threats, or policy demands. And when conceptualized in more relational, context-specific terms of power, there is reason to think that such indirect effects usually render judicial victories more empowering for social reformers than critics often recognize. Contrary to what many realist legal studies suggest, winning court cases—even when they achieve only limited advances in legal doctrine—is usually beneficial to movements. Indeed, winning in court is almost always better for political campaigns than losing, or not resorting to legal tactics at all. On the other hand, it is equally important to recognize that the focus on winning judicial remedies itself is highly misleading as a point of departure. As noted earlier, movements in many circumstances can gain tremendous advantages from winning only small doctrinal advances for a cause far short of a full remedy, from initiating actions that never get to court, and even sometimes from losing altogether in court. The animal rights, pay equity, and pro-life movements all provide evidence of these dynamics.

Finally, if behavioral social scientists tend to understate how law often matters for movements, scholars in the ideological school often overdetermine law's significance as a constraint on movements. It is true that official law does often prefigure terrains of struggle, limit the options, and constrain possible meaning-making efforts as well as deny state support in ways that routinely inhibit social movement efforts. And there is no doubt that the official legal system works far more as a brake than as an accelerator for citizen challenges to systemic hierarchies of power (class, race, gender, sexuality, etc.) in our culture. No serious student of political struggle could refute that prevailing legal conventions serve the haves more than the have-nots, and the forces of hierarchy more than the forces of equality. But the conventional focus on official law too often ignores the ways in which legal conventions are a volatile, ambiguous force in social life. As Stuart Scheingold has put it, "rights, like the law itself, do cut both ways—serving at some times and under some circumstances to reinforce privilege and at other times to provide the cutting edge of change" (1989: 76; Milner 1986). As such, this paper has attempted to outline a general approach to critically analyzing these ambiguous and variable expressions of law's power in political struggle.[14] The primary goal has been to shift emphasis away from official doctrine to the more complex manifestations of law within the larger social context of group power relations.

It is worth adding here that the constraining effects of lawyers on movements often are overstated in much the same way. The fact is that lawyers in most movements are just one of many differently situated leadership groups (Hunt 1990). Moreover, many movement lawyers are no less politically sophisticated about the limits, biases, and costs of law than are scholarly critics. As Olson (1984) has argued, a new style of critical, flexible lawyering has been apparent in many movements over recent decades (see McCann and Silverstein 1997). Again, this is not to deny that some lawyers have been limiting forces in some social struggles. Rather, the point is to redirect attention to the need for more subtle, theoretically expansive studies regarding the many contextual factors—the changing opportunities, resources, and intersubjective relations—that generate the variable significance of lawyers and legal practice.

I conclude by noting that one major contribution of recent theorizing about power has been to recognize that social struggle is far more pervasive than often presumed. My own view is that we have only begun to probe the variable significance of law's complex manifestations in such struggles, both when they do and do not escalate into what we might label a social movement. And in this unexplored terrain we can see enormous opportunities for contemporary legal scholars to contribute in socially relevant ways.

NOTES

1. For examples, see Johnson and Canon (1984); Rosenberg (1991); Becker and Feeley (1973). Handler (1978) is a variant on this model. For discussion, see McCann (1992a, 1994) and Sarat (1985).

2. Scheingold (1974); Bell (1976); Handler (1978); Medcalf (1978); Katz (1982); Bruun (1982); O'Neill (1985); Tushnet (1987); McCann (1986); Olson (1984).

3. The first type of studies tends to be positivistic in orientation, modest in theoretical orientation, and executed by behavioral social scientists. The second tend to be far more theoretical and interpretive, empirically focused on judicial decisions, and emanate from scholars in law schools. The third tend to dwell on middle-range theory, to focus on case studies, and to use eclectic empirical methods.

4. The major line of differentiation is between (often middle-class) social reform movements and (often lower-class) social protest movements. Moreover, most such studies focus on left-wing or progressive movements, even though the analytical models are equally applicable to right-wing or reactionary movements.

5. Several criticisms of resource mobilization approaches are worth noting. These include that RM tends (1) to "normalize" social movements by emphasizing their instrumental rationality and roots in conventional associations; (2) to overstate elite elements and discount insurgent mass dimensions of movements; and (3) to downplay both the ideological claims and solidaristic identities that animate most movements. My synthetic account below attempts to overcome these limitations. See McAdam (1982); Klandermans (1992).

6. This literature itself is broad and diverse. See Goodwyn (1978); Piven and Cloward (1979); Evans (1980); Fantasia (1988); Melucci (1989); Cocks (1989); Klandermans (1992); Morris (1992); Ferree (1992). On understanding culture broadly as "strategies," see Swidler (1986). Some legal scholars have made important advances in viewing law as culture and exploring "legal consciousness": Ewick and Silbey (1992); Silbey (1992); Merry (1990); Sarat (1990). On analyzing legal consciousness in social movements, see McCann (1994); Silverstein (1996); Milner (1986); Brigham (1988).

7. Studies of civil dispute processing include Merry (1990), Mather and Yngvesson (1980–81), and Galanter (1983). Studies of everyday legal resistance include Ewick and Silbey (1992) and Sarat (1990). More culturally focused studies of law and social movements include Scheingold (1974), Olson (1984), Milner (1986), and Brigham (1988). See McCann (1994) and Silverstein (1996).

8. I have worked out similar themes in my development of a "legal mobilization" framework (McCann 1991, 1994).

9. In this regard, the approach urged here challenges realist (both jurisprudential and empirical social scientific) perspectives assuming that legal indeterminacy robs legal norms of their intrinsic power. See McCann (1994).

10. For a different, much more skeptical and critical viewpoint, see Rosenberg (1991).

11. "Going public" does not always benefit disadvantaged or exploited groups in the ways that Schattschneider suggests, of course. My point is simply that mobilization of public sentiment often can provide valuable leverage for resource-poor groups in many circumstances, especially when it involves appeals to widely accepted rights claims.

12. I am skeptical about this argument, but some scholars more knowledgeable about the political history of the issue have made compelling arguments along this line.

13. Rosenberg's (1991) analysis takes judicial impact studies a long way by emphasizing contextual factors, although his view of "legal impact" remains narrowly positivistic.

14. This paper has offered few general principles for predicting when law may work one way or the other, that is, to serve hierarchy or challenges to it. On the one hand, I am skeptical that any but the most general, contingent predictions are possible regarding both the historical emergence and outcomes of particular types of political struggle. On the other hand, I think that our understanding of law in struggle can be best advanced by going beyond court-centered analysis to systematic studies of law in politics such as outlined here.

BIBLIOGRAPHY

Anderson, Michael R. 1987. Law and the Protection of Cultural Communities: The Case of Native American Fishing Rights. 9 *Law and Policy*, 125.

Atleson, James B. 1983. *Values and Assumptions in American Labor Law*. Amherst: Univ. of Massachusetts Press.

Balser, Diane. 1987. *Sisterhood and Solidarity: Feminism and Labor in Modern Times*. Boston: South End Press.

Bartholomew, Amy, and Alan Hunt. 1990. What's Wrong with Rights. 9 *Law and Inequality*, 501.

Becker, Theodore L., and Malcolm M. Feeley, eds. 1973. *The Impact of Supreme Court Decisions* 2d ed. New York: Oxford Univ. Press.

Bell, Derrick. 1976. Serving Two Masters: Integration Ideals and Client Interests in School Desegregation Litigation. 85 *Yale Law Journal*, 470.

Berger, Margaret A. 1980. *Litigation on Behalf of Women*. New York: Ford Foundation.

Blum, Linda M. 1991. *Between Feminism and Labor: The Significance of the Comparable Worth Movement*. Berkeley: Univ. of California Press.

Bookman, Ann, and Sandra Morgen, eds. 1988. *Women and the Politics of Empowerment*. Philadelphia: Temple Univ. Press.

Bourdieu, Pierre. 1987. The Force of Law: Toward a Sociology of the Juridical Field. 38 *Hastings Law Journal*, 805.

Brigham, John. 1987. *The Cult of the Court*. Philadelphia: Temple Univ. Press.

————. 1988. Right, Rage, and Remedy: Forms of Law in Political Discourse. 2 *Studies in American Political Development*, 303.

Bruun, Rita. 1982. The Boldt Decision: Legal Victory, Political Defeat. 4 *Law and Policy*, 271.

Bullock, Charles S., III, and Charles M. Lamb. 1989. Toward a Theory of Civil Rights Implementation. In *American Court Systems: Readings in Judicial Process and Behavior*, ed. Sheldon Goldman and Austin Sarat. 2d ed. New York: Longman.

Bumiller, Kristin. 1988. *The Civil Rights Society: The Social Construction of Victims*. Baltimore: Johns Hopkins Univ. Press.

Burstein, Paul. 1991. Legal Mobilization as a Social Movement Tactic: The Struggle for Equal Employment Opportunity. 96 *American Journal of Sociology*, 1201.

Burstein, Paul, and Kathleen Monaghan. 1986. Equal Employment Opportunity and the Mobilization of the Law. 20 *Law and Society Rev.*, 355.

Bussière, Elizabeth. 1997. *(Dis)Entitling the Poor: The Warren Court, Welfare Rights, and the American Political Tradition*. University Park: Pennsylvania State Univ. Press.

Chong, Dennis. 1991. *Collective Action and the Civil Rights Movement*. Chicago: Univ. of Chicago Press.

Cocks, Joan. 1989. *The Oppositional Imagination: Feminism, Critique, and Political Theory*. London: Routledge.

Copelon, Rhonda. 1989. Beyond the Liberal Idea of Privacy: Toward a Positive Right of Autonomy. In *Judging the Constitution: Critical Essays on Judicial Lawmaking*, ed. Michael W. McCann and Gerald L. Houseman. Glenview, IL: Scott, Foresman.

Costain, Anne N. 1992. *Inviting Women's Rebellion: A Political Process Interpretation of the Women's Movement*. Baltimore: Johns Hopkins Univ. Press.

Crenshaw, Kimberle Williams. 1988. Race, Reform, and Retrenchment: Transformation and Legitimation in Antidiscrimination Law. 101 *Harvard Law Rev.*, 1331.

De Certeau, Michel. 1984. *The Practice of Everyday Life*. Berkeley: Univ. of California Press.

Delgado, Richard, et al. 1985. Fairness and Formality: Minimizing the Risk of Prejudice in Alternative Dispute Resolution. 85 *Wisconsin Law Rev.*, 1359.

Dolbeare, Kenneth, and Phillip E. Hammond. 1971. *The School Prayer Decisions: From Court Policy to Local Practice*. Chicago: Univ. of Chicago Press.

Edelman, Lauren. 1990. Legal Environments and Organizational Governance: The Expansion of Due Process in the American Workplace. 97 *American Journal of Sociology*, 1531.

Epp, Charles. 1990. Connecting Litigation Levels and Legal Mobilization: Explaining Interstate Variation in Employment Civil Rights Litigation. 24 *Law and Society Rev.*, 145.

Evans, Sara M. 1980. *Personal Politics: The Roots of Women's Liberation in the Civil Rights Movement and New Left*. New York: Vintage.

Ewick, Patricia, and Susan S. Silbey. 1992. Conformity, Contestation, and Resistance: An Account of Legal Consciousness. 26 *New England Law Rev.*, 731.

Fantasia, Rick. 1988. *Cultures of Solidarity*. Berkeley: Univ. of California Press.

Feeley, Malcolm M. 1973. Power, Impact, and the Supreme Court. In *The Impact of Supreme*

Court Decisions, ed. Theodore L. Becker and Malcolm M. Feeley. New York: Oxford Univ. Press.

Ferree, Myra Marx. 1992. The Political Context of Rationality: Rational Choice Theory and Resource Mobilization. In *Frontiers in Social Movement Theory*, ed. Aldon Morris and Carol Mueller. New Haven, CT: Yale Univ. Press.

Fink, Leon. 1987. Labor, Liberty and the Law: Trade Unionism and the Problem of the American Constitutional Order. 74 *Journal of American History*, 904.

Fireman, Richard, and William Gamson. 1979. Utilitarian Logic in the Resource Mobilization Perspective. In *The Dynamics of Social Movements*, ed. Mayer Zald and John McCarthy. Cambridge, MA: Winthrop.

Flexner, Eleanor. 1973. *Century of Struggle: The Woman's Rights Movement in the United States*. New York: Atheneum.

Forbath, William E. 1991. *Law and the Shaping of the American Labor Movement*. Cambridge, MA: Harvard Univ. Press.

Freeman, Alan. 1982. Antidiscrimination Law: A Critical Review. In *The Politics of Law: A Progressive Critique*, ed. David Kairys. New York: Pantheon.

Freeman, Jo. 1975. *The Politics of Women's Liberation*. New York: David McKay.

Gabel, Peter. 1982. Reification and Legal Reasoning. In *Marxism and the Law*, ed. Piers Beirne and Richard Quinney. New York: Wiley.

————. 1984. The Phenomonology of Rights Consciousness and the Pact of Withdrawn Selves. 62 *Texas Law Rev.*, 1563.

Galanter, Marc. 1983. The Radiating Effects of Courts. In *Empirical Theories of Courts*, ed. Keith D. Boyum and Lynn Mather. New York: Longman.

Gamson, William. 1988. Political Discourse and Collective Action. In *From Structure to Action: Comparing Movement Participation Across Cultures*, ed. P. G. Klandermans, H. Kriesi, and S. Tarrow. Greenwich, CT: JAI Press.

Garth, Bryant G. 1992. Power and Legal Artifice: The Federal Class Action. 26 *Law and Society Rev.*, 237.

Gaventa, John. 1980. *Power and Powerlessness: Quiescence and Rebellion in an Appalachian Valley*. Urbana: Univ. of Illinois Press.

Gelb, Joyce, and Marian Lief Palley. 1982. *Women and Public Policies*. Princeton, NJ: Princeton Univ. Press.

Goldberg, Roberta. 1983. *Organizing Women Office Workers: Dissatisfaction, Consciousness, and Action*. New York: Praeger.

Goodwyn, Lawrence. 1978. *The Populist Moment*. New York: Oxford Univ. Press.

Handler, Joel F. 1978. *Social Movements and the Legal System: A Theory of Law Reform and Social Change*. New York: Academic Press.

Harrington, Christine, and Barbara Yngvesson. 1990. Interpretive Sociolegal Research. 15 *Law and Social Inquiry*, 135.

Horowitz, Donald L. 1977. *The Courts and Social Policy*. Washington, DC: Brookings Institute.

Hunt, Alan. 1985. The Ideology of Law: Advances and Problems in Recent Applications of the Concept of Ideology to the Analysis of Law. 19 *Law and Society Rev.*, 1.

————. 1990. Rights and Social Movements: Counter-Hegemonic Strategies. 17 *Journal of Law and Society*, 309.

Hutner, Frances C. 1986. *Equal Pay for Comparable Worth: The Working Women's Issue for the Eighties*. New York: Praeger.

Jenkins, Joseph C., and Charles Perrow. 1977. Insurgency of the Powerless: Farmworker Movements. 42 *American Sociological Rev.*, 249.

Johnson, Charles A., and Bradley C. Canon. 1984. *Judicial Policies: Implementation and Impact*. Washington, DC: Congressional Quarterly Press.

Kairys, David, ed. 1982. *The Politics of Law: A Progressive Critique*. New York: Pantheon.

————. 1990. Freedom of Speech. In *The Politics of Law: A Progressive Critique*, ed. David Kairys. 2d ed. New York: Pantheon.

Katz, Jack. 1982. *Poor People's Lawyers in Transition*. New Brunswick, NJ: Rutgers Univ. Press.

Kelman, Mark. 1987. *A Guide to Critical Legal Studies*. Cambridge, MA: Harvard Univ. Press.

Kessler, Mark. 1990. Legal Mobilization for Social Reform: Power and the Politics of Agenda Setting. 24 *Law and Society Rev.*, 121.

Kessler-Harris, Alice. 1990. *A Woman's Wage: Historical Meanings and Social Consequences*. Lexington: Univ. of Kentucky Press.

Klandermans, Bert. 1991. New Social Movements and Resource Mobilization: The European and American Approach Revisited. In *Research on Social Movements: The State of the Art in Western Europe and the USA*, ed. Dieter Rucht. Boulder, CO: Westview.

————. 1992. The Social Construction of Social Protest and Multiorganizational Fields. In *Frontiers in Social Movement Theory*, ed. Aldon Morris and Carol Mueller. New Haven, CT: Yale Univ. Press.

Klein, Ethel. 1984. *Gender Politics: From Consciousness to Mass Politics*. Cambridge, MA: Harvard Univ. Press.

Kluger, Richard. 1976. *Simple Justice: The History of Brown v. Board of Education and Black America's Struggle for Equality*. New York: Knopf.

Lears, T. J. Jackson. 1985. The Concept of Cultural Hegemony: Problems and Possibilities. 90 *American Historical Rev.*, 567.

Lefcourt, Robert, ed. 1971. *Law against the People: Essays to Demystify the Law, Order and the Courts*. New York: Vintage.

Lichterman, Andrew M. 1984. Social Movements and Legal Elites. 1984 *Wisconsin Law Rev.*, 1035.

Lowi, Theodore J. 1971. *The Politics of Disorder*. New York: Basic Books.

————. 1979. *The End of Liberalism: The Second Republic of the United States*. New York: Norton.

Lynd, Staughton. 1984. Communal Rights. 62 *Texas Law Rev.*, 1417.

Mansbridge, Jane J. 1986. *Why We Lost the ERA*. Chicago: Univ. of Chicago Press.

Mather, Lynn, and Barbara Yngvesson. 1980–81. Language, Audience, and the Transformation of Disputes. 15 *Law and Society Rev.*, 775.

McAdam, Doug. 1982. *Political Process and the Development of Black Insurgency, 1930–1970*. Chicago: Univ. of Chicago Press.

McCann, Michael W. 1986. *Taking Reform Seriously: Perspectives on Public Interest Liberalism*. Ithaca, NY: Cornell Univ. Press.

———. 1991. Legal Mobilization and Social Reform Movements: Notes on Theory and Its Applications. 11 *Studies in Law, Politics, and Society*, 225.

———. 1993a. Reform Litigation on Trial. 18 *Law and Social Inquiry*, 1101.

———. 1993b. Resistance, Reconstruction, and Romance in Legal Scholarship. 26 *Law and Society Rev.*, 601.

———. 1994. *Rights at Work: Pay Equity Reform and the Politics of Legal Mobilization*. Chicago: Univ. of Chicago Press.

McCann, Michael W., and Helena Silverstein. 1997. The "Lure of Litigation" and Other Myths about Cause Lawyers. In *The Politics and Practice of Cause Lawyering*, ed. Austin Sarat and Stuart Scheingold. New York: Oxford Univ. Press.

McGlen, Nancy, and Karen O'Connor. 1983. *Women's Rights*. New York: Praeger.

Medcalf, Linda. 1978. *Law and Identity*. Beverly Hills: Sage.

Melnick, R. Shep. 1983. *Regulation and the Courts: The Case of the Clean Air Act*. Washington, DC: Brookings Institution.

Melucci, Alberto. 1989. *Nomads of the Present: Social Movements and Individual Needs in Contemporary Society*. London: Hutchinson Radius.

Merry, Sally Engle. 1985. Concepts of Law and Justice among Working-Class Americans: Ideology as Culture. 9 *Legal Studies Forum*, 59.

———. 1988. Legal Pluralism. 22 *Law and Society Rev.*, 868.

———. 1990. *Getting Justice and Getting Even: Legal Consciousness among Working-Class Americans*. Chicago: Univ. of Chicago Press.

Milkman, Ruth. 1985. Women Workers, Feminism, and the Labor Movement Since the 1960s. In *Women, Work, and Protest*, ed. Ruth Milkman. Boston: Routledge and Kegan Paul.

Milner, Neal. 1986. The Dilemmas of Legal Mobilization: Ideologies and Strategies of Mental Patient Liberation. 8 *Law and Policy*, 105.

Minow, Martha. 1987. Interpreting Rights: An Essay for Robert Cover. 96 *Yale Law Journal*, 1860.

———. 1990. *Making All the Difference: Inclusion, Exclusion, and American Law*. Ithaca, NY: Cornell Univ. Press.

Mnookin, Robert H., and Lewis Kornhauser. 1979. Bargaining in the Shadow of Law: The Case of Divorce. 88 *Yale Law Journal*, 951.

Morris, Aldon. 1984. *The Origins of the Civil Rights Movement*. New York: Free Press.

———. 1992. Political Consciousness and Collective Action. In *Frontiers in Social Movement Theory*, ed. Aldon Morris and Carol Mueller. New Haven, CT: Yale University Press.

O'Connor, Karen. 1980. *Women's Organizations' Use of the Courts*. Lexington, MA: Lexington Books.

Olson, Susan M. 1984. *Clients and Lawyers: Securing the Rights of Disabled Persons.* Westport, CT: Greenwood.

O'Neill, Timothy J. 1985. *Bakke and the Politics of Equality.* Middletown, CT: Wesleyan Univ. Press.

Piven, Frances F., and Richard A. Cloward. 1979. *Poor People's Movements: Why They Succeed, How They Fail.* New York: Vintage.

Rose, Nikolas. 1985. Unreasonable Rights: Mental Illness and the Limits of Law. 12 *Journal of Law and Society*, 199.

Rosenberg, Gerald. 1991. *The Hollow Hope: Can Courts Bring about Social Change?* Chicago: Univ. of Chicago Press.

Rupp, Leila, and Verta Taylor. 1987. *Survival in the Doldrums: The American Women's Rights Movement.* New York: Oxford Univ. Press.

Santos, Boaventura de Sousa. 1977. The Law of the Oppressed: The Construction and Reproduction of Legality in Pasargada. 12 *Law and Society Rev.*, 5.

Sarat, Austin. 1985. Legal Effectiveness and Social Studies of Law. 9 *Legal Studies Forum*, 23.

————. 1990. " . . . The Law is All Over": Power, Resistance and the Legal Consciousness of the Welfare Poor. 2 *Yale Journal of Law and the Humanities*, 343.

Sax, Joseph L. 1971. *Defending the Environment: A Strategy for Citizen Action.* New York: Knopf.

Schattschneider, E. E. 1960. *The Semi-Sovereign People: A Realist's View of Democracy in America.* New York: Holt, Rinehart, and Winston.

Scheingold, Stuart A. 1974. *The Politics of Rights: Lawyers, Public Policy, and Political Change.* New Haven, CT: Yale Univ. Press.

————. 1989. Constitutional Rights and Social Change. In *Judging the Constitution*, ed. Michael W. McCann and Gerald L. Houseman. Glenview, IL: Scott, Foresman / Little, Brown.

Schneider, Elizabeth M. 1986. The Dialectic of Rights and Politics: Perspectives from the Women's Movement. 61 *New York Univ. Law Rev.*, 554.

Scott, James. 1985. *Weapons of the Weak: Everyday Forms of Peasant Resistance.* New Haven, CT: Yale Univ. Press.

————. 1990. *Domination and the Arts of Resistance: Hidden Transcripts.* New Haven, CT: Yale Univ. Press.

Silbey, Susan. 1992. Making a Place for Cultural Analyses of Law. 17 *Law and Social Inquiry*, 39.

Silverstein, Helena. 1996. *Unleashing Rights: Law, Meaning, and the Animal Rights Movement.* Ann Arbor: Univ. of Michigan Press.

Skocpol, Theda. 1979. *States and Social Revolution.* Cambridge: Cambridge Univ. Press.

Smart, Carol. 1989. *Feminism and the Power of Law.* London: Routledge.

Snow, D. A., and R. D. Benford. 1988. Ideology, Frame Resonance, and Participant Mobilization. In *From Structure to Action: Comparing Movement Participation across Cultures*, ed. P. G. Klandermans, H. Kriesi, and S. Tarrow. Greenwich, CT: JAI Press.

Stone, Deborah. 1989. Causal Stories and the Formation of Policy Agendas. 104 *Political Science Quarterly*, 281.

Swidler, Ann. 1986. Culture in Action: Symbols and Strategies. 51 *American Sociological Rev.*, 273.

Tarrow, Sidney. 1983. *Struggling to Reform: Social Movements and Policy Change during Cycles of Protest*. Occasional Paper no. 15, Center for International Studies, Cornell University.

Taylor, Michael. 1988. Rationality and Revolutionary Collective Action. In *Rationality and Revolution*, ed. Michael Taylor. Cambridge: Cambridge Univ. Press.

Taylor, Verta. 1989. Social Movement Continuity: The Women's Movement in Abeyance. 54 *American Sociological Rev.*, 761.

Thompson, E. P. 1975. *Whigs and Hunters: The Origin of the Black Act*. New York: Pantheon.

Tomlins, Christopher L. 1985. *The State and the Unions: Labor Relations, Law, and the Organized Labor Movement in America, 1880–1960*. New York: Cambridge Univ. Press.

Turk, Austin. 1976. Law as a Weapon in Social Conflict. 23 *Social Problems*, 276.

Tushnet, Mark. 1984. An Essay on Rights. 62 *Texas Law Rev.*, 1363.

———. 1987. *The NAACP's Legal Strategy against Segregated Education, 1925–1952*. Chapel Hill: Univ. of North Carolina.

Westin, Alan Furman. 1953. The Supreme Court, the Populist Movement, and the Campaign of 1896. 15 *Journal of Politics*, 3.

Williams, Joan C. 1989. Deconstructing Gender. 87 *Michigan Law Rev.*, 797.

Williams, Patricia. 1987. Alchemical Notes: Reconstructing Ideals from Deconstructed Rights. 22 *Harvard Civil Rights–Civil Liberties Law Rev.*, 410.

Wirt, Frederick M. 1970. *The Politics of Southern Equality: Law and Social Change in a Mississippi County*. Chicago: Aldine.

Zald, Mayer N. 1992. Looking Backward to Look Forward: Reflections on the Past and Future of the Resource Mobilization Program. In *Frontiers in Social Movement Theory*, ed. Aldon Morris and Carol Mueller. New Haven, CT: Yale Univ. Press.

HOW DOES LAW MATTER
IN THE CONSTITUTION OF
LEGAL CONSCIOUSNESS?

DAVID M. ENGEL

1. INTRODUCTION

The interest of law and society scholars in "legal consciousness" is a relatively recent phenomenon. Although references to the term can be found in scholarship of the late 1970s and early 1980s, legal consciousness has emerged as a discrete topic of widespread research interest among sociolegal scholars only within the past eight to ten years. In this essay, I suggest that the subject of legal consciousness did not grow and bloom as a new species within the law and society field, but rather that it is an offshoot of earlier law and society research traditions. It is a concept, or a cluster of ideas, that now seems promising to a group of sociolegal scholars who have arrived at the topic of legal consciousness by way of research on legal needs, legal culture, dispute processing, and legal ideology. The restless search of these scholars is a story in itself. I will try to provide a sense of what it is they are looking for, why the earlier formulations ultimately proved too constraining, and why the concept of legal consciousness now seems promising. In doing so, I point to differing assumptions about how law matters in the constitution of legal consciousness and offer tentative suggestions for bringing greater clarity to this question.

In order to provide a focus for this discussion, I base my analysis primarily on six recent[1] and reasonably representative books and articles by widely read law and society scholars. Many other works and authors might have been chosen, of course, and some of these others are cited in the discussion that follows. The six works I have selected, however, provide a sense of the diversity as well as the commonality of interests within this emerging subfield as well as a range of assumptions about the ways in which law matters. Furthermore, all six share a quality that has come to define much of the most distinctive law and society research—a commitment to examine theoretical issues as they play themselves out in the lives and experiences of actual people. The six works are: John Comaroff and Jean Comaroff, *Ethnography and the Historical Imagination* (1992); Patricia Ewick and Susan S. Silbey, "Conformity, Contestation, and Resistance: An Account of Legal Consciousness" (1992); Carol J. Greenhouse, "Courting Difference: Issues of Interpretation and Comparison in the Study of Legal Ideologies" (1988); Sally Engle Merry, *Getting Justice and Getting Even: Legal Consciousness among Working-Class Americans* (1990); Austin Sarat, " ' . . . The Law Is All Over': Power, Resistance, and the Legal Consciousness of the Welfare Poor" (1990); and Barbara Yngvesson, "Making Law at the Doorway: The Clerk, the Court, and the Construction of Community in a New England Town" (1988).[2]

The Comaroffs write about the "colonialization of consciousness" during historical encounters between British imperialists and South African peoples, a process that involved a transformation of both British and African world-views. Ewick and Silbey illustrate a theory of legal consciousness with an early example from an ongoing study: Millie Simpson, a domestic house-keeper, loses and then wins in a criminal court where she was mistakenly charged for a vehicular offense committed by a teenager who took her car without permission. Greenhouse revisits "Hopewell," Georgia, in order to show how ideologies of law and court use as well as concepts of community and history are constructed around categories of difference (insider versus outsider, newcomer versus local, those prone to engage in conflict versus those able to control themselves, those who "belong" versus those who are rootless and without faith or commitment). Merry, who studied litigation and mediation among working-class New Englanders, examines transformations in the consciousness of those who go to court to assert their rights in family or neighborhood conflicts only to find that such cases are viewed as "garbage" by clerks and judges, who try to channel them toward nonjudicial, "therapeutic" resolutions. Sarat explores the perceptions of welfare recipients who view themselves as caught in a vast web of legal rules dominating most aspects of their lives yet allowing some room for resistance and temporary, strategic victories. Yngvesson studies complaint hearings conducted by the court clerk in a district criminal court in Massachusetts and sketches the process by which this seemingly marginal actor in a seemingly peripheral judicial locale actually participates in important ways in the negotiation of concepts of community, of belonging, of appropriate behavior, and of social order.

The discussion that follows is organized into four sections. First, I examine the concepts of legal consciousness that are presented in these six works. I focus in particular on whose consciousness the authors attempt to study and on what is meant by the term "legal consciousness." Second, I suggest that similar interests and concerns appeared in earlier research by law and society scholars working under such paradigms as legal needs, legal culture, dispute processing, and legal ideology. I ask why these earlier paradigms were ultimately considered inadequate by those who now focus on issues of legal consciousness. Third, drawing on these earlier research traditions as well as the six representative works on legal consciousness, I examine differing assumptions about the extent to which law matters. Finally, I offer my own suggestions about the study of legal consciousness and some ways in which insights gained from earlier law and society research might usefully be applied to this emerging subfield.

2. CONCEPTS AND DEFINITIONS

"Legal consciousness" is by no means a self-defining term. In this section, I examine some of the meanings given to it by the scholars listed above. An overview of the concepts and definitions used by our sample of law and society scholars reveals a variety of different starting points for the discussion of legal consciousness. I hope to suggest that these differences reflect different scholarly perceptions of how law matters and what (and where) law is. Using these scholars as informants, we listen to how they talk about legal consciousness and thereby reveal their own understandings of the role of law in society.

A. WHOSE CONSCIOUSNESS?

The concept of consciousness presupposes a thinker, a cognitive self. This is not to say that the study of consciousness is necessarily a one-by-one affair, premised on notions of individual, discrete selves, each with a different way of thinking. Consciousness might be studied in this way, but in the literature we consider it is more often conceived as a collective phenomenon. Indeed, the attraction of "consciousness" as a research topic resides precisely in the commonalities that are seen by researchers to typify the thinking of groups of people or entire cultures.

To speak of the self as a repository of consciousness, then, does not necessarily imply that our starting point is one of radical individualism. Jerome Bruner tells us that even psychologists, who have been among the most tenacious investigators of individual identity and cognition, no longer dichotomize the study of the self and the groups of which the self is a member:

> [P]sychologists began to ask whether the wider circle of people about whom any person cares or in whom he or she confides might also be complicit in our narratives and our Self-constructions. Might not the complicit circle, then, be something like a "distributed Self," much as one's notes and looking-up

procedures become part of one's distributed knowledge. And just as knowledge thereby gets caught in the net of culture, so too Self becomes enmeshed in a net of others. It is this distributive picture of Self that came to prevail among "social constructionists" and "interpretive social scientists." (Bruner 1990: 113–14)

If psychologists can conceive of a self "distributed" among a wider group of persons with whom an individual interacts and influenced by the culture of which the group is a part, then we should experience no dissonance in discussing the consciousness of the self while also recognizing that consciousness may be first and foremost a phenomenon of a collectivity. Our question, then, is who are the individuals and collectivities that interest law and society researchers who write about legal consciousness? Who are the selves whose thinking seems to invite scholarly examination?

On this question, we find both agreement and ambiguity among the authors who constitute our sample. Perhaps agreement is possible precisely because of ambiguity concerning the "who" of legal consciousness. Sarat (1990) begins his discussion of definitions by quoting Trubek (1984: 592): legal consciousness is "all the ideas about the nature, function and operation of law held by anyone in society at a given time." The self, in this definition, might appear to be the individual thinker, but Sarat, in a lengthy footnote, hastens to explain that he rejects the approach of "radical individuation," that he studies consciousness rather than attitudes because the latter inappropriately presents "a picture of persons influenced by a variety of factors, thinking, choosing, deciding autonomously how and what to think." Consciousness as a research concept, by contrast to attitudes, emphasizes commonalities in thinking that grow out of the broader structures and relationships in which people are embedded:

> Consciousness and ideology [as we shall see, Sarat equates the two terms] suggest greater structure and constraint. These terms embed the study of ideas in social structure and social relations. They draw attention to the way similarly situated persons come to see the world in similar ways. They suggest that subjectivity is not free floating and autonomous but is, instead, constituted, in a historically contingent manner, by the very objects of consciousness. (Sarat 1990: 344)

Merry's definition of legal consciousness is quite similar to Sarat's with respect to its assumptions about the self. Consciousness is "the way people conceive of the 'natural' and normal way of doing things, their habitual patterns of talk and action, and their commonsense understanding of the world" (Merry 1990: 5). There is an individual aspect to consciousness (comparable to the Trubek/Sarat reference to "anyone in society at a given time"), but an individual's consciousness is shaped by the structures and relationships of which she or he is a part.

Merry also emphasizes the experiential dimension of consciousness. The ideas people have are continually tested against their experiences and are changed as a result. These experiences and transformations, in her description, might seem to suggest a more individuated emphasis than Sarat's, but Merry makes it clear that this is not her intention. Quoting Jean Comaroff, Merry emphasizes that consciousness is "embedded in the practical constitution of everyday life, part and parcel of the process whereby the subject is constituted by external sociocultural forms" (Merry 1990: 5).

Both Merry and Sarat, then, stress the interplay between the thinking self and the external forces that affect individual consciousness. Both contrast the study of consciousness with the study of attitudes, which they criticize as insufficiently sensitive to the social contexts within which consciousness is constituted. Neither Merry nor Sarat, however, provides a definition of consciousness that suggests what groups fall within particular processes of consciousness-shaping. If consciousness is not merely an individual matter but is constituted by broader structures and relationships, then what groups of people will share similar consciousnesses and where do those groups shade off into other groups whose consciousness has been constituted in different ways?

Although Merry and Sarat do not treat this question definitionally, some answers are provided in the studies themselves. Merry, for example, confines her research to working-class Americans who reside in Salem and Cambridge, Massachusetts. Her assumption, reflected throughout the book, is that working-class Americans differ in their legal consciousness from other Americans. Further, she distinguishes between two different segments of the American working class: "settled-living" and "hard-living" persons. These two groups, she suggests, have different kinds of problems and understand the world in different ways (Merry 1990: 60–61). Similarly, Sarat's article explores the consciousness of the welfare poor, a group whose experiences and understandings of the world differ from that of others:

> [T]he welfare poor construct a consciousness of law on the basis of their daily deprivation, their experience of unequal, often demeaning treatment, and their search for tools with which to cope with an often unresponsive welfare bureaucracy. . . . In all this the welfare poor recognize that their experience is different from that of others in this society, whether they be social scientists seeking to understand the welfare poor or the incompletely identified class of "the rich." (Sarat 1990: 378)

Both Sarat and Merry posit a similarity in the consciousness of classes of people who have comparable experiences and social status. For them, consciousness is shared far beyond the bounds of Bruner's "distributed self," which, as we saw, involved a group of persons linked by personal relationship and interaction over time. The groups of selves suggested by Sarat and Merry may understand the world in similar ways without ever having met or interacted with one another. Their identities have been shaped by parallel experiences, but the lines of their existence need not have intersected. Indeed, consciousness could be shared by two welfare recipients or two "hard-living" working-class Americans who spent their entire lives thousands of miles apart.

The implicit assumption is that external forces of "sociocultural production" (cf. de Certeau 1984: xiv) affect categories of similarly situated people in similar ways, as long as people within those categories have had roughly comparable experiences. In both Sarat's and Merry's work, the categories are based on social class. It is possible that their analysis could be extended to categories based on other factors, such as race, religion, or gender, yet I sense that social class is a particularly significant element in the consciousness of those who study consciousness. Perhaps the emphasis on class analysis reflects the roots of consciousness research in Marxist theory.

Research by scholars such as Yngvesson and Greenhouse reveals different assumptions about the "who" of legal consciousness. While these writers are also sensitive to cross-cutting categories such as social class, race, religion, and gender, they focus on consciousness as it is constituted and shared within groups that have some internal cohesion and share a common geographical space. For them, the issue that demands attention is how understandings of the world are negotiated and contested in specific locales in a way that constructs ideas about "community," about persons who are perceived to "belong," to share important sentiments, values, and social practices. Unlike Merry and Sarat, Yngvesson and Greenhouse do not study similarities in consciousness among persons who live parallel but separate lives. Rather, their research addresses specifically the ways people in particular localities view one another and the ways in which intersections in their lives lead to a process of social interpretation that is shared by some in the locality and contested by others.[3]

For Greenhouse, the essence of consciousness is the process of differentiation through which cultural meanings are constructed: " 'Difference' . . . is fundamental to the reproduction of social forms and values" (1988: 688). Difference, she emphasizes, is not innate but is "invented":

> [T]he interpretivist's starting premise is that differences, of any kind, are not intrinsic but are culturally defined according to extrinsic criteria of representativeness. A rough translation of this idea would be to say that difference is in the eye of the beholder, and that when an interpretivist looks at difference, it is not at any particular distinction, but at the whole system of values and meanings by which distinctions are drawn, symbolized, defended, reproduced, and modified. (Greenhouse 1988: 688)

The researcher who interprets a particular process of differentiation in a particular locality can thereby obtain insights into how communities are formed and contested, how persons are included or excluded in various social groupings, and how law is extolled or denounced in different situations. Categories such as social class are not starting points for Greenhouse. For her, we can surmise, the question would be whether social class has or has not become a significant social marker in the process of differentiation among a group of persons who have forged a set of shared understandings about the world. If social class (or religion or race) has not acquired special salience in some form, then we might expect it to drop out of the analysis in favor of the elements that figure more importantly in local understandings. We should also note that the selves that join together in this process of meaning-construction might find themselves in opposition to other groupings in the same locality that construct meaning in different ways and share a different type of consciousness.

In describing Greenhouse's work, I have taken an important—and unfair—liberty. She does not use the term "consciousness" in her article, which explores instead the concept of "ideology." There is no reason to think that Greenhouse would feel comfortable with my conclusion that her analysis of cultural interpretation is just as relevant to the concept of consciousness as it is to the concept of ideology. Yet the definitions of consciousness by Merry and Sarat, quoted above, seem to me to apply very well to the processes of meaning-construction and shared understandings of the world that are the subject matter of Greenhouse's research in Hopewell. Even though Greenhouse might, if asked, reject this use of the term "legal consciousness," her work falls well within the meanings of that term as it has been defined by others.

A similar caveat applies to the article by Yngvesson (1988). Although very much concerned with the processes by which individuals and groups construct meanings and shared understandings of the world, she does not use the term "legal consciousness" in her analysis (but see Engel and Yngvesson 1984). Like Greenhouse, Yngvesson explores the ways in which meanings and commonsense understandings emerge within particular groups in a given locality through interactions with one another and with those whose beliefs and practices they reject. She is particularly concerned with the role of the court clerk, who stands at the threshold of the judicial system and facilitates the process of meaning construction by marking boundaries between the acceptable and the unacceptable, between the proper and the improper, between "normal" problems and crime, between good citizens and "brainless" people, and between "garbage" cases and legitimate forms of court use.

Thus, like Greenhouse, Yngvesson appears to be describing what others would term the constitution of legal consciousness. Like Greenhouse, as well, she does not begin with a priori categories of people and explore the extent to which they do or do not share consciousness. Rather, within a particular locality, she asks what categories of people come to be marked out as a result of harmonious and conflictual interactions. The "who" of legal consciousness in her analysis, as in Greenhouse's, is discovered through ethnographic inquiry into the production of shared meanings. The selves whose consciousness Yngvesson and Greenhouse study are persons whose day-to-day interactions create definitions of collective identity and shared understandings of the experiences of everyday life.

B. THE MEANINGS OF LEGAL CONSCIOUSNESS

Despite the gravitational pull of the concept of legal consciousness on the work of law and society scholars, the meaning of the term is surprisingly elusive. As I have already suggested, part of the uncertainty resides in differing scholarly perceptions about the identity of the self whose consciousness is at issue. Further uncertainty, however, arises out of inconsistent assumptions about what "consciousness" means and what, if anything, the modifier "legal" might add.

We might begin with a proposition about which there is, as far as I can determine, no disagreement: "consciousness" does not refer only to the conscious thought processes of the self. Consciousness includes the unconscious and the subconscious; there is no requirement that the self be aware of the ideas and assumptions that constitute consciousness. Indeed, for some writers, the significance of consciousness resides primarily in those understandings of the world that require no self-awareness, that seem so much a part of the natural order of things that the self never reflects on them, never needs to rationalize their truth nor consider the possibility that they may be false.

Beyond this, however, we find some divergence of opinion. Sarat, after quoting Trubek's definition of legal consciousness ("all the ideas about the nature, function and operation of law held by anyone in society at a given time"), goes on to equate consciousness and ideology: "I use the term consciousness, but I could have as easily substituted ideology. Indeed, for my purposes legal consciousness and legal ideology could be used interchangeably" (Sarat 1990: 343). By contrast, the Comaroffs provide a more nuanced definition of consciousness and ideology that draws important (for them) distinctions between the two terms. To understand these distinctions, however, we should begin with their concept of culture.

The Comaroffs define culture as "the semantic space, the field of signs and practices, in which human beings construct and represent themselves and others, and hence their societies and histories" (1992: 27). They emphasize that culture is neither exclusively meaning nor exclusively behavior but a combination of the two. The interplay of signs and practices produces the possibility of pluralism, conflict, and change within a culture, as contrasted with earlier scholarly depictions of cultures as static and undifferentiated:

> Culture always contains within it polyvalent, potentially contestable messages, images, and actions. It is, in short, a historically situated, historically unfolding ensemble of signifiers-in-action. . . . Some of these, at any moment in time, will be woven into more or less tightly integrated, relatively explicit worldviews; others may be heavily contested, the stuff of counterideologies and "subcultures"; yet others may become more or less unfixed, relatively freefloating, and indeterminate in their value and meaning. (Comaroff and Comaroff 1992:27)

Given this definition of culture, it then becomes important to understand the significance of power, which can affect contests over meaning and cause some worldviews to predominate over others. The Comaroffs incorporate power into their analysis through their definitions of hegemony and ideology. Hegemony is

> that order of signs and material practices, drawn from a specific cultural field, that come to be taken for granted as the natural, universal, and true shape of social being—although its infusion into local worlds is always liable to challenge by the logic of prevailing cultural forms, is never automatic. It consists of things that go without saying: things that, being axiomatic, are not normally the subject of explication or argument. (Comaroff and Comaroff 1992: 28–29)

Schutz Gurowitz

Unlike hegemony, ideology is a particular worldview associated with a particular social group. Dominant groups attempt to impose their ideologies on other groups, who may resist and hold to their own ideologies. Whereas hegemony consists of all-pervasive, implicit, and taken-for-granted understandings, ideology consists of contestable and self-conscious systems of belief held by identifiable actors or groups: "Hegemony is beyond direct argument; ideology is more likely to be perceived as a matter of inimical opinion and interest and hence is more open to contestation. Hegemony, at its most effective, is mute; ideology invites argument." (Comaroff and Comaroff 1992: 29).

It should already be apparent that the Comaroffs' conception of ideology is different from Sarat's. It is unlikely, given their definition of ideology as the contestable opinions identified with particular social groups, that they would agree with Sarat that ideology and consciousness are equivalent terms. Indeed, at a later point in the book, the Comaroffs express impatience with those who make consciousness "a fashionable synonym for 'culture,' 'ideology,' 'thought,' or an ill-defined blend of all three" (1992: 237). A proper understanding of consciousness, the Comaroffs argue, requires a more subtle appreciation of the interrelationships between "form and content, sign and practice, intention and outcome" that shape the process by which human meanings are constructed (1992: 237).

For the Comaroffs, then, consciousness is related to, but not congruent with, the play of ideologies within a cultural space. They take pains to show that consciousness is not simply a set of explicit or implicit understandings of the world, but rather is a dynamic *process* through which human actors shape their self-awareness by invoking (and resisting) ideologies and by drawing upon systems of cultural meaning in their daily experiences and struggles:

> [C]onsciousness is best understood as the active process—sometimes implicit, sometimes explicit—in which human actors deploy historically salient cultural categories to construct their self-awareness. Its modes, we have shown, may be subtle and diverse; and it is as crucial to explore the forms in which a people choose to speak and act as it is to examine the content of their messages. (Comaroff and Comaroff 1992: 176)

Note in this definition the emphasis on <u>intentionality which the Comaroffs associate with consciousness</u>. While acknowledging, in their discussion of hegemony, that dominant groups can shape the way other people understand and experience the world, the Comaroffs' definition of consciousness stresses that people also have the capacity to construct their own meanings, albeit out of the alternatives they perceive to be available to them within a given culture.

What do the Comaroffs have to say specifically about "legal conscious-ness"? The term simply does not appear in their book. Even more surprising, perhaps, is that law itself is not singled out for discussion. This is surprising not only because one of the Comaroffs (John) is widely regarded as a leading legal anthropologist—an ascription he himself may not necessarily welcome—but also because the book is filled with discussion of subject matter that has long been a staple of law and society scholarship: the efforts of colonial governments to transform and control the practices of indigenous, non-Western peoples. I am intrigued by the omission of law, as well as legal consciousness, from a book that seems, to me, to be very much about law. Perhaps the omission should be understood as part of a continual ebb and flow in the field of legal anthropology, in which law is sometimes singled out as a subject of particular interest and importance and at other times is deliberately reabsorbed into more universal anthropological concerns with cultural interpretation.

For purposes of our discussion, however, the omission of law from the Comaroffs' analysis raises an important threshold question: How might their analysis of consciousness have been different if they had focused more specif-ically on the relationship between consciousness and law? Would they agree that there is a particular subspecies of consciousness that can be termed "legal"? If so, what does the adjective add to the Comaroffs' analysis of the ways in which humans construct meanings and self-awareness out of their experiences?

We encounter no such uncertainty in Ewick and Silbey's explication of the concept of legal consciousness. Like the Comaroffs, Ewick and Silbey define consciousness in terms of the interplay between meaning and action. They reject the scholarly approach that conceives of consciousness in terms of mere ideas and attitudes. They also reject the approach that treats con-sciousness as an epiphenomenon, that is, as a "by-product of the operations of social structures rather than as the formative agent in shaping structures" (Ewick and Silbey 1992: 739–40). Instead, they regard consciousness as a "stabilized" set of meanings that emerge out of social practices chosen by individuals from a limited "inventory" of practices available to them in a given cultural context:

> [W]e conceive of consciousness as part of a reciprocal process in which the
> meanings given by individuals to their world, and law and legal institutions
> as part of that world, become repeated, patterned and stabilized, and those
> institutionalized structures become part of the meaning systems employed by

individuals. We understand consciousness to be formed within and changed by
social action. (Ewick and Silbey 1992: 741)

Ewick and Silbey thus join Merry as well as the Comaroffs in emphasizing
the continual transformation of consciousness through a process in which
understandings of the world interact with experiences in the world. Their
interest, unlike that of the Comaroffs, is focused particularly on the meanings
given to "law and legal institutions." They suggest that these meanings change
with time and with particular experiences, such as "a dispute with a neighbor,
a criminal case, a plumber who seemed to work few hours but charged for
many" (Ewick and Silbey 1992: 742). Continual variation and transformation
in consciousness, however, is constrained by the "limited number of available
interpretations for assigning meaning to things and events" and by the access
each individual has to such meanings or to the situations in which the
meanings are constructed (Ewick and Silbey 1992: 742). With respect to legal
consciousness, in particular, we can infer that persons situated differently in a
given society would have access to different repertoires of meaning they might
assign to a dispute with a neighbor or a plumber and would have differing
capacities to use lawyers, courts, or police officers in their efforts to act on
the meanings they assign.

What is not entirely clear in the article by Ewick and Silbey is whether
the term "legal consciousness" refers to consciousness in general as it focuses
(perhaps fleetingly) on law and legal institutions or whether, on the other
hand, it refers to a particular kind of thought process that people bring to bear
whenever legal matters arise. I find this same ambiguity in the work of other
law and society scholars who write about legal consciousness. Sometimes
the term seems to refer to images of laws and legal institutions that people
carry around in their heads (among many other images and impressions
of their social environment) and occasionally act upon. For example, an
individual might view courts as sites of rampant litigiousness populated by
greedy plaintiffs and bloodthirsty lawyers. When this individual is injured,
her behavior might accordingly involve "lumping" the harm and the financial
loss (cf. Felstiner 1974). At other times, however, the term seems to refer
not to images of law but to a legalistic or law-informed style of reasoning
or problem-solving that is functionally equivalent to the reasoning process
lawyers use. For example, an individual might be aware that government
agencies are, in certain circumstances, protected from lawsuits by the doctrine of governmental immunity. When this individual is injured by such
an agency, his legal consciousness would lead him to "lump" the harm
because he knows that formal legal action would be futile. In the first case,
legal consciousness would seem to refer to perceptions or images of law
and legal institutions; in the second case, to legal aptitude, knowledge, or
competence.

The distinction I am trying to make between consciousness as perceptions or images and consciousness as aptitude or competence is central to

the question that is the subject of this chapter: how does law matter in the constitution of consciousness? Clearly, this question will be answered quite differently depending on which of the two meanings we assign to the term "legal consciousness." For example, if legal consciousness is defined in terms of perceptions or images of law rather than competence in dealing with law-related problems, then we might imagine a variety of social and cultural factors that matter a great deal more than the law matters in shaping consciousness.

On the other hand, if we define legal consciousness to mean aptitude or competence, then law might matter a great deal more. Here one thinks, for example, of Millie Simpson's encounters with lawyers and judges as she worked her way through the false accusation of leaving the scene of an accident and driving without insurance (Ewick and Silbey 1992), or of Joe, Joan, and Mary's dealings with lawyers, clerks, judges, and mediators in an intrafamilial dispute involving a deteriorating marriage and a missing emerald ring (Merry 1990: 162–70). In both of these cases, researchers are likely to conclude that law plays a very important role in constituting "legal consciousness," if the term refers to individuals' capacity to understand what the relevant legal norms and procedures are in a given dispute.

Furthermore, these two alternative meanings of the term "legal consciousness" lead us in somewhat different directions when we relate the issue of legal consciousness to the field of law and society as a whole. If legal consciousness refers primarily to perceptions or images of law, then its study becomes part of a much broader research agenda that includes analysis of meanings and practices related to any number of state institutions or other symbolically important sources of power and influence in our society. If this is what we mean by legal consciousness, then it is readily reabsorbed into general research on culture, society, and the state. As in the Comaroffs' book, the specifically legal dimension might disappear entirely.

If, by contrast, legal consciousness refers primarily to aptitude or competence or awareness of the law, then law becomes so central to the inquiry that a new set of problems arises. The researcher must struggle with the difficulty of defining those social situations that are potentially legal in character in order to determine whether an individual's competence in such situations represents legal consciousness and therefore merits study. This is an old problem for law and society researchers and is not one we should eagerly revisit. Yet the problem of sifting the potentially legal from the stuff of everyday life looms large when researchers of legal consciousness define their subject matter in terms of consciousness of what the law is and what legal actors and institutions might potentially do in a given situation.

There is, then, an ambiguity in the term "legal consciousness" that ultimately calls into question the nature of the research enterprise itself. The ambiguity could lead researchers in rather different directions as they explore legal consciousness, and, in pursuing these different paths, they are likely to confront different kinds of obstacles.

3. ANTECEDENTS IN LAW AND SOCIETY RESEARCH

Here is a scene in academic life that many of us have witnessed: A younger scholar presents his or her research to an audience of colleagues in the faculty lounge. The presentation is animated and at times passionate. Invoking new theories and terminology, the presenter attempts to break through the restrictions of earlier approaches to achieve important new insights. Drenched with perspiration, the presenter eventually concludes. The first hand in the air is that of older Colleague A, who speaks in a bemused and condescending voice. The presentation was quite interesting, but Colleague A cannot refrain from observing that, once one strips away the veneer of currently fashionable language, there is really nothing new. Why, thirty or forty years ago we were studying precisely the same questions and reaching very similar conclusions. The presenter really ought to avoid dressing up old ideas in new garb and should not pretend that there is anything innovative or original in this work.

In devoting this section of my paper to law and society research that predates the study of legal consciousness, it is not my intention to speak in the curmudgeonly voice of Colleague A nor to discredit or debunk current research efforts by showing that they offer nothing new. Rather, a brief overview of earlier research traditions will help us to understand the appeal and the promise of research on legal consciousness and may suggest some aspects of this research area that merit special scholarly consideration.

The following overview is highly selective and somewhat idiosyncratic. To analyze all relevant research in all the law and society subfields over the past thirty or more years would be impossible. Instead, I select a few illustrative examples that reveal some of the origins of current interest in legal consciousness. These examples also suggest that research on legal consciousness is part of a continuing quest in the law and society field to explore how law matters and for whom.

A. STUDIES OF POVERTY AND LEGAL NEEDS

In the late 1960s and early 1970s, some of the most important law and society research took place in a subfield that is now quiescent: legal needs. An early landmark work that helped to shape this subfield was *Civil Justice and the Poor: Issues for Sociological Research,* by Carlin, Howard, and Messinger (1967). As the title implies, the authors were concerned with the way civil courts and lawyers dealt with poor people and the extent to which the poor were able to use the civil justice system to protect their rights and interests. The monograph provided a formulation of research issues based on studies that were then available; it did not purport to present new empirical findings by the authors themselves.

The authors of *Civil Justice and the Poor* observed that courts and lawyers treat poor people differently from the rich or middle class. Courts confronted with poor people as litigants approach their task as "benevolent administrators" rather than "impartial adjudicators" (Carlin, Howard, and Messinger 1967: 25). They conceive of the poor "as having problems rather than grievances and of needing treatment not justice" (1967: 25–26). Lawyers are largely unavailable to poor people in civil cases, and when they are available, they rarely provide the same kind of representation and facilitation of legal relationships that they provide for clients of means.

Although Carlin, Howard, and Messinger cite many reasons for the unequal treatment of poor people in the civil justice system, a core concept is "legal competence." This term refers to "the ability to further and protect one's interests *through active assertion* of *legal rights*." An individual with legal competence "will have a sense of himself as a *possessor of rights,* and in seeking to validate and implement these rights through law he will be concerned with holding *authorities accountable to law*." Legal competence is "one part *awareness* and one part *assertiveness*" (Carlin, Howard, and Messinger 1967: 62, 63; emphasis in original).

"Legal competence" is an early precursor of "legal consciousness." It is based on the concept that all people have certain rights, but that some people are more cognizant of their rights than others. "Competence" entails both an awareness that one possesses these rights and a readiness to invoke them in appropriate circumstances. Because the poor live in a "narrow world" (Carlin, Howard, and Messinger 1967: 66) which diminishes their "capacity . . . to objectify events and experiences and to deal with abstract issues" in legal frameworks (1967: 67), they tend to have less legal competence than persons who are not poor. The lack of legal competence, along with their social disempowerment and the built-in biases of the legal system itself, results in a failure to satisfy the legal needs of the poor.

Like Merry, Yngvesson, and other current writers, the authors of *Civil Justice and the Poor* conceived of law and legal consciousness (if we can apply this contemporary term to their analysis) as mutually constitutive. That is, lack of legal competence prevents poor people from effectively asserting and enforcing their rights; but, at the same time, those who attempt to use the civil justice system find that it minimizes, diverts, or rejects their claims because of their lower social status. Law thus contributes to a perception among the poor that efforts to secure their rights are futile (i.e., law constitutes consciousness), and this perception in turn makes it unlikely that poor people will make the legal system a bastion of legal protection (i.e., consciousness constitutes law).

Legal needs research flowed from this interest in the nature of legal problems experienced by poor people and the kinds of resources they used—or did not use—when such problems arose. Levine and Preston, for example, surveyed low-income people in a "middle-size midwestern city" in order to determine "the extent to which people were oriented to legal and other resources in coping with common life problems" (1970: 82). They asked about hypothetical cases ("What would you do if . . .") and about actual problems ("Have you ever been . . ."). Although the study discovered a number of interesting variations in patterns of problem-solving and legal competence, the general conclusion, based on both the hypothetical and actual cases, was that their interviewees seldom thought of using outside resources to protect their interests, but, when they did, lawyers were often among the first of the possible outside resources that they considered.

Like Carlin, Howard, and Messinger, Levine and Preston found that low-income people "were not aware of many of their rights" and did not even realize that some aspects of their lives, such as the providing of welfare benefits, could be subjected to a rights analysis (Levine and Preston 1970: 109). Thus, the greater availability of legal services for the poor would not, in itself, get to the root of the problem, which was "primarily one of education and the communication of information" (1970: 112).

While some researchers focused on the legal needs of the poor, others explored the legal needs of Americans in all social classes (e.g., Mayhew and Reis 1969). A national survey directed by Curran (1977) for the American Bar Association and the American Bar Foundation was the most broad-based of these studies, involving a lengthy survey instrument administered in 2,064 households across the United States. Like the Preston and Levine study, Curran's study relied on questions about hypothetical and actual problems and about interactions with—and perceptions of—lawyers. Although her report is too lengthy and complex to summarize here, a few points are worth noting. First, Curran's study tended to support earlier findings that persons of lower social status had a more pessimistic view than persons of higher social status concerning the potential utility of lawyers and the legal system (1977: 252). Second, attitudes were influenced by actual experience: persons who had actually used lawyers tended to be somewhat more sanguine than nonusers about the benefits of seeking legal counsel (Curran 1977: 236). Third, the use of lawyers when legal needs arose was highly problem-specific. When asked about the most recent occurrences of twenty-nine different problem situations, the respondents indicated that they had used lawyers in 790 of the 1,000 most recent occurrences of estate planning problems, but only 160 out of 1,000 tort problems, 120 out of 1,000 consumer and constitutional problems, and 40 out of 1,000 employment problems (Curran 1977: 143–46).

The influence of legal needs studies on studies of legal consciousness can be seen clearly in the first two points listed above. Legal needs studies provided strong evidence that attitudes and behavior *were* related to social class and that actual experiences with lawyers and courts *did* modify "consciousness." The third point, however, which Curran (1977: 259–64) described as one of her most significant findings, is often forgotten. Studies of legal consciousness often speak of the law in undifferentiated terms. Curran and others, however, have suggested that law-related attitudes, perceptions, and behavior vary dramatically depending on the particular area or type of law involved. While undifferentiated references to the law and the legal system may be useful for some purposes, they may be misleading and reductionist in many situations.

Indeed, as I have tried to suggest elsewhere (Engel 1984), the contrasting meanings associated with different areas of the law, such as torts and contracts, can reveal fundamental aspects of legal consciousness that would be overlooked entirely by researchers who were content to speak of the law in monolithic terms.

By the mid-1970s, as Curran completed work on her final report, many law and society researchers appeared ready to leave legal needs studies behind. The concept of a "legal need" proved so elusive that it was never pinned down, not even to the satisfaction of those working in the field. Researchers became increasingly aware that legal needs were not "things" out there to be studied and that definitions of what were needs—as well as what was legal—depended largely on the perceptions and worldview of the individual. The concept of legal need thus collapsed back into problems of cognition, interpretation, and meaning. Moreover, some scholars became critical of decontextualized studies of problems and problem solving. Anonymous responses to impersonal, closed-ended survey instruments were difficult to assess, not only in terms of their reliability but also in terms of their relationship to the lives and practices of the subjects. Changes in attitudes and behavior over time could be gauged only by the self-reporting of the subjects in their brief encounter with the interviewer. Subjective meanings and the complexities of particular events were largely inaccessible. At the same time that concerns over many of these research issues became more intense, research on dispute processing was increasingly occupying the attention of many law and society scholars.

B. DISPUTE PROCESSING

In the 1970s and early 1980s, dispute processing was perhaps the most vibrant and dynamic subfield of law and society research. Closely related to the case method on which conventional legal scholarship has long relied, dispute processing grew out of work by legal anthropologists such as Llewellyn and Hoebel (1941) among the Cheyenne and Gluckman (1955; 1965) among the Barotse of Northern Rhodesia. Seminal works by Abel (1973), Galanter (1974), and Felstiner (1974), among others, provided a framework for dispute analysis that fostered contextualized, qualitative, culturally grounded studies that were nonetheless susceptible to comparative analysis. Laura Nader and her graduate students in the Berkeley Village Law Project undertook dispute-based studies in Europe, Asia, Africa, the Middle East, and Central America (see, e.g., Nader 1965; Nader and Todd 1978). Other law and society scholars turned their attention to dispute processing in North American settings (e.g., Best and Andreasen 1977; Buckle and Thomas-Buckle 1982; McEwen and Maiman 1984; Merry 1979; Perin 1977; Steele 1975; Trubek et al. 1983).

The allure of dispute processing was not only that it seemed to provide a unit of analysis that was applicable in any society during any historical period, but also that it permitted researchers to study norms and attitudes in action. Dispute analysis focused not on what people told a researcher in a detached, closed-ended interview format but on accounts—or direct observations—of complex behaviors of people who were actually confronted with difficult, multistranded interpersonal problems. Furthermore, dispute analysis seemed to provide a bridge between cases handled without courts and lawyers and those handled by more formal legal means. Unlike much of the legal needs research, the key issue for research on disputing was not whether the individual in question went to a lawyer to assert legal rights, but what varieties of formal and informal dispute processing mechanisms were available, how the individual chose among them, and what consequences flowed from that choice. By situating lawyers and courts at one end of a broad spectrum of disputing alternatives (cf. Galanter 1974; Steele 1975), researchers could obtain more nuanced understandings of how individuals actually dealt with their problems and where the formal legal system fit in this picture.

The literature on dispute processing is too vast to summarize here. The relevance of this subfield for later studies of legal consciousness, however, is clear. First, the emphasis on extended case studies in dispute processing research is reflected in all six legal consciousness studies discussed above, with the possible exception of the Comaroffs' book (although they have used the extended case method in other related works, such as Comaroff and Roberts 1981). Research on disputing revealed that legal problems or legal needs were not like cases published in case reporters. They were not neat, self-contained, and limited in content, but were messy, complicated dimensions of social relationships that tended to recur repeatedly in different forms over extended periods of time. Indeed, the tendency of disputes to enlarge, contract, and transform themselves over time was seen by some (Mather and Yngvesson 1980–81) as one of their most telling features.

Second, the decentering of courts and lawyers was an important feature of dispute processing research. Abel (1973), for example, showed that third-party intervenors could be legal officials but could just as well be other, nonofficial actors playing a comparable role but applying quite different norms and procedures. Researchers became more sensitive to the existence and importance of lawlike rules, structures, and practices in everyday life that do not necessarily depend on the formal legal system for their viability. The relationship between such nonofficial systems of social ordering and the formal legal system was not assumed but became an important subject for study.

Third, research on disputing linked the study of behavior to the interpretation of meaning. Researchers increasingly asked not only what it was that individuals did in various problem situations, but how they thought about their conflicts and what meanings they assigned to various alternatives. Some researchers (e.g., Engel 1980; Kidder 1980–81; but see Trubek 1980–81) became uncomfortable with the tendency to reify disputes as social "facts" directly equivalent to legal "cases and controversies" rather than viewing them as essentially subjective phenomena constructed differently by different people in different situations. As the search for meaning intensified, scholars found themselves drawn to earlier and earlier phases of the disputing process. That is, scholarly attention increasingly focused on variations in initial perceptions that there was a problem that could lead to the assertion of a claim (Engel and Steele 1979; Felstiner, Abel, and Sarat 1980–81). Why do some people experience particular kinds of social interactions as problematic while others experience the same interactions as a normal part of everyday life?

The movement of some dispute research toward problem perception represented a shift similar to that which we observed in the research on legal needs: an initial exploration of positively conceived social facts or events began to collapse back into an inquiry into subjectivity, meaning, and cognition. But if the real issue was meaning and perception, then the very concept of the dispute as a research paradigm was called into question. Admittedly, meaning and perception could sometimes be studied in the context of actual disputes. But researchers now seemed equally interested in nondisputes, in the absence of trouble in situations where some individuals might perceive potential grievances and legal claims. The ground of inquiry began to shift away from the dispute as the central issue and toward other concerns that we might now group under the heading of "legal consciousness."

It should also be noted that this shift in focus was part of the scholarly biography of most of the researchers whose work was discussed in the first section of this essay: their earlier work dealt with dispute processing while their later work addresses legal consciousness. Merry (1990: 6–7), for example, discusses this transition in her own study, which began in the dispute processing mode but was increasingly influenced by considerations of "meaning making" and ideology. Like the other authors, she did not abandon dispute analysis entirely, but she supplemented and changed it significantly by introducing

> the analysis of interpretation and contest over the way things are understood, an enterprise which we normally associate with the study of ideology. The focus on dispute processes is attentive to social interactions and to the way the social world is revealed in moments of fight. The focus on ideology foregrounds meaning and the power inherent in establishing systems of meaning. (Merry 1990: 6–7)

Thus, the subfield of dispute processing represents an important precursor of research on legal consciousness. Dispute analysis provided many of the insights and terms of reference that studies of legal consciousness employ, but it was ultimately viewed as too constraining and as overly positivistic, insufficiently flexible to permit the sort of inquiry scholars now deemed important.

C. LEGAL CULTURE AND LEGAL IDEOLOGY

I have suggested that the shift from dispute analysis to studies of legal consciousness was not a unique occurrence in the law and society field but that it expressed a recurring tension. The interpretive analysis of belief, perception, meaning, and subjectivity is to be found in law and society research almost from the beginning. Sometimes this emphasis is distinguished from the study of behavior and sometimes it is linked to it. Sometimes it is assumed that only qualitative research methods are suited to such analysis, but at other times a variety of research methods are seen as appropriate. Ethnographic studies of non-Western societies by law and society scholars have long reinforced this sense that it is important to consider variations in culturally based understandings, practices, perceptions, attitudes, and beliefs.

The term "legal culture" appears with particular prominence as early as the late 1960s in the work of Friedman (1969; see also 1989; 1990) and subsequently in writings by Sarat (1977), Macaulay (1987a; 1989), Yngvesson (1989), and others. Friedman described legal culture in terms of "the values and attitudes which bind the system together, and which determine the place of the legal system in the culture of the society as a whole" (1969: 34). To explore a society's legal culture, researchers would have to address such questions as:

> What kind of training and habits do the lawyers and judges have? What do people think of law? Do groups or individuals willingly go to court? For what purposes do people turn to lawyers; for what purposes do they make use of other officials and intermediaries? Is there respect for law, government, tradition? What is the relationship between class structure and the use or nonuse of legal institutions? What informal social controls exist in addition to or in place of formal ones? Who prefers which kind of controls, and why? (Friedman 1969: 34)

Friedman stresses that any legal system as a totality must be understood in terms of its structural components (legal institutions) and its substantive components (the laws themselves) as well as its cultural components. Yet legal culture affects the workings of the other two components and determines when and how they are used: "It is the legal culture, that is, the network of values and attitudes relating to law, which determines when and why and where people turn to law or government, or turn away" (Friedman 1969: 34).

Legal culture, then, determines the efficacy and the meaning of laws and legal institutions in a given culture. It determines which laws will "penetrate" into society and which ones will not. Thus, in two societies with identical laws and legal institutions but different legal cultures, there might be completely different patterns of legal administration, law use, and legal attitudes and values (see Friedman 1990: 213 for a recent, but similar, explanation of the concept of legal culture).

The concept of legal culture surfaces repeatedly in law and society research of the 1970s and 1980s. It is seen in Macaulay's (1987a; 1989) speculation on the significance of television and baseball for law in America; it is seen, as well, in Sarat's (1977) summary of survey evidence on American attitudes toward police, lawyers, courts, and civil liberties. The concept of legal culture was an early expression of an important but elusive aspect of the law and society field for which researchers have not always found a more precise name. It conveyed the culturally grounded, subjective dimension of law and society scholarship that emphasized shared attitudes, values, perceptions, and meanings. It was this set of concerns that continually tugged at law and society researchers from one direction even when they felt themselves drawn in a rather different direction by behaviorism, objectivism, and positivism, or by individualized microstudies.

The term "legal culture" is not free from its own problems and limitations, and a number of difficult questions are raised by research on legal culture: Social scientists disagree about definitions of culture, but whatever definition one settles on, should it not include law rather than requiring a separate specification of that which is legal about—or in—culture? Is culture properly understood as merely a "network of values and attitudes" rather than, in the Comaroffs' (1992: 27) words, "a historically situated, historically unfolding ensemble of signifiers-in-action"? How should we deal with the likelihood that some individuals and groups do not share in those values and attitudes and that peoples' values and attitudes, even if they could be adequately ascertained, continually change with time and experience? Is it appropriate to speak of legal culture in terms of "values and attitudes" as phenomena that can be understood apart from the everyday practices that shape and are shaped by them? Is there such a thing as the legal culture of large national groups such as the Americans, French, and Japanese, or are cultural boundaries drawn differently from national boundaries? Most important, for purposes of this essay, does law matter for the constituting of legal culture, or is legal culture significant only for its constraining or enabling effects on law?

The cluster of ideas and emphases associated with legal culture has had a remarkable resilience in law and society research over nearly three decades. Some scholars interested in pressing such issues have recently invoked the concept of "legal ideology" rather than "legal culture." The use of this term no doubt reflects the influence during the 1980s of critical legal studies and postmodern theory (particularly the work of Bourdieu, de Certeau, and Foucault) on law and society research. As we have already seen, ideology and culture are by no means cognate terms. Yet the connections between recent discussions of legal ideology by law and society scholars and earlier writings on "legal culture" by Friedman and others are quite apparent despite these differences and despite the introduction of perspectives derived from the work of critical social and legal theorists.

In a special issue of the *Law and Society Review* on legal ideology, the editors' introduction (1988; written collectively by members of the Amherst Seminar) acknowledged the multiple and often inconsistent meanings that have been associated with the term. Their approach was to define "legal ideology" in terms of four "conceptual moves" in law and society research. First, studies of legal ideology involve a shift "from focusing on concrete, tangible, and material interests to ideas and concepts in legal discourse." This "move" emphasizes the ways in which law contributes to "an authoritative image of social relations and [the] shaping [of] popular consciousness in accordance with that image" (1988: 631), rather than simply viewing law as a set of potential resources that individuals might or might not utilize to deal with their legal needs and interests. Second, studies of legal ideology "connect behavior with culture through the concept of social practice" (1988: 632). Here we see an explicit recognition of the problem raised by the concept of legal culture. The authors of the introduction emphasize that ideology must be understood in terms of the inseparability of behavior and meaning, as revealed in the everyday routines by which people carry out their lives. Third, studies of legal ideology regard power as a central subject of study, and they do so by assuming that power is apparent not just in the way resources are accumulated and deployed but that "power is organized and deployed *through law*, and through that organization and deployment provides the inescapable fabric of social life" (1988: 633, emphasis added). Fourth, studies of legal ideology necessarily involve attention to history and the changing historical contexts within which ideologies are constituted and transformed.

The concept of legal ideology provides a bridge between recent studies of legal consciousness and earlier research traditions in the law and society field. For some (e.g., Sarat 1990), as we have seen, ideology and consciousness are interchangeable terms; for others (e.g., Comaroff and Comaroff 1992), they are not. Yet the study of legal ideology infused earlier law and society analyses of poverty, legal needs, legal resources, dispute processing, and legal culture with a new set of concepts and emphases. Attention was focused much more forcefully on the culturally constitutive role of law and its capacity to affect the way people understand the world and consequently behave within the world. Rather than asking, as in the legal needs studies, when and how people choose to avail themselves of legal protections, law is now viewed in terms of its capacity to structure the choice process itself and, often, to prevent legal needs from being realized. Law is seen as a projection of the counter-interests of powerful persons and groups in the form of self-limiting understandings and practices imposed on those without power. Rather than focusing only on individual disputes, studies of legal ideology explore broad-based patterns of meaning-creation and social practice as they evolve and transform over extended periods of time. Disputes and individual case studies are useful illustrations of these patterns in action, but they are no longer the principal objects of study.

Some law and society scholars who have written about legal ideology might disagree with the assumptions or emphases of the authors of the introduction to the special issue of the *Review*. Yet all would probably agree that an important transition has occurred in the last eight to ten years. In the next section, I examine the implications of this transition for research on legal consciousness and attempt to connect earlier approaches and insights to recent efforts to employ new frameworks of analysis.

4. HOW DOES LAW MATTER?

In the preceding section, I attempted to locate research on legal consciousness in a broader tradition of law and society research. The map I drew was admittedly sketchy and, like all maps, distorted in important ways. There are many other subfields of law and society research that are relevant to the current interest in legal consciousness: I have omitted important work on, for example, legal socialization and identity, law and the family, criminology, law and gender, litigation studies, and much else. Even the few subfields I have selected for discussion were treated in a cursory and, no doubt, idiosyncratic fashion. My purpose was not to be comprehensive, however, but to emphasize through examples that research on legal consciousness has deep roots in earlier law and society studies. Although the terminology is new, the concerns are old.

I now return to the studies of legal consciousness that were the subjects of the earlier sections of this essay and examine their assumptions about how law matters. The preceding overview of some of the antecedents of legal consciousness research should now help us to understand the authors whose work we are exploring and the contribution they hope to make.

The six studies listed earlier in this essay provide a range of answers to the question, How does law matter? These answers can be grouped along a continuum where one end represents law as inevitably determinative and the other end represents law as a contingent force or symbol whose determinative role with respect to consciousness depends on local cultures and contexts. None of the studies would suggest that law does *not* matter in the construction of consciousness. This may seem a frivolous observation, but authors like Macaulay (1987a) are fond of reminding us that law, while important in some ways, often matters much less than we like to think. The issue for the authors we are considering is when and to what extent law matters, not whether it matters at all. Also, we must continue to ask what it is about law that matters: Is it the substantive content of particular kinds of law, or is it the images and ideas about law that people carry in their minds? This question corresponds to our earlier discussion of consciousness as aptitude or competence versus consciousness as perceptions or images, and relates as well to the conclusion by legal needs researchers that different areas of substantive law figure differently in the thinking and behavior of ordinary people.

A. POWER AND RESISTANCE

The articles by Ewick and Silbey and by Sarat move their authors toward the end of the continuum that sees law as powerfully determinative of legal consciousness. Both articles explain why and how law plays a crucial constitutive role, yet both articles also suggest how individuals are able to contest the power of law and find some wiggle room in an otherwise predetermined set of meanings and practices.

Both articles cite and rely, in part, on the work of de Certeau (1984), who presents a model of "practice" and "resistance." Essentially, this model conceives of power as emanating outward from the sources of sociocultural production to shape the practices of everyday life. Such practices become givens of our day-to-day existence and are associated with particular ways of organizing time and space as well as shaping the norms and values that guide everyday behavior. Thus, power is naturalized and disseminated broadly throughout most aspects of our lives, even when we are not aware that we are subject to its domination. Yet power is not totally determinative of all aspects of everyday life. Resistance to power is possible and frequently occurs in the form of "tactics." This term refers to the "art of the weak" (de Certeau 1984: 37) who attempt to "reappropriate the space organized by techniques of sociocultural production" (1984: xiv). Such reappropriations, however, always take place within the space organized by power:

> The space of a tactic is the space of the other. Thus it must play on and with a terrain imposed on it and organized by the law of a foreign power. . . . It operates in isolated actions, blow by blow. It takes advantage of "opportunities" and depends on them, being without any base where it could stockpile its winnings, build up its own position, and plan raids. What it wins it cannot keep. (de Certeau 1984: 37)

De Certeau's model is clearly apparent in both of these articles, which associate law with the externalized sources of sociocultural production and concern themselves, in somewhat different ways, with the tactics of resistance of disempowered persons. Ewick and Silbey analyze the experiences of Millie Simpson, who attempts to plead not guilty to a false accusation that she left the scene of an accident and drove an uninsured vehicle. To her surprise, the judge finds her guilty and ignores her efforts to convey the fact that her car had been driven without permission by her son's friend. Ms. Simpson achieves a minor victory by retaining her driver's license when she was supposed to turn it in and by having the court sentence her to community service at a church where she already worked as a volunteer. Yet it is not until Simpson's employers, Bob and Carol Richards, put her in contact with a lawyer from the firm that worked for Bob's company that the case is reopened and she is acquitted.

Ewick and Silbey interpret the first phase of this case, in which Simpson is convicted and sentenced for a crime of which she is innocent, as an example of power and resistance. The "terrain" of the criminal justice system is organized entirely by external sources of power, and she is forced to fit herself—without much success—into the spaces and practices that the law creates:

> The rules, taxonomies and operating procedures of the court flattened and froze time into these separate occasions. The spatialized modes of knowledge abstracted the actors from their continuing interactions and arranged them in static impersonal roles, moments, and performances. . . . The human interaction

that Millie believed was to be embodied in the paper was instead pre-empted by it. (1992: 744)

By her small acts of resistance—community service at her own church and retention of her driver's license—she merely "insinuated her life into the space of the law and, in doing so, reversed for a moment the trajectory of power," but this amounts only to "deflecting" power without actually "challenging" it (Ewick and Silbey 1992: 745, 746).

The involvement of the lawyer and the eventual reversal of her conviction is a more significant act of resistance in one sense: "Millie's contestation is now articulated explicitly within the discursive space of the law. It is a public engagement and official victory, rather than the private pleasures of her resistance" (Ewick and Silbey 1992: 746–47). Yet, in another sense, the formal legal victory only confirms her subordination to power. She has access to the lawyer only because she is a poor African American woman working in a subordinate role as housekeeper for a wealthy white woman. She is able to escape subordination within the criminal justice system only by relying on her subordinate social position within the Richards' household. As Carol Richards herself observes, "To get justice, the poor black woman needs a rich white lady." And, as Ewick and Silbey add, "the story ends with Millie's reinscription in a system of domination from which the law provides no exit" (1992: 748).

Despite Simpson's "reinscription in a system of domination," Ewick and Silbey find significance in her acts of tactical resistance. Legal consciousness is shaped and transformed through the "shifting experiences and understandings of men and women as they move through legal institutions and other arrangements of power." Acts of resistance are "memorable" and important to those who experience them and help to forge identity "in the cracks of the law" (Ewick and Silbey 1992: 749).

Ewick and Silbey thus base their analysis on a model of power and resistance resembling that of de Certeau. Law is powerfully determinative of the terrain within which Simpson must operate, yet she finds room within that terrain to resist and ultimately to prevail. Her consciousness is not constituted entirely by law but by her act of resistance as well. Law, however, shapes the form of her resistance and requires her to acknowledge and depend upon her subordinate social status. Nonetheless, the authors suggest that even such small and temporary victories on the "terrain" of the "foreign power" (to borrow de Certeau's terms) can "prefigure more formidable and strategic challenges to power" (Ewick and Silbey 1992: 749) and thus, eventually, reshape the terrain and the consciousness of those who move upon it (see also Ewick 1992: 761).

Sarat's analysis is similar in its reliance on the model of power and resistance. For the welfare poor, whom he interviewed in legal services offices in two different middle-sized New England cities, the law is a "web-like enclosure in which they are 'caught.'" The law is experienced as a series of "they say(s)," and the "sayer" is the "embodied voice of law's bureaucratic guardians" (Sarat 1990: 345). In this analysis, as in Ewick and Silbey's, law organizes the terrain within which the disempowered are left to formulate acts of resistance: "The recognition that ' . . . the law is all over' expresses, in spatial terms, the experience of power and domination; resistance involves efforts to avoid further 'spatialization' or establish unreachable spaces of personal identity and integrity" (Sarat 1990: 347).

Sarat finds that the welfare poor frequently do formulate acts of resistance, sometimes with the aid of legal services attorneys. The welfare poor, however, see no special significance in the fact that the attorneys possess expertise of a distinctively legal character. They perceive the attorney as functionally equivalent to the caseworker, in that either one can sometimes be helpful in "sending a message" to the welfare bureaucracy and creating "just a little space in which a self could claim recognition" (Sarat 1990: 364). Indeed, the primarily legal character of the welfare bureaucracy's rule structure is perceived as relatively unimportant by the welfare poor. They see the process as essentially political rather than legal, and recognize that the space within which they are "caught" is organized around personal power and "whom you know" rather than neutral legal principles administered by impartial and disinterested experts (Sarat 1990: 356).

Thus, when Sarat's interviewees try to oppose the welfare bureaucracy, they are as likely to invoke moral arguments as legal arguments couched in terms of rights violations. Whatever discourse they find expedient, however, the conversations "occur on law's terrain and depend on a vocabulary made available by law itself." Discourses of human need and of legal right both "reaffirm law's dominance even as they are used to challenge the decisions of particular legal officials" (Sarat 1990: 374). Yet the tactics and the consciousness of the welfare poor have a distinctive quality. As a group, the welfare poor tend to encounter a formal legal structure more frequently than other groups in society. Consequently, they are less likely to incorporate into their legal consciousness an abstract view of law as lofty, dignified, and impartial. Their consciousness, instead, reflects their actual encounters with law in the grunge and personal politics of the welfare bureaucracy.

In Sarat's analysis, legal consciousness is "polyvocal, contingent and variable" (1990: 375). It is shaped by the distinctive experiences of particular groups who are differently situated in society and who encounter the law in different ways. Yet legal consciousness, for groups like the welfare poor, is always formed in the context of power and resistance. Their tactical challenges never "dislodge the power of law or the dominance of legal rules and practices" (Sarat 1990: 376). Equally important, their understandings of law and their legal consciousness, however shrewd and insightful they may be, never succeed in becoming a part of the structure or the practices in which the welfare poor are enmeshed:

> [N]either their realism nor their sophistication guarantees the production of counterhegemonic views of law. Continuous, regular contact does not mean that

the welfare poor are included, or can establish themselves, as full participants in the construction of legal meanings or in the practices through which power is exercised and domination maintained. (Sarat 1990: 377)

For Sarat and for Ewick and Silbey, law matters a great deal in the constitution of legal consciousness. Yet it does not matter in the simplistic sense that it inscribes its meanings and categories directly on the minds of persons like Millie Simpson or Sarat's welfare recipients. On the contrary, Sarat and Ewick and Silbey seem to suggest at times that legal consciousness is shaped as significantly by tactics of resistance as by the imposition of power. Even when relatively powerless persons adopt a counterhegemonic view of the world, however, they construct it around the cultural shapes and forms that law helps to create. Moreover, the authors stress that the legal consciousness of resistance is not empowering in any lasting way. Tactical victories are temporary, their effects short-lived. At most, as Ewick and Silbey suggest, they may prefigure a more broadly shared consciousness that, in the future, could transform the status quo and change the framework of meaning and practice through which power is currently exercised.

B. COMMUNITIES OF MEANING

The articles by Greenhouse and Yngvesson provide a different set of answers to the question, how does law matter in the constitution of legal consciousness? As I have already noted, neither author uses the term "legal consciousness," but both explore the processes by which meanings are created and shared through social practices related to the law. In contrast to the power and resistance model adopted by Ewick and Silbey and by Sarat, both Greenhouse and Yngvesson present a model in which understandings of law and of community mutually constitute one another. Legal institutions, in particular the local courts of first instance in the towns studied by these two anthropologists, are among the sites where such meanings are constructed. Legal officials—lawyers, clerks, and judges—are important actors in this drama, but so are the litigants and the residents of the towns in which the courts are situated. The law is one agency for exercising social control, but others are found in local opinion and in the fabric of meaning local residents weave as they retell local histories and draw lines between those they perceive as insiders and outsiders. The relevant terrain is not predetermined by the law alone but is constituted by the continual struggles among local residents over their collective identity and the norms, practices, and social boundaries that should prevail in their imagined communities (to borrow a term from Anderson 1991).

Greenhouse explores the interplay between court and community in Hopewell by focusing first on the differing perspectives of the judge and the clerk of the Superior Court. The clerk is the descendant of a well-established family that has lived in Hopewell for many generations. He expresses concern about the rapid expansion of Hopewell's population and the unrestricted growth of the town caused by newcomers who have escaped from the nearby metropolis to live in the suburbs. He views the influx of newcomers as a negative social development that has produced negative consequences for the local court as well. Those he categorizes as outsiders are, in his view, quick to use the court, whereas those he considers insiders are not. The increase in litigation is thus "a signal of social fragmentation" (Greenhouse 1988: 693). The deterioration of social life is caused by people who reject the traditional Hopewell values of neighborly harmony: "I think that people are being thrown together more now, and they are quicker to go to court. People with good neighbors don't need courts—people just don't *want* to get along now" (Greenhouse 1988: 694).

The perspective of the judge is somewhat different. Although he was born and raised in Hopewell, local residents say "he is not from here" because his parents were not Hopewell natives. Like the clerk, the judge expresses concern with the rise in litigation and interprets it as "a sign of social decline" (Greenhouse 1988: 696). Unlike the clerk, however, the judge does not locate this decline in the history of Hopewell as a community but in America as a whole. Throughout the country, people are more prone to litigate because relationships and exchanges have become more distant and impersonal, because people trust each other less than before, and because the pressures of work on two-income families produce less stable marriages and family relationships. From the judge's perspective, Hopewell and its court have changed because the town has become a part of the regional and national economy.

The judge, speaking for one segment of Hopewell's residents, views growth and development in generally positive terms, while regretting its inevitable negative side effects. The clerk, speaking for a different segment, identifies more closely with the town's imagined past and is disturbed by the values and behavior of those he identifies as newcomers. His views are echoed by other longtime residents: "One woman says, 'They just came to take our money and make trouble.' Another woman refers to the people 'with dollar signs in their eyes'" (Greenhouse 1988: 696).

The Hopewell court is a site where differing perspectives are constituted and communicated and where struggles over the community itself are enacted. Greenhouse presents six short case studies and demonstrates how contending images of the community are associated with the litigants and their conflicts. She also suggests that both the judge and the clerk, as self-perceived "insiders," share certain perceptions of the cases despite their differing orientations toward social change, and that their shared perceptions draw on a "coherent set of representations" familiar to many in the town of Hopewell. These representations have four elements. First, the concept of community as a cultural category is based on "a fundamental distinction between a past predefined as harmonious and a future defined as perilous." Second, concerns about the future center on people who cannot handle conflict on their own, as contrasted with another category of people who can and who are always able to "get along." Third, approval is conferred on those who are able, through prayer and other forms of self-control, to prevent felt conflict from becoming overt. Fourth, the capacity for self-control is associated with "belonging"—to a community and to a family (Greenhouse 1988: 703, 704).

In Greenhouse's conception, these elements of what we are calling "legal consciousness" are shared by court officials and by a well-established group of longtime residents in the community. Contrary to the power and resistance model discussed above, Greenhouse assumes that the court does not deter-mine these categories of meaning but that it becomes a conspicuous stage on which they are embodied and played out:

> The symbolic role of the court is relevant here, not as an agency that can "do" anything about the encroachments of change, but as one that marks and measures those encroachments. If, as local people claim, newcomers in Hopewell are without the kinds of social ties that make other people prefer getting along, the court cannot change that situation in any fundamental way. The court reaffirms and sees reaffirmed the important distinctions out of which the local view is constructed. (Greenhouse 1988: 704)

The court thus "marks and measures" the perceived changes in Hopewell's imagined community and, in doing so, participates in a reaffirmation of the fundamental distinctions that constitute the local consciousness of an important segment of Hopewell's residents. Although this view of how law matters differs significantly from those of Ewick and Silbey and of Sarat, Greenhouse agrees with them that legal consciousness (not her term, of course) continually shifts and changes as these processes of symbolic reaf-firmation unfold. In particular, she suggests that the very reaffirmation of an ethic of harmony is used by longtime residents to justify its opposite. That is, denunciation of the selfish individualism of the "newcomers" carries with it an acknowledgement that "oldtimers" need at times to act individualistically as a matter of self-defense:

> Insiders acknowledge the importance of being able to defend themselves against the newcomers, and so justify an individualistic and materialistic discourse even as they devalue it. Insiders, then, can live in two value systems simultaneously: one (ours) that emphasizes affective ties and cooperation, the other (theirs) that centers on competitive self-interest. (Greenhouse 1988: 705)

Thus, law matters not only in the sense that it provides a symbolically im-portant stage where cultural categories and values can be reenacted but also in the sense that the reenactment leads to the continual transformation of consciousness in response to perceived social change.

Yngvesson's assumptions about how law matters resemble Greenhouse's in many ways. Like Greenhouse, she explores the ways in which locally contested meanings of community are enacted in the local court and projected back into the social context from which they emerge. Unlike Greenhouse, however, her emphasis is not on the conspicuous symbolism of the courtroom in "Riverside" but on a seemingly marginal process by which local citizens and police apply to the court clerk's office for the issuance of criminal complaints. Yngvesson suggests that the clerk's role, while less potent symbolically than that of the trial judge, is significant because he stands at the boundary between the legal system and the society of which it is a part. Because of his unique position, the clerk has to operate with skill in legal matters (although he has no legal training) but also in matters that require an understanding of Riverside's culture and history. Attentive to the system of meanings shared by various local residents, the clerk distinguishes that which is worthy of legal handling from that which is "garbage." In so doing, he participates in the construction and reaffirmation of a particular set of cultural categories that determine what the community is and who belongs to it.

Yngvesson, who observed complaint hearings in the clerk's office over an extended period of time, presents a series of case studies that demonstrate how concepts of both law and community are constructed in the interactions of the clerk and the disputants:

> By pulling the court into the most mundane areas of daily life, these hearings become forums for constructing the separateness of law while transforming the courthouse into an arena for "thinking the community," for constituting what the local community is and who is not of it, even as they involve the local community in defining the place of law. (Yngvesson 1988: 420)

The disputes become occasions for defining who is a "good neighbor," what lifestyles are undesirable, what neighborhoods are dangerous and disordered, what people are "brainless" and conflict-prone, how men, women, and children should behave toward one another, and how members of a community should conduct themselves during a time of perceived social change. The complaint hearings, in Yngvesson's view, construct the law as well as the community. While the court is defined as an inappropriate site for "garbage cases," litigation is not in itself condemned. In appropriate circumstances, it is important to define some kinds of conflict as essentially legal in order to preserve the social order and protect time-honored concepts of "rights to property, privacy, and to live in peace." The clerk has to deploy two rather different "images of order and relationship to develop the meaning of events in a complaint and to argue for issuance or denial" (Yngvesson 1988: 444). One image centers on harmonious interactions among neighbors who care about one another; the other centers on the more individualistic imagery of rights.

Yngvesson, like Greenhouse, suggests that law matters in large part because of the symbolic centrality of the local court:

> Prominently placed at the cultural and political center of New England towns, the courthouse seems to stand guard. In Riverside, as elsewhere, it recalls a colonial republican tradition in which virtuous, public-spirited citizens keep

watch, protecting the "community of visible saints" from corrupt forces within and beyond its boundaries. (Yngvesson 1988: 444)

In contrast to the studies by Ewick and Silbey and by Sarat, however, Yngvesson problematizes the concept of law and views the social construction of the legal as part of the same process as the social (and legal) construction of the community. Both aspects of this process require study; neither is taken as a given.

Thus, Yngvesson does not start with the assumption that law marks out a terrain that must be negotiated by the clerk and the disputants. Law is not simply imposed on the people Yngvesson studies. Instead, she views the legal and social terrain as mutually negotiated. The law has power, but its power is inseparable from the social context within which it functions and whose categories of meaning pervade the workings of legal institutions and actors. Yngvesson therefore poses a paradox: the clerk has power in both the legal and the social sense, yet the power is completely dependent on his ability to understand and reaffirm cultural meanings located in the community outside the courthouse:

> [W]hile he is the dominant figure in the hearings, his power is contingent, dependent not only on his authority as a legal official but also on his knowledge of, stature in, and connections to the local community, and his rhetorical skill in using these to define conflicts in particular ways. Paradoxically, then, the clerk is most powerful when he is most connected. (Yngvesson 1988: 444)

The paradox of legal power, although articulated in an especially compelling fashion in Yngvesson's work, reminds us of the line of law and society research stretching back to earlier concerns with legal culture. The law, a central symbol of power and social order, depends for its influence on the very culture it attempts to control.

C. SUMMARY

I have explored a continuum of perspectives on the question of how law matters in the constitution of legal consciousness. At one end of the continuum, the power and resistance model sees law as significant because of its capacity to organize the categories, structures, meanings, and practices which less powerful people must then negotiate as they attempt to reclaim some portion of social space for their own. At the other end of the continuum, the communities of meaning model sees law as significant because of its symbolic centrality in the struggle among social groups to develop authoritative definitions of community, of social order and belonging, of appropriate behavior, and of law itself.

The two approaches are not mutually exclusive; they are points on a continuum rather than dichotomous alternatives. There is considerable overlap in the theoretical foundations of both approaches, and it is this overlap that defines the study of legal consciousness as a subfield distinct from the earlier law and society research traditions we have considered above. Yet, in their conclusions about how law matters, the two approaches are clearly distinguishable. In part, I would suggest, the difference can be understood in terms of a point made earlier in this essay: that legal consciousness can be understood either in terms of legal aptitude or competence or in terms of perceptions and images of the law. Writers who rely on the power and resistance approach tend to emphasize the first of these two possibilities: "law" is conceptualized primarily in terms of its substantive rules and procedures, and consciousness refers to knowledge and facility in using them. Writers who focus on communities of meaning, on the other hand, tend to emphasize the second possibility: "law" for them is conceptualized primarily in terms of its symbolic power, and their research focuses on the ideas people have about legal rules and institutions rather than the extent of people's familiarity with the rules and institutions themselves. In this sense, despite the many similarities and shared assumptions of all six studies, those that emphasize power and resistance have roots extending back to the legal needs research tradition (which was concerned with knowledge of rights), while those that emphasize communities of meaning have roots in research on legal culture (which was concerned with "values and attitudes" toward law and legal institutions).

5. CONCLUSION

Law and society studies of legal consciousness are as notable for their continuities with past law and society research traditions as they are for their engagement with critical, postmodern theory. I am not suggesting that these studies are no more than old wine in new bottles. I do think, however, that the assumptions and approaches brought to these studies can best be understood in terms of the decades of law and society research on which they build. The authors of all six studies that I have discussed had previously grounded their research in the law and society subfield of dispute processing. And, as suggested in the immediately preceding section of this essay, the two differing approaches to legal consciousness I have outlined reflect law and society perspectives reaching back to studies of legal needs and legal culture in the late 1960s. The connections between legal consciousness research and other related law and society research traditions is unmistakable.

Despite these important continuities with past law and society research, it strikes me that studies of legal consciousness have sometimes forgotten important lessons from the past. In the excitement of applying contemporary social theories to the subject matter of law and society research, we have sometimes failed to reinsert some of the very insights that represent the most distinctive achievements of law and society scholarship. In this concluding section, I provide three examples of lessons from the past that should, in my opinion, figure more significantly in the emerging subfield of legal consciousness.

(1) Different substantive areas of law are associated with different perceptions, understandings, and behaviors and must therefore be distinguished in research on legal consciousness.

Studies of legal consciousness tend to speak generically of "the law" as if its constitutive effects on consciousness operate in essentially the same way regardless of its substantive content. There is reason to be cautious about such assumptions. The legal needs studies suggested that people behave and think quite differently about (for example) constitutional law or employment law than they do about wills and trusts or family law. In my own research in a midwestern community (1984), I found that people attached fundamentally different meanings and significance to the law of personal injuries and to the law of contracts.

It would be interesting to know if law matters in different ways when issues of legal consciousness involve divorces or commercial transactions or housing as contrasted with criminal or welfare law. The question is not simply one of social class, although class certainly figures differently in these different fields of law. Different substantive areas of the law represent different kinds of social relationships and interactions and involve different kinds of legal actors, procedures, and institutions. Law may matter more for consciousness associated with some of them than for others. Yet none of the studies of legal consciousness considered in this essay attempted to make comparisons across different areas of substantive law. All tended to assume that one could generalize about the relationship between law and consciousness without differentiating between different kinds of law.

(2) Law in society is multicentered and assumes many different shapes. It is not necessarily an instrument of state power, and its connection with the state is a problem to be studied rather than a fact to be assumed.

Some studies of legal consciousness tend to assume that law is a projection of state power or otherwise emanates outward from the centers of sociocultural production associated with powerful groups and interests in society. Yet law and society researchers have consistently rejected simplistic, centralized conceptions of what law is and how it operates in society. Different groups have different kinds of law, and internal rule structures of groups interact in complex ways with laws of a more formal kind (Moore 1978; Macaulay 1987b). Even if one focuses on "official" law, one still finds a significant dependence on unofficial or customary rule structures to determine norms of reasonableness or fairness. In such instances, the relationship between state power and unofficial sources of rules and meanings located elsewhere in the society becomes a problem that requires study.

Studies of legal consciousness sometimes imply a more centralized, simplified, top-down conception of law than is justified when one considers the lessons of three decades of law and society research. Prior research teaches us to be skeptical of claims that official laws are highly effective in organizing social behavior or in controlling the production of social meaning. On the contrary, much of what we have learned points to the inefficiency and ineffectiveness of state law and calls attention to the making of law "from below." Perhaps earlier research was insufficiently sensitive to the more subtle and indirect effects of state law, but such effects must always be demonstrated rather than assumed.

(3) In some instances, official law directly touches and influences the lives of individuals, but more often law is mediated through social fields that filter its effects and merge official and unofficial systems of rules and meanings.

Law and society research has long emphasized the importance of intermediate-level structures associated with the activities of social groups that may have only indirect relationships to state law. Within such groups, state law may play some role, but its effects are uncertain because of the presence of other norms, procedures, and systems of meaning. In a recent article (1993), I have described an intermediate-level structure I call the "domain," and I suggest that from one domain to the next one finds significant variation in the construction of time and space, identity, norms, and concepts of community or belonging. Variations in domains produce radical differences in the effect of state laws designed to regulate behavior (in my article, I show extreme variations from one locality to the next in the impact of a sweeping federal civil rights law for children with disabilities in the public schools).

Studies of legal consciousness sometimes ignore the significance of these intermediate structures and assume that the effects of state law are uniformly distributed throughout society. In such characterizations, state law has a direct impact on individual lives. Yet law and society research has suggested that such direct contacts are not necessarily typical, and that researchers must often concern themselves with the ways in which state law is refracted as it passes through social fields (or domains) that provide the contexts within which individuals and groups carry on their lives.

These examples of lessons from earlier law and society research are intended as cautionary reminders. I am not suggesting that the six studies discussed in this essay necessarily ignore these lessons but that, as innovative works, they call our attention to new kinds of problems where earlier research findings may nonetheless prove very useful. The question of how law matters is an old one and will never be answered definitively. But as we adopt new strategies to address the question, we are likely to get closer to the truth if we bring to bear our most important and hard-won insights into the workings of law, culture, and society.

NOTES

1. This essay was written for presentation at the Law and Society Association Summer Institute in July 1993. Literature on legal consciousness has proliferated since that time, and more recent examples—by these authors and by others—might be selected if a new and different essay were to be written now. The basic premises of the essay in its current form would not, however, require substantial change; and the argument about the roots

of legal consciousness research in earlier sociolegal research traditions would remain basically the same.

2. The articles by Greenhouse and Yngvesson were subsequently republished in a book, of which I am the third author, that examines and compares concepts of law and community in three different American towns. The book appeared the year after this essay was first presented; see Greenhouse, Yngvesson, and Engel (1994).

3. Since this essay was written, two books relevant to legal consciousness have been published by these two authors: Yngvesson (1993) and Greenhouse, Yngvesson, and Engel (1994).

BIBLIOGRAPHY

Abel, Richard L. 1973. A Comparative Theory of Dispute Institutions in Society. 8 *Law and Society Rev.*, 217.

Amherst Seminar. 1988. From the Special Issue Editors. 22 *Law and Society Rev.*, 629.

Anderson, Benedict. 1991. *Imagined Communities: Reflections on the Origins and Spread of Nationalism.* London: Verso.

Best, Arthur, and Alan Andreasen. 1977. Consumer Response to Unsatisfactory Purchases: A Survey of Perceiving Defects, Voicing Complaints, and Obtaining Redress. 11 *Law and Society Rev.*, 701.

Bruner, Jerome. 1990. *Acts of Meaning.* Cambridge, MA: Harvard.

Buckle, Leonard, and Suzann R. Thomas-Buckle. 1982. Doing unto Others: Dispute and Dispute-Processing in an Urban American Neighborhood. In *Neighborhood Justice*, ed. Roman Tomasic and Malcolm Feeley. New York: Longman.

Carlin, Jerome E., Jan Howard, and Sheldon L. Messinger. 1967. *Civil Justice and the Poor: Issues for Sociological Research.* New York: Russell Sage Foundation.

Comaroff, John and Jean Comaroff. 1992. *Ethnography and the Historical Imagination.* Boulder, CO: Westview.

Comaroff, John, and Simon Roberts. 1981. *Rules and Processes: The Cultural Logic of Dispute in an African Context.* Chicago: Univ. of Chicago Press.

Curran, Barbara A. 1977. *The Legal Needs of the Public: The Final Report of a National Survey.* Chicago: American Bar Foundation.

De Certeau, Michel. 1984. *The Practice of Everyday Life.* Trans. Steven F. Rendall. Berkeley: Univ. of California Press.

Engel, David M. 1980. Legal Pluralism in an American Community: Perspectives on a Civil Trial Court. 1980 *American Bar Foundation Research Journal*, 425.

————. 1984. The Oven Bird's Song: Insiders, Outsiders, and Personal Injuries in an American Community. 18 *Law and Society Rev.*, 551.

————. 1993. Law in the Domains of Everyday Life: The Construction of Community and Difference. In *Law in Everyday Life*, ed. Austin Sarat and Thomas R. Kearns. Ann Arbor: Univ. of Michigan Press.

Engel, David M., and Eric H. Steele. 1979. Civil Cases and Society: Process and Order in the Civil Justice System. 1979 *American Bar Foundation Research Journal*, 295.

Engel, David M., and Barbara Yngvesson. 1984. Mapping Difficult Terrain: "Legal Culture," "Legal Consciousness," and Other Hazards for the Intrepid Explorer. 6 *Law and Policy*, 299.

Ewick, Patricia. 1992. Comment on Presidential Address: Post-modern Melancholia. 26 *Law and Society Rev.*, 755.

Ewick, Patricia, and Susan S. Silbey. 1992. Conformity, Contestation, and Resistance: An Account of Legal Consciousness. 26 *New England Law Rev.*, 731.

Felstiner, William L. F. 1974. Influences of Social Organization on Dispute Processing. 9 *Law and Society Rev.*, 63.

Felstiner, William L. F., Richard L. Abel, and Austin Sarat. 1980–81. The Emergence and Transformation of Disputes: Naming, Blaming, Claiming. 15 *Law and Society Rev.*, 631.

Friedman, Lawrence M. 1969. Legal Culture and Social Development. 4 *Law and Society Rev.*, 29.

———. 1989. Law, Lawyers, and Popular Culture. 98 *Yale Law Journal*, 1579.

———. 1990. *The Republic of Choice: Law, Authority, and Culture*. Cambridge, MA: Harvard Univ. Press.

Galanter, Marc. 1974. Why the "Haves" Come Out Ahead: Speculations on the Limits of Legal Change. 9 *Law and Society Rev.*, 95.

Gluckman, Max. 1955. *The Judicial Process among the Barotse of Northern Rhodesia*. Manchester: Manchester Univ. Press.

———. 1965. *The Ideas in Barotse Jurisprudence*. New Haven, CT: Yale Univ. Press.

Greenhouse, Carol J. 1988. Courting Difference: Issues of Interpretation and Comparison in the Study of Legal Ideologies. 22 *Law and Society Rev.*, 687.

Greenhouse, Carol J., Barbara Yngvesson, and David M. Engel. 1994. *Law and Community in Three American Towns*. Ithaca, NY: Cornell Univ. Press.

Kidder, Robert L. 1980–81. The End of the Road? Problems in the Analysis of Disputes. 15 *Law and Society Rev.*, 717.

Levine, Felice J., and Elizabeth Preston. 1970. Community Resource Orientation among Low Income Groups. 1970 *Wisconsin Law Rev.*, 80.

Llewellyn, Karl, and E. Adamson Hoebel. 1941. *The Cheyenne Way: Conflict and Case Law in Primitive Jurisprudence*. Norman: Univ. of Oklahoma Press.

Macaulay, Stewart. 1987a. Images of Law in Everyday Life: The Lessons of School, Entertainment, and Spectator Sports. 21 *Law and Society Rev.*, 185.

———. 1987b. Private Government. *In Law and the Social Sciences*, ed. Leon Lipson and Stanton Wheeler. New York: Russell Sage Foundation.

———. 1989. Popular Legal Culture: An Introduction. 98 *Yale Law Journal*, 1545.

Mather, Lynn, and Barbara Yngvesson. 1980–81. Language, Audience, and the Transformation of Disputes. 15 *Law and Society Rev.*, 775.

Mayhew, Leon, and Albert J. Reiss, Jr. 1969. The Social Organization of Legal Contacts. 34 *American Sociological Review*, 309.

McEwen, Craig A. & Richard J. Maiman. 1984. Mediation in Small Claims Court: Achieving Compliance through Consent. 18 *Law and Society Rev.*, 11.

Merry, Sally Engle. 1979. Going to Court: Strategies of Dispute Management in an American Urban Neighborhood. 13 *Law and Society Rev.*, 891.

———. 1990. *Getting Justice and Getting Even: Legal Consciousness among Working-Class Americans.* Chicago: Univ. of Chicago Press.

Moore, Sally Falk. 1978. Law and Social Change: The Semi-Autonomous Social Field as an Appropriate Subject of Study. In *Law as Process: An Anthropological Approach*, ed. Sally Falk Moore. London: Routledge and Kegan Paul.

Nader, Laura. 1965. Choices in Legal Procedure: Shia Moslem and Mexican Zapotec. 67 *American Anthropologist*, 394.

Nader, Laura, and Harry F. Todd, Jr., eds. 1978. *The Disputing Process—Law in Ten Societies.* New York: Columbia Univ. Press.

Perin, Constance. 1977. *Everything in Its Place: Social Order and Use in America.* Princeton, NJ: Princeton Univ. Press.

Sarat, Austin. 1977. Studying American Legal Culture: An Assessment of Survey Evidence. 11 *Law and Society Rev.*, 427.

———. 1990. " . . . The Law Is All Over": Power, Resistance, and the Legal Consciousness of the Welfare Poor. 2 *Yale Journal of Law and the Humanities*, 343.

Steele, Eric H. 1975. Fraud, Dispute and the Consumer: Responding to Consumer Complaints. 123 *University of Pennsylvania Law Rev.*, 1107.

Trubek, David. 1980–81. The Construction and Deconstruction of a Disputes-Focused Approach: An Afterword. 15 *Law and Society Rev.*, 727.

———. 1984. Where the Action Is: Critical Legal Studies and Empiricism. 36 *Stanford Law Rev.*, 575.

Trubek, David, Austin Sarat, William L. F. Felstiner, Herbert M. Kritzer, and Joel B. Grossman. 1983. The Costs of Ordinary Litigation. 31 *UCLA Law Rev.*, 73.

Yngvesson, Barbara. 1988. Making Law at the Doorway: The Clerk, the Court, and the Construction of Community in a New England Town. 22 *Law and Society Rev.*, 409.

———. 1989. Inventing Law in Local Settings: Rethinking Popular Legal Culture. 98 *Yale Law Journal*, 1689.

———. 1993. *Virtuous Citizens, Disruptive Subjects: Order and Complaint in a New England Court.* New York: Routledge.

BODY IMAGES:
HOW DOES THE BODY MATTER
IN THE LEGAL IMAGINATION?

KRISTIN BUMILLER

1. INTRODUCTION

How does the body matter in the legal imagination? In this essay, I address this question by examining how the body is seen within legal discourses. By asking how the body is viewed within the law, I suggest that the authority, meaning, and subjectivity of the law depends on the representation of the body. I also consider how the law matters as an agent in the production of symbolic images of the body in Western culture.

These concerns do not readily follow from the perspective of political liberalism in which the epistemological status of the body is unproblematic. In liberal legal discourse, the body gains significance as the "territory of the self"—a bounded sphere of the human being preexisting legal authority. For example, Jennifer Nedelsky argues that liberals use the concept of property rights to create "a picture of human beings that envisions their freedom and security in terms of a bounded sphere" (1991: 163). In the liberal view, each person is a rights bearer whose autonomy rests metaphorically on placing the person inside rigid walls protected from the invasions of state power. When the body is seen in legal discourse, it is viewed from the outside as the bounded container of the person. A bounded body is essential if the self is to maintain its integrity and autonomy of action. By definition, to violate the body is to intrude on the autonomy of the self—to act on the body without consent. In this notion of persons within bounded spaces, the body is the "territory of the self" because it provides the terrain in which the self is both isolated from others and protected from invasion.

Despite the insistence within liberal legalism that the body is properly understood as "outside" of the law, the law's vision is often the subject of contention. Disputes arise over the authority of law's way of seeing bodies and its power to make bodies its subject. Debates that focus on law's authority over bodies, such as controversies about abortion, sexual violence, the death penalty, and pornography, raise fundamental questions about the ownership of bodies. These disputes, however, rarely question the ontological relationship between law and the regulated bodies.

In this essay I seek to move beyond the liberal conception of the relation between law and the body. As a point of departure, I assume that the law is implicated in the construction of body images, and that those images always exist in mediated social space. As Susan Suleiman suggests, the significance of the body is not its "flesh and blood entity, but that of a symbolic construct. Everything we know about the body . . . exists for us in some form of discourse; and discourse, whether verbal or visual, fictive or historical or speculative, is never unmediated, never free of interpretation, never innocent" (1986: 2). I also make the claim that the body is always inside of law—bodies exist inside the representational apparatus of the law, and that law exists in part to regulate the body produced through its representations. I will contend that liberal discourses on law and the body are positioned against a constitutive view of bodies and law, and those discourses position the body outside of law's domain in order to maintain an instrumentalist conception of law.

The purpose of this essay is to show the progression from conceptions of law in which the body is seen as a territory "to be violated" to a view of legal regulation in which bodies are produced "to be regulated." My essay is divided into two parts. I begin by considering the debate about pornography, in which both anticensorship and antipornography positions appear to present unproblematic reasons for the law's interest in bodies. According to both of these positions, bodies become subjects of the law because it is necessary to protect them against violation. On both sides of the debate, the body is treated as a bounded entity, and the scope of the state's authority to interfere with the distinct boundaries of the person is the fundamental issue. The legal question is whether these bodies, or the representation of these bodies, are inside or outside of the law's authority.

In the next section, I move to the question of how the law itself views bodily differences. I complicate the picture by considering how bodies become subjects before the law because of visually marked differences of race, gender, disability, and age. The image of the person as a holder of rights is complicated when the law recognizes that the differently marked bodies become sites of oppression. In these cases, legal authority is called on to notice, and to say when, if ever, these differences make a difference in the exercise of state power. The problematic for legal discourse becomes: how does the law speak for "bodies"? Moreover, I will argue that the law's recognition of bodily differences is part of a process of increasing the state's regulatory power over bodies. There is a proliferation of law's interest in the body beyond the containment of the pornographic. The subject of the law becomes the regulated body, the paradigmatic diseased body. This perspective describes law's agency in a system of social control over gendered subjects, in particular, control over reproductive functions. I will discuss how the law expands its power, as a regulatory discourse, and how juridical and technological interventions are justified through the production of erotic danger.

2. BOUNDED BODIES

In this section, I want to illustrate how both liberal anticensorship policy and feminist antipornography campaigns rely upon similar conceptions of bounded bodies and how both seek to define law's significance by its "effectiveness" in transforming cultural values. I also want to show that both positions define the relationship between the law and the body in similar ways, and to suggest that this has implications for how sexualized bodies become the subject of law.

A. ANTICENSORSHIP DISCOURSE

The anticensorship position holds that the regulation of "explicit sexual representations of bodies" should be outside of law's authority because the "body" is not harmed by pornography. For Hawkins and Zimring (1988), authors of a major treatise about pornography in a "free society," the exaggerated importance of pornography as a legal issue is a consequence of the failure to see bodies simply as bodies (naked, but harmless). Hawkins and Zimring reveal their sensibilities toward law's position in the viewing of bodies when they suggest that it is indeed absurd to suggest that the law could exercise control over the "anxieties and hypocrisies of sexuality" (1988: ix, xii, quoting Harry Kalven, Jr.). Pornography, they suggest, is about bodies, and the law is not well served by the pretense of aversion to naked realities. Hawkins and Zimring also imply, on the other hand, that legal authority is incapable of containing and regulating "sexualities," which are from their perspective neither fully located within or represented by the body.

The opposition of law and the body is also illustrated by the ways in which Hawkins and Zimring confront what they call the "problems of definition." Hawkins and Zimring argue that it is not sufficient (and perhaps fraudulent) to make Justice Stewart's assertion, "I know it when I see it." They claim that "[a]nnoucing that we know 'it' when we see it represents an evasion of the responsibility for saying what pornography is. Even if by means of some kind of intuitive insight we were able to instantly recognize pornography, we would still not be able to say upon inspection *what it is that is pornographic about pornography*" (Hawkins and Zimring 1988: 20; emphasis added). These authors are seeking a rationale for judgment, while criticizing the claim of visual knowability implied by Stewart-like assertions. Those who claim to see the pornographic, and to know what they see, are, Hawkins and Zimring argue, likely to be caught in their own illusions. Yet Hawkins and Zimring's critique is also an epistemological argument about law's (or a particular justice's) incapacity to "know" the meaning of sexual behavior from representations of bodies.

If there is to be a distinctive definition of the pornographic, Hawkins and Zimring argue, it must speak to how pornography arouses sexual response and behavior. For them, the issue of pornography is reduced to an empirical issue, namely arousal, and its significance in the legal arena is defined in terms of a causal linkage to violent acts. They portray arguments for censorship as attacks on the autonomy of bodies. They see the producers of pornography as persons engaged in physical acts (speaking, drawing, writing, photographing) of self-expression and they see the consumer as inhabiting bodies with sexual needs. Whether law should intervene is determined empirically—it is a question of the link between attitudes and behavior. As a form of communication, the effects of the pornographic can be determined with some precision. For example, in response to research conducted on the effects of pornography on male viewers, they conclude: "[b]ut if violent cues produce the same harmful effect without sexually arousing content, then what is harmful about the communication is not pornographic and what is pornographic about the communication is not harmful" (Hawkins and Zimring 1988: 103). Thus Hawkins and Zimring assert that law's intervention to ameliorate any of the social ills created within a pornographic culture is only justified as a response to a clearly identifiable pornographic harm.

B. ANTIPORNOGRAPHY DISCOURSE

While Hawkins and Zimring treat pornographic materials as "communication," they also define the activities of both producer and viewer as taking place around the bounded space of the aroused body. This image of the bounded body and the boundaries between law and the body provides the basis for Catherine MacKinnon's challenge to a legal system that, in her view, protects the pornographer by making it "more important to preserve the pornography than to prevent or remedy whatever harm it does" (1987: 178). MacKinnon makes her case for expanding the role of the law in controlling pornography by describing harm to "bodies." She does not challenge Hawkins and Zimring's model of harm and legal action, but rather expands their idea of harm by taking into consideration the "rights" of coerced and subordinated women.

MacKinnon's argument depends on what I would call radical "nonrepresentation" of the body. She writes: "Pornography is not imagery in some relation to a reality elsewhere constructed. It is not a distortion, reflection, projection, expression, fantasy, representation, or symbol either. It is a sexual reality" (1987: 172–73). For MacKinnon the effects of gender oppression are "socially real," by which I take her to mean that the harm of both the abuse inflicted upon pornographic models and the objectification of women perpetuated by men viewing pornography is something real being done to real bodies. In order to make this point, MacKinnon redefines the pornographic gaze from the viewing of bodies to an act of sexual oppression in itself:

> The object world is constructed according to how it looks with respect to its possible uses. Pornography defines women by how we look according to how we can be sexually used. Pornography codes how to look at women, so you know what you can do with one when you see one. Gender is an assignment made visually, both originally and in everyday life. A sex object is defined in terms of its usability for sexual pleasure, such that both the looking—the quality of the gaze, including its point of view—and the definition according to use become eroticized as part of the sex itself. (MacKinnon 1987: 173)

For MacKinnon, the gaze is instrumental to male sexuality (but not to the law?). Pornography promises to deliver "before the law" the bodies of victims "bound, battered, tortured, humiliated, and killed" in an unmediated form.

Hawkins and Zimring also treat sex and bodies, as I previously argued, as "real," but unlike MacKinnon, they see no particular sexuality displayed in pornographic representations. In so doing, they call into question both the claim of manifest offensiveness and the heterosexual appeal of pornographic material. For example, they suggest that pornography as defined by MacKinnon and Andrea Dworkin "would be regarded by many as a reflection of pathological perversity rather than material that would sexually arouse the *normal* heterosexual male" (1988: 157).

Yet the significance of Hawkins and Zimring's "normalized" construction of sexual reality is that, like MacKinnon, they claim the social reality of their bounded bodies to be indisputable. Here, the differences between the anticensorship and antipornography positions appear to emerge as vigorous disagreements about how law does and does not matter. Hawkins and Zimring's claim that it "doesn't matter" is explicated, at MacKinnon's expense, by rehearsing their distinction between attitudes and behavior:

> A sexist society produces a pornography—and not only pornography—that reflects the relative position of women in society. But what is degrading to women in such material is not inherent in the nature of pornography. There seems to be no necessary connection between who is in a literal sense on top in pornography and the roles played by men and women in the social order. In this analysis, it is the traditional missionary attitude rather than the missionary position that is the problem. (Hawkins and Zimring 1988: 174)

In their analysis, the legal suppression of pornographic material would not produce a fairer society. Rather, for them "diminishing social concern" about pornography would be seen as a "positive good."

MacKinnon, however, assigns enormous significance to law, or to the potential role of legal action, in making a world without pornography. She strongly asserts that a woman's right to be free from sexual abuse is the same as a bounded property right when she states: "The Indianapolis [antipornography ordinance] is the *Dred Scott* of the women's movement. The Supreme Court told Dred Scott, to the Constitution, you are property. It told women, to the Constitution, you are speech. The struggle against pornography is an abolition struggle to establish that just as buying and selling human beings never was anyone's property right, buying and selling women . . . is no one's civil liberty" (MacKinnon 1987: 213). MacKinnon conceives of her antipornography campaign as the consecration of women's bodies by the law.

For both Hawkins and Zimring and MacKinnon, the law matters in an instrumental sense. In Hawkins and Zimring's analysis, the desire to live in a noncensoring society simplifies, or simply answers, the question of whether legal action is necessary (1988: 210). The police power of the state is implicitly described as poised for action: restrained from using regulatory powers as a tool for censorship, the state is "employable" as an instrument to prevent the exploitation of children or "other special dangers." Whereas for MacKinnon, the law, as it exists, exercises male power. Yet, what law gives it can take away—the law participates in the ultimate violation of the female person (pornography) while, in conferring individual rights (to pornographers) it makes their rights to self-expression ultimately inviolable. In MacKinnon's terms, bodies are placed outside of law and what matters is who counts as a legally recognized person.

This returns me to my original question: How does the body matter in legal discourse? Or, more specifically, how does the viewing of the body in this policy discourse about pornography matter? Hawkins and Zimring and MacKinnon are looking differently at bodies, and are looking at different bodies, yet for the most part they foreclose our possible speculations about what they are looking at. In their efforts to define pornography, they both give too much weight to what is viewed and too little weight to how it is being viewed. As a result, MacKinnon ends up accepting the terms of liberal discourse (which pictures law as external to and acting on bodies) and making her case against pornography based on its harmful effects. She then attempts to demonstrate this harm by producing the most extreme (defined in terms of heterosexual domination) representations of sex and violence. The focus on extreme material works to render invisible the representational process in which MacKinnon denies she is participating. As Beverly Brown explains, "[extreme material takes] a short step from seeing pornography as a reproduction of acts in the image to seeing it as a reproduction of images in the act" (1990: 142). Moreover, the representation of sexuality is "not just a matter of what was seen, but how that seeing was organized" (Brown 1990: 46). MacKinnon's perspective neglects the many ways in which the organization of viewing produces images of sexuality.

Because neither the anticensorship nor antipornography positions acknowledge how bodies are contained by techniques of viewing, bodies outside of legal authority are imagined to be "free." In this policy debate, therefore, the question of how the law matters rests on its capacity to promote freedom (either of expression or from physical domination). In liberal legal discourse, the problem of pornography is fundamental in that it raises paradigmatic questions about the power of the state to protect and intrude upon bodies in a free society.

C. MARKING BODY DIFFERENCES

The treatment of the body as a kind of detriment to freedom and, therefore, as something to be liberated "from," is a pervasive tendency of Western legal thought. For example, in the case of MacKinnon's antipornography position, it suggests that all women, without regard to the bodily differences among them, share a common form of oppression—the objectification of their bodies by a pornographic culture. In MacKinnon's terms, the woman-as-person who is the object of legal protection is represented as a universal gendered subject. The tendency to associate women's oppression with their embodied lives, however, leads to strategies for liberation that begin by denying the cultural value of their bodies. Moreover, it produces a kind of thinking about the need to liberate women from their bodies that ignores differences of race, class, and characteristics of the body. This critique is developed in the work of Elizabeth Spelman, who argues that "by looking at embodiment . . . we [come] to recognize and understand the particularity of experience" (1988: 129). Spelman cautions, "[i]f, because of somatophobia, we think and write as if we are not embodied, or as if we would be better off if we were not embodied, we are likely to ignore the ways in which experiences of embodiment are correlated with different kinds of experience" (1988: 130). The fear of our bodies, or our aversion to our embodiment, is the basis of thinking that ignores bodily differences that have been culturally deemed to be unworthy.

In a similar vein Iris Young (1990) describes the ways forms of oppression depend upon aversion to the body of the "other." Drawing on the work of Franz Fanon, Young identifies cultural imperialism in an interactive dynamic of aversion to the experiences of the body. "Others" are imprisoned in their bodies by this dynamic, and the "dominant discourse defines them in terms of their bodily characteristic, and constructs those bodies as ugly, dirty, defiled, impure, contaminated, or sick" (Young 1990: 123). Young suggests that the source of the construction of excluded groups as ugly or despised bodies is the "structure of modern reason's self-made opposition to desire, body, and affectivity" (1990: 124). From her perspective, it is precisely modern reason's "opposition to affectivity and the body" that perpetuates forms of oppression that enact unconscious feelings and aversions. The oppressor's unconscious fears find their way into the construction of the "despised" body of the "other" in ways that reflect the anxieties and instabilities in the identity of dominant groups.

Young demonstrates how images of degenerate bodies are constructed through what appears to be the infallible vision of a neutral and rational subject. The gazer, or the privileged group, is disembodied, while the oppressed groups are "locked in their objectified bodies, blind, dumb, and passive" (1990: 127). Young describes the aesthetics of the creation of "otherness" as a "scaling of bodies with the authoritativeness of objective truth" (1990: 128). The scale ranges from an apex of strength and beauty to a nadir of disease and degeneracy. The gaze can view degeneracy as it appears on the surface of bodies, and thus what is seen as loathsome or undesirable is "marked" as the embodiment of "others."

Young moves from this description of oppression as a form of bodily aversion to a theory of justice which recognizes the harms imposed on those who live in "marked" bodies. Young proposes a normative theory of justice that recognizes how oppression operates through the "aversion" of the body of the "other." She is reacting against legal notions of responsibility which emphasize intention as the basis of fault, and thereby narrow legal remedies to harms perpetuated by "people who know what they are doing and why" (Young 1990: 150). This notion of intentional harms, she argues, fails to capture acts of oppression that arise from "habitual interaction, bodily reactions, unthinking speech, feelings, and symbolic associations." In a sense, she holds people responsible for their unconscious aversions, by suggesting there are goals of social justice that require us to recognize how oppression is produced and reinforced. She sees this stance as involving an essentially political process of transforming the aesthetic judgment of bodies in such a way as to bring into discussion the previously unconscious image of the body.

The conception of the "bounded body" is unsettled when liberal legalism is explicitly challenged by these theories of body differences based on characteristics of race, class, and gender. When social groups become the subject of law because of their "marked" differences the liberal legal order is confronted with the issue of how to promote the freedom of differently embodied subjects.

For example, antidiscrimination law is conventionally viewed as both color-blind and sex-blind—in other words, the body has an unseen presence. In response to the fiction of the unembodied subject, Zillah Eisenstein (1988), for example, makes an argument for antidiscrimination policy that explicitly takes account of the body. Such a policy would treat what she calls "sex class" as a heterogeneous unity—and thus recognize that "the universalized woman of the construct 'sex class' must be specified in terms of her particularity, whether that be her color, her economic class, her sexual preference, or her individuality" (Eisenstein 1988: 36). How courts see and reflect upon gender differences depends upon whether these differences are perceived as unitary and static or socially constructed and historically contingent. Eisenstein envisions a legal discourse about sexual differences that is reflective about how the female body is given a particular identity because of its reproductive role and its gendered meanings (1988: 116). She argues that such a discourse would radically transform the idea of sex equality, in which differences (including bodily differences) are not seen as oppositional or lacking, but that a "person can be different and (not un)equal" (1988: 222). Eisenstein's theory of sex equality, therefore, brings into view the "engendered body" and also sees that body as it is mediated through legal discourses.

Yet once the body is potentially seen as a site of oppression, then the law is challenged to take into account the effect of "living" in a body marked as different. For the law to see bodily difference, it would have to bring into view the different experiences of both victims and perpetrators of acts of oppression. I discuss the failure of law to see the bodies of others in *The Civil Rights Society* (1988), where I argue that antidiscrimination law's projection of anonymous and typical victims has the effect of producing uncomfortable feelings of exceptionality among people who experience race- and sex-based mistreatment. When "victims" of discrimination see themselves in their bodies, in ways that act out feelings and emotions, they have difficulty seeing their harm through the lens of the idealized victim constructed in legal discourse. And thus "victims" of discrimination play into the oppressors' vision by ascribing less dignity and authority to their own actions. In fact, they are often unable to recognize their embodied differences (in race, class, and gender terms) as recognizable according to standards of legal personhood.

Patricia Williams (1991) directly approaches the question of how "persons" are caught in law's embodiments when she asks her reader to imagine what it is like to be an "object of property." In *Pierson* v. *Post*, she constructs the analogy between her great-great-grandmother (a slave) and the fox (hunted prey) on the grounds that they both were "either owned or unowned, rights over them never filtered down to them; rights to their person were never vested in them" (1991: 156). The law rationalizes its ability to cast its objects as "fair game" for those who have rights, while those who are the "objects of the hunt" have no point of view (1991: 157). For Williams, renegotiating our embodiment is one act of reclaiming the self or the parts of the self that have been disinherited by law's contract (1991: 217). Yet does this return us to the body as the "territory of the self"?

In her analysis of antidiscrimination cases, Judith Grbich (1990) argues that judges reveal their own embodied imaginings of typical persons in their attempts to embody differences in the law. Grbich raises the question of whether the "expression of rights [can] be used by oppressed groups to change the concept of what is just and unjust" (1990: 63). For Grbich (drawing on a blend of MacKinnon and Foucault), law constructs representations of the "male experience of power." As she puts it: "Law becomes a theory of embodied imagination, the metaphors of 'being' in the world, and the feminist legal theory project becomes the task of engaging with those practices which appear to have excluded women's imaginings of life possibilities from conversations of humanity" (1990: 68). The effect of law is found in its ability to project these "embodied imaginings," which are male representations of women's bodies, as "if they are real" and to put women in the position of "simulating another's reality." In cases in which the issue is whether differential assessments of cosmetic injury to men or women are admissible, the "nondiscriminatory" standards of judging require that the experience of the injured woman be represented in the same way as that of the injured man. Grbich explains the logic by which this paradigm of the representation of the injured woman is applied in an employment discrimination case:

> The particular woman in the sex discrimination litigation still has to live the present meaning of "woman." If she is denied employment because she is disfigured, or simply not attractive enough, she is required to assert that her female body is the cause of the employer's departure from normal employment practices. The dialogue requires her to assert that employment practices are the same for men and women, that male and female bodies are, alike, not normally judged for the aesthetic qualities in the employment decision. Whether she wins or loses, a simulable female body is asserted. . . . Under the present meaning of "woman" it is always she who will be scrutinized and unveiled before a court simply because it is still women who are constituted around male aesthetics and male sexuality. (Grbich 1990: 74)

Grbich demonstrates in her reading of this case how the "gaze," when directed toward literally and figuratively "marked" bodies, reflects back an embodied imagination that reinforces a male representation of women's embodied life.

In Grbich's analysis of law's embodied imaginings, we are provided a vantage point from which to question how the law matters. In the case of antidiscrimination law, the law matters because it is actively engaged in representations of embodiment. In this context, we see law not only as an agent addressing social ills but also as constructing the meanings of sexuality, gender, and bodily identity. Grbich, however, sees women, as bodies and agents, outside of law, and as having the capacity to transform their representations within the law. Grbich suggests one direction for making law matter differently: "If we begin to conceive of legal reasoning without its 'law-ness,' that is, not as a privileged representation but as just representation, we all become its officials." Thus the project of removing the "law-ness" from law involves revealing women's resistance to representations within law's privileged discourses, and renegotiating women's representation (as well as that of other groups who are the object of law) (Grbich 1990: 70).

Spelman (1988), Young (1990), and other feminists interested in the lived experiences of women describe how the recognition of the rights of those classified as "other" depends upon the law's ability to see and recognize their differences. It matters how the law sees bodily aversions. And it matters how law becomes an agent of the unconscious fantasies of the dominant groups.

In this part of the paper, I have moved from a consideration of bounded bodies to a perspective in which the representation of the body matters, in that the law potentially serves the interest of justice by taking notice of body differences. By recognizing the role of the dominant order in constructing body aversions, the law is treated as a vehicle of power that captures and renegotiates the images of bodies.

3. REGULATED BODIES

From the perspective of those who critique law's role in constructing body aversions, law is a powerful instrument that confers meanings on the body. Those writers have in common a desire to identify and reclaim law's power, and thereby produce a rewriting of the narrative about the body in law. In this section, I emphasize a perspective that focuses on law as an agent of regulation, as an extension of disciplinary power that coincides with other forms of control over the social body. This account of the regulated body is directly influenced by Foucault, particularly his reconceptualization of power in a disciplinary society.

In Carol Smart's (1989) appropriation of Foucault for feminist legal theory she argues that modern law has created new fields of intervention over women's bodies. It has become a method of regulation and surveillance and has extended its "control through the incorporation of medicine, psychiatry, social work, and other professional discourses of the modern episteme" (1989: 96). Smart suggests that "law's power has become refracted as technology has accumulated knowledge about women's bodies and reproductive capacities" (1989: 97).

This line of analysis is further developed in Linda Singer's book, *Erotic Welfare* (1993), in which she explores the relation between the expanding regulation of women's lives and the age of the sexual epidemic. Drawing on Foucault, she suggests that a sexual epidemic brings about a "rethinking of the relationship between bodies, pleasures, and powers beyond the call for liberation from oppression" (1993: 115–16). Singer identifies the emergence of particular strategies and apparatuses associated with the sexual epidemic— in which the site of struggle "is certainly bodies, bodies already inscribed with regulatory encodings like gender and race" (1993: 27). The emergence of the epidemic provides new occasions for the intervention and regulation of bodies and new social discourses that "provide access to bodies and a series of codes for inscribing them" (1993: 117).

Singer argues that the epidemic politics brought about by the AIDS crisis has both produced associations between sexuality and danger and opened possibilities for the proliferation of interventions into women's bodies. She maintains that, because the AIDS epidemic emerged as explicitly sexual, it provided an occasion to reinscribe hegemonic relationships on gendered bodies. This increased the opportunity to apply "epidemic" strategies of control to a wide range of gendered behaviors and to provoke anxieties about unregulated female bodies:

> The establishment of a connection between epidemic and transgression has allowed for the rapid transmission of the former phenomena that are outside the sphere of disease. We are thus warned of the "epidemics" of teenage pregnancies, child molestation, pornography, and divorce. The use of this language marks all phenomena as targets for intervention because they have been designated as unacceptable, while at the same time reproducing the power that authorizes and justifies their deployment. According to this discourse, it is existing authority that is to be protected from the plague of transgression. (Singer 1993: 118)

The logic of epidemic is employed on these new areas of contagion, spreading to fields in which the incitement of anxieties about women's bodies can justify expanded forms of control.

The age of the sexual epidemic has created a sexual politics in which women are ideologically regulated according to the strategies of "safer sex" and efficient body management. Singer draws the analogy between the sexual politics of disease and reproduction: "At a time when sexual politics is being figured as a struggle between life and death, women's bodies are likely to be exploited for their life-producing capacities" (1993: 86). In this age of epidemic, there is an effort toward better management of the reproductive process. This has the consequence of inserting "technology into reproduction itself" (1993: 86). This expansion of technology has made reproduction an active site for legal regulation, including issues surrounding abortion politics, surrogacy, and conception.

In the age of epidemic, according to this analysis, not only "diseased" bodies but women's bodies are subject to disciplinary responses that, thereby, justify further juridical and technological intervention in regulating the body. The theory of the epidemic brings us a long way from the liberal legal conception of the body outside of law. It shows how the body is within law, and how legal discourse is part of the disciplinary apparatus "producing" representations of the body. This discourse then constitutes law as a necessary mechanism for safety and protection of these regulated bodies.

For example, the logic of the epidemic law extends its vision "inside" gendered bodies. Rosalind Petchesky's (1990) analysis of the visual politics of abortion provides examples of what might be described as the invasion of disciplinary technology into the womb in the age of the sexual epidemic. She begins from a challenge to personhood as it is socially and contextually constructed in moral argument about abortion. She rejects a doctrine of fetal personhood because it demeans pregnant women as "physical vessels," and it disregards that "what makes human life distinct is its capacity for consciousness and sociability" (1990: 345). This perspective takes an interesting departure from Spelman's definition of somatophobic feminism in that it comes close to characterizing the person as her body: "While the self, the *person*, cannot exist separately from its body and its sensory apparatus, which is the biological precondition for its consciousness, the body predates the self and may survive its extinction (as consciousness)" (1990: 349). Petchesky seems to argue that the body, and therefore, the self, only exists in a social context. She defines pregnancy as a mutually dependent relationship between mother and fetus, yet one that does not take on its full human dimensions until consciousness emerges out of "reciprocal sensory activity" (1990: 350).

The visual dynamics of the invasion into the womb are revealed in Petchesky's analysis of the movie *The Silent Scream*. She considers how fetal images, through the use of ultrasound technologies, become a vehicle for projecting the consciousness of pregnant women and the reality of the unborn child in contests over reproductive politics. Petchesky argues that fetal images, presented as "autonomous, atomized mini-space hero[es]" (1987: 64), rely on a form of technology that disrupts the definition of women's bodies:

> Such images blur the boundary between foetus and baby; they reinforce that idea that the foetus' identity as separate and autonomous from the mother (the "living, separate child") exists from the start. Obstetrical technologies of the visualization and electronic/surgical intervention thus disrupt the very definition, as traditionally understood, of the "inside" and "outside" of a woman's body, of pregnancy as an interior experience. Increasingly who controls the interpretations of bodily boundaries in medical hermeneutics [becomes] a major feminist issue. (Petchesky 1987: 65)

Petchesky's description of the new technologies of viewing that reach inside the woman's body shows the effects of both medical and legal discourse in making the body into a penetrable social space. The production of *The Silent Scream*, it might be argued in Singer's terms, is an advertisement in which women are positioned as "counterforces" to life. The body is repackaged and assessed by a technological apparatus of viewing. This in turn allows for the visual displacement of the woman's body in favor of the newly visualized fetus. In another sense, the "technodynamic aesthetic" (Petchesky 1987: 87) of the ultrasound devices makes sexuality of reproduction "safe," in that it regulates reproduction in socially desirable ways (for the production of new families).

Another example is found in the advent of surrogacy contracts which present a new field of regulating women's bodies that involves both technological innovations and revisions of legal doctrine. Carol Smart's analysis (1989) of the official government responses to surrogacy contracts in Britain links efforts to restrain these contracts to a process of criminalization of women's bodies. The legal response to surrogacy, Smart suggests, comes from the challenge it poses "to basic patriarchal attitudes about the ownership of women's bodies (wombs) and the idealized notion of motherhood" (1989: 109). Surrogacy is rejected largely because of its incompatibility with other forms of reproductive regulations. Singer also notes the significance of surrogacy as part of the reproductive regulatory apparatus and highlights the opportunities for the Baby M case to create discourses about how women's bodies will be circulated and managed and how "issues of sexual safety will be resolved" (1993: 90). Yet she concludes, like Smart, that legal determinations move toward the criminalization of such use of women's bodies: "The courts' decisions to withhold the baby from Mrs. Whitehead are also part of their larger strategic agendas, to limit surrogacy as a practice, and to eliminate monetary exchange from surrogacy arrangements" (Singer 1993: 96).

The political economy of surrogacy, in effect, puts economic limits on women's reproductive freedom and allows the state to both regulate the "free" use of women's bodies and defend obligations that are made freely. Therefore, "women are [reproductively] free only when they are also economically exploited." The effect of the Baby M decision, according to Singer, is to allow for the selective use of technologies in ways that advantage men and to potentially enlarge the "reproductive brigade" of women. Ultimately the result is to secure men's positions in systems of economic and reproductive exploitation (1993: 98). Singer contends that:

> The Baby M decision therefore has particular utility at a time when sexuality is figured as an epidemic that is out of control, by authorizing ways of controlling sexual exchanges by subjecting women's bodies to gender-specific regulations, technologies, and tactics. It also helps to extend male hegemony over reproduction to cover the consequences of the new fertility and social technology, while concomitantly increasing the risks accruing to women. (Singer 1993: 98)

In the case of surrogacy arrangements, legal regulations expand the scope of preexisting prerogatives of patriarchy and economic advantage.

The major consequence of the insertion of technology into the reproductive process, according to Singer, is to "increase men's control over reproduction while reducing their accountability" (1993: 86). The expansion of technology benefits men's abilities to maintain control over reproductive processes without incurring responsibilities for the consequences of reproduction. Martha Fineman provides an example of an analysis critical of this type of intervention in reproduction when she suggests that proposals made to use law to encourage male responsibility for birth control make way for more coercive policy reforms directed at "irresponsible production" (1993: 233). The result is that women are punished despite the appearance of an "incentive-disincentive system" focused on men. Fineman's analysis helps to show the way regulatory policies in the age of epidemic work. She shows how the resort to the law becomes a mechanism for "fashioning prohibitions and determining punishments" usually targeted at women.

In response to the question of how law matters in the regulation of the body, this analysis of the age of the sexual epidemic demonstrates the growing criminalization of gendered subjects. This in turn produces what Singer terms a "highly marketable excess" of criminality, in that the "regulatory power preserves and increases the very criminality that it claims to oppose, becoming the paradigm of contagious criminality that justifies its own interventionist strategies" (1993: 44). This rapid growth of criminality also has its manifestations in the production of sex crimes, in which both victims and criminals are inscribed with fears about sexual safety. In these spectacles, narratives about day-care abuse, gang rape, and family murders are projected in highly visible legal settings thereby allowing for social coding of the private sexual realms (Singer 1993: 43). For example, in my own recent work I have been interested in the way that interracial gang rape trials perpetuate erotic fantasies about racial danger that code both white women and black men as socially marked bodies. Applying Singer's analysis, these cases are examples of the intensification of forms of deviance that perpetuate discourses of criminalization and ultimately normalize the behavior of both "victims" and "criminals."

This contagious criminalization and the perpetual incitement of sexualized crime create highly visible dramas that call for law's intervention to protect women from dangerous sexualities. Epidemic conditions within late capitalism, Singer argues, create "strategic connections between advertising, marketing, and pornography; each represents and enacts a strategy of seduction" (1993: 37). Singer's analysis, in fact, enables a rethinking of the feminist interpretation of pornography, one in which pornography is seen as one of the technologies for the management of bodies rather than a social harm requiring legal protection. In Singer's terms, pornography is "an appropriate site for erotic investment in the age of sexual epidemic" (1993: 38). She argues that pornography along with advertisement places bodies in spectacles that create erotic needs and then reinscribe the body in terms of phantasmatic constructions. For Singer, pornography is not about the control of the representation of the erotic (in either Hawkins and Zimring's or MacKinnon's terms), but is instead about the production of the erotic images that can then be mobilized and maintained. In her words, "pornography is not the discourse by which one body is represented to another body. . . . In pornography the commodity is the sexual semiotic, that is, the phenomenon of sex without bodies" (1993: 38).

Singer's description of the "epidemic" of pornography brings us back to the question of how law is positioned in relation to the body. According to her analysis, the contests over the regulation of pornography are not only forms of constructed incitement about erotic dangers, but may also provide an opportunity for the law to treat bodies and sexualities as dangerous. From this perspective, legal regulations in which the law appears to be protecting the territory of the self (i.e., pornography and sexual assault) can be seen as creating social space to inscribe bodies with the sexual fears and dangers of this age of epidemic. The question becomes not how the body matters in legal discourse, but how dangerous the law might become to its embodied subjects.

4. CONCLUSION

In addressing the question "How does the law matter in the legal imagination?" this essay has critiqued the premise of liberal legalism that law exists to protect and preserve the bounded sphere of embodied subjects. Through an analysis of the pornography debate, I argued that both the anticensorship and antipornography position essentially rely on the same assumptions about the relationship between law and the body: that the law's function is to promote the agency of "free" bodies. The law matters because it must strike an appropriate balance between protection and autonomy of those subject to bodily harms.

Yet this conception of why the law matters rests on a vision of law that projects itself as without vision—all representations of the body preexist law's authority to regulate embodied persons. Liberal legal discourse, therefore, assumes that the law does not exercise its power through the viewing of subjects (i.e., its viewing is never pornographic) and that law is fully empowered to contain a concrete pornographic reality (i.e., to place boundaries on the viewing of naked bodies). This assumption unravels when the law is confronted with, and is forced to notice, differently embodied persons. Feminist theorists, in particular, have shown how the law engages in an imperialism of its own vision by reconstituting the aversions of the dominant culture. The law's gaze reinforces the embodied imagination of the dominant vision of differences based on gender, race, sexuality, and disability.

This essay provides a reformulation of the question of how the body matters in legal discourse. It turns this question on its head, by arguing that bodies are the construction of that discourse and by showing how contemporary legality has brought about a proliferation of forms of regulation of bodies. These analyses place the body firmly within the domain of law and, at the same time, raise further questions about how law constructs justifications for controlling the lives of its subjects.

BIBLIOGRAPHY

Brown, Beverley. 1990. A Feminist Interest in Pornography: Some Modest Proposals. In *The Woman in Question*, ed. Parveen Adams and Elizabeth Cowie. Cambridge, MA: MIT Press.

Bumiller, Kristin. 1988. *The Civil Rights Society*. Baltimore: Johns Hopkins Univ. Press.

Eisenstein, Zillah. 1988. *The Female Body and the Law*. Berkeley: Univ. of California Press.

Fineman, Martha. 1992. Legal Stories, Change, and Incentives—Reinforcing the Law of the Father. 37 *New York Law School Law Rev.*, 227.

Grbich, Judith. 1990. The Body in Legal Theory. In *At the Boundaries of Law*, ed. Martha Fineman and Nancy Thomadsen. New York: Routledge.

Hawkins, Gordon, and Franklin Zimring. 1988. *Pornography in a Free Society*. Cambridge: Cambridge Univ. Press.

MacKinnon, Catharine. 1987. *Feminism Unmodified: Discourses on Life and Law*. Cambridge, MA: Harvard Univ. Press.

Nedelsky, Jennifer. 1991. Law, Boundaries, and the Bounded Self. In *Law and the Order of Culture*, ed. Robert Post. Berkeley: Univ. of California Press.

Petchesky, Rosalind. 1987. Foetal Images: The Power of Visual Culture in the Politics of Reproduction. In *Reproductive Technologies: Gender, Motherhood and Medicine*, ed. Michelle Stanworth. Minneapolis: Univ. of Minnesota Press.

———. 1990. *Abortion and Woman's Choice*. Boston: Northeastern Univ. Press. Rev. ed.

Singer, Linda. 1993. *Erotic Welfare*. New York: Routledge.

Smart, Carol. 1989. *Feminism and the Power of Law*. New York: Routledge.

Spelman, Elizabeth. 1988. *Inessential Woman*. Boston: Beacon.

Suleiman, Susan. 1986. *The Female Body in Western Culture*. Cambridge, MA: Harvard Univ. Press.

Young, Iris Marion. 1990. *Justice and the Politics of Difference*. Princeton, NJ: Princeton Univ. Press.

Williams, Patricia. 1991. *The Alchemy of Race and Rights*. Cambridge, MA: Harvard Univ. Press.

LAW, SOCIAL CONTRACT THEORY, AND THE CONSTRUCTION OF COLONIAL HIERARCHIES

❖

JANE F. COLLIER

1. INTRODUCTION

Law played a central role in shaping struggles over inequality in colonial situations, at least in the colonies established by European powers since the sixteenth century. Law was the central discourse used within colonizing countries to assert and contest both political authority and control over economic resources. Inevitably, colonizers drew on legal discourses when asserting sovereignty over the peoples and lands they coveted. As a result, by claiming to institute the rule of law in their colonies, colonizers established— perhaps unwittingly—law as the authoritative discourse for claiming and resisting power over others. Colonists carried domestic conflicts over law to their overseas colonies, shaping hierarchies among colonizers, even as the discourse of law provided colonized peoples with a powerful language to invoke against those who would rule them.

In this essay, I will focus on the effects, both intended and unintended, of a particular discourse of law—social contract theory—based on the idea that equal "men" should make the laws that govern them. To highlight the historical specificity of social contract theory, I will contrast its effects on colonial struggles over inequality with the effects of another discourse of law, that based on the idea of a God-ordained hierarchy, as it was brought to the Americas by sixteenth-century Spanish colonizers. My narrow focus on social contract theory is intended to complement Sally Merry's broader essay reviewing the wealth of studies published on colonialism in the last decade

(1991). While she, too, focuses on the role of law in shaping struggles over inequality, she concentrates on law's role in promoting the cultural transformation of colonized peoples. I focus instead on contradictions within social contract theory as these played themselves out during colonizing ventures.

2. BASIC PREMISES

Discourses of law are always and inevitably fields of argument. Not only do assertions of power predictably provoke resistance (Dahrendorf 1968; Foucault 1980), but the language of justice necessarily conjures up its opposite, injustice or oppression. The two concepts of justice and injustice are mutually constructed; the absence of each establishes the existence of the other. As a result, claims to rule based on dispensing justice through law necessarily spawn competing notions of which laws are just and which are unfair or oppressive, as well as arguments about whether or not existing laws are being properly interpreted and enforced. These arguments, in turn, serve to validate the concepts of law and justice that make argument possible. As Bourdieu has observed, competing opinions establish a field of shared doxa, consisting of assumptions that tend to go without saying and so to become part of people's commonsense knowledge about the everyday world (1977: 168).

Because commonsense assumptions are rarely articulated, the contradictions they contain tend to pass unrecognized. In this essay, I want to offer some preliminary observations on how contradictions at this level of seldom contested assumptions shaped hierarchies within European colonies by shaping struggles over laws and their applications. In particular, I want to explore how a central contradiction inherent in social contract theory—the use of "equality before the law" to justify and enforce unequal distributions of power, privilege, and prestige—was played out in the colonizing efforts of northern European countries, particularly Britain, in the nineteenth century. I focus on Britain because most of the writings in English deal with British colonies in India and Africa (see also Merry 1991). But, as noted earlier, I will briefly compare the nineteenth-century colonization efforts of northern European countries to the earlier sixteenth-century colonizing ventures of imperial Spain in the New World in order to separate the effects of differences between their conceptions of law from the effects of their shared use of law as the legitimizing discourse for rule.

Since emerging from the Dark Ages, Western Europeans developed a set of interrelated concepts about sovereignty that were not shared by many of the non-European peoples they conquered and colonized. Europeans had a notion of peoples, linked to territories, who could (should) be ruled. And they conceived of rule as maintaining order through the enforcement of laws.[1] In sixteenth-century Spain, for example, "the state was fundamentally a dispenser of justice, and its officials were invariably known as 'judges' or the like" (Stern 1982: 293). But sixteenth-century Spain and the later republics and constitutional monarchies of northern Europe differed in their assumptions about the primary source of law and about the nature of human society. In Spain, the king derived his authority from God and proved his legitimacy by enforcing God's laws on earth. Rulers of post-Enlightenment republics and constitutional monarchies, in contrast, derived their authority from "the people," whose laws they were expected to implement. And sixteenth-century Spain was a hierarchical society, whereas eighteenth- and nineteenth-century northern European polities declared all "men" equal.

In sixteenth-century Spain, people were unequal on Earth, even if equal in heaven, because God, in his infinite wisdom, ensured an orderly society by allocating different privileges and obligations to different status groups.[2] "Justice," in this ideology, was defined as apportioning to each person and group the particular privileges and obligations that God had ordained for it. Predictably, this ideology spawned endless conflicts over whether particular people were assigned to the correct groups and over whether officials were correctly interpreting God's commandments. On a deeper level, the generally unquestioned assumption that laws were authored by God spawned conflicts over what God had intended and, most disruptively, over who had the authority to report God's will. Kings, as God's appointed representatives on earth, vied with priests, and both were occasionally challenged by outsiders who claimed direct access to God's mind. Such challenges became endemic with the Protestant Reformation. In fact, the dilemma posed by Protestantism, which made it impossible to resolve conflicts over which sect spoke for/to God, led Thomas Hobbes to propose a social contract among humans (Latour 1993: 9).

Substituting man for God as the author of law may have seemed a brilliant solution to the problem of Britain's religious civil wars, but it could not end conflict because central societal discourses are always fields of argument. Social contract theory merely enabled a new set of contending opinions, giving rise to a new set of commonsense assumptions whose implications and contradictions we are still exploring (and contesting). The idea that men author law has spawned not only endless surface conflicts over whether officials are correctly applying laws and interpreting the intentions of lawmakers, but also deeper-level conflicts over who counts as a man for the purpose of participating in the social contract.

Moreover, Hobbes's observation that "Nature hath made men . . . equall" ([1651] 1991: 86) has encouraged similar conflicts over "nature." Hobbes may not have intended to establish nature as an independent source of law when he declared man the author of laws governing society, but this was the result. Once Hobbes left God only the role of having endowed humans with the capacity for reason, he created the possibility that nature, too, was endowed by God only with a basic set of principles, rather than with a complete body of laws to govern all interactions. Latour (1993), for example, traces the development of modern science to debates between Hobbes and Boyle, arguing that Boyle invented the scientific method as a way of determining the laws of nature at the same time that Hobbes invented the social contract as a way of determining the laws of society.[3] Both of them relegated God to the background role of establishing basic principles, leaving humans to "discover" natural laws and to "create" social ones. "Boyle, just like Hobbes, extends God's 'constructivism' to man. God knows things because He creates them. We know the nature of facts because we have developed them in circumstances that are under our complete control" (Latour 1993: 18).[4]

The separation between natural laws discovered in laboratories and human laws passed by parliaments is not complete, however, for when Hobbes gave nature credit for making all men equal, he simultaneously established the possibility that nature created some humans less equal than others, and therefore as not entitled—by nature—to participate in the social contract. Hobbes's observation that "Nature hath made men . . . equall" has thus spawned endless arguments over what nature intends (i.e., "nature/nurture" debates) as well as controversies over who speaks for nature.[5]

In this paper, I explore how contradictions inherent in the intertwined concepts of "man" and "nature" affected struggles over hierarchical relations in the colonies established by European powers. I begin with a discussion of how these contradictions shaped relations between colonizers and the colonized, followed by a section exploring their role in constructing inequalities among colonizers, and ending with a section focusing on hierarchies within colonized groups. In each section, I will pay attention to historical processes, for the outcomes of previous struggles inevitably shaped the conflicts that succeeded them. In concluding, I will suggest how the contradictions inherent in the basic concepts of "man" and "nature" continue to shape struggles over inequality within our postcolonial world of globalized interactions.

Although I plan to explore the contradictions inherent in social contract theory by contrasting it with sixteenth-century Spanish notions of God's law, I should note that, in the early days of social contract theory, its social consequences were not very different from those of Spanish law. The first colonists from Protestant northern Europe, for example, did not establish egalitarian societies, but rather small commonwealths. The heads of such commonwealths might have claimed equality with one another, but they expected hierarchy to prevail within their domains, where dependent kin, servants, and slaves had unequal obligations and privileges.[6] Before the nineteenth century, when social contract theory became the central discourse used to assert and contest sovereignty in northern Europe, the most obvious difference between the social inequalities established in Spanish colonies and those established by Protestants from northern Europe lay in the fact that Spaniards imagined one, all-encompassing hierarchy in which everyone had a place defined by God, whereas Protestants tended to imagine a series of smaller hierarchies, each presided over by a head who participated in the social contract. But if social contract theory had little impact on social hierarchies when first proposed, its long-term effects were far reaching.

3. THE ROLE OF LAW IN CONSTRUCTING HIERARCHIES BETWEEN THE COLONIZERS AND THE COLONIZED

Sixteenth-century Spaniards who assumed sovereignty derived from God had little difficulty justifying the conquest and rule of ethnically distinct peoples. Spaniards, for example, easily interpreted their "discovery" of America and their subjugation of its peoples as a sign that God intended the New World to be governed by a Christian king. Post-Enlightenment social contract states, in contrast, found it difficult to justify ruling ethnically distinct others. If "men" were supposed to author the laws that governed them, then colonizing powers lacked a cultural justification for imposing their own laws on peoples who had had no part in making them. For a long time, northern European states avoided this problem by refusing to become rulers of native peoples— at least in theory. British colonists in North America, for example, took over "unoccupied" lands, "bought" property from native peoples, or made "treaties" with native "chiefs."[7] In other areas of the world, particularly those with dense, settled populations, such as India and Southeast Asia, northern European trading companies made "contracts" with native rulers. For most of the eighteenth century, this arrangement worked fairly well. Property-owning colonists and traders from northern Europe were governed by home country laws (which meant that their propertyless "dependents" were as deprived of rights as their counterparts in Europe), while native rulers supposedly retained sovereignty over their own peoples.[8]

This convenient fiction of nonrule, however, became increasingly difficult for European powers to maintain as native leaders became unwilling and unable to guarantee the security of persons and property required by capitalist traders and colonizers. By the end of the eighteenth century, for example, the British East India Company had ceased to be a trading company, and had become instead a military and administrative operation, directly responsible for ruling large tracts of land on the Indian subcontinent. But administrative and military operations were expensive, cutting into company profits. The company was able to make a profit for its investors only through its monopoly on opium, which it used to finance the China tea trade. Faced with a situation where it needed money to govern its Indian possessions, and where "more than half the revenue of the State was derived from taxation of land" (Stokes 1959: 38), company employees became de facto rulers, even as their efforts to collect land revenues undermined the economic basis of social relations in the Indian countryside. As famine and disorder spread, the East India Company turned to the British Parliament for help in restoring law, order, and prosperity (see Cohn 1989).

Once the British state accepted the task of ruling Indian peoples, three schools of thought emerged offering contending strategies (Stokes 1959). These schools resembled those that had emerged three centuries earlier when sixteenth-century Spaniards faced governing conquered New World civilizations (Borah 1982). One school favored retaining indigenous traditions. Britons influenced by Romanticism, for example, tended to argue for preserving (or rather, restoring) the institutions of traditional Indian rule (Cohn 1989: 134–35; Stokes 1959). Similarly, one school of sixteenth-century Spanish thought held "that the Indians, having developed their own society, were entitled to their own institutions and law" (Borah 1982: 266). A second school, supported primarily by missionaries, also favored maintaining a separation between the institutions of the colonizers and colonized, but for the purposes of radically transforming rather than maintaining indigenous traditions. Both British Protestants and earlier Spanish Catholic missionaries hoped to create utopias on Earth by settling the natives in communities where missionaries could supervise their education apart from the corrupting influence of other Europeans. A third school, reflecting the desires of government administrators, argued for transferring European institutions to the colonies. British Whigs, for example, advocated installing a British type of government in the colonies (Stokes 1959). And in sixteenth-century Spain, "crown jurists and most of the colonists, advanced the idea of one republic: the Indians should be assimilated as rapidly as possible into the European system and be moved thus to Castilian institutions and law" (Borah 1982: 267).[9]

The idea of imposing European institutions tended to prevail in the colonies of both Britain and Spain, but in both cases colonial officials adopted strategies advocated by the other schools of thought as natives' resistance and colonists' greed undermined efforts to establish "law and order." In British India, the "utilitarian" policy articulated by James Mill combined aspects of the Whig, Romantic, and missionary visions (Stokes 1959). And Borah observes that Spanish "official royal policy steered an ambiguous course among" the three schools of thought (1982: 297). In both colonial situations, those advocating respect for indigenous traditions tended to prevail to the extent that indigenous people successfully resisted attempts by colonial officials to transform their societies. And the missionary vision of radical transformation prevailed to the degree that the social, economic, and political changes introduced by colonial rule required indigenous peoples to refigure their commonsense assumptions about everyday reality (see Comaroff and Comaroff 1991).

Despite similarities in schools of thought and pragmatic politics, however, eighteenth-century Britain and sixteenth-century Spain differed in their ideas about the source and nature of law, leading to profound differences in the effects their policies produced. British policies tended to create a binary contrast between colonizers and colonized, whereas Spanish policies tended to assimilate the colonizer/colonized opposition into the set of distinctions that divided legally defined estates from one another. As already noted, sixteenth-century Spaniards assumed that God had ordained a hierarchical society, in which status groups held different privileges and obligations corresponding to their rank and social function. As a result, Spaniards—once they had decided that New World Indians had human souls—experienced little difficulty, at least conceptually, incorporating Indians into their hierarchical society as one more status group with its own particular privileges and obligations. This policy had the effect of playing down the conceptual opposition between Indians and non-Indians, making it just one contrast in the set of distinctions among status groups. This policy also had the effect of playing down differences among the colonized, encouraging Indians of various ranks and groups to unite as one legally defined status group in competition with other status groups.

Colonizing social contract states, in contrast, faced problems not only in justifying their rule over colonized peoples but also in deciding how to treat them once forced to abandon the fiction of nonrule. The ideal of equality before the law, in the double sense of equal treatment by the law and equal access to making law, would not only have been difficult to implement in colonial situations but was never intended to be implemented, even in home countries, where the ideal of equality served to justify and enforce unequal distributions of power, privilege, and prestige. Transported to the colonies, the contradictory ideal of equality fomented endless struggles, whose effect was to highlight and exacerbate the binary opposition between colonizers and colonized as well as to encourage ethnic group distinctions among the colonized.

In eighteenth-century Britain, equal treatment by the law meant equal protection for persons and (especially) property. Because "equality" was imagined primarily in contrast to the divinely ordained hierarchies of feudalism, it tended to be defined in negative terms, as government refusal to dictate the separate rights and privileges of different status groups. As a result, the ideal of equality established the concept of a "free market," governed by its own economic laws (in contrast to Spanish notions of God's hierarchy which provided no grounds for imagining an economy separate from politics or religion). Many social theorists have observed that "free" (i.e., capitalist) markets produce inequalities.[10] But this effect is actually a result of a basic contradiction within social contract theory, which, by treating unequally placed people as if they were equals, perpetuates and exacerbates existing inequalities. When the law requires equal protection of property, for example, it not only protects those fortunate enough to own property from direct actions by the propertyless but also discourages propertyless people from using political means to demand a more equal distribution of resources.

This ideal of equal treatment is well expressed by Cornwallis, a British Whig who took over as governor-general of India from 1786 to 1793. He planned to introduce

> a new order of things, which should have for its foundation, the security of individual property, and the administration of justice, criminal and civil, by rules which were to disregard all conditions of persons, and in their operation, be free of influence or control from the government itself. (Fifth Report from the Select Committee on the Affairs of the East India Company, 1812, quoted in Stokes 1959: 4)

Cornwallis's intention to guarantee the "security of individual property" actually led to endless struggles over property rights. If the contradiction inherent in using equality before the law to preserve unequal privileges fomented conflict in the home countries, it caused even greater problems in the colonies, where relations between people in respect to land tended to be based on principles other than those which the Europeans inherited from Roman law. In India, for example, people held overlapping rights in land leading to struggles among the colonizers (as well as among the colonized) over whose rights were to be considered "ownership." Cornwallis, as a Whig, treated Indian elites as owners of large estates; Romantics argued for communal tenure vested in villages; and missionaries envisioned peasants as owners of the small plots they farmed (Stokes 1959). Needless to say, the colonized took advantage of legal ambiguities and conflicts among the colonizers to argue for interpretations of the law that benefited their own families and groups.

The concept of a self-regulating free market, inherent in the ideal of a state limited to protecting persons and property, also caused problems for colonizers who claimed areas without class differences, such as parts of Sub-Saharan Africa, where the immediate families of producers tended to consume all of the goods and services produced. When such colonized peoples refused to produce a surplus for the colonizers, "irrationally" preferring to consume their produce and enjoy leisure time rather than produce goods for sale or work for wages, colonizers from social contract states found themselves having to violate their principle of equal treatment by the law. They had to impose special taxes or labor requirements on colonized peoples in order to force them into the market, creating exactly the kinds of legally differentiated status groups that social contract theory was designed to abolish.

More disruptive than the ideal of equal treatment by the law was the ideal of equal participation in making laws. As noted earlier, when Hobbes—and then Rousseau—invoked "natural equality" as the fact that required men to make their own laws rather than submitting to laws made by a king, they established "natural inequality" as the principle justification available to rulers of social contract states for denying other humans the right to participate in governing themselves. If "all men are created equal," then those who are denied the franchise must be classified as not "men," that is, as somehow less than human. Modern racism and sexism are produced by social contract theory; they are not unfortunate deviations from it (Fitzpatrick 1992). Sixteenth-century Spaniards were not free from racism and sexism but, because they believed that God had ordained a hierarchy of status groups, they tended to recognize gradations of skin color and gender instead of constructing and enforcing stark white/nonwhite and men/women dichotomies.[11]

Peter Fitzpatrick, drawing on Michel Foucault's analyses of shifts in Western thought, has written a provocative book (1992) analyzing the conceptual oppositions that rulers of social contract states developed in the process of replacing the rule of God with the rule of man. He argues that during the eighteenth century, when Western thinkers used classificatory grids to understand and manage the world, they invented the "man of reason" by conjuring up his opposite: the person who was incapable of rational, objective thought. European thinkers constructed "savages" as lawless, propertyless, promiscuous, and enslaved (to despots or custom) in the process of endowing "rational man" with the qualities of law, property, morality, and autonomy. This European image of the "savage"—constructed in the process of inventing the free (male) "citizen" of liberal democracies—proved useful to European colonizers as the fiction of nonrule broke down and they found themselves needing to justify governing people whom they wanted to exclude from participating in making laws.

In the nineteenth century, when European thinkers began using origin stories rather than classificatory grids to interpret the world, they invented evolutionary myths of progress, based on social Darwinism, to explain both the "savage" residue within rational man and why "less evolved" peoples could not govern themselves. Fitzpatrick (1992) observes that the "status-to-contract" stories told by nineteenth-century jurists and social scientists (most of whom had experience in the colonies) constructed colonized peoples as lacking the personal autonomy and private property rights supposedly enjoyed by evolved Europeans. Unlike civilized "men" who created nations through social contracts and who regulated themselves, colonized peoples were portrayed as unfit for self-government because they remained embedded in kin relations, held property communally, and were constrained from acting autonomously by fear of social sanctions. Fitzpatrick observes, ironically, that Europeans used images of dominated natives to construct themselves as self-regulating individuals at the very time when European governments were extending their control over citizens through the disciplinary mechanisms analyzed by Foucault: schools, prisons, hospitals, factories, and asylums.

The shift from classificatory grids to evolutionary origin stories coincides, roughly, with the triumph of abolitionist thinking in Europe linked to the creation of "free" laborers. Cooper and Stoler, in their discussion of the dynamics of colonialism, note a break point in "the early 19th century—when the debate over slavery brought the new universalist discourses on economy and state into the colonies" (1989: 617), forcing colonizers to find new ways to distinguish the naturally free from those to whom nature had denied the ability to govern themselves. As Europeans began condemning the enslavement of non-European peoples "in the name of a universal definition of free labor that transcended the moral vision of any one religion or any one state" (1989: 617), European colonizers turned to social Darwinism to justify uplifting and civilizing the natives whose lands and labor they coveted. Evolutionary thinking, as Fitzpatrick (1992) notes, allowed European colonizers to portray themselves as helping the colonized toward self-rule, while endlessly postponing the postcolonial moment.

Because social contract thinkers tended to construct stark oppositions between those eligible to participate in making laws and those who were not, colonizers from social contract states had a more difficult time deciding how to classify children of mixed parentage in their colonies than did sixteenth-century Spaniards, who simply proliferated categories of racial mixtures. The problem became acute for colonizers during the nineteenth century, when increasing numbers of colonists led to increases in mixed-race offspring and the abolition of slavery had destroyed the convenient fiction whereby children born to slave women were slaves unless freed by their master. Ann Stoler suggests that European colonizers—faced with increasing numbers of free persons of mixed ancestry, often with education, who were challenging the dominance of European whites—responded by importing white women from Europe to "make empire respectable" and to provide the means for drawing a clear line between white people and others (1989: 634). Most earlier accounts of colonialism had accused white women of bringing racism and rigid moral codes to colonies that had previously enjoyed relaxed sexual relations between colonizers and colonized. Ann Stoler contests this view, arguing that the correlation between white women's arrival in the colonies and the imposition of racial hierarchies is due less to women's bringing racist and moralistic ideas with them, than to the fact that white men imported white women for the express purpose of creating a racial barrier between whites and persons of mixed ancestry.

4. THE ROLE OF LAW IN CONSTRUCTING HIERARCHIES AMONG THE COLONIZERS

Recent work, particularly in anthropology, has emphasized divisions among the colonizers. Sally Merry observes that Darby (1987), in his "historical study of British imperialism in Asia and Africa from 1870 to 1970, notes that European colonial expansion incorporated three motivations: power politics, moral responsibility, and economic interest" (Merry 1991: 896). The British missionaries to South Africa, whose writings John Comaroff (1989) analyzed, also recognized these divergent, and inevitably conflicting, motivations among colonizers. And these three motivations can be distinguished among Spanish colonizers of the sixteenth century. These three motivations, however, do not correspond to the three schools of thought about governing colonized peoples discussed in the previous section. Rather, they reflect differences in the interests of colonists—roughly the differences between colonial officials concerned with ruling, missionaries concerned with saving souls, and colonists hoping to make money as settlers, mine owners, or traders.[12]

Although colonists from Europe may have exhibited the same three conflicting motivations across five centuries of colonial expansion, sixteenth-century Spanish colonists drew on a different set of legal discourses when struggling among themselves for power and privilege than did later colonists from social contract states in northern Europe. As noted earlier, sixteenth-century Spaniards did not imagine a separation between the state, the economy, and religion. Because the Spanish crown had "responsibility for reconciling life on earth with the principles of a higher, divinely ordained law" (Stern 1982: 293), colonists expected the state to establish and enforce the economic privileges and obligations of unequal status groups as well as to oversee the conversion of Indians to Christianity. As a result, the major line of struggle and cleavage among Spanish colonizers occurred within the ranks of would-be rulers—between colonial officials born in the Americas and officials sent over from Spain. This struggle between colonists and the crown over who should determine the allocation of privileges in the New World continued until the early nineteenth century, when successful revolutions ended Spain's colonial rule.

Eighteenth- and nineteenth-century colonists from northern Europe, in contrast, expected the state to refrain from interfering in colonists' freedom of religion and contract. The state, in their view, should limit itself to guaranteeing the security of persons and property. As a result, struggles and cleavages among colonists from northern Europe tended to reflect their different motivations, with missionaries, bent on saving souls, and traders or settlers, bent on making money, coming into conflict with each other and with colonial officials over what constituted proper protection of their liberties and what marked improper state interference.

Comaroff (1989), for example, identifies "three models of colonialism" that reflect the different interests and demands dividing colonists. These three models, as expressed in letters and essays written by British missionaries in South Africa during the nineteenth century, were a "state model," a missionary model of "civilizing colonialism," and a model of "settler colonialism." "The state model, according to which the colonial government was seen to oversee the territory, had, as its first priority, *Pax Britannica*: the pacification of 'tribes,' under British law" (1989: 673). After pacification, the missionaries expected the state "to 'protect the aborigines'—from internecine war, unscrupulous whites and enslavement" by Boer settlers (1989: 672). The state, according to the missionaries, should not concern itself with civilizing the natives. Comaroff observes, however, that over time the state did interfere in native life—and in the missionaries' domain—through "the imposition of taxes, the limitation of chiefly authority and many other (typically legalistic, punitive) forms of regulation" (1989: 673). Not only did colonial officials have to maintain peace in the colonies but, faced with opposition from taxpayers in their home countries, they had to find ways to make the colonies (i.e., the colonized) pay the costs of colonial administration.

The missionaries in South Africa appropriated for themselves the task of civilizing the natives, which they hoped to do without interference from other Europeans. Unlike sixteenth-century Spanish missionaries, who expected the state to help them convert the Indians, nineteenth-century missionaries in Africa expected the natives to convert of their own "free" will. Missionaries "sought to 'cultivate' the African 'desert' and its inhabitants by planting the seeds of bourgeois individualism and the nuclear family, of private property and commerce, of rational minds and healthily clad bodies, of the practical arts of refined living and devotion to God" (Comaroff 1989: 673). The missionaries wanted to use education rather than law to reform all aspects of the natives' private and public life. "The nub of the civilizing colonialism of the mission—and it was, quite explicitly a colonialism, in that it sought to subordinate Africa to the dominance of the European order—lay in replacing native economy and society with an imagined world of free, propertied, and prosperous peasant families" (1989: 674).

The model of "settler colonialism" represented all that the South African missionaries abhorred. "To them, Boers were no more than half-savages: they led degenerate, unrefined lives, lacked a true European 'spirit of improvement,' and showed their 'monstrous' character by treating blacks as prey to be hunted and enslaved" (Comaroff 1989: 673). The Boers, who sought freedom from British rule after the British abolished slavery, probably did represent the most exploitative kind of settler. But settlers, mine owners, and traders in other colonies all came into conflict with missionaries over what constituted proper protection of persons and property. Settlers wanted the state to protect "their" farms and mines from native claimants, and to uphold the "contracts" they made with native workers. They probably also wanted protection from missionary and other "agitators" who urged the natives to reclaim stolen lands and to contest exploitative work relations. Finally, settlers, like taxpayers in the home country, probably wanted to avoid, as much as possible, having to pay for the government protection they demanded.

These three nineteenth-century "models of colonialism" identified by Comaroff (1989) reflect, I believe, similar conflicting visions in the home countries linked to the contradiction within social contract theory between equality before the law and inequality of property holdings. Like owners of large properties in the home countries, capitalist settlers, mine owners, and traders emphasized the protection of private property at the expense of equality. They wanted the state to protect the rights of property owners even if that meant consigning some, or most, people to remaining propertyless (and powerless). The missionaries, like propertyless people or owners of minuscule estates at home, emphasized equality over the protection of property, at least in the sense that they wanted all their (male) converts to own enough land to support themselves and their dependent wives and children. Colonial officials were caught in the middle, trying to balance the inherent contradiction between protecting private property and ensuring political equality, while reproducing the contradiction by equating equal political rights with security of property as well as persons.

These three models of colonialism may also have paralleled different positions in debates over morality occurring at the time in England and France. After 1848, as triumphant capitalism and uncontrolled industrialization disrupted European social relations and destroyed rural landscapes, Europeans worried about the loss of morality in their society. By that time, liberal social contract theory had clearly replaced God's great chain of being as the symbolic fount of law and order, setting off a debate over how to ground moral values. Social theorists, culminating in Durkheim at the turn of the century ([1893] 1933), envisioned law as the source and repository of human moral reason, arguing against religious holdouts who wanted to create God's utopia on Earth and social Darwinists who reduced natural laws to survival of the fittest. Theorists who wanted to establish law in the position formerly occupied by God argued that law represented progressive human reason in opposition to both religious "superstition" and the "natural reason" imagined by social Darwinists. Just as human *reason* should replace religious or traditional superstitions, so *human* reason required protecting persons who lacked reason (such as children, women, and savages) from the unrestrained forces of nature's competition for survival.

These nineteenth-century struggles over morality reflect the transformation in social contract theory that occurred as it evolved from an oppositional discourse during the seventeenth and eighteenth centuries into a hegemonic one by the nineteenth century. First advocated by bourgeois property owners in their struggle against the discourse of divinely ordained kingship, its assumptions became taken-for-granted reality in later struggles between nineteenth-century capitalists and those who opposed them. A similar, albeit much accelerated, transformation occurred in the colonies, as colonial officials—who first justified governing colonized peoples on the grounds of protecting the persons and properties of their own nationals from hostile "natives"—found themselves called on to protect conquered peoples from rapacious colonists and overzealous missionaries. In Europe, and then in the colonies, a discourse once invoked against "outsiders" became a discourse used by "insiders" to argue with one another, leading to profound changes in the role of officials charged with upholding and applying the law.

A role transformation from protecting colonists to protecting the colonized may have been inevitable in colonial situations. Sixteenth-century representatives of the Spanish crown, for example, who sided with colonizers in conquering native peoples, later found themselves trying to protect Indians from colonists in order to stem the drastic decline in New World populations. In both colonial situations, as well, officials were hampered in their attempts to protect indigenous peoples by at least two factors: colonists often had influential friends and supporters at home who could engineer the recall of overly zealous colonial officials, and—given the small number of colonists relative to the masses of the colonized—officials were often reluctant to expose conflicts among the colonizers that the colonized might use to their own advantage.

Although colonial officials inevitably incurred the wrath of colonists, different discourses of law affected the ability of angry colonists to form opposition groups. In Spain's New World colonies, for example, where the proliferation of legally defined status groups muted distinctions between colonizers and colonized, liberals who argued for establishing social contract states could claim to speak for all "men" in the colonies. In the nineteenth-century colonies of northern European nations, in contrast, colonists were hampered by the deep racial cleavage between whites and nonwhites from joining with indigenous peoples to establish separate states. In fact, whites in some colonies, such as the Boers in British-ruled South Africa, declared independence for the express purpose of preserving and deepening the racial cleavage between settlers from Europe and indigenous peoples.

In this section, I have focused on conflicts between colonial officials concerned with ruling, missionaries concerned with saving souls, and colonists concerned with making money, but conflicts also occurred within these groups. Colonial bureaucracies undoubtedly experienced the usual conflicts between different agencies, as well as conflicts caused by the thwarted career ambitions of individual officials. Missionaries from different sects, religions, or religious orders fought for converts as well as with members of their own groups for precedence and resources. And those out to make money inevitably came into conflict in the process of pursuing private economic interests, even as capitalist relations fostered conflict within enterprises between owner/managers and subordinated employees. Contending parties often turned to discourses of law for managing their disputes. Stokes, for example, observes that in India, "the Supreme Courts, established in the Presidency towns and presided over by judges appointed directly by the Crown, were regarded by the English inhabitants as the shield and defence of their rights and liberties against the despotic government of the Company" (1959: 61). And Stoler notes how the Dutch state cooperated with corporate authorities to prevent lower-level European employees from marrying, thus allowing companies to pay low salaries and reap high profits (1989: 638).

5. THE ROLE OF LAW IN CONSTRUCTING HIERARCHIES AMONG THE COLONIZED

Although scholars have probably written more about the impact of colonialism on social relations among the colonized than on any other topic related to colonialism, it is hard to generalize about the role of law in shaping hierarchies among the colonized because precolonial systems of social inequality varied considerably. Colonized peoples drew on very different resources, both conceptual and material, when invoking legal discourses to contest the power of those who would rule over them. As a result, the outcomes of struggles between colonizer and colonized, and among the colonized, varied from people to people, place to place, and across time.

In a recent book, Anna Tsing notes "a central tension that divides current scholars" who write about peoples marginalized by Western imperialism. This tension revolves "around the political implications of notions of cultural difference." One side focuses on "how the notion of cultural difference has been used [by Westerners] to debase and control Third World peoples." The other side explores the "empowering aspects of self-involvement with cultural difference." For scholars who celebrate empowerment, "the discourse of domination that seems most constraining is not that of encrusted difference, but that of white privilege falsely universalized to erase the struggles, accomplishments, and dilemmas of people of color" (Tsing 1993: 15). Both sets of scholars tend to fear and oppose the current rise of racist, ethnic, and religious movements designed to purify nations by using state power to expel or incarcerate those defined as different. But they adopt separate strategies for combating intolerance. Those who focus on how European ideas of difference have been used to oppress others argue that no peoples or cultures (even European ones) are pure—all are hybrids (e.g., Said 1993).[13] Others, particularly those who deplore the rise of racist and anti-immigrant sentiments in developed nations, document the creativity of persecuted peoples who have combated oppression by invoking and reworking cultural heritages.[14]

In this section, I adopt the first strategy. I explore how Europeans developed and spread notions of racial and cultural difference in the process of using legal discourse to assert domination over colonized peoples abroad and over minorities, women, and the poor at home. This strategy, however, does tend to have the unfortunate consequence noted by scholars who celebrate cultural difference. It focuses attention on Europeans rather than on those who resisted them. Resistances, however, are difficult to analyze for two reasons. First, it is hard to generalize about them because instances of resistance, like the outcomes they produced, varied from place to place and time to time, requiring careful attention to local histories.[15] Second, evidence of resistance is hard to interpret from the written record. Because Europeans, from the sixteenth century to recent times, have assumed that humans live in societies governed by moral laws (in contrast to animals whose relations are determined by base instincts), European scholars, and those trained in Europe, have commonly found bounded societies governed by laws (or at least norms) wherever they looked. Given such misreadings of other realities, a deep knowledge of local histories and cultures, as well as a willingness to read against the grain, are required to uncover the subordinated discourses of sociality that colonized peoples invoked when contesting European rule.

Although I focus on European discourses, I will explore how such discourses changed through time, due to resistance from the colonized. Europeans who invoked law to justify conquering and ruling colonized peoples simultaneously (if unintentionally) established law as a discourse that colonized peoples could use to assert and contest relations of domination. Resistance by the colonized, in turn, tended to prompt colonizers to revise the laws they propagated and enforced. In this section, I will begin by tracing commonalities in European responses to indigenous resistance, before exploring the different resources that Spanish notions of God's law and later northern European notions of Man's law offered to resisting populations.

During conquest and the initial stages of colonization, European colonizers tended to stress differences between their own rule of law and indigenous custom, which they commonly defined as a lack of law or, at least, of proper law. But as Europeans began ruling over colonized peoples, the stark conceptual opposition between law and custom began to break down. Given their own use of law as a justification for sovereignty, Europeans had to extend the rule of law to the indigenous peoples they governed, which meant, in practice, that they had to allow the colonized access to at least some of the legal procedures that symbolized the existence of law. This tactic, however, led to a transformation in the conceptual opposition between law and custom. As native peoples rapidly began taking advantage of European legal procedures to assert and contest relations of power, they confronted the colonizers with a dilemma that colonial regimes commonly solved by instituting special legal procedures, administered by special courts, for native peoples. As a result, European colonizers, however reluctantly, tended to develop—in conjunction with the colonized—a hybrid between law and custom: customary law.

Sixteenth-century Spanish colonial rulers, for example, began by recognizing a sharp distinction between Spanish law and indigenous custom. This distinction was presupposed by their arguments over whether or not to preserve indigenous institutions or replace them with Spanish ones. At first, the Spanish crown enjoined "its governors to preserve Indian organization and custom so long as they were not contrary to reason or Christian precept" (Borah 1982: 267). This injunction, however, had contradictory consequences, for in order to preserve Indian customs that were not contrary to reason or Christian precept, Spaniards had to institute legal procedures for reviewing Indian decisions. They thus extended to Indians the Spanish right of appeal "against the acts of judicial and administrative officials" (Borah 1982: 272).

Indians in Spanish America discovered "very quickly, that any decision once rendered could be appealed up the long line of reviews provided by Castilian law" (Borah 1982: 272), allowing its implementation to be postponed and possibly avoided altogether. "As early as 1531, the Second *Audencia* reported to the crown that Indian cases, civil and criminal, were occupying a great deal of its time" (Borah 1982: 272). Similarly, Stern observes that "by the 1550s, [Indians in South America] had flooded the viceregal court, or *Audencia*, in Lima with petitions and suits—the majority of them between native communities, *ayllus* (kin groups), or ethnic groups." And "by the 1600's, [Indians] had developed legal forms of struggle into a major strategy for protecting individual, *ayllu*, and community interests" (Stern 1982: 293). Faced with overburdened courts and complaining colonists, the Spanish crown tried various means to discourage Indians from appealing every adverse decision. The Spaniards finally hit on the solution of requiring Indian "complaints, hearings, and decisions . . . to be by summary process and largely oral" (Borah 1982: 284).

Similar processes occurred in British India. Cohn reports that the British decided to establish courts in India because they "did not think that the (indigenous) procedural law and the courts, as they found them in the late eighteenth century, were adequate." But almost from the establishment of British courts in India, it was apparent to the British that there were serious faults in these courts. It took years for disputes to be resolved, and there were too many appeals from lower courts. Use of forged documents and perjury in the courts became endemic. It was evident that courts did not settle disputes, but were used either as a form of gambling . . . or as a threat in a dispute. (Cohn 1967: 154)

Like earlier Spanish colonists in the Americas, the British in India tried to stem the flood of appeals by instituting reforms, including establishing informal, oral procedures in local communities. "But," observes Cohn, "the flood of cases continues, and, at least based on my experience in 1952–3 and on a brief visit in 1958, there is no apparent abatement in this cycle of false cases" (1967: 154).[16]

Colonized people's heavy use of courts had contradictory effects for the colonized as well as for colonizers. Stern, for example, observes that "mastering the art of judicial politics" allowed "ethnic groups, *ayllus* and even individuals" in colonial Peru to win "battles on real-life issues such as [labor obligations], tribute, and land rights" (1982: 311).

But on another level, the natives' achievement cost them a great deal. . . . To the extent that reliance on a juridical system becomes a dominant strategy of protection for an oppressed class or social group, it may undermine the possibility of organizing a more ambitious assault aimed at toppling the exploitative structure itself. . . . [Because] the Indians' struggle for Spanish justice . . . could not . . . challenge colonialism itself . . . , it set into motion relationships that sustained colonial power, weakened the peasantry's capacity for independent resistance, and contributed to the oppression of Andean peoples. (Stern 1982: 311)

Colonized peoples, however, clearly understood that they could be co-opted through appealing to courts run by colonizers. Nader, for example, observes that many colonized peoples developed a "harmony ideology" encouraging them to settle their disputes within the native community (1990). The desire of the colonized to stay out of the colonizers' courts thus tended to coincide with the desire of colonizers to stem the flood of native appeals. Together they encouraged the development of local courts in indigenous communities that used informal procedures to promote reconciliation among disputants. Nevertheless, evidence suggests that although informal courts often succeeded at promoting reconciliation among people who wanted to reach an agreement, they usually failed to settle disputes between political opponents or between groups contesting access to vital resources (Starr and Yngvesson 1975).

Although native "overuse" of courts led both Spanish and northern European colonizers to establish informal local forums, differences between earlier Spanish and later northern European concepts of law led to differences in the visibility of customary law. The Spanish concept of a social hierarchy ordained by God, for example, tended to conceal the development of customary law because all officials recognized and appointed by the crown were expected to enforce God's laws. This reliance on officials, while prompting the crown to institute a comprehensive system of appeal, gave the crown no reason to notice deviations unless they were brought to its attention. As a result, native departures from Spanish rules and procedures tended to go unrecorded. This tactic of ignoring customary law was followed by Latin American liberals when they finally succeeded in taking over state power during the nineteenth century. Like the advocates of hierarchical status distinctions whom they replaced, liberal rulers tended to treat the elected and appointed officials of Indian communities as if they were indistinguishable from their counterparts in mestizo ones. Until recently, when indigenous groups demanding political autonomy have exposed the existence of customary law, anthropologists tended to be the only ones interested in observing that native communities in Latin America have legal norms and procedures that differ from those of positive state law.

Social contract theory, in contrast, tends to highlight differences among legal regimes, leading to the appearance of dual legal systems in colonial situations (see Merry 1991: 890). Because social contract theory rests on the assumption that "men" make the laws that govern them, it suggests that different groups of men will make different laws. The early inventors of social contract theory, particularly Rousseau, may not have envisioned this outcome, for they tended to imagine that all men of reason would reason similarly. But the spread of social contract theory, with its ideology of self-government, soon required groups hoping to avoid assimilation into imperialist social contract states, such as Napoleonic France, to develop unique definitions of self. When social contract theory became hegemonic in nineteenth-century Europe, it stimulated not only the development of class-based political movements but also Romanticism, with its celebration of folk cultures and concomitant rise of ethnic nationalism.

When carried to the colonies, social contract theory led colonial officials to expect different groups of natives to have different laws (in contrast to sixteenth-century Spaniards who posited a single divine law). Colonial officials thus set about codifying native laws, both as a way of predicting native behavior and to provide native judges in newly established courts with copies of the culturally distinct laws they were supposed to administer.[17] This codification process not only tended to highlight ethnic differences among colonized peoples (in contrast to the Spanish tendency to treat all native peoples as belonging to the same status group), but also to highlight differences between the customary law of the colonized and the law of the colonizers.

Customary law, by its very name, suggests that it encodes native traditions, but historians of eighteenth- and nineteenth-century European colonialism in Africa, particularly Ranger (1983), Chanock (1985), and Moore (1986), have observed that customary law is not a continuation of indigenous practices. Rather, it is a product of the colonial encounter, forged in struggles between colonizers and colonized. Ranger, for example, declares that "what were called customary law, customary land-rights, customary political structure and so on, were in fact *all* invented by colonial codification" (1983: 250, emphasis in original). "The point is not merely that so-called custom in fact concealed new balances of power and wealth, since this was precisely what custom in the past had always been able to do, but that these particular constructs of customary law became codified and rigid and unable so readily to reflect change in the future" (Ranger 1983: 250–51). The codification of customary law required by social contract theory also stimulated changes in native legal procedures. Once courts were required to keep records of their proceedings, evidence moved "away from the magical (such as oaths and ordeals) in the direction of the evidential and refutable" (MacGaffey, quoted in Ranger 1983: 251).

Historians of colonialism in Africa have argued over whether the imposition of colonial rule ameliorated or exacerbated inequalities within colonized groups. Ranger (1983) and Chanock (1985) assert that European rule, once it became established in the colonies, tended to strengthen rather than undermine traditional hierarchies, increasing the power of chiefs over commoners, elders over young men, and men over women. Recently, other historians have challenged this view with studies that suggest the empowerment of commoners, youths, and women relative to native elites (Roberts 1993). This argument, of course, presumes the value of equality inherent in social contract theory—the belief that law *should* treat all "men" equally. Instead of joining the argument, therefore, I want to shift the focus. Because I assume that European discourses of law always promoted inequalities (although of varying kinds and amounts), I prefer to explore how discourses of law affected the organization of inequality among colonized peoples by favoring some at the expense of others.

It seems reasonable to imagine that during the initial stages of conquest and pacification, all colonizing powers reduced inequalities among the colonized by supporting the enemies of elites they hoped to conquer and replace. Sixteenth-century Spaniards, for example, championed the causes of Indian groups who had been oppressed by the Aztecs and Incas. But because Spanish colonists assumed that people were inherently unequal before the law, they soon began using law to reinforce the power of native rulers. "The crown was pledged to respect the rights of Indian rulers, nobility, and commoners; the rulers were no longer sovereign but were still entitled to respect and revenue; all ranks were entitled to security of possessions and good treatment" (Borah 1982: 268).

Later colonizers from northern Europe also began by championing the causes of oppressed groups. But because social contract theory required all men to be equal before the law, colonial officials found it difficult to adopt the Spanish policy of recognizing and protecting the rights of different status groups within native populations. Cornwallis, as already noted, wanted the British administration of justice in India "to disregard all conditions of persons," such as their caste membership. Moreover, colonizers from social contract states often tried to justify their colonizing ventures by claiming to free oppressed peoples from despotic rulers (rather than by claiming to give them Christian revelation, as Spanish colonizers had). As a result, colonizers from social contract states tended to waffle in their support for disadvantaged groups within colonized populations. At times, they tried to stamp out customs they defined as oppressive. But over the long run, they, like the Spanish before them, tended to reinforce the power of native elites, particularly after pacification, when colonizers needed the support of indigenous leaders in order to govern.

When colonial officials withdrew support from disadvantaged groups, they often justified their actions by invoking the right of every group to its own traditions. Ranger, who writes about "the invention of tradition in colonial Africa" (1983), observes that "nineteenth-century Africa was *not* characterized by lack of internal social and economic competition, by the unchallenged authority of the elders, by an acceptance of custom which gave every person—young and old, male and female—a place in society which was defined and protected." Rather, "competition, movement, fluidity were as much features of small-scale communities as they were of larger groupings" (1983: 248). As European powers conquered African peoples, however, they came to see competition and movement as a threat to their rule. After 1895, "pacification came to mean immobilization of populations, re-enforcement of ethnicity and greater rigidity of social definition" (Wright 1975: 803, cited in Ranger 1983: 249). Colonial "administrators who had begun by proclaiming their support for exploited commoners against rapacious chiefs ended by backing 'traditional' chiefly authority in the interests of social control" (Ranger 1983: 249). Colonial administrators not only installed "traditional" chiefs, but helped them to invent "traditions" that exacerbated inequalities within native populations.[18] Chiefs and older men, for example, played a major role in recording customary law.[19] Not surprisingly, they tended to remember (invent?) customs that favored chiefs over commoners, elders over young people, and men over women.

Colonial administrators' waffling support for disadvantaged groups within native populations is nicely illustrated in colonial policies toward women. Social contract theory, of course, has always had problems deciding whether women are equal humans or men's natural dependents (Pateman 1988)— just as it has always had problems deciding when nature intended some people to be unequal by granting them, for example, a low IQ or a lack of initiative. Eighteenth- and nineteenth-century colonial officials carried their ambivalence about women with them to the colonies. One the one hand, they had many reasons for supporting colonized women against those who would dominate them. In nineteenth-century Europe, social Darwinists tended to judge a group's place on the evolutionary ladder by assessing men's treatment of women, thus encouraging colonizers to decry colonized women's supposed oppression as a way of justifying colonial rule. And because colonial officials from nineteenth-century Europe tended to cast their own marriages as contracts to which women freely consented, they were particularly eager to stamp out native practices they understood as denying women the possibility of consent, such as child marriage or marriage by capture.

Chatterjee, for example, observes that British officials in colonial India condemned the treatment of women as a way of discrediting Indian civilization in general and Indian men in particular (1989). British colonial writings described women as slaves of their husbands, and British officials used law to prohibit practices they regarded as particularly abhorrent, such as "sati," the custom in which a widow committed suicide by jumping on the funeral pyre of her dead husband. Indian nationalists—who belonged to the emerging bourgeoisie and who were invoking social contract theory to assert their own right to rule India—responded to this discrediting of their culture (and manliness) by "creating the image of a new woman who was superior to Western women, traditional women, and low class women" (Chatterjee 1989: 622). Indian nationalists creatively took advantage of contradictions within social contract theory to point out the oppression of women in Victorian England.

On the other hand, European colonial officials had several reasons for condoning—and encouraging—the oppression of indigenous women. Once colonial officials recognized their need for support from local elites, their belief that nature condemned women to being dependents of men allowed them to justify supporting traditions that recognized the rights of indigenous husbands and fathers. In a fascinating article about Zambia in the 1930s, Ault (1983) explains how "the coalescence of interests of colonial officials and tribal authorities" led to the invention of "traditional" marriage customs that limited women's options by requiring men to pay high bridewealth in an area where marriage had previously involved only token exchanges. During the world depression of the 1930s, colonial officials concerned to avoid union activity among African mine workers on the copperbelt, and rural elders concerned that young women were following young men to urban areas—thus depriving elders of women's services and young men's remittances—joined forces to establish Urban African Courts designed to extend "tribal authority" to the towns. Judges appointed by rural chiefs proceeded to enforce newly invented "traditional" laws regulating marriage. Young men were required to pay high bridewealths that benefited chiefs and rural elders by ensuring a steady flow of bridewealth payments from wage-earning mine workers to rural elders. Ault is concerned to show that African chiefs, rather than being predictable, inveterate traditionalists, "proved innovators in their own right" (1983: 198). He argues that urban African judges "departed from customary practice by insisting on the formal registration of marriage as a condition of its validity, by transforming the nature of bride-price, and even by usurping jurisdiction over marital disputes from kin elders." These judicial innovations, however, took away women's former ability to escape unwanted marriages, as judges used state power to prevent wives from leaving husbands who had paid for them.[20]

Just as colonizers from social contract states waffled in providing equal protection of persons, so they waffled in providing equal protection of property. In contrast to sixteenth-century Spaniards, who recognized forms of communal tenure and so had no difficulty recognizing the land rights of Indian communities in the Americas, colonizers from social contract states celebrated private ownership of property. Chanock, for example, observes that nineteenth-century British colonists in Africa viewed the "right to property as a natural human right, necessary to human nature, a just reward for labor, and the very basis of a proper political society" (Chanock 1991: 62). But efforts by colonists from social contract states to privatize land often had disastrous consequences, such as throwing subsistence farmers off their lands, causing widespread famines and massive migrations.

Historians of African colonialism have just begun to explore the role of property law in struggles over power within colonized groups, in contrast to historians of British India who have analyzed the role of property law in creating a powerful landlord class among the colonized (Guha 1963). This difference in attention is probably due to the fact that colonial officials in Africa concentrated on restructuring personal relations as a way to release labor for colonial enterprises, whereas colonial officials in British India financed their administration through land taxes. Chanock, for example, observes "that the economic transformation of Africa during the colonial period had its impact first on those laws which define the nature of control over dependents and their labor. The development of a customary law legitimizing the control of persons in new ways was followed by the emergence of a customary law of property in general, and land in particular" (1991: 62). The colonial period opened "with the dominance of ideas about the evolutionary superiority of western concepts of individual property rights. Yet communal rights to land, ideologically judged to be primitive, were eventually accorded a recognition denied to various forms of bonded labor" (Chanock 1991: 63).

6. CONCLUSION

The contradictions inherent in social contract theory continue to shape struggles over inequality in our supposedly postcolonial world. Law remains the central discourse used in national and international forums for asserting and contesting sovereignty and control over vital resources. As a result, people from former colonies, like people in colonizing countries, are likely to find that their claims, however intended, are interpreted by others within the framework of assumptions that constitute social contract theory. And to the degree that people in former colonies actively draw upon social contract theory, such as using the European idea that men should author their own laws to justify national liberation movements, they are drawn into irresolvable debates over the nature of nature and over who counts as a "man" for the purpose of participating in the social contract (Maurer 1994).

Most of the places colonized by Europe and North America have become independent nations. But dominant discourses of nature still portray their peoples as naturally inferior. Social Darwinism lives on. Not only does pseudoscience keep discovering natural differences among humans, particularly between races and sexes, but the evolutionary narrative used by nineteenth-century colonizers to justify conquering and ruling African and Asian peoples has merely undergone a facelift. The old demeaning opposition between civilized nations and savages has been replaced by an (equally demeaning) opposition between the first and third worlds. And the "civilizing mission" invoked by nineteenth-century colonists has been taken on and given new life by experts in economic development (Escobar 1991). Whereas nineteenth-century colonists promised civilization to the savages whose resources they appropriated and whose lives they invaded, twentieth-century experts from first-world nations promise development to the third-world peoples whose lands and labor they exploit for capitalist profit. Although most supposed aid to poor third-world nations is described as economic rather than political or legal, international investors, in fact, tend to demand legal protection for their persons and properties, just as colonists from Europe once did. The International Monetary Fund and the World Bank, for example, often require the governments of receiving countries to institute legal reforms, commonly establishing or enforcing private property rights, as a prerequisite to granting loans. And contemporary efforts by overdeveloped nations to spread democracy and economic prosperity around the world eerily recall Cornwallis's vision of the new order he hoped to create on the Indian subcontinent.

People from former colonies are also being drawn, willingly or not, into debates over who counts as a "man" for the purpose of participating in the social contract. As suggested earlier, social contract theory provides two main principles for delimiting the specific group of "men" entitled to participate in making the laws of a territory: "reason" and ethnic or religious "tradition." While the principle of reason does tend to exclude those who are culturally defined as denied reason by nature (such as children, women, the insane, savages, illiterates, the propertyless, etc.), it is usually conceived as an inclusive principle. It unites men across divides of religion and ethnicity, commonly on the basis of a shared economic interest in protecting their persons and properties. Hobbes, for example, writing in the context of Britain's religious civil wars, stressed men's common interest in avoiding the "warre" of each against all that rendered both life and property precarious. This intimate link between reason and economic interest has, of course, encouraged class-based resistance to the dominance of property owners. Working-class movements flourished in Europe during the late nineteenth and early twentieth centuries, after property owners had by and large succeeded in replacing divinely ordained kings with parliamentary rule.

Tradition, in contrast to reason, is usually conceived as an exclusive principle, designed to limit those eligible to participate in making laws to people who share a common ethnic or religious heritage. As noted earlier, the assumption inherent in social contract theory that men make their own laws suggests, logically, that different groups of men will make different laws. This idea was invoked and elaborated by nineteenth-century European Romantics as a defensive move to justify resisting attempts by expanding social contract states to impose their version of reason on others. And it seems to be enjoying a resurgence around the world today as leaders of militant ethnic and religious movements point out—correctly—that reason is simply another cultural tradition, imported from Europe and tainted with imperialism.

Invocations of tradition suggest, of course, a return to the past. But contemporary political leaders who invoke their ethnic or religious heritages to justify demanding self-government are operating in a modern rather than a premodern context. Whatever their intentions about preserving or restoring ancient customs, and however sincerely they believe they are following in the footsteps of their ancestors, their invocations of tradition are heard—and responded to—as challenges to power-holders who claim political dominance based on reason. Reason enjoys dominance today because during the nineteenth century, and for most of the twentieth century, it was the primary principle invoked by political leaders demanding self-government. In the twentieth century, for example, many if not most leaders of movements for national liberation invoked the principle of reason to justify throwing off the yoke of colonial or bourgeois rule, playing down ethnic and religious divisions by stressing people's shared economic interest in exploiting their territory's resources for their own benefit rather than for the benefit of foreign colonizers or capitalists. Discourses of sovereignty, however, inevitably provoke resistance. Reason's spectacular success guarantees that those who oppose the policies of current governments will find ready support for their positions if they stress religious over economic values, promise to restore their nation's glorious heritage, and/or vow to purify the nation by expelling people of the wrong religion, race, or ethnicity.

NOTES

This paper was prepared for the Law and Society Summer Institute, 1993. I would like to thank George Collier, Bryant Garth, Bill Maurer, Sally Merry, and Austin Sarat for their helpful comments on the original draft.

1. Two commonly found contrasting conceptions of "rule" are those in which a ruler's concentration of power (mana) creates both the crowds he rules and the order among them (see Anderson 1972), and those in which "big men" construct followings and ensure meaningful relations among people by orchestrating relationships of "debt" (see Collier 1988). In both types of polities, groups do not exist (either conceptually or in reality) apart from the persons who create them, and the relevant conceptual opposition tends to be power/chaos rather than justice/injustice.

2. Sixteenth-century Spain was not a multi-ethnic empire, in contrast to the Islamic empires it displaced in the Iberian peninsula. In 1492, the Spanish crown expelled both Jews and Islamic peoples, creating a Christian polity.

3. Latour argues against those who would use the concepts of social science to understand the "social construction of science," by contending that the concepts used by social scientists to study social phenomena were developed at the same time as the concepts used by the natural scientists they want to study (1993).

4. Latour observes that when Boyle established laboratory science as the method for discovering nature's laws, he did not try to ground "his work in logic, mathematics or rhetoric." Rather, he drew on "a parajudicial metaphor: credible, trustworthy, well-to-do witnesses gathered at the scene of the action can attest to the existence of a fact, the matter of fact, even if they do not know its true nature" (1993: 18). Boyle's witnesses to scientific truth were the same limited set of male property owners that Hobbes declared "equall" for the purpose of participating in the social contract.

5. In the nineteenth century, Tocqueville observed that "Democracy looses social ties, but tightens natural ones; it brings kindred more closely together, whilst it throws citizens more apart" (1984: 233).

6. In a recent book, Olwig (1993) explores the changing relation between hierarchy and equality in Britain's Caribbean colonies, arguing that during the seventeenth century, English settlers in the Caribbean incorporated African slaves into their hierarchical households, treating them as humans, albeit lesser ones. During the eighteenth century, however, as yeoman farming gave way to plantation agriculture, British colonists began invoking a language of equality that denied the basic humanity of African slaves.

7. Cohn, e.g., observes that

the British colonies in North America and the Caribbean had from their inception forms of governance that were largely an extension of the basic political and legal institutions of Great Britain. The colonizing populations, even when drawn from dissident political and religious groups in Great Britain, still were thought of as English or British. The laws of these colonies were the laws of Great Britain (1989: 131).

8. Because post-Enlightenment liberal states maintained the fiction that native rulers continued to hold sovereignty, such states have, by and large, managed to avoid assuming responsibility for the massive dislocations and deaths caused by their colonization schemes. Spain, for example, which did claim sovereignty over the New World, is commonly blamed for the drastic decline of North American Indian populations, but Britain has largely escaped blame for the terrible famine that occurred in Bengal due to the mismanagement of the supposedly independent British East India Company.

9. John Comaroff (1989) provides an excellent discussion of the three "imagined worlds" and corresponding "images of empire" held by the late eighteenth- and early nineteenth-century Britons who established a colonial empire in Africa.

10. Max Weber, for example, wrote that

It is the most elemental economic fact that the way in which the disposition over material property is distributed among a plurality of people, meeting competitively in the market for the purpose of exchange, in itself creates specific life chances. According to the law of marginal utility this mode of distribution excludes the non-owners from competing for highly valued goods; it favors the owners and, in fact, gives to them a monopoly to acquire such goods. Other things being equal, this mode of distribution monopolizes the opportunities for profitable deals for all those who, provided with goods, do not necessarily have to exchange them. It increases, at least generally, their power in price wars with those who, being propertyless, have nothing to offer but their service in native form or goods in a form constituted through their own labor, and who above all are compelled to get rid of these products in order barely to subsist. (1966: 22)

11. Lancaster, who argues that Spanish colonialism created racism in Central America, observes that Nicaraguans, in contrast to Anglo North Americans, recognize many shades of skin color, allowing almost every Nicaraguan to be both lighter and darker than someone else (1991). Similarly, Lancaster's discussion of male homosexuality in Nicaragua reveals that male and female are not cast as opposites, but rather arranged in a hierarchy according to who penetrates and who is penetrated (1988).

12. In a sense, these different colonial projects correspond to the three kinds of power identified by Etzioni (1961): the state exercised coercive power through its control of the use of force, the missionaries wielded normative power associated with morality, and the settlers, mine owners, and traders enjoyed remunerative power that came from their wealth. The missionaries were the least powerful segment, wielding only moral authority. They saw themselves as the conscience of the colonizers, a role that reflected their relative lack of power compared to state officials backed by military might and wealthy settlers able to buy favors.

13. Said, for example, observes that "because of empire, all cultures are involved in one another; none is single and pure, all are hybrid, heterogeneous, extraordinarily differentiated, and unmonolithic" (1993: xxv). Given this hybridity, essentialist movements seeking to "purify" races or cultural traditions are inherently oppressive. While "no one can deny the persisting continuities of long traditions, sustained habitations, national languages, and cultural geographies, . . . there seems no reason except fear and prejudice to keep insisting on their separation and distinctiveness" (1993: 336).

14. Feminist scholars, too, have explored the double-bind of sameness/difference, noting how scholars (generally white, Western ones) who focus on sexism have tended to miss differences among women, whereas those who document and celebrate such differences (often nonwhite scholars or those who sympathize with them) tend to overlook male privilege in the groups they write about. These scholarly positions also reflect political positions. Those who stress universal sexism usually urge all women to unite. Those who stress differences among women tend to support movements for ethnic or religious liberation.

15. Tsing, e.g., observes that interethnic subversion always entails surprises, for the fact that subordinated peoples misunderstand the intentions of their superiors means that the effects of initiatives by superiors "are always complex and unpredictable" (1993: 188).

16. Cohn attributes the prevalence of "false cases" to a clash between British and indigenous values. Because Indians did not regard British procedures as legitimate, he argues, they "did not use the courts to settle disputes but only to further them" (1967: 155). Cohn may be right about why Indians appealed to courts, but it is nevertheless true that Europeans in Europe also used courts to "further" disputes. Law, after all, was the principal discourse available to Europeans for asserting and contesting claims to power. If Europeans appeared to bring fewer "false cases" than the peoples whose lands they colonized, it may have been because falseness resides in the eye of the beholder, as well as because European countries were not undergoing the rapid social changes associated with colonization.

17. Because French colonial officials in Africa came from a civil law rather than a common law tradition, they had less respect for custom and were consequently less eager than British officials to codify the laws of colonized peoples. But when resistance by educated natives

demanding self-government threatened French colonial rule, French officials, too, sought support from traditional chiefs and began to codify customary law.

18. Ranger, e.g., writes that

Elders tended to appeal to "tradition" in order to defend their dominance of the rural means of production against challenge by the young. Men tended to appeal to "tradition" in order to ensure that the increasing role which women played in production in the rural areas did not result in any diminution of male control over women as economic assets. Paramount chiefs and ruling aristocracies in polities which included numbers of ethnic and social groupings appealed to "tradition" in order to maintain or extend their control over their subjects. Indigenous populations appealed to "tradition" in order to ensure that the migrants who settled amongst them did not achieve political or economic rights. (Ranger 1983: 254)

19. The famous Restatement of African Laws project, for example, carried out in the mid-twentieth century, assembled "knowledgeable elders" (all men) to explain their community's customs.

20. Countering such examples of how colonial rule increased the oppression of colonized women, other historians have used court records to suggest that colonial rule did, in at least some instances, increase women's power relative to their husbands and elder kin. At a recent day-long conference, "Law, Colonialism, and Control over Bodies in Africa" held at Stanford University (Roberts 1993), many participants suggested that Ranger and Channock may have been premature to conclude that colonial customary law subordinated women. The court records examined by conference participants revealed an unexpectedly high rate of female complainants, primarily women seeking divorces from their husbands. This finding suggests that women were "not merely pawns in the marriage game," as one paper title put it (Hubbell 1993), but rather people who appealed to law to advance their own interests. I question, however, whether high rates of female complainants can be taken as an accurate indication of women's power. In many, if not most, African groups, marriage was (and often still is) a process rather than an event. The degree to which women and men were married changed over time as bridewealth was paid, children born, and relations between in-laws renegotiated. Women, who tended to gain power as their children aged, often precipitated the realignment of family obligations by running away from husbands and fathers and appealing to senior kin. As a result, it would be difficult to decide without further study whether high rates of female complainants at colonial courts reflected this earlier pattern of marital negotiations, or whether it reflected a new pattern due to the fact that courts offered women an alternative, and powerful, ally against those who would constrain them.

BIBLIOGRAPHY

Anderson, Benedict. 1972. The Idea of Power in Javanese Culture. In C. Holt, ed., *Culture and Politics in Indonesia*. Ithaca, NY: Cornell Univ. Press.

Ault, James M., Jr. 1983. Making "Modern" Marriage "Traditional." 12 *Theory and Society*, 181.

Borah, Woodrow. 1982. The Spanish and Indian Law: New Spain. In *The Inca and Aztec States, 1400–1800*, ed. G. Collier, R. Rosaldo, and J. Wirth. New York: Academic Press.

Bourdieu, Pierre. 1977. *Outline of a Theory of Practice*. New York: Cambridge Univ. Press.

Chanock, Martin. 1985. *Law, Custom, and Social Order: The Colonial Experience in Malawi and Zambia*. Cambridge: Cambridge Univ. Press.

————. 1991. Paradigms, Policies and Property: A Review of the Customary Law of Land Tenure. In *Law in Colonial Africa*, ed. K. Mann and R. Roberts. Portsmouth, NH: Heinemann.

Chatterjee, Partha. 1989. Colonialism, Nationalism, and Colonized Women: The Contest in India. 16 *American Ethnologist*, 622.

Cohn, Bernard. 1967. Some Notes on Law and Change in North India. In *Law and Warfare*, ed. P. Bohannan. Garden City, NY: Natural History Press. (Reprinted from 7 *Economic Development and Cultural Change*. [Oct. 1959].)

————. 1989. Law and the Colonial State in India. In *History and Power in the Study of Law*, ed. J. Starr and J. Collier. Ithaca, NY: Cornell Univ. Press.

Collier, Jane F. 1988. *Marriage and Inequality in Classless Societies*. Stanford, CA: Stanford Univ. Press.

Comaroff, Jean, and John Comaroff. 1991. *Of Revelation and Revolution*. Vol. 1. Chicago: Univ. of Chicago Press.

Comaroff, John. 1989. Images of Empire, Contests of Conscience: Models of Colonial Domination in South Africa. 16 *American Ethnologist*, 661.

Cooper, Frederick, and Ann L. Stoler. 1989. Tensions of Empire: Colonial Control and Visions of Rule. 16 *American Ethnologist*, 609.

Dahrendorf, Ralf. 1968. On the Origin of Inequality among Men. In Dahrendorf, *Essays in the Theory of Society*. Stanford, CA: Stanford Univ. Press.

Darby, Philip. 1987. *The Three Faces of Imperialism*. New Haven, CT: Yale Univ. Press.

Durkheim, Emile. [1893] 1933. *The Division of Labor in Society*. Glencoe, IL: Free Press.

Escobar, Arturo. 1991. Anthropology and the Development Encounter. 18 *American Ethnologist*, 658.

Etzioni, Amitai. 1961. *A Comparative Analysis of Complex Organizations*. New York: Free Press.

Fitzpatrick, Peter. 1992. *The Mythology of Modern Law*. New York: Routledge.

Foucault, Michel. 1980. *Power/Knowledge: Selected Interviews and Other Writings, 1972–1977*. Ed. Colin Gordon. New York: Pantheon.

Guha, Ranajit. 1963. *A Rule of Property for Bengal*. Paris: Mouton.

Hobbes, Thomas. [1651] 1991. *Leviathan*. New York: Cambridge.

Hubbell, Andrew. 1993. Not Merely Pawns in the Marriage Game: Samo Women, Customary Law and Colonialism in Dafina (Burkina Faso), 1900–1960. In unpublished manuscript, Symposium on Law, Colonialism, and Contracts in Africa, Stanford Humanities Center, ed. R. Roberts.

Lancaster, Roger. 1988. Subject Honor and Object Shame: The Construction of Male Homosexuality and Stigma in Nicaragua. 27 *Ethnology*, 111.

————. 1991. Skin Color, Race, and Racism in Nicaragua. 30 *Ethnology*, 339.

Latour, Bruno. 1993. *We Have Never Been Modern*. Cambridge, MA: Harvard Univ. Press.

Mann, Kristin, and Richard Roberts, eds. 1991. *Law in Colonial Africa*. Portsmouth, NH: Heinemann.

Maurer, Bill. 1994. *Recharting the Caribbean: Land, Law and Citizenship in the British Virgin Islands.* Ph.D. diss., Stanford Univ.

Merry, Sally. 1991. Law and Colonialism: Review Essay. 25 *Law and Society Rev.*, 889.

Moore, Sally Falk. 1986. *Social Facts and Fabrications: "Customary Law" on Kilimajaro, 1880–1980.* Cambridge: Cambridge Univ. Press.

Nader, Laura. 1990. *Harmony Ideology: Justice and Control in a Zapotec Mountain Village.* Stanford, CA: Stanford Univ. Press.

Olwig, Karen Fogg. 1993. *Global Culture, Island Identity: Continuity and Change in the Afro-Caribbean Community of Nevis.* Chur, Switzerland: Harwood Academic.

Pateman, Carol. 1988. *The Sexual Contract.* Stanford, CA: Stanford Univ. Press.

Ranger, Terrence. 1983. The Invention of Tradition in Colonial Africa. In *The Invention of Tradition*, ed. E. J. Hobsbawm and T. Ranger. New York: Cambridge.

Roberts, Richard, ed. 1993. Symposium on Law, Colonialism, and Contracts in Africa. Stanford Humanities Center, May 20, 1993. Unpublished manuscript.

Said, Edward. 1993. *Culture and Imperialism.* New York: Knopf.

Starr, June, and Jane F. Collier, eds. 1989. *History and Power in the Study of Law.* Ithaca, NY: Cornell Univ. Press.

Starr, June, and Barbara Yngvesson. 1975. Scarcity and Disputing: Zeroing-in on Compromise Decisions. 2 *American Ethnologist*, 533.

Stern, Steve J. 1982. The Social Significance of Judicial Institutions in an Exploitative Society: Huamanga, Peru, 1570–1640. In *The Inca and Aztec States, 1400–1800*, ed. G. Collier, R. Rosaldo, and J. Wirth. New York: Academic Press.

Stokes, Eric. 1959. *The English Utilitarians and India.* Delhi: Oxford Univ. Press.

Stoler, Ann L. 1989. Making Empire Respectable: The Politics of Race and Sexual Morality in 20th Century Colonial Cultures. 16 *American Ethnologist*, 634.

Tocqueville, Alexis de. [1835–40] 1984. *Democracy in America.* Ed. and abr. Richard D. Heffner. New York: Mentor.

Tsing, Anna L. 1993. *In the Realm of the Diamond Queen.* Princeton, NJ: Princeton Univ. Press.

Wallerstein, Emmanuel. 1974. *The Modern World-System I.* New York: Academic Press.

Weber, Max. 1966. Class, Status and Party. In *Class, Status, and Power*, ed. R. Bendix and S. M. Lipset. New York: Free Press.

Wright, Marcia. 1975. Women in Peril. 20 *African Social Research*, 800.

THE JURY:
HOW DOES LAW MATTER?

❖

SHARI SEIDMAN DIAMOND

JASON SCHKLAR

In the most fundamental sense, the jury *is* a legal matter. The legal system creates the jury and, in the absence of that legal mandate, criminal charges and civil disputes in the United States would be handled as they generally are elsewhere: without the assistance of a jury.[1] Yet although the jury is a product and instrument of the law, it is the most nonlegal of legal creations. The legal system gives a group of ordinary citizens the extraordinary power to make consequential legal decisions—to determine guilt or innocence in criminal cases and to decide whether a defendant should be sentenced to death, as well as to determine liability and set damages in civil cases. Although most jury verdicts can be appealed or altered,[2] the jury as a rule is not required to explain its decisions,[3] and jury verdicts are accorded substantial deference by both trial court judges and appellate courts.

Despite or perhaps because of the formidable powers it grants to a group of laypersons, the legal system reveals considerable ambivalence toward the jury. For example, legal doctrine assumes that the jury will base its verdict solely on the facts and law presented in court, and that jurors will not be influenced by prejudice or legally irrelevant information. Yet concern about the jury's ability to sift and to evaluate information fairly has produced a myriad of legal rules that orchestrate and restrict the presentation of facts and law that jurors receive in the course of a trial—all aimed at controlling and channeling jury decision making. Nor is there consistent agreement on how the jury should exercise its discretion in applying legal doctrine to the facts it finds. Although the jury is told that it is obligated to follow the court's instructions on the law, one of the jury system's acknowledged strengths is its occasional deviation from the law a judge would be expected to apply. Thus, after a jury acquitted a young bartender with no criminal record who was prosecuted for possession of a single stolen television set, choosing to believe that the defendant did not know it was stolen, a federal judge expressed relief in the acquittal. As the judge explained, he would have had to convict on the evidence in a bench trial, although he believed that the jury's verdict was the better outcome. An appreciation for the jury's power to stretch the law—or to impose a legal standard codified only in the community's sense of justice— has a long tradition (Green 1985; see also Constable 1994). Moreover, it is not confined to so-called nullification cases involving criminal defendants; the jury's tempering of the strict rule of contributory negligence barring a plaintiff's recovery for injuries unless the defendant was totally responsible preceded the modern comparative negligence statutes that permit partial recovery by a negligent plaintiff.

The rules of evidence and instructions on the law that the judge delivers to the jury are the most conspicuous legal efforts to control jury decision making, but they are not the only ones. In addition, legal standards specify the size of the jury, influence how the jury is selected, and determine the structure of an acceptable verdict (e.g., unanimous or based on a majority vote, a special or general verdict). Each of these decisions too reflects the tension between conflicting values in controlling and relying on the jury: attempting to achieve both representativeness and impartiality, to provide for full debate while reducing costs and minimizing hung juries, and to structure decision making while leaving the jury free to soften some of the inflexibilities of the statutory and judge-made law.

If the legal system is ambivalent about the jury, it is perhaps no surprise that jurors sometimes express ambivalence in their reactions to the law. Thus, in asking how law matters for the jury, we must ask not only how the jury exercises the powers that the legal system grants to it, but also how the jury interprets and reacts to and sometimes resists the legal controls used to structure and constrain its actions and to channel its influence. Research on the jury indicates that it exercises its powers and handles its constraints actively, functioning not as the passive recipient of information and compliant decision maker that the law sometimes appears to expect, but as an active collaborator in the production of verdicts (see, e.g., Diamond and Casper 1992; Diamond, Casper, and Ostergren 1989). This picture of the active jury will be helpful as we examine the thicket of inconsistent and often ineffective approaches used by the legal system ostensibly to guide and channel jury behavior.

We begin by considering how law explicitly and implicitly influences which cases go to juries rather than to judges, what kind of verdicts juries can reach, and which citizens become jury members. We then examine how the law organizes the content of a jury trial, including legal arrangements invisible or only partially visible to the jury as well as legal directives explicitly communicated to the jury. We also discuss some obstacles to legal control of the jury. Finally, we consider the sources and consequences of the ambiguous legal efforts exerted in the name of jury control.

1. HOW LAW MATTERS IN PRODUCING A JURY TRIAL

A. When Jury Trials Occur

Most criminal offenses carry a constitutional right to trial by jury, but even this right has important limits. The United States Supreme Court has interpreted the Sixth Amendment's right to trial by jury in all criminal prosecutions to apply only if the verdict can carry the potential of at least six months imprisonment (*Baldwin v. New York* 1970).[4] Juveniles, however, even when charged with the same crimes as adults, are not entitled to a jury trial (*McKeiver v. Pennsylvania* 1971). Moreover, convicted defendants have no constitutional right to a jury decision on penalty and in most states the jury does not participate in felony sentencing decisions.[5] Even in capital cases, the Constitution does not guarantee the right to a jury in determining whether the defendant will be sentenced to death (e.g., *Walton v. Arizona* 1990). Although the federal government and thirty-four of the thirty-eight states with death penalty statutes do use juries in some form,[6] four of the thirty-four use the jury only in an advisory capacity, leaving the final decision to the judge.[7] The U.S. Supreme Court has explicitly endorsed advisory juries on the ground that this reduced role must be permissible if it is constitutional to eliminate the jury entirely from the capital punishment decision. Some recent work in Indiana by Hoffman (1995) suggests that the jury's advisory role may affect jury decisions by reducing juror concerns about the consequences of their decision. If judges in turn use the jury's recommendation for guidance, the legal framework putting the jury in an advisory role may have the significant and presumably unintended consequence of reducing the deliberation associated with decisions on death—an example of the way in which attempts to control the jury can undermine the jury's performance.

The right to a jury trial in the civil arena also takes its pedigree from the U.S. Constitution, but there is considerable controversy about when that heritage entitles litigants to a jury. In federal courts the Seventh Amendment preserves the right to jury trial in suits at common law, but the U.S. Supreme Court has not made the right to trial by jury in civil cases binding on the states by incorporating the Seventh Amendment into the Fourteenth Amendment. Nonetheless, all state constitutions currently contain provisions protecting the right to a jury trial in civil suits. The primary legal limitation on the right to a civil jury trial turns on the definition of "suits at common law,"[8] and many pages of court opinions and law review analysis have been spent in the attempt to delineate what this phrase encompasses (e.g., If a statute provides for civil penalties and not merely damages, does a party have the right to a civil jury trial on the issue of liability?[9] If Congress uses the magic word "equitable" to describe the relief provided under the employment discrimination provisions of Title VII of the Civil Rights Act, but not under the fair housing provisions of Title VIII, is the right to a jury trial to be denied in the former but not in the latter?).[10] Although some scholars believe that recent court decisions have expanded the reach of the civil jury (e.g., Cecil, Hans, and Wiggins 1991), efforts have also been made, albeit unsuccessfully, to carve out a "complexity" exception to the right to trial by jury in civil cases (*In re Japanese Electronic Products Antitrust Litigation* 1980). The boundaries of the right to a civil jury trial are likely to continue to be contested ground as new causes of action are identified and as the legal system continues to struggle with its ambivalence about the power and competence of the lay jury.

There is thus noticeable ambiguity in and dispute about the formal rules of the legal system that control the characteristics of the cases that are or should be eligible for jury trial. In contrast, there is substantial agreement about the quantity of cases that juries actually decide. Both civil and criminal jury trials are rare events. Most criminal indictments are disposed of without any trial.[11] The majority of convictions are obtained as a result of guilty pleas.[12] On the civil side, most claims are dismissed or settled before trial.[13] Even when trials do occur, the decision maker may be a judge rather than a jury. This rate of jury trial activity suggests that we should look elsewhere for the sources that shape court outcomes. But the small number of jury trials is a misleading measure of the jury's influence on participants in the legal system. The jury, through what Galanter (1990) calls its threat-and-signal function, shapes the pretrial, and even the prelitigation decisions of prospective trial participants. Predictions about what a jury would be likely to do affect the probability of a guilty plea, the sentence a defendant is willing to accept in order to avoid trial, the settlement offer a defendant is willing to make, and the amount a plaintiff is willing to accept. This image of what the jury would do does not of course assume that predictions are always accurate. Indeed there is ample evidence to suggest that some pictures of the jury's likely behavior are systematically distorted. For example, Daniels (1989) and Saks (1992) have demonstrated that media coverage of jury decisions and, in particular, strategic publicity by the insurance industry create a false picture of pro-plaintiff juries and runaway jury awards that purport to inflate insurance rates and threaten business health.[14] Nonetheless, false or correct, different expectations about what the jury is likely to do are the stuff that jury trials are made of. After all, if the parties agreed in advance on what the jury's verdict would be, they generally would settle, agree to drop the charges, or plead, avoiding the anguish and work of trial.

B. WHAT VERDICT A JURY CAN RETURN

The general verdict is the standard form of jury verdict. The jury delivering a general verdict indicates only whether it finds the defendant guilty or not guilty, liable in the amount of X dollars or not liable. One critic of the jury has called the general verdict "the great procedural opiate" (Frank 1949) because it provides no information about whether the jury's verdict was based on error or bias. Others have praised the general verdict for the scope it leaves the jury to do what the law officially forbids: to compromise (Casper 1993). Unease with the general verdict is thus one more area that reveals the law's ambiguous relationship to the jury. The inscrutable nature of the general verdict is acceptable only if the jury is a trustworthy decision maker. If it is deemed necessary to monitor the structure of the jury's decision making, the form of the verdict can be adjusted to reveal that structure. One approach used in some civil cases gives the jury a list of questions to answer that together determine whether and how much a plaintiff will recover (e.g., Do you find that the defendant behaved recklessly? Do you find that the defendant's behavior was a cause of the plaintiff's injury?). A verdict that consists entirely of the answers to such questions is called a special verdict. Alternatively, the jury may be asked to provide a general verdict as well as to answer a set of questions called interrogatories. The notion is that these more specific verdict forms will both help the jury to organize its consideration of the evidence and will permit closer supervision of the jury's behavior by the trial and appellate courts. Inconsistencies can be detected and, where necessary, a retrial can occur on only the unresolved issues.

The debate about the effects of special verdicts and interrogatories has thus far been minimally informed by data. Some scholars have identified plausible systematic biases that could accompany a shift to special verdicts (Casper 1993). For example, Lempert (1981) has suggested that plaintiffs would be disadvantaged because jurors would be required to reach a series of favorable decisions and failure on any one would preclude a finding of liability. More recently, Lombardero (1996) has pointed to the logical advantage a plaintiff may have with a special verdict: if the jury answers all of the special verdict questions in favor of the plaintiff, the judge will enter a judgment for the plaintiff. Yet suppose that the answers were independent[15] and in each instance the jury thought it was only 75 percent likely that the answer favored the plaintiff (and 25 percent likely it favored the defendant). If there were four questions, the probability that the verdict would favor the plaintiff should be $(.75)^4$ or .32, logically supporting a verdict for the defendant. Of course, jurors may not answer each question without considering the answer to the remaining questions, and thus this model may not reflect the way jurors actually behave.

Little is known about whether or how special versus general verdicts actually affect jury behavior. In the single study that compared juror performance using general versus special verdict structures, Wiggins and Breckler

(1990) examined how jurors responded to a simulated defamation trial. They found that verdict structure did not affect the frequency of liability verdicts. Jurors who delivered special verdicts did give significantly higher compensatory damages awards than jurors who reached general verdicts, but there were no differences in the size of punitive awards. In addition, special verdict jurors did not show better comprehension of the evidence, although they did understand the legal standard on the burden of proof better than jurors who reached a general verdict, possibly because they were exposed to it twice, once during instructions and again on the verdict form. The mixture of findings from this lone study leaves us with fundamental questions about how the special verdict affects jury behavior, whether it achieves the shaping function it was designed to serve, and how it affects other values more easily expressed through the jury discretion implicitly conferred by the general verdict.

C. HOW THE JURY TRIAL IS STRUCTURED

1. The Role and Consequences of Law in the Composition of the Jury

Jury service has evolved since colonial days when jurors were selected for their personal knowledge of the events at issue in the trial (Thayer 1898; Dawson 1960) and only men of property were eligible to sit as jurors.[16] This limited pool of prospective jurors expanded gradually as U.S. courts determined, based on constitutional mandate, that jurors must be drawn from a fair cross-section of the community.[17] In 1880 the U.S. Supreme Court ruled that black male citizens could not be excluded from jury service[18] but women were regularly excluded from serving in some jurisdictions even after 1946.[19] Some recent state decisions have been sensitive to more subtle forms of systematic underrepresentation. In 1984, the California Supreme Court found that voter lists used to select prospective jurors were not, as a general rule, sufficiently representative of the jurisdiction.[20] California state courts now merge voter and driver lists in selecting prospective jurors (Munsterman and Munsterman 1986).[21] Yet there is no doubt that the selection process that begins with the population at large and ends with the empaneling of a jury produces substantial differences in demographic and other characteristics between the jury and the population at large (Fukurai, Butler, and Krooth 1993; Van Dyke 1977). This path leading to the selection of the jury highlights the conflict between the legal rhetoric that endorses jury representativeness and the selection processes deemed necessary to obtain a competent and impartial jury.

The legal system thus provides numerous opportunities for the most representative prospective cross-section of citizens to be transformed by the time that the jury is seated. First, most jurisdictions have until very recently permitted statutory exemptions from jury service. It was only in 1975 that the U.S. Supreme Court declared Louisiana's method of selecting women as jurors unconstitutional. At that point, Louisiana summoned men to the courthouse for jury service, but called women only if they went to the courthouse and filed notice of their desire to serve.[22] More subtle forms of exclusion occurred and occur in the granting of excuses for individuals in certain occupations. Recently, with the advent of one-day/one-trial procedures in many jurisdictions, states have reduced statutory exemptions (even attorneys are called to serve) and become less generous in granting excuses. The apparent result is that lists of prospective jurors are more heterogeneous and representative than they have ever been. Nonetheless, the process of qualifying jurors itself affects the shape of the jury venire. For example, citizens who move frequently are less likely to appear on the juror roles, and mobility is associated with socioeconomic status (Fukurai, Butler, and Krooth 1993). Moreover, potential jurors with family and other pressing responsibilities, burdens not distributed randomly in the population, are regularly excused from jury service.

Even if the qualified sample of citizens summoned for jury duty formed a random subset of citizens, the empaneled jury would not. The yield for a jury summons reflects substantial loss—as much as 50 percent in some large cities, and courts rarely engage in the vigorous follow-up that would be required to ensure that the majority of these qualified no-shows eventually appeared as prospective jurors. One explanation for this failure to pursue recalcitrant prospective jurors, in addition to the costs involved, is the suspicion that citizens reluctant to serve will be less motivated to serve well. In fact, the limited evidence we have suggests that jurors tend to come away with more favorable attitudes toward jury duty than they had before serving, including those jurors who report that they had attempted to avoid jury service (Diamond 1993). Thus, by failing to press all eligible citizens to serve as jurors, the legal system may unnecessarily reduce the representativeness and threaten the legitimacy of the juries it empanels.

Before they are seated, prospective trial jurors are subjected to further screening, which often involves detailed questioning about their backgrounds and their attitudes on issues related to the case they may be asked to decide. If they explicitly display or admit an inability to be fair to any party, they will be excused for cause.[23] In addition, however, all parties are allotted a number of peremptory challenges that they can exercise to remove a juror for any or no reason.[24] Because these challenges are not exercised randomly,[25] the jury selected is not a random sample of six or twelve drawn from among those awaiting assignment.[26] From both within and outside the legal system, some of the most vociferous criticism of the way jurors are selected has focused on this final stage of the selection process (e.g., *Batson v. Kentucky* 1984; Alschuler 1995).

The attempt to ensure participation of jurors drawn from a cross-section of the community can be justified on constitutional grounds or because of the greater legitimacy that is likely to flow from democratically selected juries, but we can also ask about its effect on the decisions juries reach. Does systematic exclusion of particular citizens affect jury decision making itself in predictable ways? Do the decisions of juries drawn from a representative jury pool differ from those that would be reached by more homogeneous sets of jurors? The competing values served by the jury system are squarely implicated in this final stage of jury selection because the peremptory challenge, while not constitutionally mandated, is a well-entrenched tradition in American legal procedure. Peremptory challenges permit the parties in a case to have a voice in the composition of the jury that will be exerting its power over them, a recognized component of procedural justice (Lind and Tyler 1988). At the same time, the interests of the community at large in the appearance of fairness to all trial participants, including jurors as well as parties, argue for limits on the form taken by this exercise of voice—thus, the U.S. Supreme Court has ruled in a series of recent cases that a party cannot base a peremptory challenge on the race or gender of the prospective juror.[27]

In principle, the race or gender of any trial participant, witness, party, or juror can influence juror verdict preferences. Although some color-blind and gender-neutral models of legal decision making view any relationship between race or gender and jury decisions as unacceptable bias in a purportedly neutral system (and indeed some of the U.S. Supreme Court's language in *Batson* and its progeny and in *J. E. B.* have this flavor—e.g., "we hold that gender, like race, is an unconstitutional proxy for juror competence and impartiality" [p. 1421]), the color-blind gender-neutral perspective ignores the social context that jurors may legitimately reflect in their decision making. Race and gender may be indicators of differences in life experiences that can lead jurors to evaluate the same testimony differently—indeed the pooling of those different perspectives is arguably one of the major strengths of the jury system. To the extent that the experience of jurors who differ in their racial backgrounds or gender leads those jurors to see evidence in different ways (e.g., if the experience of some black jurors with police officers leads them to view the police with greater suspicion, if some women find a claim of self-defense more plausible because of their own experience with the threat of violence), they sometimes may evaluate witness credibility differently and consequently favor different verdicts. To the extent that race and gender affect jury decisions by reflecting the multiple perspectives of jurors with different experiences, ensuring widespread participation on juries across race and gender may expand the pool of experience that the jury has at its disposal. Thus, while legal institutions are charged with ensuring that litigants do not receive different outcomes based on their race or gender, there are ways in which race and gender can affect the legal process legitimately. In evaluating evidence for the effects of race and gender, we attempt to distinguish between these different forms of race and gender effects.

a. The Effects of Race on Jury Decision Making
The evidence for racial effects on verdict preferences is surprisingly mixed. Although several researchers have shown higher conviction rates for black defendants than for white defendants by white respondents (e.g., McGlynn, Megas, and Benson 1976; Poulson 1990; for reviews, see Johnson 1985 and King 1993), a recent meta-analysis of twenty-nine juror simulation studies revealed no consistent effect of race of defendant on conviction rates across studies (Mazzella and Feingold 1994). This mixed pattern of racial results may reflect a complex web of interactions, but a few regularities emerge. First, there is some evidence that white jurors are *less* likely to convict when the victim and defendant are both minority members. At least some juries, according to the judges surveyed by Kalven and Zeisel (1966), showed an unusual willingness to acquit when both the defendant and the victim were black, exhibiting a form of racism that benefited the black defendant—but only at the expense of a black victim. This finding has been replicated by Myers (1980) and by Foley and Chamblin (1982).

Second, both white and black jurors show some evidence of an own-race bonus. Although most researchers have focused on the behavior of white jurors, a few studies have examined the verdicts of both black and white jurors. For example, a comparison of conviction rates for defendants tried by biracial or all-white juries in Florida (Freedberg 1984) showed a conviction rate for black defendants to be higher before all-white juries than before biracial juries (79 versus 51 percent), but higher for white defendants before biracial juries than all white juries (73 versus 56 percent). Although the study was based on a small number of cases (37 cases before all-white juries and 144 before biracial juries) and there were no controls for the weight of the evidence and make-up of the jury on nonracial characteristics, the pattern is consistent with results from two simulation studies in which the case facts were held constant. Both Ugwuegbu (1979) and Bernard (1979) asked black and white college students to judge a simulated case and found that white respondents were more likely to convict a black defendant than a white defendant, while black respondents were more likely to convict a white defendant than a black defendant.[28] If both black and white jurors favor same-race defendants, that pattern provides an additional justification (apart from juror rights and concerns about jury legitimacy) for court judicial and administrative efforts to avoid procedures that reduce minority representation on juries.

Only a few of the many researchers who have used simulations to investigate racial effects on the verdicts of jurors have given the jurors judicial instructions on the law or have obtained their verdicts after allowing them to deliberate as a group. In a study by Pfeiffer and Ogloff (1991), white jurors who received no judicial instructions showed an increased conviction rate for black defendants on trial for a crime involving a white victim, but the race of the victim and the defendant had no effect on jurors who had received instructions. Similarly, uninstructed jurors showed an increased conviction rate for black defendants that did not occur for instructed jurors in a study by Rector, Bagby, and Nicholson (1993). A parallel attenuation of ethnic effects occurred with deliberations in a study by Lipton (1983) comparing the verdicts of Hispanic and Anglo student jurors. It is of course unclear whether such procedures would eliminate or reduce race effects outside the laboratory.

Thus, despite an inconsistent pattern of results, there is evidence that societal issues of race do not stop at the jury room door, although they may be muted. There are also some data suggesting that judges too may be influenced by racial stereotypes that affect their decisions. Uhlman (1979) found that both white and black judges were more likely to convict black defendants than white defendants, even after controlling for crime severity, but the difference was smaller for black judges.

Several scholars (e.g., Alschuler 1995) have suggested racial quotas to ensure minority representation on juries in every trial. This proposal puts in sharp focus the ambiguous status of the juror as a representative of the community at large as opposed to a particular subcommunity, as a presumptively impartial blank slate or as a repository of particular experiences. It also raises serious questions about the effect of labeling jurors as racial representatives in an effort to reflect the community in the jury room.

b. The Effects of Gender on Jury Decision Making

Like race, a juror's or other trial participant's gender is a potential source of influence on the outcome of a jury trial. In *J. E. B. v. Alabama* (1994) the Supreme Court noted that even if the judgments of men and women were found to differ from each other in some statistically significant way, gender could not be used as a proxy for bias to justify a gender-based peremptory challenge. In fact, research has produced little evidence that systematic differences in verdicts are associated with gender for most offenses (e.g., Bray and Noble 1978; Eisen and McArthur 1979; Gray and Ashmore 1976; Hastie, Penrod, and Pennington 1983). The two exceptions arise in studies of sexual assault (e.g., Bottoms and Goodman 1994; Sealy and Cornish 1973; for a recent meta-analysis of mock juror reactions to sexual assault cases finding a higher conviction rate by women, see Schutte and Hosch 1996) and wife-battering (e.g., Pierce and Harris 1993). In cases involving these offenses, women appear to be more willing to convict. Note, however, that such cases typically involve a male defendant and a female victim, so that it is impossible to distinguish among potential explanations for the gender pattern that emerges in these cases. Are women simply more likely to show sympathy and empathy for the victim who is similar to them? Do they find the victim's story more credible because their life experiences or increased knowledge about crimes of sexual assault lead them to find it more plausible?

As in the case of racial effects, there is some evidence that judicial instructions and deliberations may attenuate gender effects. Studies of gender in real cases as opposed to simulations have revealed few differences (e.g., Bridgeman and Marlowe 1979; LaFree, Reskin, and Visher 1985; Visher 1987). Moreover, the addition of deliberations to jury simulations also appears to mute gender differences in verdict preferences (Crowley, O'Callaghan, and Ball 1994; Davis et al. 1975; Kerr et al. 1976) or cause them to disappear (Davis et al. 1977; Epstein and Bottoms 1996; Swim, Borgida, and McCoy 1993).

Although the Supreme Court specified in *J. E. B.* that gender could not be used as a proxy for bias when making peremptory challenges, the court explicitly noted that other characteristics were still permissible reasons for peremptorily striking jurors, even if one gender was disproportionately represented in, for example, a particular employment status. Thus, under *J. E. B.* it would presumably be appropriate to challenge an unemployed spouse because of his/her lack of paid employment. Researchers have identified some juror characteristics strongly correlated with gender that are associated with verdict (e.g., housewives were significantly less likely to acquit a defendant by reason of insanity in an incest case than were both women who worked outside the home and men [Simon 1967]; sex role stereotypes and rape empathy were associated with both gender and verdict preferences (Weir and Wrightsman 1990; Willis 1992). Under the reasoning expressed in *J. E. B.* it would be legitimate to peremptorily strike jurors based on attitudes or occupational characteristics even when they are closely related to gender.

c. The Effects of Juror Heterogeneity on Jury Decision Making
Thus far we have considered the effect of specific juror characteristics on individual verdict preferences, but we can also take a more multidimensional approach to the effect of juror composition on the behavior of the jury, asking how heterogeneity on the jury affects the process of decision making. Several pieces of evidence suggest that juror heterogeneity improves the deliberative process by encouraging a more thorough evaluation of possible alternative interpretations of evidence. For example, Pennington and Hastie (1990) report that jurors in their research responded differently to the fact that the defendant was carrying a knife. Jurors from wealthier suburbs found the defendant's possession of a knife remarkable, leading them to infer that the defendant had culpable intent, while jurors from poorer neighborhoods were more willing to believe the defendant was carrying the knife as a habit or for protection.

A more detailed exploration of the effects of heterogeneity was conducted by Cowan, Thompson, and Ellsworth (1984), who varied the homogeneity of juries according to jurors' willingness to consider giving the death penalty. They found that jurors who served on heterogeneous juries were more critical after deliberations in their evaluations of all witnesses than jurors who served on more homogeneous juries. The jurors on heterogeneous juries were also more accurate in their recall of the testimony, providing evidence that heterogeneity promoted more critical analysis of all issues. Thus, they suggest, "[H]omogeneity may hush the voice of a dissenting minority, whose criticisms of the majority viewpoint would have fostered the careful scrutiny of all relevant issues" (Cowan, Thompson, and Ellsworth 1984: 60). More recently, Diamond et al. (1996) found that in close cases (in which members of the jury pool were substantially divided on the appropriate verdict), juries that reflected that heterogeneity in their individual predeliberation verdict preferences covered more different facts in their deliberations than did juries that were less representative (and more homogeneous) in their initial preferences. Heterogeneous juries thus engaged in deliberations that more thoroughly reflected the evidence at trial.

At various times, the legal system has limited heterogeneity on the jury by using special so-called blue-ribbon juries composed of jurors who meet special educational or training qualifications. The assumption is that such jurors bring special skills to and as a result increase the competence level of the jury. Under current federal law, such special juries are specifically prohibited[29] but it is unclear that any constitutional obstacle exists. In 1947 the U.S. Supreme Court upheld a New York statute authorizing special juries selected from the general jury lists in cases involving "important, intricate, or widely-publicized" issues. It survived several constitutional challenges before being repealed in 1965. In recent years, a number of commentators have suggested that blue-ribbon juries be used in at least some complex cases (e.g., Drazan 1989; Luneburg and Nordenberg 1981).

Proposals for special juries generally do not consider the potential costs of blue-ribbon juries for the jury's political and legitimizing role. In suggesting them for complex civil cases, advocates would effectively create a two-tiered jury system in which large corporate defendants draw blue-ribbon juries and individual tort defendants go before traditional juries. The proponents of blue-ribbon juries also fail to provide any empirical foundation to support this dramatic curtailment of juror eligibility (Casper 1993). There is some intuitive plausibility to the notion that individual jurors with higher education levels or particularly relevant experience might show better comprehension for complex or technical evidence, but some recent work indicates that heterogeneous juries can draw on the special expertise of their members without sacrificing the advantages of heterogeneity (Diamond et al. 1996).

In sum, there may be more rhetorical heat than substance to the assumed trade-off between jury representativeness and jury competence that fuels much of the legal struggle to define the boundaries of jury composition. Reducing exclusions and removing obstacles to wide jury participation may stimulate a more complete representation of diverse views and more thorough debate about the evidence during jury deliberations and at the same time produce greater legitimacy for the resulting jury decisions.

2. How Big Will the Jury Be?
Must the Verdict Be Unanimous?

The traditional jury is a group of twelve citizens instructed that its verdict must be unanimous. What then was the source of the movement to reduce the size of the jury and to permit non-unanimous verdicts? One explanation is that those arguing for the change genuinely believed that it would be possible to reduce costs with no effect on the quality of jury deliberative processes. An alternative explanation is that the movement expressed an image of the jury as a decision producer, whose particular verdict is less important than the fact that a verdict is produced.

In a series of cases during the 1970s, the U.S. Supreme Court ruled that juries with as few as six members were permissible and that unanimity was not required for jury verdicts in civil and criminal cases.[30] Many of the early court opinions cited substantially flawed research which purported to show no effect of jury size or a unanimity requirement on jury decisions or deliberations (Zeisel and Diamond 1974). Since those rulings, smaller and non-unanimous juries have become more common. Courts adopted these changed procedures primarily in the name of cost savings and with the expectation that the rate of hung juries would drop.

More carefully designed studies of the effects of the smaller and non-unanimous juries have found evidence that the cost savings produced by these changes are minimal (Guinther 1988), and that the changes have additional consequences: smaller juries are significantly less representative (Zeisel 1971) and are less accurate in their recall of the evidence (Padawer-Singer 1977); non-unanimous jury members are less likely than those on unanimous juries to correct factual errors, are less satisfied with deliberations, and report that deliberation has been less thorough (Hastie, Penrod, and Pennington 1983).

As Paul Carrington (1990) has pointed out, at the same time that legal shifts have produced more representative jury pools, the reduction in jury size has reduced opportunities for obtaining representative juries. The loss associated with the reduction in jury size has been compounded by a failure to reduce the number of peremptory challenges, so that the attorneys can exert more substantial control over the ultimate membership on the jury. Thus, these apparently value-free cost-saving measures have altered the distribution of control over jury membership and reduced the ability of juries to reflect the sense of the community.

2. HOW LAW MATTERS IN SHAPING THE CONTENT OF THE JURY TRIAL AND THE VERDICT OF THE JURY

So far we have considered aspects of the trial that the jurors can influence only in limited ways. They can fail to cooperate in becoming jurors or they can fabricate responses during jury selection, but in general the judge and the parties and their attorneys control who will be seated on the jury. The potential for control shifts dramatically once the jury is chosen and faces the content of the trial itself. Here the jury in reaching its verdict can, if it chooses, ignore evidence or disregard the judge's admonitions and instructions on the law. If it decides to acquit a defendant in a criminal trial, the decision will be final. As we shall see, although the jury possesses these powers, its rule departures occur relatively infrequently. When they do, they are often the result of inadequacies in legal instruction and fundamental human information processing and attributional processes, rather than overt rebellion against the applicable legal standard. Even in those instances when the jury intentionally deviates from what it understands the law to be, the legal standard provides a yardstick which the jury considers in exercising its power.

There are a number of reasons to expect rule departures by juries. Much legal doctrine proceeds on the assumption that the jury is a passive and docile receptacle for evidence and instructions on the law. The rules of evidence create a selective picture of what the jurors are told about the events that led to the trial. Curious omissions, objections, and admonitions to disregard information dot the presentation of evidence. Jurors are told not to discuss the case and generally cannot ask questions during the trial. They are instructed not to form impressions or make judgments about their ultimate verdict until all the testimony is completed and the judicial instructions have been issued. Although most judges and attorneys would probably not claim that jurors actually achieve this model of passivity, the legal system proceeds as if it assumes they do.

Evidence from behavioral science paints a very different picture. Like other human decision makers, jurors bring expectations and preconceptions with them to the jury box, actively search for causal explanations to make sense of the events about which they are told, and consciously or unconsciously process information, filling in blanks or interpreting ambiguities in testimony in ways that may strongly influence their decisions (Casper, Benedict, and Perry 1989; Diamond and Casper 1992; Hastie, Penrod, and Pennington 1983). Like all human information processors, jurors do not absorb everything they are exposed to (Fiske and Taylor 1991), instead drawing selectively from the factual and legal information that the trial presents. As a result, the jury's verdict may be guided less by the intended legal lessons of the jury instructions and more by the jury's own construction of the case evidence in light of the jury's own sense of justice.

A. THE RULES OF EVIDENCE

The rules of evidence determine what evidence the jury will be permitted to hear. Not only is irrelevant[31] information excluded from the trial, but also some relevant information is excluded if the legal system determines that it will cause prejudice or confusion, or mislead the jury.[32]

Jurors know that the story they hear in the courtroom is incomplete (Diamond 1993). Sidebars during the trials, objections, and instances in which the jurors are excused from the courtroom all convey to jurors that they are not being permitted to learn all that there is to know. Although jurors are instructed to base their decisions only on the evidence presented in court, it can be difficult for them to avoid speculating about matters they view as omissions or limitations. For example, in a survey of jurors who served in thirty-eight federal and state civil cases in Pennsylvania, 51 percent of the jurors said they wondered why certain people who were mentioned during the trial didn't testify (Guinther 1988). One-fourth (27 percent) said they "held it against the side that did not call certain people to testify who might have added important information." Thus, by limiting the jurors' access to some forms of evidence, legal controls only partially succeed in focusing the jurors solely on the events that transpire in the courtroom.

B. PARTIALLY VISIBLE CONTROLS: ADMONITIONS TO DISREGARD, LIMITING INSTRUCTIONS, AND BLINDFOLDING

In the course of a trial, a witness may say something that is precluded by the rules of evidence (e.g., the witness may refer to the defendant's liability insurance in a jurisdiction that forbids the mention of insurance). Or a judge will instruct jurors to consider the defendant's criminal record only for the limited purpose of judging credibility and not as evidence that the defendant committed the offense. Or jurors who are deciding whether the defendant should be sentenced to death send a note to the judge asking what will happen if the defendant is not sentenced to death. Although the statute requires the judge to sentence the defendant to life in prison without the possibility of parole, the jurors are blindfolded to the consequences of their decision. They are told that their only responsibility is to determine whether the defendant should be sentenced to death.

In each instance, the legal system asks the jurors to ignore a case attribute that may fundamentally affect their perceptions of the parties and the case. Research indicates that on some of these occasions jurors are unable to comply fully with the legal demand. The most studied instance involves the defendant with a criminal record who takes the stand. As Wissler and Saks (1985) demonstrated, jurors told about the defendant's prior record tend to convict at a higher rate than those not told of the defendant's record, particularly if the defendant has a prior conviction for a crime identical to the current charge. Moreover, there is persuasive evidence that this effect is not a product simply of discounting the defendant's exculpatory testimony, but rather is produced by the existence of the criminal record itself.

When legal policies attempt to control jury behavior by simply forbidding juries access to available information or demanding that they use the information in limited ways, the policies are ignoring the role of the juror as an active collaborator in the production of the trial verdict. Although it may not always be possible to meet the jury's cognitive needs and gain the jury's cooperation, one strategy is to do what Judge Schwarzer of the Federal Judicial Center calls "level" with the jury. Jonathan Casper and one of us (S. D.) tested juror responses to several versions of an antitrust jury instruction (Diamond and Casper 1992). Some of the jurors were informed that their verdict would be automatically trebled by statute and the jurors gave significantly lower awards as a result of that information, presumably to avoid a plaintiff windfall. Other jurors were told about the trebling provision and were simply admonished not to lower their awards. That admonition did not prevent them from giving reduced awards. In contrast, a third condition treated the jurors as collaborators and explained why Congress had passed the automatic trebling provision—for purposes of punishment and deterrence—and how they would be undermining Congress's purpose if they reduced their award below the amount necessary to compensate the plaintiff. In this third condition, the jurors did not give reduced awards. Although the strategy of blindfolding may occasionally be preferred (if jurors are unlikely to think of a particular topic or fact unless it is introduced in the courtroom), leveling with jurors may in many cases facilitate rather than impair legal control. Again, a system ambivalent in its willingness to trust lay decision makers may fail to gauge when the cost of withholding information is greater than the danger of providing it.

C. EXPLICIT LEGAL DIRECTIVES: JURY INSTRUCTIONS

In every American jury trial today, the jurors begin their deliberations only after receiving instructions from the judge on the law they are to apply in reaching a verdict. These judicial instructions are a relatively recent development in the history of the American jury. Early juries in the United States were regarded as equal to the judge in their ability to interpret the common law (Perlman 1986). The rationale was that juries shared the values and knew the rules of ordinary transactions on which the common law was built. It was not until the end of the nineteenth century, as part of the increasing efforts at jury control, that state legislatures and courts began to require the trial judge to instruct the jury and empowered the judge to grant a new trial when the jury's verdict was deemed inconsistent with the law. In 1895, the U.S. Supreme Court held in *Sparf and Hansen v. United States*[33] that jurors did not have the right to decide questions of law, even in criminal cases. If jurors did not have that right, the trial judge had to give the jury instructions so that the jury could base its verdict on the applicable law.

Appellate courts began to review the instructions that the judges gave to juries, reversing jury decisions or ordering a new trial when judges failed to state the applicable law accurately. To increase the likelihood that their instructions would be accurate and to decrease their chance of being reversed, judges formed committees, usually with representatives from the practicing bar, to draft pattern jury instructions that could be endorsed for use in all applicable cases. Almost all jurisdictions have developed some form of pattern jury instructions (Nieland 1978) and in some states judges are required to give the pattern jury instruction whenever one is available that is applicable to the case.[34]

This history reveals the dominant force that motivated the way in which jury instructions were written: a determination to present the applicable law accurately. It also provides a clue like the one that came from the silent dog in the Sherlock Holmes tale:[35] nowhere in this history was any concern expressed about whether the judicial instructions were being written in a way that would effectively instruct the jury on the applicable law. The audience of concern was and continues to be the appellate court, not the jury.

Jurors encounter a series of difficulties in attempting to follow the judicial instructions they typically receive. These include problems of comprehension, memory failure, and problems in applying the legal standards.[36] Researchers have conducted a number of empirical studies that reveal the breadth and depth of these obstacles and which raise serious questions about the ability of standard jury instructions to control or even to affect jury decision making.

1. Rewriting Jury Instructions

In the late 1970s and early 1980s several teams of psychologists and legal scholars presented citizens with selections from judicial instructions and tested juror comprehension of the instructions. For example, Charrow and Charrow (1979) read a set of instructions drawn from the official set of California pattern jury instructions, one at a time,[37] to a panel of prospective jurors in California and asked each juror to paraphrase the instruction after listening to it. Across the fourteen pattern jury instructions they tested, the Charrows found that jurors averaged approximately 45 percent correct.[38] By altering the grammatical structure of the instructions without changing their meaning, the Charrows were able to improve significantly the overall juror performance to approximately 59 percent correct. Performance on several individual instructions improved by more than 20 percent. This result provided evidence that lack of clarity in judicial instructions was not solely the result of inherent complexity in legal concepts, but rather was at least in part due to unnecessary lack of clarity in presentation.

Later researchers have described in detail how rewriting can improve the clarity and comprehensibility of judicial instructions. Elwork, Sales, and Alfini (1982), in the most extensive attempt to address problems of opaque instructions and describe ways to overcome them, presented jurors with trial evidence from a simple burglary case or a complex criminal case involving a defense of insanity. They then gave the jurors a set of judicial instructions. To some jurors they gave the original instructions. To other jurors they gave rewritten instructions which were simplified and clarified using standard psycholinguistic techniques (e.g., exchanging unfamiliar words like "conjecture" for more familiar ones like "guess," substituting active for passive voice, reorganizing sentences to avoid complicated embedded clauses, etc.). By rewriting the instructions, Elwork and his colleagues were able to increase juror performance on a multiple choice test from 51 percent in the complex criminal case and 65 percent in the simple burglary case to 80 percent in both cases.

If the goal is to guide juror decision making with a set of legal standards, communicating the content of the rules is an obvious first step. But good performance on a comprehension task does not ensure that the jurors will be able to apply the instructions accurately. Severance and Loftus (1982) tested their respondents' comprehension.[39] They then gave the respondents a series of fact patterns and assessed the rate of agreement and disagreement by the respondents with correct and incorrect applications of the law. On the critical concepts they studied, jurors began with low comprehension levels (between 24 and 47 percent on a multiple-choice test). By rewriting jury instructions on those concepts (like reasonable doubt and the meaning of intent) that appeared to cause jurors difficulty,[40] Severance and Loftus were able to produce some significant increases in both comprehension and correct application. The increases, however, were small, and even with the revised instructions the mean percentage correct on the application measures averaged 68 percent.

The efforts to rewrite jury instructions generally have shown significant improvements in comprehension, but the level of jury miscomprehension researchers have found with standard jury instructions and the size of the effects produced by rewriting the instructions have varied considerably. In part, the differences may be due to the variations in the procedures used. Some researchers studying comprehension of jury instructions have had jurors paraphrase the instructions (e.g., Charrow and Charrow 1979), some have asked questions that required short answers (e.g., Elwork, Sales, and Alfini 1977), some have asked true/false questions (e.g., Ellsworth 1989; Reifman, Gusick, and Ellsworth 1992), and others have used multiple-choice measures (e.g., Strawn and Buchanan 1976). Some have permitted jurors to refer to written copies of the instructions (e.g., Severance, Greene, and Loftus 1984), while others have read the instructions to the jurors so that the jurors were left to rely on their memories (Ellsworth 1989).[41] Some have used student respondents (e.g., Severance and Loftus 1982) and others have tested jurors (e.g., Elwork, Sales, and Alfini 1982). Some have allowed jurors to deliberate (e.g., Severance, Greene, and Loftus 1984) and some have not (e.g., Strawn and Buchanan 1976). In all cases, however, researchers have been able to produce some improvements in comprehension by clarifying the instructions.

2. Deliberations

Two recent investigations have conducted thorough examinations of the role played by instructions during deliberations (Ellsworth 1989; Hastie, Penrod, and Pennington 1983). Both showed jurors the same videotaped criminal murder trial[42] in which jurors were asked to reach one of four possible verdict categories.[43] Hastie, Penrod, and Pennington report that approximately 25 percent of the remarks jurors made during deliberations referred to the instructions. Similarly, Ellsworth found that jurors spent an average of 21 percent of their time discussing the judge's instructions. This substantial attention to instructions might suggest that low comprehension levels are cured in the course of normal trial procedures. Further analysis, however, indicates that any optimism would be misplaced.

Hastie, Penrod, and Pennington (1983) found that jurors averaged less than 30 percent correct on questions that concerned the instructions although they showed an average performance of 60 percent on factual issues in the testimony. Ellsworth (1989) coded the accuracy of juror discussion of both instructions and factual issues during deliberations as well as postdeliberation comprehension levels. Using what she characterized as generous coding, Ellsworth (1989) found that only half of the references to the law were correct. Moreover, although inaccurate statements of fact tended to be corrected during deliberations, incorrect references to the law were not corrected. Because she had a sample of jurors who were not asked to deliberate, she was also able to test directly the impact of deliberations on juror comprehension. Although deliberating jurors performed quite well on the test of factual issues and significantly better than jurors who did not deliberate, both deliberators and nondeliberators performed equally poorly, at no better than chance levels, on the test assessing comprehension of the judge's instructions.

The dismal overall performance of the jurors in dealing with judicial instructions in these two studies might have been partially cured if the instructions had been rewritten following the model proposed by Elwork, Sales, and Alfini (1982). In a recent study, Diamond and Levi (1996) tested the effects of deliberation on juror comprehension of a set of death penalty instructions that had been revised to improve clarity. Although revising the instructions improved performance on all three of the issues they were designed to address, deliberation affected only the one issue on which a substantial portion of jurors individually demonstrated comprehension: that is, deliberation helped only when the deliberating jurors were more likely to share correct rather than incorrect information.

3. Written Instructions

Numerous commentators have advocated providing jurors with written instructions to increase comprehension (e.g., Cunningham 1958; Elwork, Sales, and Alfini 1982; Sand and Reiss 1985). Moreover, cognitive psychology has repeatedly demonstrated the comprehension benefits of multiple exposure (e.g., Nelson 1977), and educational psychology has shown that the opportunity to go over material several times—not possible when listening but possible when reading—generally makes reading comprehension superior to listening comprehension (Young 1973). Nonetheless, many jurisdictions currently do not allow and most do not require that jurors be provided with a written copy of the judge's instructions on the law.

Neither of the two studies that have directly assessed the impact of written instructions provide evidence that written instructions can be relied on to ensure juror comprehension. Hastie (1983) randomly assigned simulated juries to a written or an oral instruction condition. The jurors then watched a videotape of an armed robbery trial and deliberated to a verdict. The jurors who received written instructions performed *less* well on a recall measure than those who received oral instructions. Hastie suggests that jurors who can refer to the instructions do not process them as deeply as those who must rely on their memories, but he was not able directly to test that explanation because he did not have comprehension measures or measures that tested how jurors applied the instructions to fact situations.

Heuer and Penrod (1989) tested the effect of written instructions by randomly assigning real criminal and civil trials to written or oral instruction conditions.[44] Jurors filled out questionnaires at the end of each trial, including a set of multiple-choice questions that assessed juror memory for the judge's instructions. Jurors who received written instructions did not differ in their performance from those who received them orally. Because even the jurors who received written instructions filled out the questionnaire and returned it through the mail after the trial, the measure assessed memory rather than simply comprehension. Moreover, the test was not able to evaluate the effect of written instructions on many issues of substantive law because all of the questions were designed to apply to every trial.[45] Nonetheless, these two studies suggest that the problems associated with judicial instructions may not be solved merely by supplying written copies.

4. Preinstruction

Preinstruction is another procedure designed to improve juror comprehension. Jurors traditionally are instructed on the law only after they have heard the evidence. By failing to provide a framework of relevant legal considerations at the outset, the system assumes that jurors will attend to and recall all relevant evidence for later use in reaching a verdict, an expectation that strains credulity. In a larceny trial, for example, testimony about whether the defendant intended to permanently deprive the victim of his property is relevant to the definition of the crime. If jurors begin the trial thinking that larceny consists simply of taking property, they may not attend closely to testimony that relates to the defendant's plans for the property's return. Although some evidence suggests better recall for instructions delivered both before and at the end of the trial (Smith 1991), as with written instructions, preinstruction does not appear to eliminate the comprehension deficit.

In general, then, if jury instructions are intended to control jury decision making, there is substantial evidence that they are not achieving that goal. Why have efforts to improve communication been so limited (Tanford 1991)? In some areas of the law, the reluctance may be understandable, if not justified, because there is considerable disagreement about the meaning of a particular legal standard or principle. The best example of this may be the phrase "beyond a reasonable doubt," a phrase that jurors regularly raise questions about (Severance and Loftus 1982) and apparently have some difficulty applying in a consistent fashion (e.g., Kagehiro and Stanton 1985). Courts have been ambivalent about how and even whether to define the phrase (e.g., Newman 1996; *Victor v. Nebraska* 1994). In most areas, however, communication can be improved although the effort entails two costs. First, the task requires some effort both in writing and in testing proposed alternatives. Second, the committees generally responsible for drafting pattern instructions must deal with the not insignificant challenge of pleasing diverse constituencies with competing interests (e.g., prosecutors and plaintiffs' attorneys as well as defense counsel).

Does a failure to communicate applicable legal standards to the jury matter? One possibility is that jurors faced with opaque instructions apply their own sense of justice (Saks 1993). Thus, in such cases, the legal system may by default (or by benign neglect or design?) encourage jurors to turn to custom and practice rather than doctrine in reaching their decisions.

5. Resistance and Jury Nullification

There is no clear standard for gauging the correctness of a jury verdict or even its consistency with the law. Judicial behavior was the standard used by Kalven and Zeisel (1966) in their survey of American judges. They asked judges across the country to report on the jury trials they presided over. After each of the more than seven thousand criminal and civil trials in the study, the judge filled out a questionnaire indicating the characteristics of the trial, the nature of the evidence presented, what the jury decided, and how the judge would have decided the case. The rate of agreement between judge and jury was 78 percent for criminal cases (Kalven and Zeisel 1966) and 79 percent for civil cases (Kalven 1964). If we assume that the judges reached decisions consistent with the law, the room for the jury's resistance would be confined to the remaining 20 percent of cases.[46] Kalven and Zeisel, based on their analysis of the case characteristics that produced disagreements between judge and jury, concluded that even among the 22 percent of criminal cases involving judge-jury verdict differences, few reflected a war with the law.[47] Jurors were less likely to convict when the offense involved an unpopular law (e.g., gaming), or the defendant appeared to be acting in self-defense but used more force than was permissible under the law, and jurors seemed to recognize contributory fault in the victim that the law would find irrelevant. In general, however, Kalven and Zeisel (1966) attribute most of the disagreements to evidentiary disputes, reporting that the jury is engaged in only a modest rewriting of the law in cases that are close on the evidence.

In one important respect, the Kalven and Zeisel data provide only a limited correlational view of how much the law influences the jury's behavior.

We cannot tell whether or how much of the agreement they report is the result of the law's influence on the jury and how much is due simply to a convergence of the jury's perspective and the law's guidance. The data on juror comprehension of judicial instructions indicate that many attempts to instruct the jury on the law are more ritual than communication. To the extent that communication about legal standards is fuzzy or unclear, it may be that a large portion of the high agreement is the spurious result of legal standards that are consistent with jurors' doctrinally unfettered sense of justice.

This assessment is consistent with our evidence from those limited occasions when the jury does refuse to apply the law, the jury nullification cases. These cases reveal the limited nature of the jury's overt disagreement with legal standards or their application. Some of these instances have a political tinge, like those involving juries who refused to convict young men who failed to register for the draft during the Vietnam era. Others express what may be the beginning of a move to change the law, as in some acquittals or manslaughter convictions of battered women charged with the murder of the men who brutalized them and the occasional acquittals in cases of euthanasia.

In a third category is a more diverse collection of cases in which the jury's mercy simply exceeds that of the law. The young bartender we described at the beginning of this chapter is one of this group, and the background of the case is telling. The stolen television he bought for such an unexpectedly low price had been part of a large shipment that the prosecutor said had been sitting in a truck in the adjacent parking lot. Behind the scenes, it emerged that the prosecutor had brought the case to trial because he believed that the young man knew and refused to disclose the name of the person responsible for the shipment. The judge, who applauded the jury's acquittal saying that based on the evidence he would have been forced to convict if it had been a bench trial, was annoyed with the prosecutor for bringing the case to trial. Some of the jurors said they believed that the defendant must have known that the television set was stolen.[48]

In a second case, the defendant was a longtime mail handler on disability leave from a job-related injury. He was accused of stealing a test sack of mail with a lock on it that indicated the sack contained money. Using periscope-like equipment to watch the employees from the ceiling of the building, postal security was able to document that he had moved the sack from its proper place to an out-of-the-way location. Some jurors felt that the postal authorities should have waited until he removed or opened the bag, but they did not seem to doubt that he had intentionally moved the bag so that he could obtain its contents. Some of the jurors said that they suspected that the post office was trying to get rid of a disabled employee. All of the jurors objected to what they called the "spy-in-the-sky" surveillance system. The judge told one of us (S. D.) he would have convicted, albeit reluctantly. The jury acquitted.

A final example comes from the film of an actual deliberating jury in the case of *Wisconsin v. Leroy Reed* (Herzberg 1990).[49] After an agonizing deliberation, the jurors acquitted the mentally deficient defendant on a weapons charge although the evidence clearly indicated that he possessed a gun, in direct violation of the terms of his parole. Although recognizing the extenuating circumstances, the last juror agreed to acquit with the greatest of difficulty. His struggle reflected discomfort with the conflict between an acquittal and the apparent demands of the law.

Throughout the history of the jury, the appropriate role of jury nullification has been a source of extensive and continuing debate. In particular, courts and commentators have argued about whether the jury should be told about its power to nullify. In *United States v. Dougherty* (1972), which grew out of protests against the Vietnam War, the majority opinion found that although juries have the power to nullify, they do not have the right to be told explicitly that they have that power. Judge Leventhal contended that to make the power explicit would loosen appropriate restraint. In his dissent Judge Bazelon argued for candor. In the federal courts and in all but two states,[50] jurors are not told that they are entitled to nullify.[51] Although they occasionally do, the power is used sparingly. Some limited empirical evidence suggests that Judge Leventhal may have been correct in assuming that nullification would be more common if jurors received an explicit instruction. In a series of jury simulations Horowitz and his colleagues (Horowitz and Willging 1991) have shown that jurors are more willing to acquit in certain circumstances when they hear an explicit instruction on nullification. Horowitz found that increased acquittals occurred only when the offense and defendant were admirable (e.g., a devoted nurse in a case of euthanasia), and that an unexpected increase in guilty verdicts occurred for unsympathetic defendants (e.g., a drunk driving case). Thus, the release of restraint caused by the explicit instruction may have unanticipated and objectionable consequences. In the absence of instruction, nullification currently operates as a limited restraint on the inflexibility of the legal context in which the jury operates.

3. COMPARING JURIES AND JUDGES

One assumption in our discussion of the jury—and indeed in all of the legal efforts aimed at jury control—has been that the jury, without special efforts at channeling and guiding, will be less likely to follow legal standards than would a professionally trained judge. Recent critics of the jury have claimed that jurors cannot be trusted to apply legal standards. Thus, an important question is: How do lay judges compare with their professional counterparts in their ability to follow the law and arrive at reasonable verdicts?

One way to answer this question is to find out whether judges and jurors make the same verdict choices given an identical set of case facts. Kalven and Zeisel (1966), based on their comparison of judge and jury verdicts, concluded that disagreements between the judge and jury were rarely the product of disagreement over legal standards. Furthermore, when they did disagree it was not likely due to the jury simply misunderstanding the evidence or law involved in the more complex cases, as the level of disagreement was the same whether the case was rated by judges as "easy to understand" or "difficult to understand."[52]

The few other studies that have examined decision making by judges and jurors have shown a surprising correspondence, even in response to case characteristics that might be expected to influence laypersons more than professionals. Wells (1992) asked both judges and jury-eligible undergraduates to evaluate naked statistical evidence in a series of mock civil cases. Both sets of decision makers were reluctant to find for the plaintiff when presented with this kind of evidence, even though both assessed the meaning of the probability information similarly. Furthermore, a substantial proportion of judges who chose not to apply statistical evidence gave weak or flawed reasons for discounting it.

More recently, Vidmar and Rice (1993) compared the medical malpractice awards of professional judges (experienced arbitrators) and jurors (who volunteered to participate while waiting to be called to the courtroom) in a simulated case. Decision makers were informed that liability and economic damages had already been agreed on, but that noneconomic damages for disfigurement and pain and suffering were still in dispute. The authors found no significant differences in the total amount of money that the arbitrators and jurors awarded the plaintiff. More importantly, no differences between arbitrator and juror awards emerged when the total awards were disaggregated into their component parts (economic damages, pain and suffering, and disfigurement). Based on these findings the authors argued that the reasoning of jurors does not differ substantially from that of their professional counterparts.

Based on some of the above data (and other data by Diamond and Stalans 1989; Howe 1991; Howe and Loftus 1992), Landsman and Rakos (1994) questioned whether judges consistently reach verdicts that are more legally justifiable than the verdicts of jurors. They tested the legal system's assumption that judges can "compartmentalize" and discount legally inadmissible information when they are exposed to it. In a mock civil products liability case they found that judges and jurors who were exposed to information that had been ruled inadmissible were influenced by that information to a similar extent. This finding calls into question the traditional assumption that judges (though not juries) can ignore prejudicial information they may be exposed to during pretrial hearings and outside the presence of a jury. Moreover, it suggests that under some circumstances law can matter more in a jury trial than in a bench trial, precisely because the structure of the jury trial avoids burdening the decision maker with much potentially biasing information which the judge must confront in any trial.

4. THE LAW'S AMBIVALENT REACTIONS TO THE JURY: SOURCES AND CONSEQUENCES

The jury has changed in substantial ways since its early days when it consisted of knowledgeable citizens who were familiar with the events that formed the foundation for the conflict they were to judge. These early jurors knew more than the judge did about the facts and were expected to determine the applicable legal standards based on custom and practice. They were drawn from a relatively narrow population of eligible citizens (white male property-owners) and only limited efforts were mounted to control them. Over the years, both the demands and the constraints on the jury have grown, interacting in unanticipated ways.

Our examination of legal controls on the jury reveals a mixed picture of attempts to direct the jury along the pathways of formal legal doctrine. While granting substantial decision making power to the jury, the legal system imposes formidable blindfolds and barriers that limit the jury's base of information. While engaging in increasing efforts to maximize heterogeneity in the pool of potential jurors, the legal system permits a selection process that limits the diversity of jurors who actually are seated on the jury. Despite substantial ritual in the design and policing of jury instructions, there is evidence of a persistent failure to communicate and little serious effort to facilitate juror comprehension of legal standards. What explains these inconsistent efforts to regulate the jury?

The answer may lie in the multiple roles that the jury is called on to play and in the fact that the roles themselves are often inconsistent. When one demand on the jury seems paramount, we bolster the structures that promise to fill that demand. Thus, in addressing concerns about the jury's ability to resolve complex fact-laden disputes, we focus on ways to maximize the jury's rational information-processing skills. A natural response is the expansion of methods aimed at channeling the jury's attention and limiting its access to potentially distracting but persuasive evidence. When concerns are raised about the jury's ability to perform its symbolic and political role in reflecting community values, attention shifts to procedures that control heterogeneity and structures that limit the jury's ability to express a distinctive voice. Not surprisingly, conflicting demands produce conflicting responses.

The jury is an instrument of the formal legal structure—law does matter—and jury decisions generally mirror those of its judicial counterpart. But much of the value and vitality of the jury, embedded in the legal rules and structures that only partially restrain it, lies in the jury's power to, and indeed in the expectation that it will on occasion, deviate from formal doctrinal paths or from what a judge would do. In that role, the jury acts as a safety valve, able to respond to the particulars of an individual case without disturbing or creating legal precedents.

The jury, however, is not simply a safety valve. Nor does it merely soften the law's hard edges. Jury verdicts may also reflect community legal standards more accurately than do the decisions of professional judges even when they are attempting to represent those community standards. When the jury is called upon to define community norms, it is *the* voice of the law, and that voice, permitted to carry weight, can act as a constraint on judicial deviation from those uncodified standards. For example, does the jury or the judge better represent the law when the decision is whether or not to sentence a defendant to death? In thirty of thirty-eight states with capital sentencing, the jury is the ultimate barrier to a death sentence: no judge can impose death after a jury determination that death is not appropriate. In Alabama and three other states, juries provide advisory verdicts in capital cases and the judge retains final authority to decide on the sentence. In a recent survey in Alabama, judges overrode the nondeath recommendation of the jury in forty-seven cases and spared five defendants for whom the jury had recommended death.[53] Justice Stevens (*Harris v. Alabama* 1995) argues that this disproportionate rate of judicial override in favor of death can be explained by prejudicial extralegal pressure on the judges: "The 'higher authority' to whom present-day judges may be 'too responsive' is a political climate in which judges who covet higher office—or who merely wish to remain judges—must constantly profess their fealty to the death penalty. . . . Alabama trial judges face partisan election every six years. The danger that they will bend to political pressures when pronouncing sentence in highly publicized capital cases is the same danger confronted by judges beholden to King George III" (p. 1039). Although the polls show that a majority of citizens support the death penalty, they do not show how a majority of citizens would vote in a particular trial. Thus, if a judge attempts to reflect community norms by applying a generalized community sentiment, that reflection will provide an imperfect guide to relevant community standards applied to the facts of that case.

The legal system's ambivalence about the jury is thus both understandable and unavoidable. The jury plays an important, if not always predictable, role not just in applying legal doctrine, but also in interpreting it, defining and redefining it. As a result, those responsible for granting power and discretion to the jury will always be ambivalent about sharing power with a group of amateurs. That ambivalence will continue to express itself in periodic efforts to control and constrain the jury. The form taken by these efforts, and the response of the jury to them, will continue to shape how law matters to the jury.

NOTES

1. The jury is primarily an Anglo-American phenomenon. In Great Britain, juries decide cases involving serious criminal offenses, but juries in civil cases were abolished in most circumstances by the Administration of Justice Act of 1920.

2. Decisions to acquit in criminal cases cannot be overturned due to constitutional protection from double jeopardy.

3. The standard jury decision is a general verdict unaccompanied by any explanation or delineation of the steps that led the jury to its finding on guilt or liability. In civil cases, however, the general verdict occasionally is either replaced with a special verdict which requires the jury to answer a series of specific questions on the factual issues involved in the case or is supplemented with a set of special interrogatories. Unlike the extensive findings of fact that characterize a judicial opinion, special verdicts and interrogatories are limited to conclusions about the crucial legal elements that would be required to produce liability or determine the amount of damages that would be awarded (e.g., Did the defendant exercise ordinary care? Did the defendant have a duty to warn the plaintiff? What percentage of fault was attributable to the plaintiff?).

4. In *Blanton v. North Las Vegas* (1989), the court extended this coverage, suggesting that there may be a right to a jury trial even when the possible penalty is less than a six-month sentence if there are other penalties that are so severe that they indicate the legislature viewed the crime as serious rather than petty.

5. States that do have jury sentencing in some noncapital felony cases include Georgia, Indiana, Kentucky, Texas, and Virginia.

6. The judge is responsible for capital sentencing in Arizona, Idaho, Montana, and Nebraska.

7. The jury plays an advisory role in Alabama, Delaware, Florida, and Indiana (Russell 1994).

8. This phrase entails two distinctions: (1) between law and equity jurisdiction; and (2) causes of action that existed or are according to some analysis comparable to causes of action that existed at the time the Bill of Rights was passed

9. The party does, according to *Tull v. United States*, pp. 417–27 (1987).

10. Carrington (1990: 83) describes this distinction as a "Solomonic result . . . that cannot be persuasively explained to the practical political observer," but that provides a way for a motivated Congress to deny the right to a civil jury trial in private actions.

11. National Center for State Courts (1983), p. 37.

12. U.S. Department of Justice (1983).

13. Galanter (1990) reports that jury trials take place in less than one percent of cases terminated in state courts and in just over two percent of terminations in federal courts.

14. This coverage not only presents unrepresentative damages awards, it also portrays the jury as eager to believe plaintiff claims, an image that sharply conflicts with evidence from studies of actual jurors (e.g., Hans and Lofquist 1992).

15. For some special verdicts, the answers are not independent because the answer to some questions may be contingent on the answer to an earlier question. For example, in a products liability suit, the jury may be asked first whether the product at issue caused the plaintiff's injury and then whether that product was manufactured by the defendant (versus some other manufacturer).

16. The property requirement provided an easy way to discipline jurors who delivered unacceptable verdicts. Jurors could be punished by having their property seized.

17. Case law has interpreted the constitutional mandate for an impartial jury to require "a body truly representative of the community and not an organ of any special group or class" (*Glasser v. U.S.*, 1942). This requirement has generally been interpreted to preclude

systematic exclusion or underrepresentation of distinctive groups in the jury selection process (e.g., *Duren v. Missouri*, 1979).

18. *Strauder v. W. Virginia* (1880).

19. The decision was *Ballard v. United States* (1946), which reversed a federal conviction by an all-male jury because in limiting jury service to males, the federal court had not followed practice in state court. *Ballard* was subsequently seen as simply interpreting the statute that required federal courts to follow state practice and not as establishing a constitutional standard for all courts (Van Dyke 1977: 66).

20. *People v. Harris* (1984).

21. Federal courts have been willing to accept the sole use of voter lists as the source for jurors.

22. *Taylor v. Louisiana* (1975).

23. For example, when a criminal case involves substantial pretrial publicity, jurors will be excused for cause if they admit to having preconceived notions about the guilt or innocence of the defendant that they say they would be unable to set aside. Other kinds of cases, too, may generate excuses based on cause. For example, in a federal case involving the sale of heroin, the judge excused jurors who said that the nature of the case would prevent them from being fair. The elimination of biased jurors through the challenge for cause depends largely on the willingness of jurors to recognize and admit an inability to be fair. An interesting empirical question is whether jurors who admit to such bias would in fact be less objective in response to evidence presented at trial than jurors who do not see themselves as biased (i.e., "Yes, although my father and brother are police officers, I can be fair to the accused who allegedly shot a police officer").

24. Race and gender are currently the only attributes whose use is forbidden in the exercise of peremptory challenge. In *Batson v. Kentucky* (1984), the U.S. Supreme Court applied to peremptory challenge the concerns about the systematic exclusion of jurors on the basis of race that it formerly applied only to the jury venire. In *Batson*, the court concluded that the government's use of peremptory challenges to exclude blacks during voir dire violated the black defendant's rights under the Equal Protection Clause. In later cases, the court shifted its focus and extended relief from racial discrimination to all litigants, granting them the standing to raise the equal protection rights of the prospective jurors. Thus, in *Powers v. Ohio* (1991), the court reversed the conviction of a white defendant based on systematic exclusion of black jurors by the government. *Edmonson v. Leesville Concrete* (1991) prohibited a civil litigant from basing challenges on race. Finally, *Georgia v. McCollum* (1992) held that a criminal defendant may not exercise peremptory challenges on the basis of race.

    In *J. E. B. v. Alabama ex rel. T. B.* (1994), the court extended the prohibition on the systematic use of peremptory challenges to gender in a paternity and child support suit in which the government used nine of its ten peremptory challenges to remove male jurors and thereby obtain an all female jury.

25. Attorneys show some ability systematically to exclude jurors likely to be unfriendly to their side (see, e.g., Zeisel and Diamond 1978).

26. A lucrative industry in jury-consulting supplies attorneys with advice in jury selection techniques. Evidence on the ability of social scientists to predict juror behavior based on the information typically available during jury selection suggests that the promise of scientific jury selection in most cases is overrated (see Diamond 1990).

27. See n. 24.

28. Of course even if the bias were evenhanded and always expressed toward the outgroup

it would disadvantage the minority group members, particularly when they are disproportionately represented among defendants. Note, however, that the impact would be quite different for men and women, at least in jurisdictions where they are equally represented in the jury venire.

29. 28 U.S.C. sec. 1865(a) (1970).

30. The cases included *Williams v. Florida* (1970), *Johnson v. Louisiana* (1972), *Apodaca v. Oregon* (1972), *Colgrove v. Battin* (1973), and *Ballew v. Georgia* (1978).

31. Relevance is defined as "evidence having any tendency to make the existence of any fact that is of consequence to the determinations of the action more probable or less probable than it would be without the evidence." Federal Rule of Evidence 401.

32. Federal Rule of Evidence 403.

33. *Sparf* applied only to federal trials, but most states followed its ruling.

34. See, e.g., Illinois Revised Stat., ch. 110A, sections 239 (civil) and 451 (criminal).

35. The story was "Silver Blaze," in which the dog's silence told Holmes that the dog knew the thief.

36. This discussion assumes that the juror is motivated to apply the law as it has been described by the judge. Below we will discuss the case of jury nullification when the jury chooses to depart from the legally endorsed standard.

37. Each instruction was read twice.

38. See table 14 (Charrow 1979).

39. The respondents were college students rather than jurors.

40. Severance and Loftus (1982) studied the questions that jurors ask during deliberations and they rewrote the instructions involving concepts that appeared to cause jurors trouble.

41. Ellsworth (1989) was following the standard practice in California courts.

42. Ellsworth (1989) modified the tape slightly, deleting one defense witness whose testimony added little and replacing the original judge's instructions which were based on Massachusetts law with the applicable California instructions.

43. The possible verdicts were murder in the first degree, murder in the second degree, manslaughter, and not guilty (by reason of self-defense).

44. Because litigants in Wisconsin are entitled to written instructions, the random assignment did not entirely determine the instruction condition that the trial actually received. An objection from one of the attorneys in twelve of the forty-four cases assigned to the nonwritten instruction condition resulted in that case being dropped from the study.

45. That is, the same six test items were used on all civil trials and the same nine test items were used on all criminal trials. Performance was generally better on the test given in the criminal cases (mean = 75 percent) than on the one given in the civil cases (mean = 53 percent).

46. Note, however, that if both judge and jury determined their verdicts by flipping a coin, they would agree in roughly half of the cases.

47. Although a full report was produced on the criminal jury data, the civil jury analysis was never completed.

48. Myers (1979) found that the few instances of rule departures she detected occurred in cases like this one involving young sympathetic defendants.

49. This filming was legally possible under Wisconsin law with the permission of both parties.

50. In Indiana and Maryland, judges tell jurors that they are the judges of the law as well as the facts.

51. Herzberg (1986) interviewed the juror in the *Wisconsin v. Leroy Reed* case who held out until the last and asked him if he thought jurors should be informed about their power to nullify. Although such an instruction clearly would have made his life easier, the juror said that he didn't think jurors should receive such an instruction because he thought it *should* be a difficult decision.

52. For civil trials, Kalven (1964) reports that judges and jurors agreed on the issue of liability 79 percent of the time. Unfortunately he did not present any data on whether the level of agreement differed by case difficulty.

53. These figures are grossly disproportional to the rate of death sentences recommended by juries in Alabama. According to figures for 1994 and 1995 obtained from Eva Ansley of the Equal Justice Institute, juries sentence capital defendants to death roughly half the time they find the defendant guilty of capital murder. If judges were equally likely to override death and nondeath sentences, the number of death and nondeath overrides should also be similar. Instead, the ratio of nondeath overrides to death overrides is more than 8:1.

BIBLIOGRAPHY

Alschuler, Albert W. 1995. Racial Quotas and the Jury. 44 *Duke Law Journal,* 704.

Bernard, J. L. 1979. Interaction between the Race of the Defendant and That of Jurors in Determining Verdicts. 5 *Law and Psychology Rev.,* 103.

Bottoms, Bette L., and Gail S. Goodman. 1994. Perceptions of Children's Credibility in Sexual Assault Cases. 24 *Journal of Applied Social Psychology,* 702.

Bray, Robert M., and Audrey M. Noble. 1978. Authoritarianism and Decisions of Mock Juries: Evidence of Jury Bias and Group Polarization. 36 *Journal of Personality and Social Psychology,* 1424.

Bridgeman, Diane L., and David Marlowe. 1979. Jury Decision Making: An Empirical Study Based on Actual Felony Trials. 64 *Journal of Applied Psychology,* 91.

Carrington, Paul D. 1990. The Seventh Amendment: Some Bicentennial Reflections. 1990 *Univ. of Chicago Legal Forum,* 33.

Casper, Jonathan D. 1993. Restructuring the Traditional Civil Jury: The Effects of Changes in Composition and Procedures. In *Verdict: Assessing the Civil Jury System,* ed. R. E. Litan. Washington, DC: Brookings Institution.

Casper, Jonathan D., Kennette Benedict, and Jo L. Perry. 1989. Juror Decision-making, Attitudes, and the Hindsight Bias. 13 *Law and Human Behavior,* 291.

Cecil, Joe S., Valerie P. Hans, and Elizabeth C. Wiggins. 1991. Citizen Comprehension of Difficult Issues: Lessons from Civil Jury Trials. 40 *American University Law Rev.,* 727.

Charrow, Robert P., and Veda R. Charrow. 1979. Making Legal Language Understandable: A Psycholinguistic Study of Jury Instructions. 79 *Columbia Law Rev.,* 1306.

Constable, Marianne. 1994. *The Law of the Other: The Mixed Jury and Changing Conceptions of Citizenship, Law, and Knowledge.* Chicago: Univ. Of Chicago Press.

Cowan, Claudia L., William C. Thompson, and Phoebe C. Ellsworth. 1984. The Effects of Death Qualification on Jurors' Predisposition to Convict and on the Quality of Deliberation. 8 *Law and Human Behavior*, 53.

Crowley, Michael J., M. Gemma O'Callaghan, and Peter J. Ball. 1994. The Juridical Impact of Psychological Expert Testimony in a Simulated Child Sexual Abuse Trial. 18 *Law and Human Behavior*, 89.

Cunningham, Thomas J. 1958. Should Instructions Go into the Jury Room? 33 *California State Bar Journal*, 278.

Daniels, Stephen. 1989. The Question of Jury Competence and the Politics of Civil Justice Reform: Symbols, Rhetoric and Agenda-building. 52 *Law and Contemporary Problems*, 269.

Davis, James H., Norbert L. Kerr, Robert S. Atkin, Robert Holt, and David Meek. 1975. The Decision Processes of 6- and 12-person Mock Juries Assigned Unanimous and Two-thirds Majority Rules. 32 *Journal of Personality and Social Psychology*, 1.

Davis, James H., Norbert L. Kerr, Garold Stasser, David Meek, and Robert Holt. 1977. Victim Consequences, Sentence Severity, and Decision Processes in Mock Juries. 18 *Organizational Behavior and Human Performance*, 346.

Dawson, John P. 1960. *A History of Lay Judges*. Cambridge, MA: Harvard Univ. Press.

Diamond, Shari S. 1990. Scientific Jury Selection: What Social Scientists Know and Do Not Know. 73 *Judicature*, 178.

——. 1993. What Jurors Think: Expectations and Reactions of Citizens Who Serve as Jurors. In *Verdict: Assessing the Civil Jury System*, ed R. E. Litan. Washington, DC: The Brookings Institution.

Diamond, Shari S., and Jonathan D. Casper. 1992. Blindfolding the Jury to Verdict Consequences: Damages, Experts, and the Civil Jury. 26 *Law and Society Rev.*, 513.

Diamond, Shari S., Jonathan D. Casper, Anna-Maria Marshall, and Jason Schklar. 1996. Deliberative Processes and Democratic Decisionmaking: Listening to the Jury. Presented at the Annual Meeting of the Law and Society Association in Glasgow, Scotland.

Diamond, Shari S., Jonathan D. Casper, and Lynne Ostergren. 1989. Blindfolding the Jury. 52 *Law and Contemporary Problems*, 247.

Diamond, Shari S., and Judith N. Levi. 1996. Improving Decisions on Death by Revising and Testing Jury Instructions. 79 *Judicature*, 224.

Diamond, Shari S., and Loretta Stalans. 1989. The Myth of Judicial Leniency in Sentencing. 7 *Behavioral Sciences and the Law*, 73.

Drazan, Dan. 1989. The Case for Special Juries in Toxic Tort Litigation. 72 *Judicature*, 292.

Eisen, Susan V., and Leslie Z. McArthur. 1979. Evaluating and Sentencing a Defendant as a Function of His Salience and the Perceiver's Set. 5 *Personality and Social Psychology Bulletin*, 48.

Ellsworth, Phoebe C. 1989. Are Twelve Heads Better than One? 52 *Law and Contemporary Problems*, 205.

Elwork, Amiram, Bruce D. Sales, and James J. Alfini. 1977. Juridic Decisions: In Ignorance of the Law or in Light of It? 1 *Law and Human Behavior*, 163.

——. 1982. *Making Jury Instructions Understandable*. Charlottesville, VA: Michie.

Epstein, Michelle A., and Bette L. Bottoms. 1996. Gender Differences in Child Sexual

Assault Case Judgments: What Happens after Deliberation and Why. Unpublished manuscript, Symposium on Jurors' Decisions in Child Sexual Assault Cases, Biennial American Psychology-Law Society, Hilton Head, South Carolina.

Fiske, Susan T., and Shelley E. Taylor. 1991. *Social Cognition.* New York: McGraw-Hill.

Foley, Linda A., and Minor H. Chamblin. 1982. The Effect of Race and Personality on Mock Jurors' Decisions. 112 *Journal of Psychology,* 47.

Frank, Jerome. 1949. *Courts on Trial: Myth and Reality in American Justice.* Princeton, NJ: Princeton Univ. Press.

Freedberg, Sydney P. 1984. Report Shows Race a Factor in Verdicts. *Miami Herald,* May 11, 1984, p. 1c.

Fukurai, Hiroshi, Edgar W. Butler, and Richard Krooth. 1993. *Race and the Jury: Racial Disenfranchisement and the Search for Justice.* New York: Plenum.

Galanter, Marc. 1990. The Civil Jury as Regulator of the Litigation Process. 1990 *Univ. of Chicago Legal Forum,* 201.

Gray, D. B., and Ashmore, R. D. 1976. Biasing Influence of Defendants' Characteristics on Simulated Sentencing. 38 *Psychological Reports,* 727.

Green, Thomas A. 1985. *Verdict According to Conscience: Perspectives on the English Criminal Trial Jury.* Chicago: Univ. of Chicago Press.

Guinther, John. 1988. *The Jury in America.* New York: Facts on File.

Hans, Valerie P., and William S. Lofquist. 1992. Jurors' Judgments of Business Liability in Tort Cases: Implications for the Litigation Explosion Debate. 26 *Law and Society Rev.,* 85.

Hastie, Reid. 1983. Final Report to the National Institute for Law Enforcement and Criminal Justice. Unpublished manuscript, Northwestern University.

Hastie, Reid, Steven D. Penrod, and Nancy Pennington. 1983. *Inside the Jury.* Cambridge, MA: Harvard Univ. Press.

Herzberg, Stephen J. 1986. Inside the Jury Room. Videotape available through the University of Wisconsin–Madison Law Library.

————. 1990. Presentation to the Seventh Circuit Judicial Conference. Cleveland, OH. May.

Heuer, Larry, and Steven D. Penrod. 1989. Instructing Jurors: A Field Experiment with Written and Preliminary Instructions. 13 *Law and Human Behavior,* 409.

Hoffman, Joseph. 1995. Where's the Buck?—Juror Misperception of Sentencing Responsibility in Death Penalty Cases. 70 *Indiana Law Journal,* 1137.

Horowitz, Irving A., and Thomas E. Willging. 1991. Changing Views of Jury Power: The Jury Nullification Debate, 1787–1988. 15 *Law and Human Behavior,* 165.

Howe, Edmund. 1991. Integration of Mitigation, Intention, and Outcome Damage Information by Students and Circuit Court Judges. 21 *Journal of Applied Social Psychology,* 875.

Howe, Edmund S., and Thomas C. Loftus. 1992. Integration of Intention and Outcome Information by Students and Circuit Judges: Design Economy and Individual Differences. 22 *Journal of Applied Social Psychology,* 102.

Johnson, Sheri L. 1985. Black Innocence and the White Jury. 83 *Univ. of Michigan Law Rev.,* 1611.

Kagehiro, Dorothy K., and W. Clark Stanton. 1985. Legal vs. Quantified Definitions of Standards of Proof. 9 *Law and Human Behavior*, 159.

Kalven, Harry, Jr. 1964. The Dignity of the Civil Jury. 50 *Virginia Law Rev.*, 1055.

Kalven, Harry, Jr., and Hans Zeisel. 1966. *The American Jury.* Chicago: Univ. of Chicago Press.

Kerr, Nobert L., Robert S. Atkin, Garold Stasser, David Meek, Robert Holt, and James H. Davis. 1976. Guilt beyond a Reasonable Doubt: Effects of Concept Definition and Assigned Decision Rule on the Judgments of Mock Jurors. 34 *Journal of Personality and Social Psychology*, 282.

King, Nancy J. 1993. Postconviction Review of Jury Discrimination: Measuring the Effects of Juror Race on Jury Decisions. 92 *Michigan Law Rev.*, 63.

LaFree, Gary D., Barbara F. Reskin, and Christy A. Visher. 1985. Jurors' Responses to Victims' Behavior and Legal Issues in Sexual Assault Trials. 32 *Social Problems*, 389.

Landsman, Stephen, and Richard F. Rakos. 1994. A Preliminary Inquiry into the Effect of Potentially Biasing Information on Judges and Jurors in Civil Litigation. 12 *Behavioral Sciences and the Law*, 113.

Lempert, Richard O. 1981. Civil Juries and Complex Cases: Let's Not Rush to Judgment. 80 *Michigan Law Rev.*, 68.

Lind, E. Allen, and Tom Tyler. 1988. *The Social Psychology of Procedural Justice.* New York: Plenum.

Lipton, Jack P. 1983. Racism in the Jury Box: The Hispanic Defendant. 5 *Hispanic Journal of Behavioral Sciences*, 275.

Lombardero, David A. 1996. Do Special Verdicts Improve the Structure of Jury Decisionmaking? 36 *Jurimetrics Journal*, 275.

Luneburg, William V., and Mark A. Nordenberg. 1981. Specially Qualified Juries and Expert Non-jury Tribunals: Alternatives for Coping with the Complexities of Modern Civil Litigation. 67 *Virginia Law Rev.*, 887.

Mazzella, Ronald, and Alan Feingold. 1994. The Effects of Physical Attractiveness, Race, Socioeconomic Status, and Gender of Defendants and Victims on Judgments of Mock Jurors: A Meta-analysis. 24 *Journal of Applied Social Psychology*, 1315.

McGlynn, Richard P., James C. Megas, and Daniel H. Benson. 1976. Sex and Race as Factors Affecting the Attribution of Insanity in a Murder Trial. 93 *Journal of Psychology*, 93.

Munsterman, G. Thomas, and Janice T. Munsterman. 1986. The Search for Jury Representativeness. 11 *Justice System Journal*, 59.

Myers, Martha A. 1979. Rule Departures and Making Law: Juries and Their Verdicts. 13 *Law and Society Rev.*, 781.

———. 1980. Social Contexts and Attributions of Criminal Responsibility. 43 *Social Psychology Quarterly*, 405.

National Center for State Courts. 1983. *Business of State Trial Courts.* Williamsburg, VA.

Nelson, Thomas O. 1977. Repetition and Depth of Processing. 16 *Journal of Verbal Learning and Verbal Behavior*, 151.

Nemeth, Charlan. 1977. Interactions between Jurors as a Function of Majority vs. Unanimity Decision Rules. 7 *Journal of Applied Social Psychology*, 38.

Newman, Jon O. 1996. Beyond "Reasonable Doubt." 68 *New York Univ. Law Rev.*, 979.

Nieland, Robert G. 1978. Assessing the Impact of Pattern Jury Instructions. 62 *Judicature*, 185.

Padawer-Singer, Alice M. 1977. Justice or Judgments. In *The American Jury System.* Final Report of the Annual Chief Justice Earl Warren Conference on Advocacy in the United States. Cambridge, MA: The Roscoe Pound-American Trial Lawyers Foundation.

Pennington, Nancy, and Reid Hastie. 1990. Practical Implications of Psychological Research on Juror and Jury Decision Making. 16 *Personality and Social Psychology Bulletin*, 90.

Perlman, Harvey S. 1986. Pattern Jury Instructions: The Application of Social Science Research. 65 *Nebraska Law Rev.*, 520.

Pfeiffer, Jeffrey E., and James R. P. Ogloff. 1991. Ambiguity and Guilt Determinations: A Modern Racism Perspective. 21 *Journal of Applied Social Psychology*, 1713.

Pierce, Maureen C., and Richard J. Harris. 1993. The Effect of Provocation, Race, and Injury Description on Men's and Women's Perceptions of a Wife Battering Incident. 23 *Journal of Applied Social Psychology*, 767.

Poulson, Ronald L. 1990. Mock Juror Attribution of Criminal Responsibility: Effects of Race and the Guilty but Mentally Ill (GBMI) Verdict Option. 20 *Journal of Applied Social Psychology*, 1596.

Rector, Neil A., R. Michael Bagby, and R. Nicholson. 1993. The Effect of Prejudice and Judicial Ambiguity on Defendant Guilt Ratings. 133 *Journal of Social Psychology*, 651.

Reifman, Alan, Spencer M. Gusick, and Phoebe C. Ellsworth. 1992. Real Jurors' Understanding of Law in Real Cases. 16 *Law and Human Behavior*, 539.

Russell, Kathryn K. 1994. The Constitutionality of Jury Override in Alabama Death Penalty Cases. 46 *Alabama Law Rev.,* 5.

Saks, Michael J. 1992. Do We Really Know Anything about the Behavior of the Tort Litigation System—and Why Not? 140 *Univ. of Pennsylvania Law Rev.*, 1147.

———. 1993. Judicial Nullification. 68 *Indiana Law Journal*, 1281.

Sand, Leonard B., and Steven A. Reiss. 1985. A Report on Seven Experiments Conducted by District Court Judges in the Second Circuit. 60 *New York Univ. Law Rev.*, 423.

Schutte, James W., and Harmon M. Hosch. 1996. Gender Differences in Sexual Assault Verdicts: a Meta-Analysis. Unpublished manuscript.

Sealy, P., and W. R. Cornish. 1973. Jurors and Their Verdicts. 36 *Modern Law Rev.*, 496.

Severance, Lawrence J., Edith Greene, and Elizabeth F. Loftus. 1984. Toward Criminal Jury Instructions That Jurors Can Understand. 75 *Journal of Criminal Law and Criminology*, 198.

Severance, Lawrence J., and Elizabeth F. Loftus. 1982. Improving the Ability of Jurors to Comprehend and Apply Criminal Jury Instructions. 17 *Law and Society Rev.*, 153.

Simon, Rita J. 1967. *The Jury and the Defense of Insanity.* Boston: Little, Brown.

Smith, Vicki L. 1991. Impact of Pretrial Instruction on Jurors' Information Processing and Decision Making. 76 *Journal of Applied Psychology*, 220.

Steele, Walter W., and Elizabeth G. Thornburg. 1988. Jury Instructions: A Persistent Failure to Communicate. 67 *North Carolina Law Rev.*, 77.

Strawn, David U., and Raymond W. Buchanan. 1976. Jury Confusion: A Threat to Justice. 59 *Judicature*, 478.

Swim, Janet K., Eugene Borgida, and Kathy McCoy. 1993. Videotape Versus In-Court Witness Testimony: Does Protecting the Child Witness Jeopardize Due Process? 23 *Journal of Applied Social Psychology*, 603.

Tanford, J. Alexander. 1991. Law Reform by Courts, Legislatures, and Commissions Following Empirical Research on Jury Instructions. 25 *Law and Society Rev.*, 155.

Thayer, James B. 1898. *A Preliminary Treatise on Evidence at the Common Law*. Boston: Little, Brown.

Ugwuegbu, Denis C. E. 1979. Racial and Evidential Factors in Juror Attribution of Legal Responsibility. 15 *Journal of Experimental Social Psychology*, 133.

Uhlman, Thomas M. 1979. *Racial Justice: Black Judges and Defendants in an Urban Trial Court*. Toronto: Lexington Books.

U.S. Department of Justice. 1983. *Report to the Nation on Crime and Justice*. Washington, DC.

Van Dyke, Jon M. 1977. *Jury Selection Procedures: Our Uncertain Commitment to Representative Panels*. Cambridge, MA: Ballinger.

Vidmar, Neil, and Jeffrey J. Rice. 1993. Assessments of Noneconomic Damage Awards in Medical Negligence: A Comparison of Jurors with Legal Professionals. 78 *Iowa Law Rev.*, 883.

Visher, Christy A. 1987. Juror Decision Making: The Importance of Evidence. 11 *Law and Human Behavior*, 1.

Weir, Julie A., and Lawrence S. Wrightsman. 1990. The Determinants of Mock Jurors' Verdicts in a Rape Case. 20 *Journal of Applied Social Psychology*, 901.

Wells, Gary L. 1992. Naked Statistical Evidence of Liability: Is Subjective Probability Enough? 62 *Journal of Personality and Social Psychology*, 739.

Wiggins, Elizabeth C., and Steven J. Breckler. 1990. Special Verdicts as Guides to Jury Decision Making. 14 *Law and Psychology Rev.*, 1.

Willis, Cynthia E. 1992. The Effect of Sex Role Stereotype, Victim and Defendant Race, and Prior Relationship on Rape Culpability Attributions. 26 *Sex Roles*, 213.

Wissler, Roselle, and Michael J. Saks. 1985. On the Inefficacy of Limiting Instructions: When Jurors Use Prior Conviction to Decide upon Guilty. 9 *Law and Human Behavior*, 37.

Young, Robert Q. 1973. A Comparison of Reading and Listening Comprehension with Rate of Presentation Controlled. 21 *AV Communication Rev.*, 327.

Zeisel, Hans. 1971. . . . And Then There Were None: The Diminution of the Federal Jury. 38 *Univ. of Chicago Law Rev.*, 710.

Zeisel, Hans, and Shari S. Diamond. 1978. The Effect of Peremptory Challenges on Jury and Verdict: An Experiment in a Federal District Court. 30 *Stanford Law Rev.*, 491.

———. 1974. Convincing Empirical Evidence on the Six-Member Jury. 41 *Univ. of Chicago Law Rev.*, 281.

CASES

Apodaca v. Oregon, 406 U.S. 404 (1972).

Baldwin v. New York, 399 U.S. 66 (1970).

Ballard v. United States, 329 U.S. 173 (1946).

Ballew v. Georgia, 435 U.S. 223 (1978).

Batson v. Kentucky, 476 U.S. 339 (1984).

Blanton v. North Las Vegas, 489 U.S. 539 (1989).

Colgrove v. Battin, 413 U.S. 149 (1973).

Duren v. Missouri, 439 U.S. 357 (1979).

Edmonson v. Leesville Concrete, 500 U.S. 614 (1991).

Georgia v. McCullom, 505 U.S. 42 (1992).

Glasser v. U.S., 315 U.S. 60 (1942).

Harris v. Alabama, 513 U.S. 504 (1995).

In re Japanese Electronic Products Antitrust Litigation, 631 F.2d 1069 (3rd Cir. 1980).

J. E. B. v. Alabama ex Rel. T. B., 511 U.S. 127 (1994).

Johnson v. Louisiana, 406 U.S. 356 (1972).

McKeiver v. Pennsylvania, 403 U.S. 528 (1971).

People v. Harris, 36 CA 3d 36 (1984).

Powers v. Ohio, 499 U.S. 400 (1991).

Sparf and Hansen v. U.S., 156 U.S. 51 (1895).

Strauder v. W. Virginia, 100 U.S. 303 (1880).

Taylor v. Louisiana, 419 U.S. 522 (1975).

Tull v. United States, 481 U.S. 412 (1987).

U.S. v. Dougherty, 472 F.2d 1113 (D.C. Cir.1972).

Victor v. Nebraska, 511 U.S. 1 (1994).

Walton v. Arizona, 497 U.S. 639 (1990).

Williams v. Florida, 399 U.S. 78 (1970).

Statutes and Jury Instructions

Ill. Rev. Stat. (1991) Ch. 38 Sec. 9–1.

A RESOURCE THEORY

OF THE CRIMINAL LAW:

EXPLORING WHEN IT MATTERS

❖

RICHARD LEMPERT

1. INTRODUCTION

This paper might look very different had I been asked a sensible question. Instead, I was told that the focus of the program for which this paper was originally prepared was "Does law matter?" and that my particular assignment was to discuss the question of whether the criminal law mattered. Of course criminal law matters. One hardly need be a committed functionalist to conclude from the dense net of criminal laws that envelop modern societies that criminal law must matter or else we would not have so much of it or, conversely, because we have so much of it, it must matter. And if this abstract exercise were not satisfying, one could go to any prison and ask the men or women therein whether the criminal law mattered. They would tell you it did; if it didn't they would not be forfeiting years of their lives. Moreover, there is a long tradition of research on the deterrent and other preventive functions of the criminal law (Lempert 1981–82; Gibbs 1975). The evidence, ranging from Andenaes's (1966) anecdotal evidence of a crime wave during a Montreal police strike to the most sophisticated modern quantitative research (e.g., Loftin, McDowall, and Wiersma 1992) is that people's actions are sometimes ordered at least in part by fear of criminal sanctions, and it may be that other aspects of the criminal law, such as its presumed educative effects, also affect behavior.

The situation is, to be sure, somewhat more complicated than this. Certainty of punishment appears far more important in ordering behavior than differences in the severity of the punishment that violators receive (Gibbs 1975; Lempert 1981–82). Thus, what matters most is that some sort of police force catch those who violate legal norms. The legally specified penalties and those actually inflicted appear less important; and marginal differences in penalty severity, such as the symbolically important difference between the death penalty and life imprisonment, may not matter at all (Lempert 1981).

Indeed, it may not be fear of the law's penalty which mediates the criminal law's impact. In many cases, particularly involving minor offenses, the implications for personal relations of being caught—including the anticipated embarrassment—may account for most of law's impact. Thus, various researchers have reported that for minor crimes like shoplifting or smoking marijuana, anticipated peer sanctions are more important than legal sanctions as determinants of behavior (Anderson, Chiricos, and Waldo 1977; Burkett and Jensen 1975; Saltzman, Waldo, and Paternoster 1983). Even in the case of serious felonies which can result in long sentences, the law's efficacy may depend more on the threat of breaking up relationships or destroying them than it does on the actual apprehension of violators or the sentences they receive (Lieb, Zurcher, and Ekland-Olson 1984). Moreover, deterrence is a subjective phenomenon. Lon Fuller (1964), the eminent jurisprudent, was more than philosophically right: a law that is not communicated is no law at all. Indeed, how a law is communicated and the degree of threat inherent in the communication may be more important in ordering behavior than the law's specific content. Thus Ross (1982), who investigated crackdowns on drunk driving throughout the world, consistently found marked deterrent effects in the early days of highly publicized crackdowns, but, except in rare instances, the effects did not endure the dissipation of publicity over time, even when neither the law nor enforcement patterns reverted to their pre-crackdown patterns (Ross 1982).

These contingencies, while interesting in their own right, do not, however, problematize the fundamental question of whether the criminal law matters. The quick answer, "of course it matters," is still the most obvious and the most obviously correct. Only John Griffiths's (1979) tactic of separating law from power and criminal law from its enforcement seems to problematize the question. But power is not something that can be separated from law. As sociolegal theorists from Weber (1968) through Black (1976) have recognized, power, which is to say the potential for enforcement, is built into law's very definition.

So why was I asked to address the question, "Does (the criminal) law matter?" Why wasn't the answer presupposed and the more sensible question asked, "How does (the criminal) law matter?" The latter was the question I would have to address in any event, but the former question started my thinking. Contemplating it, I was reminded of a comic strip I had seen some years ago. An older man is reflecting on love and marriage. In the strip's first panel, he is recalling the innocence of a youth when, fueled by romantic novels and Hollywood movies, he envisioned marriage as a state of continual love in which one lives happily ever after. In the second panel, he is recalling his college and early postcollege years. Failed affairs rendered him cynical and he came to believe that there was no such thing as enduring love and that marriage was largely an institution of convenience. In the final panel, he is reflecting on twenty years of married life and says of love in marriage, "I had no idea it was every other day."

If we make our L-word not "love" but "law," and criminal law in particular, we have here (1) a nice metaphor for the mattering of criminal law; and (2) a reason why it was perhaps not so silly to ask the question "Does (the criminal) law matter?" in the first instance. The metaphor is nice in two ways. First, if we look to where we expect to see criminal law mattering, we do not always see effects we associate with law. With respect to the criminal law as a mechanism for ordering behavior, for example, most often when we see behavior ordered in accordance with the criminal law's norms, we give the criminal law's norms no weight whatsoever in explaining perceived compliance. If people are not killing each other, it is not because criminal law proscribes killing but because people know, totally apart from criminal law, that killing is morally wrong and that killers are detested. In subgroups or situations where this is not true, where, for example, killing is a way of proving manhood, murder, despite criminal law, occurs with alarming frequency. Yet occasionally, as is revealed in some of the deterrence studies previously cited, law affects the behavior of enough people so that its measurable aggregate impact is unmistakable.[1] Thus the effects of criminal law on social order are not always obvious, but from time to time they appear. Second, as with marriage and love, the relationship which allows law's effects to appear and disappear continues. Without an enduring marriage, the love that our comic strip character spoke of would not be felt every other day. Similarly, without the ongoing applicability of criminal law and a continually viable enforcement apparatus, the world would not occasionally appear ordered by the application of criminal law.

2. LEGITIMACY

But now I wish to get away from compliance mechanisms like deterrence to discuss other (and in my view more interesting) ways in which criminal law has this "now you see it, now you don't" form of mattering. Criminal law is symbolic. It not only symbolizes a society's abhorrence of certain behavior (Durkheim 1984; Garland 1990), it also and perhaps more powerfully symbolizes the restraints that a society puts on itself and on the government that is its agent in dealing coercively with its members. Indeed, when we speak of the "rule of law," we largely have in mind criminal law and its associated regulatory law, like rules of criminal procedure, that condition the application of criminal sanctions. If criminal law is largely what we have in mind when we speak of the "rule of law," criminal law must matter or at least must appear to matter, for if criminal law clearly did not matter, the rule of law could not be a dominant motif in ideologies of capitalist democracies.

In ascribing this role to criminal law, I am following the lead of E. P. Thompson (1975), Douglas Hay (1975), Isaac Balbus (1973), and others (e.g., Genovese 1972) who have agreed that the idea of the rule of law, as worked out through the visible play of the criminal justice system, is a central feature in capitalist systems of domination. In their view, fairness—exemplified by occasions on which criminal law honors its own restraints to free less powerful social actors from the threat of social sanctions or respects its own norms in punitively sanctioning powerful social actors—is the central mechanism by which criminal law legitimates an unequal social order.

Thus, Thompson describes the workings of the Black Acts—draconian legislation which punished severely (often capitally) such seemingly small (to modern eyes) violations of the forest order as poaching deer and breaking fish dams. Some people were hung for these crimes; but others, known in the country to be equally guilty, were acquitted because the law's rigorous requirements for proof could not be surmounted. With known poachers going free, even those most oppressed by the acts could not dismiss the legal cloak for oppression as mere window dressing. Hay (1975) recounts the tale of Lord Ferrers, a British nobleman hanged and then dissected like a common criminal for murdering his steward. Not only was his hanging a contemporary subject of story and song; his story was still being told in the countryside half a century after the event. The story's inescapable conclusion is the lesson that no one is above the law, but it seemed to have fascinated most not those who might reasonably have aspired to be above the law but rather the classes who would be subject to law in any event.

Isaac Balbus (1973) describes the fates of many black citizens arrested for race rioting in the 1960s. Low bail was eventually set for most of them, and many cases foundered for want of proof. Again, these are the kinds of outcomes that law formally demands; they are unexpected only to the extent that when class interests are palpable one might expect the rule of law to give way.

This expectation, which accords most closely with an instrumental Marxist worldview, is, however, naive. The point which each of the above authors in his own way makes is that the interests of capitalists as a class are by and large independent of the outcomes of any particular clash of capitalist and noncapitalist or even anticapitalist interests. Capitalist systems of government are more viable and their domination is more complete when the governed are prone to accept the legitimacy of laws the elite has enacted than when subordinate classes view capitalist law simply as an instrument of class warfare. If legitimacy can be enhanced by hanging the occasional nobleman or not hanging a known poacher, the collective interest of the capitalist class is thereby advanced, not threatened.

One might, of course, argue that criminal law need not matter to achieve these ends. All that is needed is for people to think the law is being applied fairly, and to achieve this end widespread false consciousness suffices.

Theoretically, this is true, but the empirical examples belie the argument. The law mattered to those Black Act violators who lived because the state could not muster sufficient proof. It also mattered to Lord Ferrers who was convicted because he had broken the law and was sentenced to death and executed according to the law's strictures. He would not have believed that his execution was mere appearance. More generally, if these arguments about the connection between the rule of law and legitimacy are correct, I do not think that there is any escape from the notion that criminal law as a set of punitive norms and state constraints sometimes matters. The best and sometimes only way to get people to think that law applies is to apply it.

People confronted with examples like those mentioned above are not mistaken if they think law mattered in these instances: surely it did. Their mistake, if they make one, is to think that the clear, visible appearance of law's importance means that law always matters in the same way as it does in its visible appearances. The fact that there are cases in which law matters more than immediate instrumental class interests does not mean that powerful interests cannot in large measure determine when law matters. The Black Acts mattered not only when the law freed some accused but when the law hanged, punished, or deterred others. Thus, both the punitive substantive and restraining procedural aspects of the criminal law seemed to have served class interests. Moreover, prosecutions and convictions under the Black Acts were not uniform over time; rather there was an ebb and flow which may have reflected the felt needs of dominant classes for the protections these laws accorded their interests. This does not mean dominant classes necessarily turn on and off the two sides of criminal law as if they were working a spigot; rather a less than fully conscious sense of urgency may motivate the application of law and the degree to which law matters.

Where the felt need for punitive measures is great, constraints that inhere in proceeding through criminal law may not for a time matter. A good example of this is the application of law in the riots that Balbus discusses. While the riots were ongoing, rioters arrested were often not brought immediately before judges as the law required; or if brought, there was no serious effort made to determine whether charged felonies were really misdemeanors or whether there was enough evidence to constitute probable cause to hold a person. Bail, when it was set, was set far out of proportion to the charged crime. Some days later, when the rioting had ended and it was becoming costly to hold those arrested, proper forms were followed. Bail was set or alleged participants were released on recognizance, felony charges were dropped, and the like.

Even more instructive is the "exception that proves the rule." Judge George Crockett, Jr., a black Recorder's Court judge in Detroit, was almost alone among judges hearing riot cases in Detroit in that he tried to make law matter even while the riot was ongoing. Rioters brought to his court had reasonable bail set based on the charges brought against them even if it meant releasing them to the streets before calm prevailed. For this he was excoriated in the press as if he were acting illegally. In a sense, the press was not too far from the mark. Judge Crockett was not acting illegally, but he was not acting role-responsibly if his role was to be a social control agent. Arguably, this is a judge's most fundamental role; it is simply one that in democratic societies is latent most of the time, for it ordinarily does not clash with the judge's manifest role as an agent of the rule of law. But in the midst of a riot, the roles can clash.

During the riot, Judge Crockett was a hero only in portions of the black community and at some local law schools, segments of the community that are atypical in the seriousness with which they are likely to take a judge's rule-of-law role. When the riot was safely ended, praise for Crockett grew and his performance during the riot eventually sent him to Congress where he served for many years in the House of Representatives.

Those who continued to excoriate Judge Crockett for his role in the riots were not acting in completely bad faith, even from a rule of law perspective. They wanted to believe that when Crockett freed alleged rioters in the midst of the riot there was some aspect of his manifest role responsibility—his responsibility as an agent of the law—that he was violating. They could not believe that a good faith interpretation of the law not only allowed him to act as he had but in fact required it. The intuition that "there ought to be a law," an intuition that elevated the judge's social control responsibilities above his legal duties, was a strong one. I still recall the Wayne County prosecutor, who in the spring following the Detroit riots visited a seminar I was teaching on riots. When he learned that Judge Crockett had participated a week earlier, he tried to pump me for information about what Judge Crockett had said. He was sure that there was evidence somewhere that the judge had acted in bad faith or from illegal motives. And he assumed that I as a law professor would share this view.

To recapitulate briefly, the criminal law in both its procedural restraining and its substantive punitive aspects typically has an on-again/off-again quality. In order to fulfill a legitimating function, the criminal law must sometimes matter in the sense that the norms inherent in the law's rules are occasionally applied, to the apparent frustration of a dominant class's interests. But the criminal law need not always matter in this way to fill a legitimating function. Indeed, law that matters too much is potentially counterproductive. Too many instances of contravening the dominant class's interests could aggregate to the point where their total cost to the dominant group outweighed the benefits they brought. However, so long as the dominant group largely controls the content of legal norms in the first place, this danger, even in an avowedly liberal legal system, is unlikely to be great.

A second implication of this analysis is that criminal law matters in a different, larger sense, whether or not it matters in the sense that its norms are applied in individual cases. It matters because the on-again/off-again pattern of mattering at the case level lends legitimacy to a system of domination at the macrolevel. This is essentially the argument of the three authors I have focused on most closely in this section. There is a problem with this implication, however. No one has ever proven that law matters in this larger sense. Although the arguments of such scholars as Thompson, Hays, and Balbus are plausible, and are additionally attractive in their ability to rescue us from a simplistic, empirically untenable instrumental Marxism, there is no proof that the rule of dominant classes is legitimated by the occasional legal victories of the dominated or by instances in which those on top are criminally prosecuted. And it is hard to see how this legitimation hypothesis could be rigorously tested. Although contrary to the views of some skeptics (Hyde 1983), it is clear that legal procedures can have legitimating functions (Thibaut and Walker 1975; Lind and Tyler 1988; Tyler 1984). These functions, however, operate at the case level and largely turn on procedures that allow parties to feel that they have participated in legal decisions affecting them. To this extent, the implementations of the procedural protections that the criminal law grants the accused may affect how criminals regard their treatment by the law (Casper 1972, 1978). The hypothesis that the criminal law matters because it legitimates class domination through the support it renders the rule-of-law ideology must, however, remain an hypothesis.

3. LAW'S INTERMITTENCY

The idea of the rule of law does not, of course, just apply at the macrolevel. The processing of each case is supposed to be an occasion for the application of the rule of law, but here too the criminal law sometimes matters and sometimes does not. Let me give two mundane examples which illustrate the themes of the appearance, disappearance, and reappearance of the rule of criminal law in case processing and the tension between the need for social control and the genuine pull that the rule of law ideology has on actors within the criminal justice system.

Consider first the initial case in a string of narcotics cases. In this case, the arresting officer, when pressed, admits that the only reason he searched the defendant and found the heroin he uncovered is because the defendant appeared to be a suspicious-looking person. The judge, applying the *Mapp* exclusionary rule, suppresses the heroin as the fruit of an unreasonable search, and the criminal goes free. Here the criminal law which proscribes unreasonable searches and seizures clearly matters. Without this norm, the accused would no doubt have been convicted of drug possession.

The next case is similar, except that the officer testifies that he saw the suspect reach into his pocket for a cigarette lighter and pull out not just the lighter but a clear plastic packet containing white powder, which fell to the ground. Since the powder looked like heroin, the officer picked it up and arrested the accused. The judge finds that there was probable cause for arrest; she denies the motion to suppress, and the accused is convicted of drug possession. Again the criminal law appears to have mattered. In this instance, the requisites of a reasonable search and seizure were met; and in accordance with the law, the evidence was allowed.

The case, however, has the surprising consequence of spawning a generation of clumsy criminals. In hundreds of cases that follow, police officers testify that they made arrests for drug possession after they saw suspects accidentally drop packets containing illicit drugs like heroin, marijuana, cocaine. Such testimony becomes so common that cases of this type are given a name: the "dropsy" cases. In each case, motions to suppress the evidence are made. In each case, the motions are denied on the ground that an officer who sees a suspicious pack drop to the ground acts reasonably when she picks it up and, if it looks as if it contains drugs, has probable cause to seize it and to make an arrest. Now it appears that criminal law as a set of authoritative legal norms does not matter, for surely most of these officers are lying.

In fact, the situation is more complex and illustrates the many ways in which criminal law can matter, for whether or not it matters depends on whose perspective one takes. From the defendant's point of view, law does not matter because he is being convicted despite the law's norms and his actual behavior. From the judge's point of view, law does matter, because had she heard a different story, such as the suspicious appearance story in our first example, she would have suppressed the evidence. Experienced judges, to be sure, will be suspicious of dropsy cases. But what should a judge do? One judge put it something like this, "I have heard enough dropsy stories that I am suspicious. But what am I to do? In any given case a police officer's testimony appears more credible than that of a self-interested defendant."[2]

From the police officer's view, the story is mixed, for two criminal law norms are involved. The first, the criminal proscription of perjury, appears not to matter at all, for to make good pinches officers are willing to lie with abandon. However, search and seizure law does matter—not in the way that it should, which is channeling an officer's behavior on the streets, but in channeling behavior in court, which is to say in specifying the content of an efficacious lie. As Weber ([1922] 1978) long ago pointed out, the lawbreaker who operates by stealth is just as surely orienting himself to the demands of the criminal law as the person who refrains from tempting behavior because it is illegal. Each is acting differently than he would if the law's norms were different.

Finally, to continue with this example, dropsy cases are sufficiently publicized, get such a bad name, and threaten to give the law such a bad name that crucial actors decide they have had enough. In one New York case the New York County District Attorney even urged the state's highest court to overturn dropsy seizures by shifting the burden of persuasion on the issue.[3] Other judges also express skepticism of dropsy testimony, and its incidence seems to diminish. Indeed, in one instance long after the great concern over dropsy testimony had dissipated, a police officer was actually indicted for telling a dropsy story from the stand (Gellman 1988). Again criminal law matters. Although dropsy testimony has not disappeared and some of it may have been replaced by different, more acceptable lies, to some extent law mattered.

Both the complexity and the on/off nature of how criminal law matters are also nicely illustrated when we consider trials. In criminal cases, a steady but small source of reversals is due to error in instructing the jury. Considering the incidence of errors at trial, reversals for erroneous instructions are proportionately more common than reversals for violating procedural rules of evidence because instructions often state the law as it applies to cases, and it is stretching things to hold such errors harmless.[4] When courts do reverse for instruction errors, it is easy to see that criminal law, as enunciated in instructions, matters.

However, research consistently reveals that jurors have great difficulty in comprehending instructions, sometimes performing at no better than chance levels (Charrow and Charrow 1979; Hastie, Penrod, and Pennington 1983; Ellsworth 1989; Reifman, Gusick, and Ellsworth 1992).[5] Thus, it would seem that criminal law as enunciated in instructions hardly matters, for if jurors do not understand the instructions, how can instructions influence their decisions? An implication is that when appellate courts reverse for errors in instructions, thus making law matter, they are likely to be reversing for reasons that wouldn't have mattered had the jury heard the law stated correctly in the first instance.

The puzzle here is that jurors often appear to decide cases correctly (Kalven and Zeisel 1966; Hastie, Penrod, and Pennington 1983). How can they do this if the law as given to them by the court does not matter?[6] The obvious explanation is that their folk norms of what constitutes particular crimes largely coincide with the law's formal definitions, and it is folk norms rather than legal norms that matter. But where do the jurors' popular conceptions of what constitutes particular crimes come from? They may in some measure come from the criminal law's norms as conveyed to jurors through various media. At the same time, the law's norms in many areas reflect popular conceptions of what constitutes specific crimes. Thus, when jurors judge criminals, the law's norms probably matter whether or not the jurors fully understand their instructions. At the same time, the law's norms may in large measure (depending on the crime) define behavior that jurors would have regarded as conviction-worthy regardless of the law. Thus, law matters; but so do popular views, and one cannot separate out their effects on each other.

To add a further wrinkle, there is another way in which instructions that state the law can matter. It appears that jurors late in their deliberations often have instructions reread as an aid in breaking deadlocks. The tactic may work because it gives one or two dissenting jurors a face-saving way to withdraw from a minority position. They can claim that although they continue to subscribe to the factual story they have been advocating, they realize that for technical legal reasons even their factual portrait does not mandate their verdict preference. Here the law matters simply because it exists. Indeed, a hard-to-understand instruction may be more helpful in this respect than a clear one because dissenting jurors can read into the instruction whatever is needed to justify their switch to the majority. Alternatively jurors may understand or misunderstand an instruction as reread, and may use their new sense of understanding to break their deadlock. Whether legal norms matter in this situation depends on whether they have been correctly understood.

4. LAW AS RESOURCE

The argument thus far is that criminal law matters, sometimes in unexpected ways, both at the macro (societal) level and at the micro (case) level. At each level, however, criminal law norms or their potential availability do not determine occasions of mattering. Rather, criminal law has what I have called a "now you see it/now you don't" or "on-again/off-again" character. In one situation, where the law's norms lead one to expect it will matter, it does; but in another situation where there is the same normative expectation that the law will matter, it does not. In the remainder of the chapter, I will offer a general explanation for this phenomenon, as I illustrate the law's intermittent mattering in other settings.

The criminal law (indeed all law) matters in some settings where it is supposed to matter and not in others because it is a resource. At one time, I thought that to speak this way was to speak metaphorically—that the law was not really a resource but was simply like one. But upon further reflection I think that to call law a resource is to speak precisely. It is a source of support that people may draw on in the same way they draw on other resources in their environment such as savings accounts, accumulated human capital, and the availability of others to help them achieve their goals. Law may be an intangible resource, as when one invokes the law's authority to order another's behavior, or a tangible one, as when one calls the police to achieve the same end.

In one sense, however, criminal law is a special resource. Its norms specify when it is to be deployed.[7] But criminal law is not self-deploying. People must do this. More than occasionally, particularly in more formal legal settings, people draw on law as a resource in the way law "intends." People are arrested because they have violated the law; they are charged with crimes their behavior best fits, and the rights that criminal procedure grants to the accused are honored throughout the guilt-determining process. More often, however, people treat law as they would any other resource available to them. Legal norms do not determine law's activation. Rather people draw on law when it is handy, convenient, and cheaper than alternative means to particular goals. Even when law is invoked as its norms specify it should be, the invocation is less likely to reflect respect for the law's norms than the sense that invoking those norms precisely is a cheap way to achieve an actor's interests.

This helps explain the law's on-again/off-again quality. The law's norms specify a wide area where it should be deployed (i.e., where it should matter).

But people generally invoke law—which is to say, make it matter—only when invocation is an efficacious route to their ends. So often when it appears law might or even should matter, it does not, for its authority is not needed. Conversely, the law's authority may be invoked in situations where its own norms appear to preclude this. This occurs because law can limit its own authority only when those who are responsible for enforcing law respect those limits. This does not always happen. Ironically, those specially responsible for enforcing law are often in the best position to avoid its limits.

5. INDIVIDUAL USE

Whether law is handier, cheaper and more convenient than alternative ways to achieve particular ends depends not just on what the law as a set of rules is, but also, and usually more importantly, on how law can be mobilized; that is, on those institutional arrangements that allow people to invoke the law. Two examples, drawn from the literature on policing, illustrate this point.

First, consider policing of skid rows. As both Bittner (1967) and Spradley (1970) emphasize, skid row policing is not so much about law enforcement as it is about order maintenance or peacekeeping. Indeed, Bittner's motivation to look at skid row was his interest in how police functioned as peacekeepers. He believed skid row would provide him with the purest example of maintaining order without law, but he found this could not be done. His conclusion in this respect is worth quoting:

> Though our interest was focused initially on those police procedures that did not involve invoking the law, we found that the two cannot be separated. The reason for the connection is not given in the circumstance that the roles of the "law officer" and of the "peace officer" are enacted by the same person and thus are contiguous. According to our observations, patrolmen do not act alternatively as one or the other, with certain actions being determined by the intended objective of keeping the peace and others being determined by the duty to enforce the law. Instead, we have found that *peace keeping occasionally acquires the external aspects of law enforcement.* (Bittner 1967: 714, emphasis in original)

The police it seems are almost totally confused—or perhaps it is better to say "fused"—with the law they enforce. The skid row situation reminds one of the classic Western movie scene in which a stranger in town taps an old timer on the shoulder and asks him, "Is there any law in this burgh?" The old timer points to the marshal and replies, "Yep, you're looking at him." If the same question were asked of a skid row denizen, he would answer "yes" and point to the policeman. Indeed, most people would find the linkage a natural one.

Phenomenologically, the connection between law and enforcer cannot be disputed, but one may nonetheless ask whether the link is conceptually justified. From the legal perspective, it is not. The criminal law distinguishes between its norms and those that enforce them. Indeed, as we have already noted, there is a special subset of criminal law norms—rules of criminal procedure—that is intended to control the behavior of the criminal law's enforcers.

From a sociological perspective, the situation is more interesting. Whether the fusion of law and enforcer is conceptually justified depends on how law is defined. Black's (1976) definition of law as governmental social control suggests that if there is any divergence between the law's norms and the actions of governmental control agents, it is the latter rather than the former which defines the law. More classic definitions of law, like Weber's (1978) or Llewellyn and Hoebel's (1941), have two ingredients: a set of authoritative norms and an enforcement staff. The assumption is that the latter will act in conformity with the former. But this only sometimes happens. For example, on skid row the criminal law is sometimes appropriately enforced in full conformity with its norms, as when a drunk is arrested for his drunken behavior. On other occasions, the law's requirements for enforcement are fully met, but the invocation of the law is pretextual. Thus, Bittner describes a situation in which, in order to break up a group and forestall the possibility of a fight, one of four equally drunk men was arrested while the others were simply sent on their way. On still other occasions, legal norms are largely irrelevant. Thus, a person who has been drinking but is not drunk may be arrested on a drunkenness charge when his real "crime" is cursing the police officer or, as in another of Bittner's examples, the paddy wagon is handy, and it is more efficient to arrest the drinker at the time than to wait until he is actually drunk and send again for the paddy wagon.

From the point of view of the arrestee, what matters is the police officer's action rather than the norms that also figure in law's definition.[8] But is it law that is mattering to an arrestee when an officer acts? Where the officer's actions and legal norms are congruent, it is easy to conclude that it is law that matters. Where, however, the law is a pretext for action, the question of whether law matters has no simple answer, even conceptually. To the extent law is a set of rules, law appears not to matter since legal norms are not being correctly applied; but to the extent that law consists of the actions of an authorized enforcement staff, law matters, for actors with a generalized legal authority to act are so acting, even if the specific reasons they invoke are inapposite. Thus, it is law which allows police to make arrests, even if law in a narrower, rule-reverential sense does not authorize it. One might say in these situations that law matters, but that the law is not working as intended. Yet even this conclusion is risky because it assumes the intent behind law is obvious from the language of a law's provisions. In applying drunkenness or vagrancy statutes to people who are not actually drunk or legally vagrant, the police officer may nevertheless be using the law for precisely the peacekeeping purposes the law's drafters intended (cf. Wilson and Kelling 1982). Indeed, such laws often only vaguely define forbidden behavior in order to provide police, and through them society, with generalized order maintenance resources.

In some situations where police conduct differs from the commands of law, there is a clear sense in which criminal law does not matter because police action does not simply fail to conform with the literal requisites of legal norms; it positively violates them. Examples include police who solicit bribes to tear up traffic tickets or who charge those they have beaten with resisting arrest in order to provide cover stories for their abuse. But in another sense, the law matters here as well. It is the police officer's privileged position with respect to legal resources that allows the officer to transform criminal law, a public resource, into an instrument for private benefit. In exploiting these resources for personal gain, the officer is acting much like the office worker who copies her tax return on an office xerox machine. The difference between the two is the easy access to resources that their institutional positions allow. The office worker is fortuitously situated with respect to a xerox machine, while a police officer is fortuitously situated with respect to the law.

In most circumstances, of course, the police are not violating the law. Most of the time, the criminal law in its normative sense matters to the police, and so it matters to us as well. Motorists who have not been speeding are seldom stopped for speeding, and those given speeding tickets usually have been traveling at least five miles per hour over the speed limit. *Miranda* warnings are real and given, and the "third degree" has largely disappeared from the repertoire of police interrogation techniques. Arrested drug dealers have typically been dealing drugs, arrested murderers are usually likely to have killed or are legitimately suspected of doing so, and so on. In short, the police typically use the public resource that is law for public ends and invoke the criminal law in ways consistent with the law's norms. Their major failing, if it is a failing, is that they do not invoke the law in many situations where the law apparently intends its own invocation. Thus the criminal law often does not matter the way it should, or it does not matter at all because of limited institutional capacities for enforcement. Some legal scholars (Goldstein 1960) have been quite troubled by this, while other, more sociologically oriented students of the police (Skolnick 1975) see underenforcement as inherent in the nature of police work.

Criminal law is, of course, a resource not just for the police but for all of us. Anyone can "call the cops," and many people do. Indeed, the police are a resource apart from the law, for many calls to the police seek aid, such as help in transporting a sick person to the hospital, that the caller knows is not part of the police's law enforcement mission (Wilson 1968). Even where the police are called because the law has been broken, there is a tendency among both police and citizens to privatize the public resource that is law. Black (1971), for example, found in his study of the social organization of arrest, that complainants' preferences were a major factor in determining whether an alleged lawbreaker was arrested. The other two major factors predicting arrest in Black's study were whether the offense complained about was a felony (arrest more likely) or a misdemeanor and whether the suspect in the field was disrespectful (arrest more likely) or not. We have thus, in one study, a nice illustration of the three ways that criminal law as a resource is most commonly employed. First, it is employed by police for the public end of crime control. Second, it is employed by police as a private resource to revenge affronts. And third, it is employed by complainants as a private resource to control others' behavior.

Returning our attention to the last of these uses, that is to the use of criminal law as a resource for citizens, one can ask how effective it is in this respect. This depends on both legal and institutional considerations. Sometimes laws that citizens wish to draw on do not exist. Thus, until recently most states did not have legislation that prevented "stalking." Police receiving complaints of stalking often purported to be helpless. The best they could offer terrorized victims was "if he attacks call us," which was, no doubt, of small solace. Ultimately, stalking incidents culminating in beatings or homicides persuaded legislatures to pass laws making stalking itself a crime. These laws provide a new resource for both citizens and police.

Passing a law, however, is not enough to provide citizens with a viable resource. Legal resources are of limited value to citizens unless they can mobilize law. With respect to criminal law, this most often means mobilizing the police—which can be problematic. Indeed, members of the same minority groups that disproportionately feel victimized by police exploitation of the criminal law for police ends (such as enforcing respect) also disproportionately feel victimized by their inability to exploit the law for their own ends. The police, they complain, often show up late when they call, or fail to respond at all (Hacker 1992; Skolnick and Fyfe 1993).

Merely mobilizing police, however, is not enough to privatize law as a resource, for there is no guarantee police will respect a complainant's private preferences. Consider the situation of a woman who has called the police because her husband has struck her. Once police are on the scene, they have many options. They may ignore a caller's request for leniency and reaffirm the public nature of the law; as when the police, following department policy, arrest an abuser that the complainant wants only to be warned. Alternatively, once the police are on the scene they may appropriate the law to their own ends, as when they ignore a complainant's preferences and arrest a man because he has been disrespectful toward them. In other situations, both public and private claims to the use of law are denied as when police refuse to arrest an abuser despite the complainant's preference. Another police response devalues the legal resource by giving a caller less enforcement than the law provides, as when an abuser is only separated from a spouse who wants him arrested. Finally, police may follow a complainant's preferences, privatizing the legal resource in a way which may or may not conflict with the public's interest in how law is deployed. Only the last of these options allows those who mobilize the police to fully privatize the law as resource. In each of these circumstances, except where nothing is done, criminal law clearly matters, but it matters for different ends. And even where nothing is done, law matters in a more limited sense, for it provided the excuse that brought police to the scene, and the event that precipitated the call is at least likely to have been transformed (Sherman and Berk 1984).

I have chosen the police to illustrate how criminal law can be used as a resource and to show how the same cost-benefit considerations that mean that any resource will be used only intermittently depending on circumstances apply to the use of the criminal law. Thus, it is not surprising that the scope of criminal law's mattering is not defined by criminal law's self-proclaimed scope of applicability, but instead turns on the contexts in which it might be applied and on alternative means to achieve goals within these contexts. The same point could have been made in the context of other institutional sectors. Totalitarian regimes, for example, need not free offenders whose actions challenge state interests on legal technicalities because the overwhelming force at their disposal means that they need not depend on legal legitimacy to maintain order. In some regimes at some times it is, in other words, less costly to rely on mechanisms like secret police than on law. Public defenders and prosecutors need not agree on pleas which comply precisely with the law a defendant has violated. Subject to certain constraints, they may use the array of laws as a resource for fitting a punishment to the degree of crime (Sudnow 1965; Maynard 1984). Judges can ignore penalties that law puts at their disposal when they feel that lectures or other "situational sanctions" will have an adequate punitive and deterrent effect (Mileski 1971; Wheeler et al. 1968; Merry 1990). Prison officials can turn much of the social control of prisons over to the inmates, and prison guards can prefer "tune ups" to formal legal proceedings when prisoners have behaved improperly (Sykes 1958; Jacobs 1977; Marquart and Couch 1985).

6. GROUP USE

The examples I have used to develop this resource theory are instances where individuals seek to privatize the ostensibly public criminal law. Groups may do the same thing with both the criminal and civil law. The classic example from the civil law is the interest group which secures a special subsidy or tax benefit, but this is just one way in which groups promote laws, including criminal laws, that turn portions of the wealth or power of the state into group rather than public ends. Less obvious is that the state itself and entities within the state are often such interest groups. Calavita (1992), for example, describes the *Bracero* program which, in allowing the temporary importation of Mexican farm workers, seems to have been ideally designed to provide growers in the South and West with cheap labor. Yet she tells us the Immigration and Naturalization Service (INS) originally had to sell the program to skeptical farmers. They persuaded farmers that the *Bracero* program would solve their labor problems because the program was even better designed to solve the

INS's core problem, keeping control of the Mexican-United States border. While parts of the program were refined or adjusted so that it better served farmers' needs, in those rare instances when clashes arose between farmers' interests and the INS's interests, the INS often had sufficient strength to adjust its policies for its own bureaucratic ends.

Groups may also use the law in conflict with other groups. In the first portion of this paper we noted how law may be an instrument of domination in that its restrained use can help legitimate regimes, which is ordinarily a cheaper way of maintaining superiority than force of arms. Piven and Cloward (1993) show that from the sixteenth century on, laws implementing poor relief have been used by the state or dominant groups within it both as devices to regulate labor markets and as "pressure release valves" that serve to contain potential revolts from below in the hardest of times. Thus, early in Franklin Roosevelt's first term, when the threat of social upheaval was greatest, there was strong general support for direct relief. As recovery proceeded and the threat of revolt receded, the consensus broke down and the welfare system became increasingly suffused with elements of labor market control (e.g., benefit cutoffs in rural areas when the spring planting season commenced). It may be no coincidence that today, with competition from low-cost foreign workers rising, welfare "as we know it" has ended and been replaced by a system designed to force welfare recipients to work without guaranteeing that jobs paying enough to replace lost welfare income will be available.

Even before the sixteenth century, vagrancy laws were used to assure a steady supply of cheap labor in the English countryside by prohibiting workers in times of labor shortage (e.g., after the black death had decimated the countryside) from leaving their native villages to sell their labor to those who would pay the most (Chambliss 1964; Piven and Cloward 1993). Monsma (1990; 1992) has documented an attempt to use vagrancy law for the same purposes in colonial Argentina. When there were no labor shortages, enforcement of such laws was lax because labor could be secured more cheaply through ordinary labor market activity.

Perhaps the most interesting use of the law as a group resource is a twist on the legitimation function I describe early in this chapter. Rather than use the law to legitimate its own rule, a group may use the law to legitimate its own values, often by delegitimizing the values of some group with which it is in conflict. Gusfield (1963) provides a good example of this in his book *Symbolic Crusade*, which calls attention to the Protestant, nativist elements of the prohibition movement and the extent to which the movement was fueled by a desire to distinguish native Protestant American from immigrant Catholic (especially Irish) cultures and to establish the moral security of the former. The goal of establishing cultural superiority seems to be a similarly strong motivating force for activists on both sides of the abortion controversy (Luker 1984).

When law is used this way, it seems to be chosen because there is no easier way of securing social validation for the morality a group asserts. Indeed, such movements often take to politics and seek legal change only after voluntary efforts at "converting the heathen" have failed. Unlike the situation where law is used to legitimate a group's domination of the state, groups that seek to legitimate a moral position seldom are in full control of the state, although they may be more powerful than those whom they seek to morally dominate, and they may be able to secure powerful allies who see acquiescence in the group's morality as a small price to pay for support that can further cement their own rule.

Groups that sponsor symbolic crusades are, however, seldom part of a ruling class. Moral status groups often cut across lines of social power, and it may be a lack of real power that motivates group members to demonstrate their moral superiority. Moreover, going to law for these purposes presupposes a strong state or a willingness to fight, for it makes ruling over the less dominant group more rather than less difficult. It also seems to presuppose state authorities more powerful than either group, because part of the motivation for seeking laws of this sort is to secure the state's imprimatur on what would otherwise be a contestable moral claim. Thus, as the prohibition movement advanced, whether a politician drank on the sly seemed less important than whether he supported the proposed Eighteenth Amendment, and anti-abortion activists hold no grudge against those who have had abortions so long as they support the movement.

7. CONCLUSION

Whereas I was reminded of a comic strip at the start of this chapter, I am reminded of a W. S. Gilbert lyric at its conclusion. In the operetta *Ruddigore*, at the conclusion of one of Gilbert's finest patter songs, the characters sing:

> This particularly rapid, unintelligible patter
> Isn't generally heard, and if it is it doesn't matter!

If the patter songs were not generally heard, there would be no sense in writing them; nor would there be a point to the quoted lines, if hearing them did not matter. But as Gilbert well knew, his patter songs were showstoppers. They were the standout features of the most popular Gilbert and Sullivan operettas and made for the few memorable moments in the less popular ones.[9] Gilbert could mock them because they mattered so much. So I think it is with criminal law. If we expect law to matter as it is enunciated, we can spot many situations in which it does not matter. We can even spot situations where apparently applicable criminal law does not matter by any standards. But ultimately the question, "Does the law matter?" is worth asking not because the law's mattering is problematic, but because it matters in so many ways that we are well advised to sort them out. I have begun that task in this paper.

NOTES

This paper was originally prepared for the Law and Society Association's 1993 Summer Institute for Sociolegal Studies. I would like to thank Paul Hunt for his research assistance and Gail Ristow for preparing the manuscript and tracking down numerous citations. I am grateful to Howard Kimeldorf, Debra Livingston, and Jennifer Whiting for their comments on an earlier version of this manuscript.

1. Even when the parallel between law and morality is as close as it is in the case of murder, we cannot be certain that some of the compliance we attribute to morality is not, in fact, a result of the law's threat (Andenaes 1966; Stephen 1883).

2. I have no citation for this quote—I read something like this once, but I no longer remember where. The reader will have to accept my claim that at least in gist it is accurate. For a similar sentiment expressed by a former district attorney, see Heilbroner (1990).

3. *People v. Berrios*, 28 N.Y. 2d 3rd, 279 N.E. 2d 709, 321 N.Y.S. 2d 884 (1971).

4. Courts often do so, however, by looking at the instructions as a whole. In fact, the Supreme Court permits harmless error analysis even when instructions are constitutionally flawed. There are some limits however. Recently the court held that an erroneous instruction on the meaning of the "beyond a reasonable doubt" burden of proof could never be harmless error. Sullivan v. Louisiana; 508 U.S. 275 (1993).

5. From a rhetorical standpoint, instructions are often written in prose that even the college educated have great difficulty understanding. I have long speculated that one reason that may contribute to this is that marginally correct, difficult to understand instructions are most likely to be appealed. Appellate courts faced, as they usually are, with criminals who appear factually guilty strain not to overturn merited convictions and approve dubious instructions. These instructions, bearing an appellate court's stamp of approval and widely disseminated through appellate opinions, then become safe instructions. Judges know they have been approved and that they will not get reversed for using them. I have, however, no way of testing this hypothesis; the most I can say is that it seems plausible to me.

6. I am now assuming an extreme situation which probably only characterizes a minority of instructions. Even if some or most jurors do not understand difficult instructions, those who do can sometimes educate their fellow jurors in what these instructions mean. The empirical research, however, does not give one great confidence in such educational efforts (Ellsworth 1989; Hastie, Penrod, and Pennington 1983).

7. In this, criminal law differs from much civil law. Civil law provides norms that may be deployed but does not specify that they should be simply because occasions for their application exist (Lempert 1972).

8. The latter may come to matter as the arrestee is further processed.

9. E.g., "My name is John Wellington Wells" in *The Sorcerer*.

BIBLIOGRAPHY

Andenaes, Johannes. 1966. The General Preventive Effects of Punishment. 114 *Univ. of Pennsylvania Law Rev.*, 949.

Anderson, Linda S., Theodore G. Chiricos, and Gordon P. Waldo. 1977. Formal and Informal Sanctions: A Comparison of Deterrent Effects. 25 *Social Problems*, 103.

Balbus, Isaac D. 1973. *The Dialectics of Legal Repression; Black Rebels before the American Criminal Courts.* New York: Russell Sage Foundation.

Bittner, Egon. 1967. The Police on Skid Row: A Study of Peace Keeping. 32 *American Sociological Rev.*, 699.

Black, Donald J. 1971. The Social Organization of Arrest. 23 *Stanford Law Rev.*, 1087.

———. 1976. *The Behavior of Law.* New York: Academic Press.

Burkett, Steven R., and Eric L. Jensen. 1975. Conventional Ties, Peer Influence, and the Fear of Apprehension: A Study of Adolescent Marijuana Use. 16 *Sociological Quarterly*, 522.

Calavita, Kitty. 1992. *Inside the State: The Bracero Program, Immigration, and the I.N.S.* New York: Routledge.

Casper, Jonathan D. 1972. *American Criminal Justice: The Defendant's Perspective.* Englewood Cliffs, NJ: Prentice-Hall.

———. 1978. *Criminal Courts: The Defendant's Perspective: Executive Summary.* Washington, DC: National Institute of Law Enforcement and Criminal Justice, Law Enforcement Assistance Administration, U.S. Department of Justice, U.S. Government Printing Office.

Chambliss, William J. 1964. A Sociological Analysis of the Law of Vagrancy. 12 *Social Problems*, 67.

Charrow, Robert P., and Veda R. Charrow. 1979. Making Legal Language Understandable: A Psycholinguistic Study of Jury Instructions. 79 *Columbia Law Rev.*, 1306.

Couch, Ben M. and James W. Marquart. 1989. *An Appeal to Justice: Litigated Reform of Texas Prisons.* Austin: Univ. of Texas Press.

Durkheim, Emile. 1984. *Division of Labor in Society.* New York: Free Press.

Ellsworth, Phoebe C. 1989. Are Twelve Heads Better Than One? (Is the Jury Competent?) 52 *Law and Contemporary Problems*, 205.

Fuller, Lon L. 1964. *The Morality of Law.* New Haven, CT: Yale Univ. Press.

Garland, David. 1990. *Punishment in Modern Society: A Study in Social Theory.* Oxford: Clarendon.

Gellman, Barton. 1988. D.C. Officer Charged with Lying on Stand. *Washington Post*, Nov. 30, 1988, p. D1.

Genovese, Eugene. 1972. *Roll Jordan, Roll: The World the Slaves Made.* New York: Vintage.

Gibbs, Jack. 1975. *Crime, Punishment and Deterrence.* New York: Elsevier.

Goldstein, Joseph. 1960. Police Discretion Not to Invoke the Criminal Process: Low Visibility Decisions in the Administration of Justice. 69 *Yale Law Journal*, 543.

Griffiths, John. 1979. Is Law Important? 54 *New York Univ. Law Rev.*, 339.

Gusfield, Joseph. 1963. *Symbolic Crusade: Status Politics and the American Temperance Movement.* Urbana: Univ. of Illinois Press.

Hacker, Andrew. 1992. *Two Nations: Black and White, Separate, Hostile, Unequal.* New York: Scribner's.

Hastie, Reid, Steven D. Penrod, and Nancy Pennington. 1983. *Inside the Jury.* Cambridge, MA: Harvard Univ. Press.

Hay, Douglas. 1975. Property, Authority and the Criminal Law. In Hay et al. 1975.

Hay, Douglas, Peter Linebaugh, John Rule, E. P. Thompson, and Carl Winslow, eds. 1975. *Albion's Fatal Tree: Crime and Society in Eighteenth-Century England.* New York: Pantheon.

Heilbroner, David. 1990. *Rough Justice: Days and Nights of a Young D.A.* New York: Pantheon.

Hyde, Alan. 1983. The Conception of Legitimation in the Sociology of Law. 1983 *Wisconsin Law Rev.*, 379.

Jacobs, James B. 1977. *Stateville: The Penitentiary in Mass Society.* Chicago: Univ. of Chicago Press.

Kalven, Harry, and Hans Zeisel. 1966. *The American Jury.* Chicago: Univ. of Chicago Press.

Lempert, Richard. 1972. Norm-Making in Social Exchange: A Contract Law Model. 7 *Law and Society Rev.*, 1.

———. 1981. Desert and Deterrence: An Assessment of the Moral Bases for Capital Punishment. 79 *Michigan Law Rev.*, 1177.

———. 1981–82. Organizing for Deterrence: Lessons from a Study of Child Support. 16 *Law and Society Rev.*, 513.

Lieb, John, Louis Zurcher, and Sheldon Ekland-Olson. 1984. The Paradoxical Impact of Criminal Sanctions: Some Microstructural Findings 18 *Law and Society Rev.*, 159.

Lind, E. Allen and Tom R. Tyler. 1988. *The Social Psychology of Procedural Justice.* New York: Plenum.

Llewellyn, K. N., and E. Adamson Hoebel. 1941. *The Cheyenne Way: Conflict and Case Law in Primitive Jurisprudence.* Norman: Univ. of Oklahoma Press.

Loftin, Colin, David McDowall, and Brian Wiersma. 1992. A Comparative Study of the Preventive Effects of Mandatory Sentencing Laws for Gun Crimes. 83 *Journal of Criminal Law and Criminology*, 378.

Luker, Kristin. 1984. *Abortion and the Politics of Motherhood.* Berkeley: Univ. of California Press.

Marquart, James W., and Ben M. Couch. 1985. Social Reform and Prisoner Control: The Impact of *Ruiz v. Estelle* on a Texas Penitentiary. 19 *Law and Society Rev.*, 557.

Maynard, Douglas W. 1984. *Inside Plea Bargaining.* New York: Plenum.

Merry, Sally Engle. 1990. *Getting Justice and Getting Even: Legal Consciousness among Working-Class Americans.* Chicago: Univ. of Chicago Press.

Mileski, Maureen. 1971. Courtroom Encounters: An Observation Study of a Lower Criminal Court. 5 *Law and Society Rev.*, 473.

Monsma, Karl. 1990. Controlling Frontier Labor in Early Nineteenth Century Argentina, Paper presented at the annual meetings of the Social Science History Association, Minneapolis.

———. 1992. Ranchers, Rural People, and the State in Post-Colonial Argentina. Ph.D. diss., Univ. of Michigan.

Piven, Frances Fox, and Richard A. Cloward, eds. 1993. *The Politics of Turmoil: Essays on Poverty, Race, and the Urban Crisis.* New York: Vintage.

Reifman, Alan, Spencer M. Gusick, and Phoebe C. Ellsworth. 1992. Real Jurors' Understanding of the Law in Real Cases. 16 *Law and Human Behavior*, 539.

Ross, H. Laurence. 1982. *Deterring the Drinking Driver: Legal Policy and Social Control.* Lexington, MA: Lexington Books.

Saltzman, Linda E., Gordon P. Waldo, and Raymond Paternoster. 1983. Perceived Risk and Social Control: Do Sanctions Really Deter? 17 *Law and Society Rev.*, 457.

Sherman, Lawrence W., and Richard A. Berk. 1984. The Specific Deterrent Effects of Arrest for Domestic Assault. *American Sociological Rev.*, 261.

Skolnick, Jerome H. 1975. *Justice without Trial: Law Enforcement in Democratic Society*, 2d ed. New York: Wiley.

Skolnick, Jerome H., and James J. Fyfe. 1993. Response to Mastrofski and Vchida. 3. *Journal of Research in Crime and Delinquency*, 359.

Spradley, James P. 1970. *You Owe Yourself a Drunk: An Ethnography of Urban Nomads.* Boston: Little, Brown.

Stephen, James Fitzjames. 1883. *A History of the Criminal Law in England.* London: Macmillan.

Sudnow, David. 1965. Normal Crimes: Sociological Features in the Penal Code in a Public Defender's Office. 12 *Social Problem*, 255.

Sykes, Gresham. 1958. *The Society of Captives: A Study of a Maximum Security Prison.* Princeton, NJ: Princeton Univ. Press.

Thibaut, John, and Laurens Walker. 1975. *Procedural Justice: A Psychological Analysis.* Hillsdale, NJ: Lawrence Erlbaum Associates.

Thompson, E.P. 1975. *Whigs and Hunters: The Origin of the Black Act.* New York: Pantheon.

Tyler, Tom R. 1984. The Role of Perceived Injustice in Defendant's Evaluations of Their Courtroom Experience. 18 *Law and Society Rev.*, 51.

Weber, Max. 1968. *Economy and Society.* Vols. 1 and 2. Ed. Guenther Roth and Claus Wittich. New York: Bedminster.

Weber, Max. [1922] 1978. *Economy and Society: An Outline of Interpretive Sociology.* Ed. Guenther Roth and Claus Wittich; trans. Ephraim Fischoff et al. Berkeley: Univ. of California Press.

Wheeler, Stanton, ed. 1968. *Controlling Delinquents.* New York: Wiley.

Wheeler, Stanton, Edna Bonacich, M. Richard Cramer, and Irving K. Zola. 1968. Agents of Delinquency Control: A Comparative Analysis. In Wheeler 1968.

Wilson, James Q. 1968. *Varieties of Police Behavior: The Management of Law and Order in Eight Communities.* Cambridge, MA: Harvard Univ. Press.

Wilson, James Q., and George L. Kelling. 1982. Broken Windows: The Police and Neighborhood Safety. *Atlantic* (March) 249:29–38.

Kristin Bumiller is professor of political science and women's studies at Amherst College.

Mia Cahill is a graduate student in sociology at the University of Wisconsin–Madison.

Jane F. Collier is professor of anthropology at Stanford University.

Shari Seidman Diamond is professor of psychology at the University of Illinois–Chicago.

John J. Donohue is professor of law at Stanford Law School.

Lauren B. Edelman is professor at the School of Jurisprudence and Social Policy at the University of California–Berkeley.

David M. Engel is professor of law at the State University of New York–Buffalo.

Bryant G. Garth is director of the American Bar Foundation.

Richard Lempert is the Francis A. Allen Collegiate Professor of Law and professor of sociology at the University of Michigan.

Michael W. McCann is professor of political science at the University of Washington.

Austin Sarat is the Oliver Wendell Holmes Professor of Law and Jurisprudence at Amherst College.

Jason Schklar is a graduate student in psychology at the University of Illinois–Chicago.

Said, Edward, 187n. 13
Saks, Michael J., 194, 205
Sales, Bruce D., 207, 209
sanctioning techniques, 28
Sarat, Austin, 110; on consciousness and
    ideology, 116; de Certeau influence
    on, 131; on ideology, 117; on legal
    consciousness as determinative, 130,
    133–34; legal consciousness definition,
    112; on legal culture, 127; welfare
    bureaucracy study, 132–33
Saulsbury, Eli, 51
Schattschneider, E. E., 91, 102n. 11
Scheingold, Stuart A., 6, 83, 91, 100
Schklar, Jason, 10–11
Schneider, Elizabeth M., 83, 97
school segregation, 50
Schwarzer, Judge, 205
Scott, James, 97
search and seizure law, 233–34; dropsy cases
    and, 234–35
self, territory of, 145–46
settlements, social advantage, 16
settler model, colonialism, 172, 173
Severance, Lawrence J., 208, 219n. 40
sex crimes, growth in, 158–59
sexual violence, 146
Silbey, Susan S., 110; on continual
    consciousness transformation, 119; de
    Certeau influence on, 131; on legal
    consciousness as determinative, 130,
    132, 134; power and resistance model,
    131–32
Silent Scream, The (film), 157
Silverstein, Helena, 92
Singer, Linda, 155–56, 157–58, 159
skid row policing, 237, 238
Smart, Carol, 155, 157
Smith, James, 67, 68
social change, 6–7 (see also social
    movements); legal tactics versus
    political/cultural factors in, 4–5,
    98–99, 102n. 14
social contract theory, 162–88; children
    of mixed parentage and, 171;
    development of modern science and,
    164–65, 186n. 3; equality before
    law and, 163–64, 168; European
    colonialists, 166, 172–73; local regime

differences and, 179, 185; morality
    debates and, 173–74; postcolonial
    inequality and, 183–85; racism/sexism
    and, 169; security of individual property
    and, 169; social Darwinism and, 170;
    sovereignty concepts and, 163–64
social Darwinism, 170, 174
social issues, regulation and, 8–9
social movements, 76–102, 78–79,
    102n. 11; building, 83–86; civil
    dispute processing scholarship, 78;
    conflict-oriented approach, 98;
    context/extralegal factors and, 89–91,
    99–100; cycles theory, 97–98; definition
    of, 77, 101n. 4; dynamic stages of,
    79; group roles in, 79; institutional
    access and, 95–96; legacy of law in,
    96–98; legal cooptation of, 86–89,
    101n. 10; legal mobilization and,
    90–97; legal resources available to,
    82; legal scholarship studies, 76–77,
    101n. 6, 101nn. 1–3; models, 79–82;
    opportunities structure of, 82, 99;
    political process approach, 81–82;
    power relations studies, 79; research
    mobilization (RM) theory of, 78;
    resources/tactics of, 79, 99–100; social
    reform approach, 81; studies of, 77–78,
    81–82; "war of position," 89
social relations: become constitutive of, 8–9;
    communities of meaning and, 140
social science, 3–5, 10
somatophobic feminism, 156–57
South Africa, 172–73
Southeast Asia, contracts with natives, 166
Southern black education. See black
    education in South
sovereignty: Europeans; sixteenth-century
    notions of, 163–64; native rulers and,
    166, 186n. 8; resistance and, 185
Spain: colonialism, social contract, and voice,
    174–75, 186n. 2; colonial motivations,
    171–72; ethnically distinct peoples
    and, 166; inequality of colonized and,
    180; review of Indian judicial decisions,
    177; source/nature of law, 167–68;
    sovereignty concept and, 163–64
Sparf and Hansen v. United States 1895,
    206, 219n. 33

258

Spelman, Elizabeth, 151, 154
Spradley, James P., 237
state antidiscrimination laws, 66, 71n. 13
state model, colonialism, 172
statutory exemptions from jury, 197; decision-making and, 198
Stern, Steve J., 177, 178
Stevens, John Paul, 216
Stewart, Potter, 147
Stier, Serena, 28
Stokes, Eric, 175
Stoler, Ann L., 170, 171, 175
Strauder v. W. Virginia 1880, 218n. 18
subjectivity, culturally embedded views of, 80
Sulieman, Susan, 146
surrogacy, 157–58; political economy of, 158
Symbolic Crusade (Gusfield), 242
systemic opportunities, social movements, 80

Tarrow, Sidney, 77, 97–98
Taylor, Verta, 96
Taylor v. Louisiana 1975, 218n. 22
technology, body images regulation and, 155; reproduction and, 158
territory of self, 145–46
therapeutic paradigm, 5; institutionalization, 20; nature of, 23
third-world development, 184
Thompson, E. P., 81, 230
Thompson, William C., 201
Tocqueville, Alexis de, 186n. 5
totalitarian regimes, 241
Trubeck, David: on legal consciousness, 112, 116
Tsing, Anna, 175, 187n. 15
Tull v. United States 1987, 217n. 9
Turner, Margery Austin, 70n. 1

Ugwuegbu, Denis C. E., 199

Uhlman, Thomas M., 200
United States v. Dougherty 1972, 213
unreasonable search, 233

vagrancy laws, 242
Vidmar, Neil, 214

wage gap. *See* gender-based wage equity movement
Weber, Max, 186–87n. 10, 228, 234, 238
Welch, Elizabeth, 27–28
Welch, Finis, 68
welfare recipients, legal consciousness and, 110
welfare rights movement, 84
Wells, Gary L., 214
Whatley, Warren, 65
White, Lucie, 8
Wiggins, Elizabeth C., 195–96
Williams, Patricia, 153
Williams v. Florida 1970, 219n. 30
Wisconsin v. Leroy Reed 1990, 213, 220n. 51
Wissler, Roselle, 205
women, status of colonized, 181–82, 187n. 14, 188nn. 18–20
women's movement: effect of litigation in, 87–88; legacy of law in, 96, 97–98
working-class Americans: legal consciousness and, 110; segments of, 113
World Bank, 184
Wright, Gavin, 65

Yngvesson, Barbara, 110; on court clerk role, 115, 134, 136–37; law, community and, 137–38; on legal consciousness, 113; on legal culture, 126
Young, Iris Marion, 151–52, 154

Zambia, status of colonized women in, 182
Zeichner, Oscar, 64
Zeisel, Hans, 11, 199, 211, 214
Zimring, Franklin, 147–48, 149